5 STEPS TO A 5

AP Computer Science A

5 STEPS TO A 5™

AP Computer Science A

Deborah B. Klipp

Kimberly A. Hermans-Chopp

New York   Chicago   San Francisco   Athens   London   Madrid
Mexico City   Milan   New Delhi   Singapore   Sydney   Toronto

The series editor was Grace Freedson, and the project editor was Del Franz.

Series design by Jane Tenenbaum.

Contents

STEP 5   Building Your Test-Taking Confidence

Way to go! By taking the AP Computer Science A course and exam, you've decided to gain a deeper knowledge of the world around you. This knowledge will give you an advantage no matter what field you study in the future.

Computer science, ironically, is a much misunderstood subject. Even in this digital age, where people are dependent on their smartphones, they see their phone as a mysterious "black box." They receive messages and notifications on a daily basis, but, for some reason, they don't understand that someone had to write the software that makes their life richer. Software developers write the computer programs that people use every day.

The purpose of this book is to help you score a 5 on the AP Computer Science A Exam. Along the way, your Java programming skills and your ability to problem-solve should dramatically improve.

Here are some pieces of advice for you:

- **Be persistent.** Software developers hate it when they can't figure out how to make a program work and even when they succeed, they always try to think of better ways to solve the problem.
- **Try to see the big picture**. This is good advice not only when studying for this exam, but for life in general. The more you see problems from multiple perspectives, the more likely it is that you will understand how to solve them. Complex program designs require you to step back and view from a distance.
- **Be patient with yourself and others.** Everyone learns at a different rate. Some of the topics in AP Computer Science A are quite challenging, so you may have to reread concepts in this book until you understand them. If you are learning this with other students, help each other out. As a programmer, you should live by the mantra that "we are all in this together."
- **Too much of a good thing is a bad thing**. Software developers need to strike a balance between structure and creativity. That is, a good developer must understand how to do the technical things (structure) or else their program won't run. But programmers also need to be creative in order to solve problems in a clever way. Work on improving both of these two skills simultaneously so you can become the best programmer you can be.
- **Above all else, work toward original thought.** You are going to need to learn how to think for yourself in order to become a good programmer. Be curious and learn how things work so that you can apply skills and techniques to new situations. Also, learn how to explain things to other people, as this will develop you as a programmer and leader.

Acknowledgments

I am very grateful that I have been given the opportunity to make revisions to this book so it follows the outline of the ten units in AP Computer Science A Course and Exam Description. First, I'd like to thank Julie Sway, 5 *Steps to a 5 AP Computer Science Principles* author, for recommending me to her publisher for this project. Second, to Grace Freedson from The Publishing Network and Anya Kozorez from McGraw Hill a huge thank you for giving me this opportunity. And lastly to Poonam Bisht for managing the reorganizing that this book required and understanding my descriptions of the copying/pasting/inserting that was needed.

This revision wouldn't have been possible without the awesome work done by the original authors Dean Johnson, Carol Paymer, and Aaron Chamberlain. All I did was rearrange their material and add additional material. At first it seemed a simple task, but it morphed into so much more. They did all of the heavy lifting and I hope I that I made them proud.

I would like to thank my husband, Doug, and daughters, Melissa and Samantha, for all of the support they have given me over the years while I travel doing AP work, and to a few of my fellow AP readers and consultants who share this passion and inspire me (Rob Schultz, Sandy Czajka, Kim Hermans, Kelly Schultz, J.P. O'Hara, Judy Hromcik, Ria Galanos, Tim Gallagher, Lester Wainwright, Steve Adriannoff, Cody Henrichsen, Maria Litvin, David Levine, Kathy Larson)—AP CS Rocks!

To my AP Computer Science A students and AP Computer Science A colleagues both past and present, this book is dedicated to you.

Deborah B. Klipp

My deepest gratitude goes to my dear friend, fellow reader, and trivia whiz, Debbie Klipp, for recommending me to Grace Freedson from The Publishing Network and Bob O'Sullivan from McGraw Hill. Of course, this revision would not be possible without the original authors: Dean Johnson, Carol Paymer, and Aaron Chamberlain, whose legacy I am so honored to continue.

To my husband, Tony Chopp, thank you for being so supportive, even when my work involves frequent travel and time away from you. To my parents, Rich and Pat Hermans, thank you for buying me my first computer and always encouraging me to work hard and continue learning.

A special thanks to my fellow computer science colleagues turned trivia players and friends: J.P. O'Hara, Rob Schultz, Sandy Czajka, Ria Galanos, Cody Henrichsen, Christopher Moretti, Amanda Lattimore, Jim Huggins, Tim Gallagher, Mark Bailey, Kelly Schultz, Andy Grover, and Dr. Jeffrey Forbes. Your willingness to share and support never goes unnoticed.

To my mentors, Dr. Jan Cuny and Dr. Debra Richardson, thank you for inspiring me as strong women in computer science.

To everyone who has embarked on their AP Computer Science A journey with me, both students and colleagues, thank you for shaping me into the educator I am today. My immense gratitude goes out to you all.

And finally, I would like to dedicate this book to the memory of Dr. Alistair Campbell. You are such an important part of the AP Computer Science A community, and you will be deeply missed.

Kimberly A. Hermans-Chopp

About the Authors

DEBORAH B. KLIPP began teaching AP Computer Science in 1987 at Mainland Regional High School in Linwood, New Jersey. After teaching math and computer science at Mainland for 25 years, she moved to Florida with her husband and two daughters. She worked at Hillsborough County schools for six years and is currently working at Florida Virtual School. She received a Bachelor of Science in Mathematics, Computer Science minor from Pennsylvania State University and a Master of Arts degree in Education from Rowan University. She has been an AP Computer Science A reader, table leader, and question leader since 1999 and has been an AP College Board Consultant since 2001. She enjoys teaching and sharing her love and passion of AP CSA to teachers during AP Summer Institutes and College Board workshops across the country.

KIMBERLY A. HERMANS-CHOPP teaches AP Computer Science A and AP Computer Science Principles at Troy High School in Fullerton, California. She has 18 years of experience teaching high school students and has lectured at California State University, Fullerton, and the University of California, Irvine, for 7 years. She has taught AP Computer Science A for 14 years and has taught AP Computer Science Principles since the pilot program's inception in 2013. Kimberly holds a BS and an MS in computer science, along with a National Board Certification in CTE. A former Albert Einstein Distinguished Educator Fellow and Ocean Exploration Trust Science Communication Fellow, Kimberly's dedication to computer science education led her to design a four-year pathway at her previous institution. Outside of teaching, Kimberly instructs preservice teachers pursuing a computer science credential in California, contributes as a College Board consultant, and participates as an AP reader. In addition to her instructional roles, Kimberly is actively involved in various initiatives aimed at broadening participation in computing. She directs the community college working group for Expanding Computing Education Pathways (ECEP), chairs the Equity Committee for her local teacher union, and serves on the Board of Directors and AAPI Steering Committee for CSTA. Despite her busy schedule, Kimberly finds joy in spending time near the ocean with her husband, Tony, at their home in Newport Beach, California.

Introduction

Computer science provides limitless possibilities. It gives you power. It drives innovation. Computer science teaches skills that transfer to other disciplines: creativity, adaptability, structured processing, strategic problem solving, reflective analysis, relevant verification, and usability. Most importantly, it will define the future leaders of our world.

—Dr. Thomas Halbert, computer science teacher, Houston, Texas

Organization of the Book

This book was created to help you earn a 5 on the AP Computer Science A Exam. It is important that you understand how this book has been written specifically for you.

This book contains the following:

- An explanation of the highly successful Five-Step Program
- A suggested calendar based on how you want to prepare for the AP Computer Science A Exam
- A series of test-taking strategies
- A diagnostic test
- A thorough explanation of each topic on the AP Computer Science A Exam
- Two practice exams with explanations

Computer science is one of those fields that can be taught in many completely different ways; even the order in which things are taught can be different. Sure, there are some concepts that you have to understand before you can move on to others, but the reality is, there is a lot of flexibility when it comes to how to learn programming.

For instance, throw a dozen computer science teachers in a room and ask them if classes and objects should be taught first, or if the fundamentals of programming should be taught first. Then, grab a bag of popcorn and sit back and enjoy the show. Computer science teachers have been arguing which way is best for years. I have taught high school students both ways, and I believe there are valid arguments on both sides. This is one of those personal decisions that each teacher gets to make.

I have chosen to follow the College Board Course and Exam Description ordering of topics. This way, when I introduce and explain classes and objects, I will reinforce these fundamental programming concepts. If your teacher teaches the concepts in a different order, don't worry, it will all work out in the end.

> The order that you learn the concepts in your computer science class may be different from the order that is presented in this book. And that's OK.

Advice from My Students

I asked my students for advice on writing this book. One thing they told me is to never explain a new topic using concepts that haven't been introduced yet. Students hate it when authors say, "Oh, I'm going to use something that I won't be explaining right now, but we'll get to it in a later chapter." I have tried really hard to design this book in a linear fashion, so I hope that I never do this to you.

> **No Forward Referencing**
> The concepts in this book move from easiest to hardest, and some of the concepts are even split into two sections (Basic and Advanced) so that the flow of the book is more natural. I will use earlier concepts to explain later concepts, but not the other way around.

One of my goals in writing this book was to strike the right balance between explaining topics in a way that *any* high school student can understand but still technical enough so students can earn a 5 on the exam. My students recommended that I start off by explaining each concept in a simple way so that anyone can understand it, and then go into greater detail. I hope you will appreciate my attempts at this. In other words, I've tried to make the book easy enough for beginning Java programmers to understand the basics so they are not completely lost, but hard enough so that advanced students have the potential to earn a 5 on the AP Computer Science A exam.

Basic and Advanced Levels

It is for this reason that I have also chosen to create two levels of questions for each of the main concepts: Basic and Advanced. As a teacher, I have learned that students like to know that they know the basics of a concept before moving on to harder questions. If a book only has really hard practice questions, then most of the beginning students find them impossible to do, start feeling like failures, lose interest, and eventually drop out because they can't relate to anything the book is talking about.

I've also learned that it helps to try to find something that the student can relate to and explain the concept using that. I have tried to use examples that high school students can identify with.

The Unit Summary

Each unit begins with a unit summary. The summary tells what's covered in the unit, and it should give you a reason why you would want to learn the material covered in that unit. It also is a great tool for deciding if you need to look further at that topic.

The Rapid Review

Each unit ends with a "Rapid Review," which is a complete summary of the important ideas relating to the concept. The lists are full of wonderful one-liners that you should understand before taking the AP Computer Science A Exam. Make sure that you understand every line in the Rapid Review before taking the exam.

> **Learn the Rapid Review Content**
> Read every line in every Rapid Review and know what each means!

The Graphics Used in This Book

 Powerful Tip: This graphic identifies a helpful tip for taking the AP Computer Science A Exam.

 Fun Fact: This graphic identifies fun deviations from the subject matter.

 Warning: This graphic points out a common error to avoid.

> If you have any questions, suggestions, or would like to report an error, we'd love to hear from you. Email us at 5stepstoa5apcsa@gmail.com.

The Five-Step Program

This guide conducts you through the five steps necessary to prepare yourself for success on the exam. These steps will provide you with the skills and strategies that are vital to the exam as well as the practice that can lead you toward the perfect 5. Reading this guide will not guarantee you a 5 when you take the AP Computer Science A Exam in May. However, by understanding what's on the exam, using the test-taking strategies provided for each section of the test, and carefully reviewing the concepts covered on the exam, you will definitely be on your way!

Step One gives you the basic information you need to know about the exam and helps you determine which type of exam preparation you want to commit to. In Step One, you'll find:

- The goals of the AP Computer Science A course
- Frequently asked questions about the exam
- An explanation of how you will be graded
- Calendars for three different preparation plan:
  - Full School Year Plan (September through May)
  - One-Semester Plan (January through May)
  - Six-Week Plan (six weeks prior to the exam)

Step Two introduces you to the types of questions you'll find on the actual test and, by identifying the content areas where you are weak, allows you to prioritize the areas you most need to review. In Step Two, you'll find:

- A diagnostic exam in AP Computer Science A. This test is just like the real test.
- Answers and explanations for all the exam questions. Read the explanations not just for the questions you miss, but also for all the questions and answer choices you didn't completely understand.

Step Three helps you develop the strategies and techniques you need in order to do your best on the exam. In Step Three, you'll learn:

- Strategies to tackle the Multiple-choice questions efficiently and effectively
- Strategies to maximize your score on the Free-response questions

Step Four develops the knowledge and skills necessary to do well on the exam. This is organized into 10 key units. In Step Four, you'll review by using:

- Complete, but easy-to-follow, explanations of all of the concepts covered on the exam
- Review questions—both basic and advanced levels—for each unit, followed by step-by-step explanations so you'll understand anything you missed
- Rapid Reviews for each unit that you can use to make sure you have the knowledge and skills you'll need

Step Five will give you test-taking practice and develop your confidence for taking the exam. In Step Five, you'll find:

- Two full-length practice exams that closely resemble the actual AP Computer Science A Exam. As well as checking your mastery of the concepts, you can use these exams to practice pacing and using the test-taking strategies given in Step Three.
- Step-by-step explanations for all the exam questions so you can understand anything you missed and learn from your mistakes.
- Scoring guidelines so you can assess your performance and estimate your score in order to see if you have reached your goal.

5 STEPS TO A 5™

AP Computer Science A

STEP **1**

Set Up Your Study Program

What You Need to Know About the AP Computer Science A Exam

IN THIS CHAPTER

Summary: This chapter provides you with background information on the AP Computer Science A Exam. Learn about the exam, how exams are graded, what types of questions are asked, what topics are tested, and basic test-taking information.

Key Ideas

✪ The AP Computer Science A Exam is about problem solving and the Java programming language.

✪ The exam has two parts: Multiple choice and Free response.

✪ Scoring a 3, 4, or 5 will earn credit and/or advanced placement at most colleges and universities.

Background Information

A Brief History of the Exam

The first AP Computer Science exam was given in 1984, and the coding language used was Pascal. In 1999, C++ replaced Pascal. In 2004, Java replaced C++. Today, AP Computer Science is one of the fastest-growing AP exams.

Goals of the Course

According to the College Board, the AP Computer Science A course reflects what computer science teachers, professors, and researchers have indicated are the main goals of an introductory, college-level computer science programming course. These goals are:

- **Program Design and Algorithm Development**—Determine required code segments to produce a given output.
- **Code Logic**—Determine the output, value, or result of given program code given initial values.
- **Code Implementation**—Write and implement program code.
- **Code Testing**—Analyze program code for correctness, equivalence, and errors.
- **Documentation**—Describe the behavior and conditions that produce the specified results in a program.
- **Ethical Computing**—Understand the ethical and social implications of computer use.

This list may seem rather ambiguous and open-ended; that's because it is. Just keep in mind that this test is all about learning how to solve different kinds of problems using Java. The best way to prepare for the exam is to follow the steps in this book and get plenty of practice designing and writing code.

> **Goal of the AP Computer Science A Exam**
> The main goals of the AP Computer Science A Exam are to test how proficient you are at problem solving and how well you know the Java programming language.

Frequently Asked Questions About the Exam

Who Writes the AP Computer Science A Exams? Who Grades Them?

The AP Computer Science A Exam is designed by a committee of college professors and high school AP Computer Science A teachers. The process takes years to ensure that the exam questions reflect the high quality and fairness that is expected of the College Board.

Similarly, the Free-response questions are scored by hundreds of college professors and high school AP Computer Science A teachers. The AP exam readers are thoroughly trained so that exams are graded consistently.

Why Take the AP Computer Science A Exam?

There are several benefits of taking the AP Computer Science A Exam. First is the college credit. If you score a 3, 4, or 5 on the exam, you can earn credit and/or placement from most colleges or universities. This saves you money. Second, you will start off at a higher level in your college coursework so that you can advance faster.

Finally, and my favorite, is that learning computer science will improve your ability to think for yourself and problem solve. Even if you do not plan on becoming a computer scientist, or you fear that you will not pass the exam, the skills and thought process that you learn in computer science will benefit you. Your world will be filled with rainbows and flying unicorns. Well, maybe not, but I'm just seeing if you are reading this.

Computer Science Makes You Think
Learning how to program improves your ability to think. You learn how things work.

When Is the Exam and How Do I Register for It?

The College Board publishes an exam schedule each year. The schedule for the various AP exams is two weeks long and starts on the first Monday of May. In the past, the AP Computer Science A Exam has been given during the first week.

If you are taking an AP Computer Science A class, you will probably get information from someone called an AP coordinator at your school. The College Board deadline to order an exam is in November, but check with the policy at your school regarding when to notify your school you will be taking the exam. If you are not taking an AP Computer Science A class and just taking this exam on your own, contact the AP coordinator for your local school district by November 1. That person will help you locate the testing site and help you register. You can take as many AP exams as you want (even if you didn't take a class!), but they cost just under $100 per exam. Your school may add additional fees to cover the cost of administering the exam.

What Is the Format of the AP Computer Science A Exam?

The exam is three hours long and there are two sections: Multiple choice and Free response.

| Section I | Multiple Choice | 40 Questions | 90 Minutes | 40 points (1 point per problem) | 50% of Exam Score |
| Section II | Free Response | 4 Questions | 90 Minutes | 36 points (9 points per problem) | 50% of Exam Score |

How Is My Final Score Calculated?

Each question in the Multiple-choice section is worth 1 point (total of 40 points). Each of the Free-response questions is worth 9 points (total of 36 points). Since there are an unequal number of points for the Multiple-choice and the Free-response sections, the total from the Free-response section is multiplied by 1.1111. This makes each section worth 50 percent.

The total from the two sections is fed into a chart similar to the one below and your final score is decided. This chart from the 2015 released exam is intended to serve as a guide, and the ranges will vary slightly from year to year.

Composite Score Range	AP Score	Interpretation
62–80	5	Extremely Well Qualified
44–61	4	Well Qualified
31–43	3	Qualified
25–30	2	Possibly Qualified
0–24	1	No Recommendation

> **Example: Computing a Score on the AP Computer Science A Exam**
> You score 31 on Section I (Multiple choice).
> You score 28 on Section II (Free response).
> Multiply 28 by 1.1111. This equals 31.1108.
> Your total is 31 + 31.1108 = 62.1108, which is rounded to 62.
> Your composite score is 62. Your AP score is a 5. Congratulations!

What Concepts Are Included in the Multiple-Choice Section?

The table below shows what topics are covered on the Multiple-choice section of the test. The percentages change from year to year, but the emphasis stays about the same. Keep in mind that many of the questions belong to more than one category, which is why the percentages do not add up to 100 percent.

Concept	Percent of Multiple-choice questions
Unit 1: Primitive Types	2.5–5%
Unit 2: Using Objects	5–7.5%
Unit 3: Boolean Expressions and if Statements	15–17.5%
Unit 4: Iteration	17.5–22.5%
Unit 5: Writing Classes	5–7.5%
Unit 6: Array	10–15%
Unit 7: ArrayList	2.5–7.5%
Unit 8: 2D Array	7.5–10%
Unit 9: Inheritance	5–10%
Unit 10: Recursion	5–7.5%

What Concepts Are Included in the Free-Response Section?

The Free-response section consists of four questions:

- Question 1 will require you to implement and call methods. The methods will use control structures like loops and `if` statements, but there will be no data structures involved.
- Question 2 will require you to design and implement a complete class.
- Question 3 will require the use of arrays and/or `ArrayLists`.
- Question 4 will require the use of 2D arrays.

What Is the Lab Requirement for the Exam?

The AP Computer Science A course must include a minimum of 20 hours of hands-on, structured lab experience. Your teacher should provide you with a chance to work with a big, complex set of related classes that helps you understand concepts like inheritance and polymorphism. Your teacher has the choice of either using the labs that are provided by the College Board or using something completely different.

The seven labs that are provided by the College Board are:

1. Magpie Lab—An exploration of some of the basics of Natural Language Processing. You'll work with strings and parse them for recognizable information. This lab can be done when studying Unit 4.
2. Consumer Lab—Ever wonder how online reviews are constructed? This lab will explore ways reviews are created. This lab can be done when studying Unit 4.
3. Data Lab—Being able to search for a data set to find answers to questions is explored in this lab. This lab can be done when studying Unit 7.
4. Picture Lab—This lab uses 2D arrays to modify digital pictures. This lab can be done when studying Unit 8.
5. Steganography Lab—Learn how to conceal messages within images. This lab can be done when studying Unit 8.
6. Elevens Lab—You'll play the solitaire card game of elevens while designing several interacting classes. This lab can be done when studying Unit 9.
7. Celebrity Lab—Design a guessing game. This lab can be done when studying Unit 9.

I See Materials on the GridWorld Case Study Online. What's with That?

That is old news. The GridWorld case study is no longer tested on the AP Computer Science A Exam. It was dropped after the 2014 exam. If you want to check it out, there are some pretty interesting things you can do with it, but the GridWorld case study won't be on your exam.

What Is the Difference Between the AP Computer Science A and the AP Computer Science Principles Exams?

Starting with the 2016–2017 school year, a new AP Computer Science course called AP Computer Science Principles began being offered. The AP Computer Science Principles course introduces students to computational thinking skills and promotes understanding of the impact of computers in our world. The biggest difference between these two courses is that AP Computer Science A focuses mainly on programming, whereas only a small part of the AP Computer Science Principles course is devoted to actual programming.

CHAPTER 2

How to Plan Your Time

IN THIS CHAPTER

Summary: The right preparation plan for you depends on your study habits, your own strengths and weaknesses, and the amount of time you have to prepare for the test. This chapter recommends some possible plans to get you started.

Key Ideas

✪ It helps to have a plan—and stick with it!

✪ You should select the study plan that best suits your situation and adapt it to fit your needs.

Three Approaches to Preparing for the AP Computer Science A Exam

It's up to you to decide how you want to use this book to study for the AP Computer Science A Exam. In this chapter you'll find three plans, each of which provides a different schedule for your review effort. Choose one or combine them if you want. Adapt the plan to your strengths and weaknesses and the way you like to study. If you are taking an AP Computer Science A course at your school, you will have more flexibility than someone learning the material independently.

The Full School-Year Plan

Choose this plan if you like taking your time going through the material. Following this path will allow you to practice your skills and develop your confidence gradually. This is a good choice if you want to use this book as a resource while taking an AP Computer Science A course.

The One-Semester Plan

Choose this plan if you are OK with learning a lot of material in a fairly short amount of time. You'll need to be a pretty diligent student who can grasp concepts quickly. This plan is also a good choice if you are currently taking an AP Computer Science A course.

The Six-Week Plan

This option is available if any one of these sounds like you:

- You are enrolled in an AP Computer Science A course and want to do a final review before the exam.
- You are enrolled in an AP Computer Science A course and want to use this book as a reference to refresh your memory.
- You are not currently enrolled in an AP Computer Science A course, but you are a fluent Java programmer and want to know what is tested on the exam.

When to Take the Practice Exams
You should take the practice exams *prior* to May. The AP Computer Science A Exam is usually given during the first week of May. If you wait until May to take the practice exams, you won't have enough time to review the concepts that you do not fully understand.

The Three Plans Compared

The chart summarizes and compares the three study plans.

Month	Full School-Year Plan	One-Semester Plan	Six-Week Plan
September	Diagnostic Exam Unit 0 Unit 1	—	—
October	Unit 2 Unit 3	—	—
November	Unit 4	—	—
December	Unit 5	—	—
January	Unit 6 Unit 7	Diagnostic Exam Units 0–3	—
February	Unit 8	Units 4–7	—
March	Unit 9 Unit 10	Units 8–10	Diagnostic Exam Units 0–10
April	Practice Exam 1 Review all concepts Practice Exam 2 Review all concepts	Practice Exam 1 Review all concepts Practice Exam 2 Review all concepts	Practice Exam 1 Review all concepts Practice Exam 2 Review all concepts
May	Review all concepts	Review all concepts	Review all concepts

Calendars for Preparing for Each of the Plans

The Full School-Year Plan

SEPTEMBER
- Learn how the book is organized.
- Determine your approach.
- Skim the practice exams.
- Take the diagnostic exam.
- Choose an IDE, the *integrated development environment* in which you will write your code.
- Read Units 0–1.
- Learn about variables, data types, and casting.
- Learn about arithmetic expressions and assignment statements.

OCTOBER
- Read Units 2–3.
- Learn about using objects and how to call their methods correctly.
- Learn about `String` objects and their methods.
- Learn how to use the methods from the `Math` class.
- Learn Boolean expressions.
- Learn to use conditional statements.

NOVEMBER
- Read Unit 4.
- Learn basic looping structures.
- Learn nested iteration.

DECEMBER
- Read Unit 5.
- Learn how to write your own class.
- Learn how to write your own methods.
- Learn how to use documentation.

JANUARY
- Read Units 6–7.
- Learn how to create and use an array.
- Learn how to create and use an `ArrayList`.
- Learn the enhanced `for` loop for arrays.
- Learn basic algorithms for using arrays.
- Learn searching and sorting algorithms.

FEBRUARY
- Read Unit 8.
- Learn how to create and use a 2D array.
- Learn basic algorithms for using 2D arrays.

MARCH
- Read Units 9–10.
- Learn inheritance and how to extend a class.
- Learn polymorphism.

- Learn how to read recursive code.
- Learn recursive searching and sorting algorithms.

APRIL
- Take Practice Exam 1.
- Review the material on the exam.
- Take Practice Exam 2.
- Review the material on the exam.

MAY
- Do any last-minute reviewing.
- Take and ace the exam. Good luck!

The One-Semester Plan

JANUARY
- Learn how the book is organized.
- Determine your approach.
- Skim the practice exams.
- Take the diagnostic exam.
- Choose an IDE, the *integrated development environment* in which you will write your code.
- Read Units 0–3.
- Learn about variables, data types, and casting.
- Learn about arithmetic expressions and assignment statements.
- Learn about using objects and how to call their methods correctly.
- Learn about `String` objects and their methods.
- Learn how to use the methods from the `Math` class.
- Learn Boolean expressions.
- Learn to use conditional statements.

FEBRUARY
- Read Units 4–7.
- Learn the basic looping structures.
- Learn nested iteration.
- Learn how to write your own class.
- Learn how to write your own methods.
- Learn how to use documentation.
- Learn how to create and use an array.
- Learn how to create and use an `ArrayList`.
- Learn the enhanced `for` loop for arrays.
- Learn basic algorithms for using arrays.
- Learn searching and sorting algorithms.

MARCH
- Read Units 8–10.
- Learn how to create and use a 2D array.
- Learn the basic algorithms for using 2D arrays.
- Learn inheritance and how to extend a class.
- Learn polymorphism.

- Learn how to read recursive code.
- Learn recursive searching and sorting algorithms.

APRIL
- Take Practice Exam 1.
- Review the material on the exam.
- Take Practice Exam 2.
- Review the material on the exam.

MAY
- Do any last-minute reviewing.
- Take and ace the exam. Good luck!

The Six-Week Plan

WEEK 1
- Take the diagnostic exam.
- Read Units 0–2.
- Learn
  - variables and assignment statements.
  - how to use objects.
  - methods in the Math and String classes.

WEEK 2
- Read Units 3–5.
- Learn
  - Boolean expressions and if statements.
  - how to use while loops and for loops.
  - how to write and use class constructors and methods.

WEEK 3
- Read Units 6–8.
- Learn
  - to use an array, ArrayList, and 2D array.
  - searching and sorting algorithms.

WEEK 4
- Read Units 9–10.
- Learn
  - inheritance and polymorphism.
  - how to read recursive code.
- Take Practice Exam 1.
- Review the material on the exam.

WEEK 5
- Take Practice Exam 2.
- Review the material on the exam.

WEEK 6
- Do any last-minute reviewing.
- Take and ace the exam. Good luck!

STEP **2**

Determine Your Test Readiness

CHAPTER **3**   Take a Diagnostic Exam

CHAPTER 3

Take a Diagnostic Exam

IN THIS CHAPTER

Summary: This step contains a diagnostic exam that closely matches what you can expect to find on the actual test. Use this test to familiarize yourself with the AP Computer Science A Exam and to assess your strengths and weaknesses as you begin your review for the test.

Key Ideas

✪ Familiarize yourself with the types of questions and the level of difficulty of the actual AP Computer Science A Exam early in your test preparation process.

✪ Use the diagnostic exam to identify the content areas on which you need to focus your test preparation efforts.

Using the Diagnostic Exam

The purpose of the diagnostic exam is to give you a feel for what the actual AP Computer Science A Exam will be like and to identify content areas that you most need to review.

When to Take the Diagnostic Exam

Since one purpose of the diagnostic exam is to give you a preview of what to expect on the AP Computer Science A Exam, you should take the exam earlier rather than later. However, if you are attempting the diagnostic exam without having studied Java yet, you may feel overwhelmed and confused. If you are starting this book in September, you may want to read a sampling of questions from the diagnostic exam, but then save the test until later when you know some Java. Taking the diagnostic exam when you begin to review will help you identify what content you already know and what content you need to revisit; then you can alter your test prep plan accordingly.

Take the diagnostic exam in this step when you begin your review, but save both of the full-length practice exams at the end of this book until after you have covered all of the material and are ready to test your abilities.

How to Administer the Exam

When you take the diagnostic exam, try to reproduce the actual testing environment as closely as possible. Find a quiet place where you will not be interrupted. Do not listen to music or watch a movie while taking the exam! You will not be able to do this on the real exam. Set a timer and stop working when the 90 minutes are up for each section. Note how far you have gotten so you can learn to pace yourself, but take some extra time to complete all the questions so you can find your areas of weakness. Use the answer sheet provided and fill in the correct ovals with a #2 pencil. Although this is a computer science exam, the AP Computer Science A exam is a paper-and-pencil test.

Part I of the exam contains Multiple-choice questions. For this diagnostic exam, give yourself 90 minutes to complete the 40 Multiple-choice questions. Note that there is no penalty for guessing on the exam, so if you're not sure of an answer, eliminate obviously wrong answer choices and guess. You'll find more helpful strategies to use in answering the Multiple-choice questions in Step 3.

Part II of the exam consists of Free-response questions. On this diagnostic exam, give yourself 90 minutes to complete the four Free-response questions. Strategies you can use to approach the Free-response question efficiently and effectively can be found in Step 3. Read those strategies after you've tried the diagnostic exam and become familiar with the types of questions on the exam.

After Taking the Diagnostic Exam

Following the exam, you'll find not only the answers to the test questions, but also complete explanations for each answer. Do not just read the explanations for the questions you missed; you also need to understand the explanations for the questions you got right but weren't sure of. In fact, it's a good idea to work through the explanations for *all* the questions. Working through the step-by-step explanations is one of the most effective review tools in this book.

If you missed a lot of questions on the diagnostic exam or are just starting out learning how to program in Java, do not stress out! Step 4 of this book explains all of the concepts that will appear on the AP Computer Science A Exam. Read Units 0–10 in Step 4, do the practice questions for each unit, and read the explanations so you understand what the correct answer is and why it is correct. Then you'll be well prepared for the AP Computer Science A Exam.

On the other hand, if you did well on some of the questions on the diagnostic exam and understand the explanations for these questions, you may be able to skip some of the units in Step 4. Look at the summaries and key ideas that begin each of the units in Step 4. If you're reasonably sure you understand a concept already, you may want to skip to that unit's review questions or the "Rapid Review" and then move on to the next unit. A good test prep plan focuses on the areas you most need to review.

Now let's get started.

Diagnostic Exam

Multiple-Choice Questions
ANSWER SHEET

1 (A) (B) (C) (D) (E)   21 (A) (B) (C) (D) (E)
2 (A) (B) (C) (D) (E)   22 (A) (B) (C) (D) (E)
3 (A) (B) (C) (D) (E)   23 (A) (B) (C) (D) (E)
4 (A) (B) (C) (D) (E)   24 (A) (B) (C) (D) (E)
5 (A) (B) (C) (D) (E)   25 (A) (B) (C) (D) (E)
6 (A) (B) (C) (D) (E)   26 (A) (B) (C) (D) (E)
7 (A) (B) (C) (D) (E)   27 (A) (B) (C) (D) (E)
8 (A) (B) (C) (D) (E)   28 (A) (B) (C) (D) (E)
9 (A) (B) (C) (D) (E)   29 (A) (B) (C) (D) (E)
10 (A) (B) (C) (D) (E)   30 (A) (B) (C) (D) (E)
11 (A) (B) (C) (D) (E)   31 (A) (B) (C) (D) (E)
12 (A) (B) (C) (D) (E)   32 (A) (B) (C) (D) (E)
13 (A) (B) (C) (D) (E)   33 (A) (B) (C) (D) (E)
14 (A) (B) (C) (D) (E)   34 (A) (B) (C) (D) (E)
15 (A) (B) (C) (D) (E)   35 (A) (B) (C) (D) (E)
16 (A) (B) (C) (D) (E)   36 (A) (B) (C) (D) (E)
17 (A) (B) (C) (D) (E)   37 (A) (B) (C) (D) (E)
18 (A) (B) (C) (D) (E)   38 (A) (B) (C) (D) (E)
19 (A) (B) (C) (D) (E)   39 (A) (B) (C) (D) (E)
20 (A) (B) (C) (D) (E)   40 (A) (B) (C) (D) (E)

AP Computer Science A
Diagnostic Exam

Part I
Multiple Choice
Time: 90 minutes
Number of questions: 40
Percent of total score: 50

Directions: Choose the best answer for each problem. Use available space for scratch work and hand tracing. Some problems take longer than others. Consider how much time you have left before spending too much time on any one problem.

Notes:
- You may assume that all import statements have been included where they are needed.
- You may assume that the parameters in method calls are not null and the methods are called when their preconditions are met.
- You may assume that declarations of variables and methods appear within the context of an enclosing class.
- You may refer to the Java Quick Reference sheet as needed.

1. Consider the following method.

```
public int someMethod(int val)
{
    for (int i = 2; i < 7; i++)
    {
        if((val + i) % 2 == 0)
        {
            val += 3;
        }
    }
    return val;
}
```

What value is returned by the call `someMethod(13)`?
(A) 17
(B) 25
(C) 28
(D) 31
(E) Nothing is returned. There is a compile-time error.

2. Consider the following code segment.

```
int num1 = 2;
int num2 = 13;
int result = 4;

if ((num1 < 5) && (num2 < 5))
    result = num1 - num2;
else if ((num1 == 2) && (num2 < 2))
    result = num2 - num1;
else
    result = num1 + num2;
System.out.println(result);
```

What is printed as a result of executing the code segment?
(A) -11
(B) 4
(C) 11
(D) 13
(E) 15

3. Assume `list` is an `ArrayList<Integer>` that has been correctly constructed and populated with the following items.

```
[13, 7, 0, 5, 12, 6, 10]
```

Consider the following method.

```java
public int calculate(ArrayList<Integer> numbers)
{
    int sum = 0;

    for (Integer n : numbers)
    {
        if (n - 8 > 0)
        {
            sum = sum + n;
        }
    }
    return sum;
}
```

What value is returned by the call `calculate(list)`?

(A) `10`
(B) `11`
(C) `13`
(D) `35`
(E) `45`

4. Consider the following class declarations.

```
public class Planet
{
    private String name;
    private double mass;
    private int position;

    public Planet()
    {  /* implementation not shown  */  }

    public Planet(String name)
    {  /* implementation not shown  */  }

    public Planet(String name, int position)
    {  /* implementation not shown  */  }

}

public class DwarfPlanet extends Planet
{
    private double distance;
    public DwarfPlanet(String name)
    {  /* implementation not shown  */  }
}
```

Which of the following declarations compiles without error?

I.   `Planet mars = new Planet();`

II. `Planet pluto = new DwarfPlanet("Pluto");`

III. `Planet ceres = new DwarfPlanet();`

(A) I only
(B) II only
(C) I and II only
(D) I and III only
(E) I, II, and III

5. Consider the following code segment.

```
ArrayList<String> supernatural = new ArrayList<String>();

supernatural.add("Vampire");
supernatural.add("Werewolf");
supernatural.add("Ghost");
supernatural.set(0, "Zombie");
supernatural.add(2, "Mummy");
supernatural.add("Witch");
supernatural.remove(3);
System.out.println(supernatural);
```

What is printed as a result of executing the code segment?
(A) `[Zombie, Werewolf, Mummy, Witch]`
(B) `[Zombie, Werewolf, Ghost, Witch]`
(C) `[Zombie, Werewolf, Mummy, Ghost]`
(D) `[Zombie, Vampire, Werewolf, Mummy, Ghost]`
(E) `[Zombie, Vampire, Werewolf, Mummy, Witch]`

6. Suppose that grid has been initialized as n-by-n 2D array of integers. Which code segment will add all values that are along the two diagonals?

A.
```
int sum = 0;
for (int row = 0; row < grid.length; row++)
    for (int col = 0; col < grid[0].length; col++)
    {
        sum += grid[row][row];
        sum += grid[row][grid.length-1 - row];
    }
```

B.
```
int sum = 0;
for (int row = 0; row < grid.length; row++)
    for (int col = 0; col < grid[0].length; col++)
    {
        sum += grid[row][row];
        sum += grid[row][grid.length-1 - row];
    }
if(grid.length % 2 == 1)
    sum -= grid[grid.length/2][grid.length/2];
```

C.
```
int sum = 0;
for (int row = 0; row < grid.length; row++)
{
    sum += grid[row][row];
    sum += grid[row][grid.length-1 - row];
}
```

D.
```
int sum = 0;
for (int row = 0; row < grid.length; row++)
{
    sum += grid[row][row];
    sum += grid[row][grid.length-1 - row];
}
sum -= grid[grid.length/2][grid.length/2];
```

E.
```
int sum = 0;
for (int row = 0; row < grid.length; row++)
{
    sum += grid[row][row];
    sum += grid[row][grid.length-1 - row];
}
if(grid.length % 2 == 1)
    sum -= grid[grid.length/2][grid.length/2];
```

7. Consider the following partial class declaration.

```
public class Park
{
    private String name;
    private boolean playground;
    private int acres;

    public Park(String myName, boolean myPlayground, int myAcres)
    {
        name = myName;
        playground = myPlayground;
        acres = myAcres;
    }

    public String getName()
    {   return name;   }

    public boolean hasPlayground()
    {   return playground;   }

    public int getAcres()
    {   return acres;   }

    /* Additional implementation not shown */
}
```

Assume that the following declaration has been made in the main method of another class.

```
Park park = new Park("Central", true, 300);
```

Which of the following statements compiles without error?

(A) `int num = park.acres;`

(B) `String name = central.getName();`

(C) `boolean play = park.hasPlayground();`

(D) `int num = park.getAcres(acres);`

(E) `park.hasPlayground = true;`

8. Consider the following code segment.

```
String idk = "mnomnomno";
for (int i = 0; i < idk.length(); i++)
{
    if (idk.substring(i, i + 1).equals("m"))
    {
        idk = idk.substring(0, i) + idk.substring(i + 1, idk.length());
    }
}
System.out.println(idk);
```

What is printed as a result of executing the code segment?

(A) mmm
(B) nonono
(C) mnomno
(D) nomnono
(E) mnomnomno

9. Consider the following method.

```
public int loopy(int n)
{
    if (n % 7 == 0)
    {
        return n;
    }
    return loopy(n + 3) + 2;
}
```

What value is returned by the call loopy(12)?

(A) 12
(B) 21
(C) 23
(D) 27
(E) 29

10. Consider the following class declarations.

```
public class Letter
{
    private String letter = "letter";

    public String toString()
    {   return letter;   }

    /* Additional implementation not shown */
}

public class ALetter extends Letter
{
    private String letter = "a";

    public String toString()
    {   return letter;   }

    /* Additional implementation not shown */
}

public class BLetter extends Letter
{
    private String letter = "b";

    public String toString()
    {   return letter;   }

    /* Additional implementation not shown */
}

public class CapALetter extends ALetter
{
    private String letter = "A";

    /* Additional implementation not shown */
}
```

Consider the following code segment.

```
Letter x = new ALetter();
Letter y = new BLetter();
ALetter z = new CapALetter();

System.out.print(x);
System.out.print(y);
System.out.print(z);
```

What is printed as a result of executing the code segment?
(A) `abA`
(B) `aba`
(C) `letterlettera`
(D) `letterletterletter`
(E) Nothing is printed. There is a compile-time error.

11. Consider the following method.

```java
public String lengthen(String word)
{
    int index = 0;
    while (index < word.length())
    {
        word = word + word.substring(index, index + 1);
        index += 2;
    }
    return word;
}
```

What is returned by the call `lengthen("APCS")`?

(A) `"APCS"`

(B) `"APCSACAA"`

(C) `"APCSAPCS"`

(D) Nothing is returned. Run-time error: `StringIndexOutOfBoundsException`

(E) Nothing is returned. The call will result in an infinite loop.

12. Consider the following code segment.

```java
int[] array = {-3, 0, 2, 4, 5, 9, 13, 1, 5};
for (int n = 1; n < array.length - 1; n++)
{
    if (array[n] - array[n - 1] <= array[n] - array[n + 1])
        System.out.print(array[n] + "   ");
}
```

What is printed as a result of executing the code segment?

(A) `1`

(B) `13`

(C) `13 1`

(D) `2 4 5`

(E) `2 4 5 9`

13. Assume that `k`, `m`, and `n` have been declared and correctly initialized with `int` values. Consider the following statement.

```java
boolean b1 = (n >= 4) || ((m == 5 || k < 2) && (n > 12));
```

For which statement below does `b2 = !b1` for all values of `k`, `m`, and `n`?

(A) `boolean b2 = (n >= 4) && ((m == 5 && k < 2) || (n > 12));`

(B) `boolean b2 = (n < 4) || ((m != 5 || k >= 2) && (n <= 12));`

(C) `boolean b2 = (n < 4) && (m != 5) && (k >= 2) || (n <= 12);`

(D) `boolean b2 = (m == 5 || k < 2) && (n > 12);`

(E) `boolean b2 = (n < 4);`

14. Consider the following code segment.

```
int[] ray = new int[11];

for (int i = 0; i < ray.length; i++)
{
    ray[i] = i * 2;
}

for (int m = 0; m < 5; m++)
{
    for (int n = 0; n < 7; n += 2)
    {
        if (m + n > 8)
        {
            System.out.print(ray[m + n]);
        }
    }
}
```

What is printed as a result of executing the code segment?
(A) Nothing is printed. Runtime error: `ArrayIndexOutOfBounds`
(B) `18`
(C) `181620`
(D) `68`
(E) `1820`

15. Consider the following method.

```
public int mystery(String code, int index)
{
    if (code.indexOf("c") == index)
    {
        return index;
    }
    return mystery(code.substring(2), index + 1);
}
```

Assume that the string `codeword` has been declared and initialized as follows.

```
String codeword = "advanced placement";
```

What value is returned by the call `mystery(codeword, 9)`?
(A) `5`
(B) `6`
(C) `7`
(D) Nothing is returned. Infinite recursion causes a stack overflow error.
(E) Nothing is returned. Run-time error: `StringIndexOutOfBoundsException`

16. Consider the following method.

```
public void switcheroo(int num, int index, int[] nums)
{
    int temp = num;
    num = nums[index];
    nums[index] = temp;
    index++;
}
```

Consider the following code segment.

```
int[] val = {5, 7, 4, -2, 8, 12};
int num = 10;
int index = 3;
switcheroo(num, index, val);

System.out.println("num = " + num + "   val[" + index + "] = " + val[index]);
```

What is printed as a result of executing the code segment?
(A) num = 10   val[3] = 10
(B) num = 10   val[3] = -2
(C) num = 10   val[4] = 8
(D) num = -2   val[3] = 10
(E) num = -2   val[4] = 8

17. Consider the following code segment.

```
for (int h = 2; h <= 6; h += 2)
{
    for (int k = 30; k > 0; k -= 10)
    {
        System.out.print(h + k + "    ");
    }
}
```

Consider these additional code segments.

I.
```
int num = 32;
int count = 0;
for (int i = 0; i < 9; i++)
{
    System.out.print(num + "    ");
    num += 2;
    if (count % 3 == 0)
    {
        count = 0;
        num -= 14;
    }
}
```

II.
```
int num = 32;
while (num < 38)
{
    System.out.print(num + "    ");
    num -= 10;
    if (num < 10)
    {
        num += 32;
    }
}
```

III.
```
for (int h = 0; h <= 3; h++)
{
    for (int k = 30; k > 0; k -= 10)
    {
        System.out.print(k + h + "    ");
    }
}
```

Which of the code segments produce the same output as the original code segment?
(A) I only
(B) II only
(C) III only
(D) II and III only
(E) I, II, and III

18. Consider the following method.

```
public void mystery (int[] array)
{
    for (int i = 1; i < array.length; i++)
    {
        int j;
        int key = array[i];
        for (j = i - 1; j >= 0 && array[j] > key; j--)
        {
            array[j + 1] = array[j];
        }
        array[j + 1] = key;
    }
}
```

The method above could be best described as an implementation of which of the following?
(A) Insertion Sort
(B) Binary Search
(C) Selection Sort
(D) Merge Sort
(E) Sequential Sort

19. Consider the following statement.

```
int number = (int)(Math.random() * 21 + 13);
```

After executing the statement, what are the possible values for the variable `number`?
(A) All integers from 13 to 21 (inclusive).
(B) All real numbers from 13 to 34 (not including 34).
(C) All integers from 13 to 34 (inclusive).
(D) All integers from 13 to 33 (inclusive).
(E) All real numbers from 0 to 21 (not including 21).

20. Consider the following class declaration.

```
public class City
{
    private String name;
    private int population;

    public City(String myName, int myPop)
    {
        name = myName;
        population = myPop;
    }

    public String getName()
    {   return name;   }

    public int getPopulation()
    {   return population;   }

    /*  Additional implementation not shown */
}
```

Assume `ArrayList<City> cities` has been properly instantiated and populated with `City` objects.

Consider the following code segment.

```
int maxPop = Integer.MIN_VALUE;
for (int i = 0; i < cities.size(); i++)
{
    /* missing code */
}
```

Which of the following should replace `/* missing code */` so that, after execution is complete, `maxPop` will contain the largest population that exists in the `ArrayList`?

(A)
```
City temp = cities[i];
if (temp.getPopulation() > maxPop)
{
    maxPop = temp.getPopulation();
}
```

(B)
```
City temp = cities.get(i);
if (temp.population > maxPop)
{
    maxPop = temp.population;
}
```

(C)
```
if (cities.get(i + 1).getPopulation() > cities.get(i).getPopulation())
{
    maxPop = cities.get(i + 1).getPopulation();
}
```

(D)
```
if (cities.get(i).getPopulation() > maxPop)
{
    maxPop = cities.get(i).getPopulation();
}
```

(E) `maxPop` should have been set to `Integer.MAX_VALUE`. This cannot work as written.

21. Consider the following method.

```
public static int mystery(int n){
    int a, b, c = 0;
    while (n > 0){
        a = n/10;
        b = n % 10;
        c *= 10;
        c += b;
        n = a;
    }
    return c;
}
```

Which statement best describes the value that is returned by mystery?

(A) Ten to the nth power is returned.

(B) The number of digits in n is returned.

(C) The number of times 10 is a factor of n is returned.

(D) The number whose digits are the reverse of n is returned.

(E) The sum of the digits in n is returned.

22. Consider the following code segment.

```
int x = 2;
int y = 4;
x += y;
y += x;
System.out.println("x = " + x + ", y = " + y);
```

What output is produced by executing this code?

(A) x = 2, y = 4

(B) x = 6, y = 6

(C) x = 6, y = 10

(D) x = 6, y = 12

(E) x = 24, y = 42

Questions 23 and 24 refer to the following class hierarchy.

```
public class Alpha
{
    public void eeny(int a,  int b)
    {
        System.out.print("alpha eeny ");
    }
    // other methods not shown
}
public class Beta extends Alpha
{
    public void miny(int x)
    {
        System.out.print("miny ");
    }
    // other methods not shown
}
public class Gamma extends Beta
{
    public void eeny(int a, int b)
    {
        System.out.print("gamma eeny ");
    }
    // other methods not shown
}
public class Delta extends Alpha
{
    public void eeny(int x)
    {
        System.out.print("delta eeny ");
    }
    // other methods not shown
}
```

23. What is printed as a result of executing the following code? (Assume that all the classes have parameterless constructors.)

```
Beta b = new Beta();
Alpha a = new Gamma();
b.eeny(1,1);
a.eeny(0,1);
```

(A) Nothing; the code does not compile.
(B) `alpha eeny`
(C) `alpha eeny alpha eeny`
(D) `alpha eeny gamma eeny`
(E) `miny gamma eeny`

24. What is printed as a result of executing the following code? (Assume that all the classes have parameterless constructors.)

```
Delta d = new Delta();
d.eeny(2);
d.eeny(0,1);
```

(A) Nothing; the code does not compile.
(B) `alpha eeny alpha eeny`
(C) `delta eeny`
(D) `delta eeny alpha eeny`
(E) `delta eeny delta eeny alpha eeny`

25. Assume that an `ArrayList` names holds the following values.

```
{"Debbie", "Rob", "Kelly", "Sandy", "Kim", "J.P. ", "Andy", "Tim", "Alistair",
    "Judy"}
```

What values does this `ArrayList` hold after executing the following code?

```
for (int i = 1; i <= 4; i++)
  names.remove(i);
```

(A) Debbie, Rob, Kelly, Sandy, Kim, J.P.
(B) Debbie, J.P., Andy, Tim, Alistair, Judy
(C) Debbie, Kelly, Kim, Andy, Alistair, Judy
(D) Rob, Sandy, J.P., Tim, Alistair, Judy
(E) Kim, J.P., Andy, Tim, Alistair, Judy

26. Consider the following method.

```
// precondition : n > 1
public static double solve(int n)
{
    double answer = 1.0;
    for (int k = 1; k < n; k++)
        answer *= (double)k/(k + 1);
    return answer;
}
```

What value is returned by a call to method `solve`?
(A) 0.0
(B) The kth root of n
(C) 1/n
(D) 1/(n-1)
(E) $(1/2)^n$

27. Consider the following method.

```
public boolean evaluate(boolean p, boolean q)
{
    return ((p && q) || !(p || q))
}
```

What is returned by `evaluate`?
(A) `evaluate` always returns `false`
(B) `evaluate` returns `true` when p and q are both `true` or both `false`
(C) `evaluate` returns `true` only when p and q are both `true`
(D) `evaluate` returns `true` only when p and q are both `false`
(E) `evaluate` returns `true` when either p or q is `true` and the other is `false`

28. Consider the following class declaration.

```
public class SeatLocation
{    private String row; // "A", "B", "C", ... , "Z", "AA", "BB", ... , "ZZ"
     private int seatNumber;
     public String getRow()  { }// implementation not shown
     public int getSeatNumber() { }// implementation not shown
     // constructor and other methods not shown
}

public class Ticket
{    private double price;
     private SeatLocation loc;
     public void setPrice(double p)
     {
         price = p;
     }

     public void setSeatLocation (SeatLocation s)
     {
         loc = s;
     }

     public double getPrice()
     {
         return price;
     }

     public SeatLocation getSeatLocation()
     {
         return loc;
     }
     // constructor and other methods not shown
}
```

Assume the following valid declarations have been made.

```
SeatLocation s = new SeatLocation("Q",107);
Ticket t = new Ticket(85.00, s);
double totalCost = 0.0;
```

Which of the following statements in a client program is valid?
(A) if (s.row > "M") System.out.println("Too far back");
(B) t.setSeatLocation("E",19);
(C) System.out.println(t.getSeatLocation(s.getRow(),s.getSeatNumber()));
(D) t.setPrice(0.5 * t.getPrice());
(E) for (String row = "A"; row.compareTo("Z") < 0; row++)
        totalCost += t.getPrice();

29. Suppose that `glop` is an `ArrayList` of `DooHickeys`. Consider the following code fragment that is meant to print out the ID numbers of all `DooHickeys` whose mass is greater than zero.

```
for (int num = 0; num < glop.size(); num++)
{
  if (/* missing code */)
      System.out.println(glop.get(num).getId());
}
```

Which of the following expressions will complete the code fragment correctly?
(A) `Doohickeys.get(num).getMass() > 0`
(B) `getNum(glop).getMass() > 0`
(C) `glop[num].getMass() > 0`
(D) `glop.get(num).getMass() >0`
(E) `glop.get(glop.getMass(num)) > 0`

30. Consider the following method, which is intended to count the number of times a value is doubled before it is at least as large as a target value.

```
// precondition: d > 0
public void doubleUp(double d)
{
    static final double TARGET = 100.0;
    int count;
    while (d < TARGET)
    {
        count = 0;
        d *= 2;
        count++;
    }
    System.out.println(count);
}
```

Of the following, which best describes the error in `doubleUp`?
(A) The static modifier cannot be used with a constant.
(B) A variable is used without being initialized.
(C) A double cannot be multiplied by an int.
(D) The counter is incremented in the wrong place.
(E) A variable is initialized in the wrong place.

Question 31 and 32 refer to the following method.

```
private int n;

public static boolean check(int[ ] arr)
{
   boolean theCheck = true;
   for (int k = 0; k < n - 1; k++)
   {
      if (arr[k] >= arr[k+1])
         theCheck = !theCheck;
   }
   return theCheck;
}
```

31. Which of the following is the best precondition for method `check`?
   (A) `0 <= n < arr.length`
   (B) `n < arr.length`
   (C) `n <= arr.length`
   (D) `n >= 0`
   (E) No precondition is necessary.

32. Which of the following is the best postcondition for method `check`?
   (A) returns `true` if there are no duplicates in the first n elements of `arr`; otherwise, returns `false`
   (B) returns `true` if the (n-1)th element of `arr` is less than the nth element; otherwise, returns `false`
   (C) returns `true` if the first n elements of `arr` are all the same value; otherwise, returns `false`
   (D) returns `true` if the first n elements of `arr` are in strictly increasing order; otherwise, returns `false`
   (E) returns `true` if there are an even number of times when an element is at least as large as its successor among the first n elements of `arr`; otherwise, returns `false`

33. Assuming that b is a boolean variable, what will be the result of executing the code?

```
b = (b != b)
```

   (A) Sets b to `false`
   (B) Sets b to `true`
   (C) Changes the value of b to its opposite
   (D) Leaves the value of b unchanged
   (E) The code will not compile.

34. Consider the following class declaration.

```
public class SimpleInt
{
   private int myInt;

   public void setVal(int v)
   {
      myInt = v;
   }


   public int getVal()
   {
       return myInt;
   }
}
```

Assuming that x is a properly constructed SimpleInt, which of the following statements will compile in a program that uses SimpleInt?

```
I.   System.out.println (x.getVal());
II.  System.out.println (x.myInt);
III. System.out.println (x.setVal(10));
```

(A) I only
(B) II only
(C) I and II only
(D) I and III only
(E) I, II, and III

35. Which expression below is equivalent to the following? (Assume x and y are Strings.)

```
((x != null) && (x.compareTo(y) > 0))
```

(A) ((x.equals(null))||(x.compareTo(y) > 0)
(B) ((x.equals(null)) && (x.compareTo(y) == 0)
(C) !((x != null) || (x.compareTo(y) >= 0))
(D) !((x == null) && (x.compareTo(y) < 0))
(E) !((x == null) || (x.compareTo(y) <= 0))

36. A programmer has mistakenly placed a semicolon at the end of the while statement in the following code fragment. What will be the result of executing the code?

```
while (j < n);   // mistaken semicolon
{
    System.out.println("in loop");
    j++;
}
```

(A) The code will behave in the same manner as if the semicolon were not included.
(B) The program will get caught in an infinite loop, appearing to do nothing.
(C) The program will get caught in an infinite loop, repeatedly printing the message, "in loop".
(D) Depending on the code that precedes this loop within the program, either an infinite loop will result or the "in loop" message will be printed one time.
(E) The code will not compile because of the presence of the semicolon at the end of the while statement.

37. Consider the following incomplete method that is intended to determine if the corresponding elements of two parallel arrays are equal.

```
// precondition: arr1.length = arr2.length
// postcondition: returns true if for all k, 0 <= k < n, arr1[k] = arr2[k]
public static boolean match(String [] arr1, String[] arr2)
{
    int n = arr1.length;
    < missing code>
}
```

Which of the following is a valid replacement for < missing code>?

(A)
```
for (int k = 0; k < n; k++)
    return arr1[k].equals(arr2[k]);
```

(B)
```
for (int k = 0; k < n; k++)
    if (arr1[k].equals(arr2[k]))
      return true;
return false;
```

(C)
```
boolean same = true;
for (int k = 0; k < n; k++)
  if (!arr1[k].equals(arr2[k]))
    same = false;
  else
    same = true;
return same;
```

(D)
```
boolean same = true;
int k = 0;
while (same && k < n)
  k++;
return same;
```

(E)
```
int k = 0;
while (k < n && arr1[k].equals(arr2[k]))
  k++;
return k == n;
```

For questions 38 and 39, consider the inheritance hierarchy shown below.

38. Suppose that we wish to add the class Snake to this hierarchy. Which of the two implementation schemes below is more appropriate and why?
  I.   The class Snake should extend the class Animal
  II. The class Snake should extend the class Cat

  (A) Implementation I is a better choice because it is the case that Snake IS-A Animal, but it is not the case that Snake IS-A Cat.
  (B) Implementation I is a better choice because the code will be shorter and easier to understand.
  (C) Implementation II is a better choice because the Snake class can inherit most of its operations from the Cat class.
  (D) Implementation II is a better choice because it leads to a deeper inheritance hierarchy.
  (E) The two implementations are approximately equivalent.

39. Which of the following is NOT true about the data and methods in the various classes?
  (A) A Dog object may use public instance variables declared in the Animal class.
  (B) An Animal object may use public instance variables associated with a separate Dog object.
  (C) A Cat object may use private instance variables declared in the Animal class.
  (D) A Cat object may invoke public methods declared in the Animal class.
  (E) A Cat object may use private instance variables associated with a separate Dog object whenever appropriate access methods are provided.

40. Consider the following recursive method.

```
public static int mystery(int x)
{
  if (x <= 1 || x == 3)
    return x;
  else
    return (mystery(x - 1) + mystery(x - 2));
}
```

What value will be printed by the call mystery(5)?
  (A) 1
  (B) 3
  (C) 4
  (D) 7
  (E) 11

STOP. End of Part I.

AP Computer Science A
Diagnostic Exam

Part II
Free Response
Time: 90 minutes
Number of questions: 4
Percent of total score: 50%

Directions: Write all of your code in Java. Show all your work.

Notes:

- You may assume all import statements have been included where they are needed.
- You may assume that all preconditions are met when making calls to methods.
- You may assume that all parameters within method calls are not null.
- Be aware that you should, when possible, use methods that are defined in the classes provided as opposed to duplicating them by writing your own code. Doing so you will not receive full credit.
- You may use the Java Quick Reference sheet as needed.

1. The `StringRotation` class contains methods used to determine if a string is a rotation of another string. The declaration of the `StringRotation` class is shown below. You will write two methods of this class.

```
public class StringRotation
{

    /** Returns the number of rotations necessary for rotation to be the same value as base.
     * If no rotations are possible for rotation to be the same value as base, -1 is returned.
     /
    public static int findNumberOfRotations(String base, String rotation)
    {        /* to be implemented in part (a) */
    }


    /** Returns true if rotation is a reverse rotation of base and false otherwise.
     */
    public static boolean isReverseRotation(String base, String rotation)
    {        /* to be implemented in part (b) */
    }


    // There may be instance variables, constructors, and methods that are not shown.

}
```

(a) Write the static method `findNumberOfRotations`, which returns the number of rotations necessary for `rotation` and `base` to have the same value. A `String` is considered a rotation of another `String` if the order of the letters remains the same, but the positions of the letters are shifted, causing the letters at the end of the `String` to shift to the beginning of the `String`. If no rotations are possible for the values of `rotation` and `base` to be the same, then `-1` is returned.
The chart contains a sample code execution and the corresponding result.

Statement	Value returned
`StringRotation.findNumberOfRotations("happy", "happy")`	0
`StringRotation.findNumberOfRotations("happy", "happiness")`	-1
`StringRotation.findNumberOfRotations("happy", "appyh")`	4
`StringRotation.findNumberOfRotations("happy", "yhapp")`	1
`StringRotation.findNumberOfRotations("happy", "pyhap")`	2
`StringRotation.findNumberOfRotations("care", "race")`	-1

(b) Write the static method `isReverseRotation`, which returns `true` if `rotation` is a reverse rotation of `base` and `false` otherwise. A `String` is considered a reverse rotation of another `String` if the `Strings` are the reverse of one another and one has been rotated. You may call on `findNumberOfRotations` and assume it works as intended, regardless of your implementation.
The chart contains a sample code execution and the corresponding result.

Statement	Value returned
`StringRotation.isReverseRotation("computer", "retupmoc")`	true
`StringRotation.isReverseRotation("computer", "mocretup")`	true
`StringRotation.isReverseRotation("computer", "putercom")`	false
`StringRotation.isReverseRotation("computer", "mocsretup")`	false

2. The class `FurnitureItem` represents a furniture item sold at a local furniture store.

```
public class FurnitureItem
{
    /** Returns the product ID of this item. */
    public String getProductId()
    {   /* implementation not shown */   }


    /** Returns the price of this item. */
    public double getPrice()
    {   /* implementation not shown */   }


    // There may be instance variables, constructors, and methods that are not shown.
}
```

The furniture store offers a special summer promotion that includes a discount if two items are purchased from the same set. You will write a class `SummerSpecial` to represent the result of purchasing two `FurnitureItem` objects, based on the following rules and the examples in the chart that follows.

- The set to which a `FurnitureItem` belongs is identified by the last five characters of the item's product ID. For example, a chair with product ID `C-123456-APCSA` and a table with product ID `T-987-APCSA` both belong to the `APCSA` furniture set. Note that product IDs from different items may differ in length.
- If two items belong to the same set, the total price is calculated by deducting 25% from the price of the more expensive item and then adding the price of the less expensive item.
- If two items do not belong to the same set, the total price is calculated by deducting 10% from the price of the least expensive item and then adding the price of the more expensive item.

Assume `FurnitureItem` objects `item1`, `item2`, and `item3` have been created as follows.
- `FurnitureItem item1` is a chair with product ID `C-123456-APCSA` and a price of $250.
- `FurnitureItem item2` is a table with product ID `T-9876-APCSA` and a price of $500.
- `FurnitureItem item3` is a chair with product ID `C-2468-APCSP` and a price of $125.

The chart contains a sample code execution sequence and the corresponding results.

Statement	Value Returned (blank if no value)	Class Specifications
`SummerSpecial ss1 = new` `    SummerSpecial(item1, item2)`		A `SummerSpecial` is composed of two `FurnitureItem` objects.
`ss1.isSet()`	true	Since its two furniture items have product IDs that end with the same five characters, the two items belong to the same set.
`ss1.getPrice()`	625.0	Because its two furniture items belong to the same set, the total price is the sum of the price of the most expensive item minus 25% plus the price of the least expensive item. 500.0 * 0.75 + 250.0 = 625.0
`SummerSpecial ss2 = new` `    SummerSpecial(item1, item3)`		A `SummerSpecial` is composed of two `FurnitureItem` objects.
`ss2.isSet()`	false	Since its two furniture items have product IDs that do not end with the same 5 characters, the two items do not belong to the same set.
`ss2.getPrice()`	362.5	Because its two furniture items do not belong to the same set, the total price is the sum of the price of the least expensive item minus 10% plus the price of the most expensive item. 125.0 * 0.90 + 250.0 = 362.5

Write the complete `SummerSpecial` class. Your implementation must meet all specifications and conform to the examples shown in the preceding chart. Note that you must call `isSet()` from within the `getPrice()` method to earn full credit.

3. The class `Route` represents a route that can be stored in a `GPSRouter` object.

```
public class Route
{
    /** Returns the route's name */
    public String getName() {  /* implementation not shown */  }

    /** Returns the mileage of the route */
    public int getMiles(){  /* implementation not shown */  }

    /** Sets the mileage of this route to the specified quantity */
    public void setMiles(int num) {  /* implementation not shown */  }

    // There may be instance variables, constructors, and methods that are not shown.
}
```

The class `GPSRouter` represents a collection of `Route` objects. Assume that the collection `routes` has been initialized.

```
public class GPSRouter
{
    private ArrayList<Route> routes; // Collection of routes
    /** Returns the Route object with the largest number of miles in the
     * GPS' collection
     */
    public Route maxMileage(){  /* implemented in part a */  }
    /** Adds the given mileage to the existing Route from the GPS, if it
     * exists. If this route is already in the collection, it updates the
     * mileage. If a route with the given name does not exist, it adds a
     * new route with the given name and mileage.
     */
    public void addMiles (String routeName, int mileage)
    { /* implemented in part b */  }
    // There may be instance variables, constructors, and methods that are not shown.
}
```

You will write two methods from the class GPSRouter as follows:
- The method maxMileage will find the Route object in the GPSRouter object with the largest number of miles and return it. If the GPSRouter object has no routes, then the method will return null.
- The method addMiles will add a route to the GPSRouter object with the given name based on the following requirements:
  - Routes in a GPSRouter object are identified by name. All routes in a GPSRouter object have unique names.
  - If the route is already represented in the GPSRouter object (has the same name as the given name routeName), then increase the mileage in the corresponding route by the given amount mileage.
  - If the route is not already represented in the GPSRouter object (the given name routeName does not match any name in the collection), then add a new Route to the collection with the given name routeName and mileage mileage.

Assume a GPSRouter object gps has been created and the following routes (already created) have been added into it.
- Route route1 is a Route with name "Kalamazoo" and a mileage of 5200.
- Route route2 is a Route with name "Tampa" and a mileage of 7000.
- Route route3 is a Route with name "Dayton" and a mileage of 1000.

The chart contains a sample code execution sequence and the corresponding results.

Statement	Value Returned (blank if no value)	Class Specifications
gps.maxMileage()	route2	
gps.addMiles("Dayton", 500);		The gps collection routes will have three items. The one with name "Dayton" will now have a mileage of 1500, which is the sum of 1000 + 500.
gps.addMiles("Chicago", 7500);		The gps collection routes will have four items with the one of them being a route with name "Chicago" and a mileage of 7500.
gps.maxMileage()	The Route with name "Chicago" and mileage 7500	

a) Write the implementation for the maxMileage method of the GPSRouter class, which will return the Route object with the largest number of miles. If there are no routes in the GPSRouter object, return null.
/** Returns the Route object with the largest number of miles in the GPS' collection   */
```
    public Route maxMileage()
```

b) Write the implementation of the addMiles method of the GPSRouter class, which updates the mileage of the given Route if it exists in the collection and adds the given Route to the collection if it does not.
/** Adds the given mileage to the existing Route from the GPS, if it exists. If this route is already
* in the collection, it updates the mileage. If a route with the given name does not exist, it
* adds a new route with the given name and mileage.
*/
```
    public void addMiles (String routeName, int mileage)
```

4. Coin Collector

The High School Coin Collection Club needs new software to help organize its coin collections. Each coin in the collection is represented by an object of the Coin class. The Coin class maintains three pieces of information for each coin: its country of origin, the year it was minted, and the type of coin it is. Because coin denominations vary from country to country, the club has decided to assign a coin type of 1 to the coin of lowest denomination, 2 to the next lowest, and so on. For American coins, coinType is assigned like this:

Coin Name	Value	coinType
Penny	$0.01	1
Nickel	$0.05	2
Dime	$0.10	3
Quarter	$0.25	4
Half-Dollar	$0.50	5
Dollar	$1.00	6

```
public class Coin
{
    private String country;
    private int year;
    private int coinType;

    public Coin(String cCountry, int cYear, int cType)
    {
        country = cCountry;
        year = cYear;
        coinType = cType;
    }

    public String getCountry()
    {   return country;   }

    public int getYear()
    {   return year;   }

    public int getCoinType()
    {   return coinType;   }
}
```

The Coin Club currently keeps track of its coins by maintaining an ArrayList of Coin objects for each country. The coins in the ArrayList are in order by year, oldest to newest. If two or more coins were minted in the same year, those coins appear in a random order with respect to the other coins from the same year.

The Coin Club has acquired some new collection boxes of various sizes to store their coins. The boxes are rectangular and contain many small compartments in a grid of rows and columns. The club will store coins from different countries in different boxes.

The `CoinCollectionTools` class below assists the Coin Club in organizing and maintaining their collection.

```
public class CoinCollectionTools
{
    private Coin[][] coinBox;

    /** Constructor instantiates coinBox and fills it with
     *  default Coin objects
     *
     *  @param country the country of origin of the coins in this box
     *  @param rows the number of rows in the coin box
     *  @param columns the number of columns in the coin box
     */
    public CoinCollectionTools(String country, int rows, int columns)
    {
        /* to be completed in part (a) */
    }


    /** Creates and returns a completed coinBox grid by adding the
     *  Coin objects from the parameter ArrayList to the coinBox
     *  in column-major order.
     *
     *  @param myCoins the list of Coin objects to be added
     *                 to the coinBox
     *  Precondition:  myCoins is in order by year
     *  Precondition:  the size of myCoins is not greater than the
     *                 the total number of compartments available
     *  @return coinBox the completed 2D array of Coin objects
     */
    public Coin[][] fillCoinBox(ArrayList<Coin> myCoins)
    {
        /*  to be implemented in part (b)  */
    }


    /** Returns an ArrayList of Coin objects sorted by coinType
     *
     *  @return ArrayList of Coin objects
     *  Precondition: all cells in coinBox contain a valid Coin object
     *  Precondition: coinBox is ordered by year in column-major
     *                order followed by default Coin objects
     *  Postcondition: Coins in ArrayList are in order grouped by coinType
     */
    public ArrayList<Coin> fillCoinTypeList()
    {
        /*  to be implemented in part (c)  */
    }

    /* Additional implementation not shown */
}
```

(a) The `CoinCollectionTools` class constructor initializes the instance variable `coinBox` as a two-dimensional array of `Coin` objects with dimensions specified by the parameters. It then instantiates each of the `Coin` objects in the array as a default `Coin` object with `country` equal to the country name passed as a parameter, `year` equal to 0, and `coinType` equal to 0.

   Complete the `CoinCollectionTools` class constructor.

```
/** Constructor instantiates coinBox and fills it with
 * default Coin objects
 *
 * @param country the country of origin of the coins in this box
 * @param rows the number of rows in the coin box
 * @param columns the number of columns in the coin box
 */
public CoinCollectionTools(String country, int rows, int columns)
```

(b) The Coin Club intends to fill the collection boxes from their list of coins, starting in the upper-left corner and moving down the columns in order until all `Coin` objects have been placed in a compartment.

   The `fillCoinBox` method takes as a parameter an `ArrayList` of `Coin` objects in order by year minted and returns a chart showing their position in the box, filled in column-major order.

   You may assume that `coinBox` is initialized as intended, regardless of what you wrote in part (a).

   Complete the method `fillCoinBox`.

```
/** Creates and returns a completed coinBox chart by adding the
 *  Coin objects from the parameter ArrayList to the coinBox
 *  in column-major order.
 *
 *  @param myCoins the list of Coin objects to be added
 *                 to the coinBox
 *  Precondition:  myCoins is in order by year
 *  Precondition:  the size of myCoins is not greater than the
 *                 the total number of compartments available
 *  @return coinBox the completed two-dimensional array of Coin objects
 */
public Coin[][] fillCoinBox(ArrayList<Coin> myCoins)
```

(c) Sometimes the Coin Club would prefer to see a list of its coins organized by coin type.

   The `fillCoinTypeList` method uses the values in `coinBox` to create and return an `ArrayList` of `Coin` objects filled first with all the `Coin` objects of type 1, then type 2, and so on through type 6. You may assume that no country has more than 6 coin types. Note that the number of coins from any specific type may be 0.

   Since the original `coinBox` was filled in column-major order, `Coin` objects should be retrieved from the `coinBox` in column-major order. This will maintain ordering by year within each coin type.

   Remember that the `CoinCollectionTools` class constructor filled the `coinBox` with default `Coin` objects with a `coinType` of 0, so no entry in the `coinBox` is null.

   You may assume that `coinBox` is initialized and filled as intended, regardless of what you wrote in parts (a) and (b).

   Complete the method `fillCoinTypeList`.

```
/** Returns an ArrayList of Coin objects sorted by coinType
 *
 *  @return ArrayList of Coin objects
 *  Precondition: all cells in coinBox contain a valid Coin object
 *  Precondition: coinBox is ordered by year in column-major
 *                order followed by default Coin objects
 *  Postcondition: Coins in ArrayList are in order grouped by coinType
 */
public ArrayList<Coin> fillCoinTypeList()
```

STOP. End of Part II.

Diagnostic Exam Answers and Explanations

Part I (Multiple Choice) Answers and Unit Mapping

#	Answer	Learning Objectives	Unit
1	B	MOD-1.G, CON-1.E, CON-2.E	2, 3, 4
2	E	MOD-1.A, CON-2.A	1, 3
3	D	MOD-1.G, VAR-2.Eb, CON-2.A	2, 3, 7
4	C	MOD-3.B, MOD-3.C	9
5	A	MOD-1.A, VAR-2.D	1, 7
6	E	VAR-2.G, CON-1.E, CON-2.N	3, 8
7	C	MOD-1.Db, MOD-1.G	2
8	B	MOD-1.A, CON-2.A, VAR-1.E	1, 2, 4
9	D	MOD-1.G, CON-2.A	2, 3
10	B	MOD-1.A, MOD-3.C	1, 8
11	B	MOD-1.G, VAR-1.Eb, CON-2.C	2, 4
12	C	MOD-1.A, VAR-2.A, VAR-2.B	1, 6
13	C	CON-1.E	3
14	E	MOD-1.A, VAR-2.B, CON-2.G	1, 4, 6
15	E	MOD-1.G, VAR-1.Eb, CON-2.D	2, 10
16	A	MOD-1.A, MOD-1.G, VAR-2.A	1, 2, 6
17	B	MOD-1.A, CON-1.E, CON-2.G	1, 3, 4
18	A	CON-2.L, CON-2.K	7
19	D	CON-1.D	2
20	D	CON-2.J	7
21	D	MOD-1.G, CON-2.C	2, 4
22	C	MOD-1.A, VAR-1.C	1
23	D	MOD-1.A, MOD-3.B, MOD-3.D	1, 9
24	D	MOD-1.A, MOD-3.B, MOD-3.D	1, 9
25	C	VAR-2.D, CON-2.J	7
26	C	MOD-1.H, CON-2.E	2, 4
27	B	CON-1.E	3
28	D	MOD-1.Db, MOD-1.G	2
29	D	MOD-1.A, VAR-2.D, VAR-2.Ea	1, 7
30	E	MOD-1.F, VAR-1.D, CON-2.C	2, 4
31	C	MOD-2.C	5
32	E	MOD-2.C	5
33	A	CON-1.E	3
34	A	MOD-1.A, MOD-1.G	1, 2
35	E	CON-1.E, VAR-1.Eb	2, 3
36	D	MOD-1.A, CON-2.C, CON-2.H	1, 4
37	E	VAR-2.B	6
38	A	MOD-3.B	9
39	C	MOD-3.D	9
40	D	CON-2.D	10

Part I (Multiple-Choice) Answers and Explanations

Bullets mark each step in the process of arriving at the correct solution.

1. The answer is B.
   - When we first enter the loop, val = 13 and i = 2. The if condition is looking for even numbers. Since val + i is odd, we skip the if clause. Increment i to 3. i < 7 so we continue.
   - val = 13, i = 3. This time val + i is even, so add 3 to val. val = 16, increment i to 4, i < 7 so we continue.
   - val = 16, i = 4. val + i is even, add 3 to val. val = 19, increment i to 5, i < 7, continue.
   - val = 19, i = 5. val + i is even, add 3 to val. val = 22, increment i to 6, i < 7, continue.
   - val = 22, i = 6. val + i is even, add 3 to val. val = 25, increment i to 7. This time, when we check the loop condition, i is too big, so we exit the loop.
   - val = 25 and that is what is returned.

2. The answer is E.
   - The first if condition evaluates to (2 < 5 && 13 < 5), which is false, so we skip to the else clause.
   - The else clause has its own if statement. The condition evaluates to (2 == 2 && 13 < 2), which is false, so we skip to the else clause.
   - result = 2 + 13 = 15, which is what is printed.

3. The answer is D.
   - The for-each loop can be read like this: for each integer in numbers, which I am going to call n.
   - The if clause is executed only when the element is > 8, so the loop adds all the elements greater than 8 to the sum variable.
   - The elements greater than 8 are 13, 12, and 10, so sum = 35, and that is what the method returns.

4. The answer is C.
   - Option I is correct. The reference variable type Planet matches the Planet object being instantiated, and the Planet class contains a no-argument constructor.
   - Option II is correct. The reference variable type Planet is a superclass of the DwarfPlanet object being instantiated, and the DwarfPlanet class contains a constructor that takes one String parameter.
   - Option III is not correct. Although the reference variable type Planet is a superclass of the DwarfPlanet object being instantiated, the DwarfPlanet class does not contain a no-argument constructor. Unlike a method, the constructor of the parent class is not inherited.

5. The answer is A.

- Let's picture the contents of our `ArrayList` in a table. After the 3 adds, we have:

0	1	2
Vampire	Werewolf	Ghost

Setting 0 to Zombie gives us:

0	1	2
Zombie	Werewolf	Ghost

Adding Mummy at position 2 pushes Ghost over one position:

0	1	2	3
Zombie	Werewolf	Mummy	Ghost

Witch gets added at the end:

0	1	2	3	4
Zombie	Werewolf	Mummy	Ghost	Witch

After the remove at index 3, Ghost goes away and Witch shifts over one:

0	1	2	3
Zombie	Werewolf	Mummy	Witch

6. The correct answer is E.

- Options A and B are incorrect. The inner column loop is not necessary and includes more values than along the diagonal to be included in the sum.
- Option C is incorrect. If the grid has odd dimensions, the center value will be counted twice.
- Option D is incorrect. If the grid has even dimensions, one value in the main diagonal will be subtracted out of the sum at the end.
- Option E works correctly. If the grid has odd dimensions, the center value will only be counted once.

7. The answer is C.

- Option A will not compile, because acres is a private instance variable.
- Option B will not compile, because the name of the object is park, not central.
- Option C is correct. The method is called properly and it returns a `boolean`.
- Option D will not compile, because `getAcres` does not take a parameter.
- Option E will not compile, because `hasPlayground` is not a public `boolean` variable.

8. The answer is B.

- The `for` loop goes through the entire string, looking at each character individually. If the character is an `m`, the substrings add the section of the string *before* the `m` to the section of the string *after* the `m`, leaving out the `m`.
- The result is that all the `m`'s are removed from the string, and the rest of the string is untouched.

9. The answer is D.

- This is a recursive method. Let's trace the calls. The parts in *italics* were filled in on the way back up. That is, the calls in the plain type were written top to bottom until the base case returned a value. Then the answers were filled in *bottom to top*.

```
loopy(12) = loopy(15) + 2 = 25 + 2 = 27, which gives us our final answer.
loopy(15) = loopy(18) + 2 = 23 + 2 = 25
loopy(18) = loopy(21) + 2 = 21 + 2 = 23
loopy(21) Base Case! return 21
```

10. The answer is B.
- The compiler looks at the left side of the equals sign and checks to be sure that whatever methods are called are available to variables of that type. Since `Letter` and `ALetter` both contain `toString` methods, the compiler is fine with the code. Option E is incorrect.
- The run-time environment looks at the right side of the equals sign and calls the version of the method that is appropriate for that type.
- `System.out.print(x)` results in an implicit call to the `ALetter` `toString` method, and prints "a".
- `System.out.print(y)` results in an implicit call to the `BLetter` `toString` method and prints "b".
- `System.out.print(z)` tries to make an implicit call to a `CapALetter` `toString` method, but there isn't one, so it moves up the hierarchy and calls the `toString` method of the ALetter class and prints "a".

11. The correct answer is B.
- On entry, word = "APCS" and index = 0.
  `word = word + its substring from 0 to 1, or "A". word = "APCSA".`
- Add 2 to index, index = 2. word.length() is 5, 2 < 5 so continue.
  `word = word + its substring from 2 to 3, or "C". word = "APCSAC".`
- Add 2 to index, index = 4. word.length() is 6, 4 < 6, so continue.
  `word = word + its substring from 4 to 5, or "A". word = "APCSACA".`
- Add 2 to index, index = 6. word.length() is 7, 6 < 7, so continue.
  `word = word + its substring from 6 to 7, or "A". word = "APCSACAA".`
- Add 2 to index, index = 8. wordlength() is 8, 8 is not < 8 so the loop exits.
- Notice that since word is altered in the loop, word.length() is different each time we evaluate it at the top of the loop. You can't just replace it with 4, the length of word at the beginning of the method. You must re-evaluate it each time through the loop.

12. The answer is C.
- Each time through the loop:
  - We are considering element n.
  - We calculate array[n] − array[n − 1] and compare it to array[n] − array[n + 1]. In other words, subtract the element *before* from the nth element, then subtract the element *after* from the nth element. If the *before* subtraction <= the *after* subtraction, print n.
  - Let's make a table. As a reminder, here is our array:
    `{-3, 0, 2, 4, 5, 9, 13, 1, 5}`

n	array[n] – array[n – 1]	array[n] – array[n + 1]	<= ?
1	0 − (-3) = 3	0 − 2 = -2	no
2	2 − 0 = 2	2 − 4 = -2	no
3	4 − 2 = 2	4 − 5 = -1	no
4	5 − 4 = 1	5 − 9 = -4	no
5	9 − 5 = 4	9 − 13 = -4	no
6	13 − 9 = 4	13 − 1 = 12	YES
7	1 − 13 = -12	1 − 5 = -4	YES

- Printing array[n] in the YES cases gives us 13 1. Remember that we are printing the *element*, not the *index*.

13. The answer is C.
- We want to negate our expression, so we are trying to solve this (note the added ! at the beginning).

```
!((n >= 4) || ((m == 5 || k < 2) && (n > 12)))
```

- DeMorgan's theorem tells us that we can distribute the !, but we must change AND to OR and OR to AND when we do that. Let's take it step by step.
- Distribute the ! to the 2 expressions around the || (which will change to &&).

```
!(n >= 4) && !((m == 5 || k < 2) && (n > 12)))
```

- !(n >=4) is the same as (n < 4).

```
(n < 4) && !((m == 5 || k < 2) && (n > 12)))
```

- Now let's distribute the ! to the expression around the second && (which becomes ||).

```
(n < 4) && !(m == 5 || k < 2) || !(n > 12)
```

- Fix the !(n > 12) because that's easy.

```
(n < 4) && !(m == 5 || k < 2) || (n <= 12)
```

- One to go! Distribute the ! around the || in parentheses (which becomes &&).

```
(n < 4) && !(m == 5) && !(k < 2) || (n <= 12)
```

- Simplify those last two simple expressions.

```
(n < 4) && (m != 5) && (k >= 2) || (n <= 12)
```

- A good way to double-check your solution is to assign values to m, n, and k and plug them in. If you do not think you can simplify the expression correctly, assigning values and plugging them in is another way to find the answer, though you may need to check several sets of values to be sure you've found the expression that works every time.

14. The answer is E.
- Consider Option A. Can an index be out of bounds? The largest values m and n will reach are 4 and 6, respectively. 4 + 6 = 10, and ray[10] is the 11th element in the array (because we start counting at 0). The array has a length of 11, so we will not index out of bounds.
- Look at the first for loop. The array is being filled with elements that are equal to twice their indices, so the contents of the array look like { 0, 2, 4, 6, 8, ... }.
- Look at the nested for loop. The outer loop will start at m = 0 and continue through m = 4. For each value of m, n will loop through 0, 2, 4, 6, because n is being incremented by 2. (It's easy to assume all loops use n++. Look!)
- We are looking for m + n > 8. Since the largest value for n is 6, that will not happen when m is 0, 1, or 2.
- The first time m + n is greater than 8 is when m = 3 and n = 6.

ray[3 + 6] = ray[9] = 2 * 9 = 18. Print 18.

- The next time m + n is greater than 8 is when m = 4 and n = 6.

ray[4 + 6] = ray[10] = 2 * 10 = 20. Print 20.

- Notice that we aren't printing any spaces, so the 1820 are printed right next to each other.

15. The answer is E.
- This is a recursive method. Let's trace the calls.
  ```
  mystery("advanced placement", 9) = mystery("vanced placement", 10)
  mystery("vanced placement", 10) = mystery("nced placement", 11)
  mystery("nced placement", 11) = mystery("ed placement", 12)
  mystery("ed placement", 12) = mystery ("placement", 13)
  ```
- By this point we should have noticed that we are getting farther and farther from the base case. What will happen when we run out of characters? Let's keep going and see.
  ```
  mystery("placement", 13) = mystery("lacement", 14)
  mystery("lacement", 14) = mystery("cement", 15)
  mystery("cement", 15) = mystery("ment", 16)
  mystery ("ment", 16)= mystery("nt", 17)
  ```
- `"nt".substring(2)` is, somewhat surprisingly, a valid expression. You are allowed to begin a substring just past the end of a string. This call will return an empty string.
  ```
  mystery ("nt", 17) = mystery("", 18)
  ```
- This time code.substring(2) fails: `StringIndexOutOfBoundsException`.

16. The answer is A.
- This problem requires you to understand that primitives are passed by value and objects are passed by reference.
- When a primitive argument (or actual parameter) is passed to a method, its value is copied into the formal parameter. Changing the formal parameter inside the method will have no effect on the value of the variable passed in; num and index will not be changed by the method.
- When an object is passed to a method, its reference is copied into the formal parameter. The actual and formal parameters become aliases of each other; that is, they both point to the same object. Therefore, when the object is changed inside the method, those changes will be seen outside of the method. Changes to array nums inside the method will be seen in array val outside of the method.
- num and index remain equal to 10 and 3, respectively, but val[3] has been changed to 10.

17. The answer is B.
- The original code segment is a nested loop. The outer loop has an index, which will take on the values 2, 4, 6. For each of those values, the inner loop has an index, which will take on the values 30, 20, 10. The code segment will print:
  ```
  (2+30) (2+20) (2+10) (4+30) (4+20) (4+10) (6+30) (6+20) (6+10)
  = 32 22 12 34 24 14 36 26 16
  ```
  We need to see which of I, II, III also produce that output.
- Option I is a for loop. On entry, num = 32, count = 0, i = 0.
  - 32 is printed, num = 34, count % 3 = 0, so we execute the if clause and set count = 0 and num = 20.
  - Next time through the loop, 20 is printed . . . oops, no good! Eliminate option I.
- Option II is a while loop. On entry, num = 32.
  - 32 is printed, num = 22, if condition is false.
  - Next time through the loop, 22 is printed, num = 12, if condition is false.
  - 12 is printed, num = 2, if condition is true, num = 34.
  - 34 is printed, num = 24, if condition is false.
  - 24 is printed, num = 14, if condition is false.
  - 14 is printed num = 4, if condition is true, num = 36.
  - 36 is printed, num = 26, if condition is false.
  - 26 is printed, num = 16, if condition is false.
  - 16 is printed, num = 6, if condition is true, num = 38.
  - Loop terminates – looks good! Option II is correct.
- Option III is a nested for loop.
  - The first time through the loops, h = 0, k = 30.
  - h + k = 30, so 30 is printed. That's incorrect. Eliminate option III.

18. The answer is A.
- This is one way of implementing the Insertion Sort algorithm. The interesting thing about this implementation is the use of a compound condition in the `for` loop. This condition says "Continue until you reach the beginning of the array OR until the element we are looking at is bigger than the key." When the `for` loop exits, the "key" is put into the open slot at position j. That's an Insertion Sort algorithm.
- Looking at this problem a different way:
  - It can't be B. If this were a search algorithm, there would have to be a parameter to tell us what element we are looking for, and that isn't the case.
  - It can't be D because Merge Sort is recursive and there's no recursion in this code segment.
  - It can't be E, because we know Sequential *Search* but there isn't a Sequential Sort.
  - That just leaves Selection Sort. Selection Sort has nested `for` loops, but the loops have no conditional exit. They always go to the end of the array. And on exit, elements are swapped. There's no swap code here.

19. The answer is D.
- The general form for generating a random number between *high* and *low* is

```
(int)(Math.random * (high - low + 1) + low
```

- high – low + 1 = 21, low = 13, so high = 33.
- The correct answer is integers between 13 and 33 inclusive.

20. The answer is D.
- Option A is incorrect. It uses array syntax rather than `ArrayList` syntax to retrieve the element.
- Option B is incorrect. It attempts to access the instance variable population directly, but population is private (as it should be).
- Option C is incorrect. First of all, the algorithm is wrong. It is only comparing the population in consecutive elements of the `ArrayList`, not in the `ArrayList` overall. In addition, it will end with an `IndexOutOfBoundsException`, because it uses (i + 1) as an index.
- Option D works correctly. It accesses the population using the getter method, and it compares the accessed population to the previous max.
- Option E is incorrect. If we began by setting `maxPop = Integer.MAX_VALUE`, then that is the value `maxPop` will have when the code segment completes.

21. The answer is D.
- Variable a holds the integer quotient of n divided by 10 and b the remainder of the division.
- To reverse n, variable c is multiplied by 10, and the new remainder is added.
- The process continues, multiplying by 10 to move the current value over one place value, until the integer quotient is 0.

22. The answer is C.
- In the third line of code x = x + y = 2 + 4 = 6.
- In the fourth line of code y = y + x = 4 + 6 = 10.

23. The answer is D.
- `Beta` extends `Alpha`. `Beta` does not have a method `eeny` so `b.eeny` invokes `eeny` from the superclass.
- The second invocation is made on a `Gamma` object, so *that* code generates the second portion of the output.
- Note that `a` is defined as a new `Gamma`, and a `Gamma` IS-A `Alpha`.
- Look first to the subclass, `Gamma`, to see if it has overridden method `eeny` before looking to the superclass, `Alpha`.
- It has an overridden method, so `a.eeny` invokes `eeny` from the `Gamma` class.

24. The answer is D.
- When methods are overloaded, the parameters determine which version of the method will be invoked.
- The second statement calls the `eeny` method from the `Delta` class (there is one parameter).
- The third statement calls the `eeny` method from the `Alpha` class (there are two parameters).

25. The answer is C.
- When the element in position 1 is removed, all remaining elements shift "down" one position.
- The element that was in position 2 fills in for the removed element and, therefore, is now in position 1.
- The loop counter moves to position 2, resulting in a skipped name.
- In fact, because the list shrinks with each iteration, every other name is skipped.

26. The answer is C.
- The code keeps a running product: $(1/2)(2/3)(3/4) \cdots [n/(n+1)]$.
- The result of this multiplication is $1/n$.

27. The answer is B.
- If p and q are different, then the first part of the expression is always false.
- If p and q are different, then p || q is true, thus the negation will be false.
- So, the expression is false whenever p and q are different.

A truth table might also help.

p	q	p && q	p || q	!(p || q)	(p && q) || !(p || q)
T	T	T	T	F	T
T	F	F	T	F	F
F	T	F	T	F	F
F	F	F	F	T	T

28. The answer is D.
- Option A is not correct for two reasons. `row` is a private instance variable and cannot be accessed outside the class. Strings must be compared using either the `equal` or `compareTo` method.
- Option B is not correct since the `setSeatLocation` method needs to be passed a `SeatLocation` parameter.
- Option C is not correct since the `getSeatLocation` method should not be passed any parameters.
- Option D is correct. The call to `setPrice` correctly takes a double parameter and the call to `getPrice` is called correctly without parameters.
- Option E is not correct. The `for` loop cannot traverse through the rows as shown.

29. The answer is D.
- Option A is incorrect since the `get` method must be called on the ArrayList `glop`, not on the class `DooHickey`.
- Option B is incorrect since there is no `getNum` method defined.
- Option C incorrectly uses array syntax for accessing the element.
- Option E uses an improper invocation of a parameterless method.

30. The answer is E.
- The count is reinitialized to 0 on each pass through the loop.

31. The answer is C.
- To avoid an exception, we must know that only valid subscripts are used to index the array.
- Each time through the loop, we access the (k+1)th cell, so we must be sure that k < arr.length-1.
- The loop condition guarantees the k < n-1, thus n can be no larger than arr.length.

32. The answer is E.
- Each time a value is found that is not less than its successor, the boolean variable `theCheck` is set to the opposite value.
- If this happens an even number of times, `theCheck` will be true; otherwise, it will be false.

33. The answer is A.
- The test for b not being equal to itself will be `false` in all cases.

34. The answer is A.
- Statement I correctly calls a method of the class.
- Statement II incorrectly attempts to access private data in the class.
- Statement III incorrectly attempts to use data from a void method.

35. The answer is E.
- Options A and B incorrectly use the `.equals` method with `null`.
- Option E correctly applies DeMorgan's Law.

36. The answer is D.
- If j < n is true, the program will get caught in an infinite loop.
- If j >= n, the while loop condition is `false` and the loop will not be executed. The body of the loop will be treated as the next statement to be executed, and the "in loop" message will be printed one time.

37. The answer is E.
- Option A will return after the first elements are checked for equality.
- Option B will return `true` as soon as two parallel elements are found to be equal. It will not determine if *all* the parallel elements are equal.
- Option C will test each parallel elements for equality, but will only return the result of the test for the last two elements.
- Option D always returns `true` since `same` is never changed inside the loop.
- Option E returns `true` if the loop counter traverses the entire list; otherwise, there is an early exit from the loop and `false` is returned.

38. The answer is A.
- Inheritance should always reflect the IS-A relationship between classes.
- The claims of options B and C may or may not be true, but they would be less important than the IS-A relationship in any case.
- Option D implies that deeper inheritance hierarchies are somehow better than shallow ones, which is not necessarily true.

39. The answer is C.
- Options A and B are true, but classes should declare all instance variables private.
- Subclasses do not have direct access to private information in the superclass. An accessor method must be used.
- Public variables and methods are always available for other objects to use.

40. The answer is D.
- Let's trace the code. The parts in italics were filled in on the way back up. That is, the calls in the plain type were written top to bottom until the base case returned a value. Then the answers were filled in bottom to top.

  mystery(5) → mystery(4) + mystery(3) → *4 + 3 = 7*

  mystery(4) → mystery(3) + mystery(2) → *3 + 1 = 4*

  mystery(3) → *3*

  mystery(2) → mystery (1) + mystery(0) → *1 + 0 = 1*

Part II (Free-Response) Solutions

Please keep in mind that there are multiple ways to write the solution to a Free-response question, but the general and refined statements of the problem should be pretty much the same for everyone. Look at the algorithms and coded solutions, and determine if yours accomplishes the same task.

General penalties (assessed only once per problem):
-1 using a local variable without first declaring it
-1 returning a value from a void method or constructor
-1 accessing an array or `ArrayList` incorrectly
-1 overwriting information passed as a parameter
-1 including unnecessary code that causes a side effect like a compile error or console output

1. `StringRotation`
   (a) **General Problem**: Write the `findNumberOfRotations` method of the `StringRotation` class.

   Refined Problem: Traverse through the `rotation` string and check for equality with the `base` string.

   Algorithm:
   - If the lengths of the strings are different, return -1.
   - Write a loop that will traverse the `rotation` string one letter at a time.
   - Create a substring that combines two parts of the `rotation` string.
     - The first part is a substring that starts at position `i`.
     - The second part is a substring that starts at position 0 up to position i-1.
   - If that substring is equal to the `base` string, return i.
   - Return -1 if the loop completes without having equal strings.

   (b) **General Problem**: Write the `isReverseRotation` method of the `StringRotation` class.

   Refined Problem: Reverse the `rotation` string and determine if it is a rotation of the `base` string.

   Algorithm:
   - If the lengths of the strings are different, return `false`.
   - Write a loop that will traverse the `rotation` string one letter at a time.
   - Create a substring that combines two parts of a string.
     - The first part is the current letter of the base string.
     - The second part is the built reverse string.
   - Call the `numberOfRotations` method passing the two strings as parameters.
   - If the result is -1, return `false`; otherwise return `true`.

Java Code

```java
public int findNumberOfRotations(String base, String rotation)
{
    if(base.length() != rotation.length())
        return -1;

    for(int i = 0; i < base.length(); i++)
    {
    if(base.equals(rotation.substring(i) + rotation.substring(0, i)))
        return i;
    }

    return -1;
}

public boolean isReverseRotation(String base, String rotation)
{
    if(base.length() != rotation.length())
        return false;
    String reverse = "";
    for(int i = 0; i < base.length(); i++)
    {
        reverse = base.substring(i, i + 1) + reverse;
    }

    if( findNumberOfRotations(reverse, rotation) != -1 )
        return true;

        return false;
}
```

Common Errors:
- Not traversing the string correctly or failing to access each element as needed.
- Incorrectly calling string methods.
- Not returning a value.

Scoring Guidelines: StringRotation

Part (a)   findNumberOfRotations   **5 points**
+1   Creates a loop that traverses the length of one of the strings (no bounds error)
+1   Calls at least one String method appropriately and all String method calls are syntactically valid
+1   Assembles rotated String appropriately based on characters in rotation string
+1   Compares the base string and the constructed string for equality
+1   On exit, returns the correct rotation count

Part (b)   isReverseRotation   **4 points**
+1   Creates a loop that traverses the length of one of the strings (no bounds error)
+1   Assembles reversed rotation string and all string method calls are syntactically valid
+1   Calls findNumberOfRotations with correct parameters
+1   On exit, returns the correct boolean value

Sample Driver:

There are many ways to write these methods. Maybe yours is a bit different from the sample solutions shown here and you are not sure if it works. Here is a sample driver program. Running it will let you see if your code works and will help you debug it if it does not.

Copy RotationDriver into your IDE along with the complete StringRotation class methods (your solution).

```
public class StringRotation
{
  public static int findNumberOfRotations(String base, String rotation)
  {
    if(base.length() != rotation.length())
        return -1;

    for(int i = 0; i < base.length(); i++)
    {
       if(base.equals(rotation.substring(i) + rotation.substring(0, i)))
          return i;
    }

       return -1;
  }
  public static boolean isReverseRotation(String base, String rotation)
  {
     String reverse = "";
     for(int i = 0; i < base.length(); i++)
     {
        reverse = base.substring(i, i + 1) + reverse;
     }

     if(findNumberOfRotations(reverse, rotation) == -1 )
        return false;

  return true;
  }
}
```

```
public class RotationDriver  {
   public static void main(String[] args)  {
        String one = "happy";
        String two = "happy";
        int num = StringRotation.findNumberOfRotations(one, two);
        System.out.println("The number of rotations between " + one + " and " + two +
            " is " + num);


        two = "happiness";
        num = StringRotation.findNumberOfRotations(one, two);
        System.out.println("The number of rotations between " + one + " and " + two +
            " is " + num);


        two = "appyh";
        num = StringRotation.findNumberOfRotations(one, two);
        System.out.println("The number of rotations between " + one + " and " + two +
            " is " + num);


        two = "yhapp";
        num = StringRotation.findNumberOfRotations(one, two);
        System.out.println("The number of rotations between " + one + " and " + two +
            " is " + num);


        two = "pyhap";
        num = StringRotation.findNumberOfRotations(one, two);
        System.out.println("The number of rotations between " + one + " and " + two +
            " is " + num);


        one = "care";
        two = "race";
        num = StringRotation.findNumberOfRotations(one, two);
        System.out.println("The number of rotations between " + one + " and " + two +
            " is " + num);


        one = "computer";
        two = "retupmoc";
        boolean reverse = StringRotation.isReverseRotation(one, two);
        if (reverse)
              System.out.println(one + " and " + two + " are reverses of each other");
        else
              System.out.println(one + " and " + two + " are not reverses of each other");

        two = "mocretup";
        reverse = StringRotation.isReverseRotation(one, two);
        if (reverse)
              System.out.println(one + " and " + two + " are reverses of each
                  other");
        else
              System.out.println(one + " and " + two + " are not reverses of each other");

        two = "putercom";
        reverse = StringRotation.isReverseRotation(one, two);
        if (reverse)
              System.out.println(one + " and " + two + " are reverses of each other");
        else
```

```
            System.out.println(one + " and " + two + " are not reverses of each other");

        two = "mocsertup";
        reverse = StringRotation.isReverseRotation(one, two);
        if (reverse)
                System.out.println(one + " and " + two + " are reverses of each other");
        else
                System.out.println(one + " and " + two + " are not reverses of each other");
    } }
```

2. SummerSpecial

General Problem: Write the SummerSpecial class.

Refined Problem: Create the SummerSpecial class with two instance variables and one two-parameter constructor. The two methods isSet and getPrice will need to be defined.

Algorithm:
- Write a class header for SummerSpecial.
- Declare two instance variables of type FurnitureItem to store the values of the furniture items.
- Write a constructor with two parameters of type FurnitureItem that represent two furniture items and assign the parameters to the corresponding instance variables.
- Write method isSet.
    - Determine the last five characters of each item.
    - Test the last five characters of each item for equality.
- Write method getPrice.
    - Determine which furniture item is the most expensive and which furniture item is the least expensive.
    - Call isSet to determine if the two pieces are a set.
    - Based on the result of that call, calculate the price of the items.

Java Code:

```java
public class SummerSpecial
{
    private FurnitureItem furnItem1;
    private FurnitureItem furnItem2;

    public SummerSpecial(FurnitureItem f1, FurnitureItem f2)
    {
        furnItem1 = f1;
        furnItem2 = f2;
    }

    public boolean isSet()
    {
        String id1 = furnItem1.getProductId();
        String id2 = furnItem2.getProductId();

        String set1 = id1.substring(id1.length()-5);
        String set2 = id2.substring(id2.length()-5);

        if (set1.equals(set2))
          return true;
        else
          return false;
    }
}
```

```
public double getPrice()
    {
        double mostExpensive = furnItem1.getPrice();
        double leastExpensive = furnItem2.getPrice();

        if (furnItem1.getPrice() < furnItem2.getPrice())
        {
            mostExpensive = furnItem2.getPrice();
            leastExpensive = furnItem1.getPrice();
        }
        if (isSet())
            return mostExpensive * 0.75 + leastExpensive;
        else
            return leastExpensive * 0.9 + mostExpensive;

    }
}
```

Common Errors:
- The instance variables must be declared private.
- Strings must be compared using .equals or .compareTo methods.
- The substring method must be used to obtain the last 5 characters in the string.

Scoring Guidelines: SummerSpecial

SummerSpecial class   **1 point**

+1 Correct class header for SummerSpecial: class SummerSpecial
    (must not be private)

state maintenance   1 point

+1 Declares at least two private instance variables capable of storing two FurnitureItem objects

SummerSpecial Constructor   **1 point**

+1 Correct method header: SummerSpecial(FurnitureItem ___, FurnitureItem ___)
    (must not be private)

method headers   **1 point**

+1 Declares two method headers: boolean isSet() and double getPrice()
    (must not be private)

isSet   **3 points**

+1 Calls getProductId on a FurnitureItem object
+1 Identifies the last 5 characters of a FurnitureItem object using both substring and length methods
+1 isSet() returns true if and only if the last 5 characters of each item's product ID are found to be equivalent using .equals comparison

getPrice   **2 points**

+1 Calls isSet to determine if the two items belong to the same set
+1 Computes the correct price given the result of the call to isSet

Sample Driver:

There are many ways to write these methods. Maybe yours is a bit different from the sample solutions shown here and you are not sure if it works. Here is a sample driver program. Running it will let you see if your code works and will help you debug it if it does not.

Copy SummerDriver and FurnitureItem into your IDE along with the complete SummerSpecial class (your solution).

```java
public class FurnitureItem{
    private String productId;
    private double price;

    public FurnitureItem(String id, double pr)
    {
        productId = id;
        price = pr;
    }
     /** Returns the product ID of this item.   */
     public String getProductId()
    {
        return productId;
    }


   /** Returns the price of this item. */
    public double getPrice()
    {
        return price;
    }
  }
    public class SummerDriver
{
   public static void main(String[] args)
    {
        FurnitureItem item1 = new FurnitureItem("C-123456-APCSA",250.00);
        FurnitureItem item2 = new FurnitureItem("T-9876-APCSA",500.00);
        FurnitureItem item3 = new FurnitureItem("C9-246-APCSP",125.00);
        SummerSpecial ss1 = new SummerSpecial(item1, item2);
        boolean set = ss1.isSet();
        if (set)
          System.out.println("is a set");
        else
          System.out.println("is not a set");
        System.out.println("The price is " + ss1.getPrice());


        SummerSpecial ss2 = new SummerSpecial(item1, item3);
        set = ss2.isSet();
        if (set)
          System.out.println("is a set");
        else
          System.out.println("is not a set");
        System.out.println("The price is " + ss2.getPrice());
    }
}
```

3. GPSRouter

(a) General Problem: Write the maxMileage method of the GPSRouter class.

Refined Problem: Traverse through the ArrayList routes to find the element with the highest mileage.

Algorithm:
- If the size of the ArrayList routes is 0, then return null.
- Create a temporary variable highest of type Route and initialize it to the 0th element of routes.
- Write a loop to traverse the routes ArrayList.
- Compare each element with highest.
- If a larger value is found, replace highest with that value.
- Return highest.

(b) General Problem: Write the addMiles method of the GPSRouter class.

Refined Problem: Traverse through the ArrayList routes looking at the names of the routes. If the name is already an element of routes, add the mileage to the existing Route element, otherwise create and add a new Route element to the routes ArrayList.

Algorithm:
- Write a loop to traverse the routes ArrayList.
- For each element in routes, compare the route name to the parameter that was passed.
- If the route name matches, add the miles that were passed as a parameter to the currently stored mileage in routes.
- If the route name was not found, create a new Route object and add that element to routes.

Java Code

```java
public Route maxMileage()
{
    if (routes.size() == 0)
      return null;

    Route highest = routes.get(0);

    for (int i = 1; i < routes.size(); i++)
    {
        Route temp = routes.get(i);
        if (temp.getMiles() > highest.getMiles())
            highest = temp;
    }
    return highest;
}


public void addMiles (String routeName, int mileage)
{
  boolean found = false;
  for (int i = 0; i < routes.size(); i++)
  {
     Route temp = routes.get(i);
     if (temp.getName().equals(routeName))
     {
        temp.setMiles(temp.getMiles()+ mileage);
        found = true;
     }
  }
  if (!found)
     routes.add(new Route(routeName, mileage));
}
```

Note: the code fragment in both part a and part b

```
    for (int i = 0; i < routes.size(); i++)
{
    Route temp = routes.get(i);
```
could be replaced with the following for each loop:

```
    for (Route temp : routes)
    {
```
without loss of functionality.

Common Errors:
- Not traversing the ArrayList correctly or failing to access each element as needed.
- Incorrectly calling `Route` methods.
- Strings must be compared using `.equals` or `.compareTo` methods.

Scoring Guidelines: `GPSRouter`

Part (a)   `maxMilage`   **4 points**
+1   Returns `null` if the list is empty
+1   Traverses the list `routes` with no bound errors and appropriate access
+1   Compares the miles of each route with an appropriately initialized maximum (algorithm)
+1   Returns the correct `Route` object in all cases

Part (b)   `addMiles`   **5 points**
+1   Traverses the list `routes` with no bound errors and appropriate access
+1   Compares the given `routeName` with a name from each `Route` object
+1   Sets the number of miles correctly using the `setMiles` method
+1   Adds a new route with the given name and mileage to `routes` when appropriate
+1   On exit, the collection `routes` has the correct `Route` objects with the correct mileage

Sample Driver:

There are many ways to write these methods. Maybe yours is a bit different from the sample solutions shown here and you are not sure if it works. Here is a sample driver program. Running it will let you see if your code works and will help you debug it if it does not.

Copy GPSDriver and Route into your IDE along with the complete GPSRouter class methods (your solution).

```java
public class Route
{
    private String name;
    private int miles;

    public Route(String name, int miles)
    {
        this.name = name;
        this.miles = miles;
    }

    public String getName()
    {
        return name;
    }

    public int getMiles()
    {
        return miles;
    }
    public void setMiles(int num)
    {
        miles = num;
    }
}


import java.util.ArrayList;
public class GPSDriver
{
  public static void main(String[] args)
  {
    Route route1 = new Route("Kalamazoo", 5200);
    Route route2 = new Route("Tampa", 7000);
    Route route3 = new Route("Dayton",1000);
    ArrayList <Route> routes = new ArrayList<Route>();
    routes.add(route1);
    routes.add(route2);
    routes.add(route3);
    GPSRouter gps = new GPSRouter(routes);
    Route mostMiles = gps.maxMileage();
    System.out.println("The maximum mileage is " + mostMiles.getMiles());
    gps.addMiles("Dayton", 500);
    gps.addMiles("Chicago", 7500);
    mostMiles = gps.maxMileage();
    System.out.println("The maximum mileage is " + mostMiles.getMiles());
  }
}
```

```java
import java.util.ArrayList;
public class GPSRouter
{
    private ArrayList<Route> routes;

    public GPSRouter(ArrayList <Route> r)
    {
        routes = r;
    }
    public Route maxMileage()
    {
      if (routes.size() == 0)
        return null;

      Route highest = routes.get(0);

      for (int i = 1; i < routes.size(); i++)
      {
          Route temp = routes.get(i);
          if (temp.getMiles() > highest.getMiles())
              highest = temp;
      }
      return highest;
    }

    public void addMiles (String routeName, int mileage)
    {
      for (int i = 0; i < routes.size(); i++)
      {
          Route temp = routes.get(i);
          if (temp.getName().equals(routeName))
          {
              temp.setMiles(temp.getMiles()+ mileage);
              return;
          }
      }
    routes.add(new Route(routeName, mileage));
    }
}
```

4. Coin Collector
   (a) **General Problem:** Complete the CoinCollectionTools class constructor.

   Refined Problem: Instantiate the instance variable coinBox as a new array of the size specified by the parameters. Traverse the array filling every cell with a Coin object instantiated with country = the country parameter, year = 0, and coinType = 0.

   Algorithm:
   - Instantiate coinBox as a new array of Coin objects with dimensions [rows] [columns].
   - Outer loop: traverse the rows of the array.
     Inner loop: traverse the columns of the array.
     - Instantiate a new Coin object, passing parameters (country, 0, 0).

   Java Code:

   ```
   public CoinCollectionTools(String country, int rows, int columns)
   {
       coinBox = new Coin[rows][columns];
       for (int row = 0; row < rows; row++)
           for (int col = 0; col < columns; col++)
               coinBox[row][col] = new Coin(country,0,0);
   }
   ```

   Common Errors:
   - If you look above the constructor in the code for the class, you will see that the coinBox has been declared as an instance variable. If you write:

   ```
   int[][] coinBox = new int[rows][columns];
   ```

   then you are declaring a different array named coinBox that exists only within the constructor. The instance variable coinBox has not been instantiated.

   Java Code Alternate Solution:
   If you read the whole problem before starting to code, you might have noticed that the other two parts work in column-major order. You can write this in column-major order also. Since you are filling every cell with the same information, it doesn't make any difference.

   ```
   public CoinCollectionTools(String country, int rows, int columns)
   {
       coinBox = new Coin[rows][columns];
       for (int col = 0; col < columns; col++)
           for (int row = 0; row < rows; row++)
               coinBox[row][col] = new Coin(country,0,0);
   }
   ```

(b) General Problem: Complete the `fillCoinBox` method.

Refined Problem: The parameter `myCoins` is an `ArrayList` of `Coin` objects in order by year minted. Assign them to the `coinBox` grid in column-major order.

Algorithm:
- Create a count variable.
- Loop through all of the `Coin` objects in `myCoins` using variable count as the loop counter.
  - Update the row and column variables based on count.
  - Get the next `Coin` object from the `ArrayList`, and place it in the `coinBox` location specified by the row and column variables.
  - Increment the `count` variable.
- Return the completed `coinBox`.

Java Code:

```
public Coin[][] fillCoinBox(ArrayList<Coin> myCoins)
{
    int count = 0;
    int row;
    int column;
    while (count < myCoins.size())
    {
        row = count % coinBox.length;
        column = count / coinBox.length;
        coinBox[row][column] = myCoins.get(count);
        count++;
    }
    return coinBox;
}
```

Java Code Alternate Solution #1:
You may not have thought of using % and / to keep track of column and row. Here's another way to do it.

```java
public Coin[][] fillCoinBox(ArrayList<Coin> myCoins)
{
    int count = 0;
    int row = 0;
    int column = 0;
    while (count < myCoins.size())
    {
        coinBox[row][column] = myCoins.get(count);
        if (row < coinBox.length - 1)
        {
            row++;
        }
        else
        {
            row = 0;
            column++;
        }
        count++;
    }
    return coinBox;
}
```

Java Code Alternate Solution #2:
This solution bases its loops on the grid, rather than the ArrayList.

```java
public Coin[][] fillCoinBox(ArrayList<Coin> myCoins)
{
    int row = 0;
    int column = 0;
    int count = 0;

    // The first condition in the outer loop is not actually
    // necessary, because myCoins will run out before coinBox
    // goes out of bounds.
    while (column < coinBox[0].length && myCoins.size() > count)
    {
        while (row < coinBox.length && myCoins.size() > count)
        {
            coinBox[row][column] = myCoins.get(count);
            count++;
            row++;
        }
        row = 0;
        column++;
    }
    return coinBox;
}
```

Common Errors:
- Do not count on the fact that you can fill the entire grid. It is tempting to write nested `for` loops that traverse the whole grid, but if there are fewer `Coin` objects in the `ArrayList` than elements in the grid, your program will terminate with an `IndexOutOfBoundsException`.
- It is common to write the row and column loops in the wrong order. In column-major order, columns vary slower than rows (we do all the rows before we change columns), so the column loop is the outer loop. In row-major order, the row loop is the outer loop.
- Even though we are filling our array in column-major order, the syntax for specifying the element we want to fill is `coinBox[row][column]`, not the other way around.
- If you used remove instead of get when accessing the `Coin` objects in the `ArrayList`, you modified the list and that's not allowed. It's called *destruction of persistent data* and may be penalized.
- In the solutions that loop through the grid (Alternates #2 and #3), be careful not to use incorrect notation for the end conditions. In general, the number of rows is `arrayName.length` and the number of columns is `arrayName[row].length`. When processing in column-major order, the loop that varies the column is the outer loop. We cannot use the loop variable row as the array index when finding the length of a column, because it does not exist outside of the inner loop. Since this is not a ragged array, it is safe to use `[0]` as our index.

(c) General Problem: Complete the `fillCoinTypeList` method.

Refined Problem: Given a `coinBox` as created by part (a) and filled in part (b), create a list that contains `Coins` in order by coin type (1–6). If `Coins` are retrieved from the `coinBox` in column-major order, they will already be in order by year.

Algorithm:
- Loop 1: Complete the inner loops 6 times, once for each coin type 1–6.
- Loop 2: Loop through the columns.
- Loop 3: Loop through the rows.
- If the `Coin` object at the row-column location specified by the loop counters of loops 2 and 3 matches the `coinType` specified from the loop counter of loop 1:
  - Add the `Coin` object to the `ArrayList`.
- Return the `ArrayList` of `Coin` objects.

Java Code:
```java
public ArrayList<Coin> fillCoinTypeList()
{
    ArrayList<Coin> myCoins = new ArrayList<Coin>();
    for (int type = 1; type <= 6; type++)
        for (int col = 0; col < coinBox[0].length; col++)
            for (int row = 0; row < coinBox.length; row++)
                if (coinBox[row][col].getCoinType() == type)
                    myCoins.add(coinBox[row][col]);
    return myCoins;
}
```

Common Errors:
- You should not create a new `Coin` object to add to the `myCoins` list. The `Coin` object already exists in the array.
- Do not worry about the default `Coins` added in the constructor. Since they have a `coinType` of 0, they will be ignored.

Scoring Guidelines:

Part (a):	CoinCollectionTools constructor	2 points

+1 Traverses the array using a nested loop. No bounds errors, no missed elements

+1 Instantiates new `Coin` objects for each cell in the array

Part (b):	fillCoinBox	4 points

+1 Accesses every element in `myCoins`. No bounds errors, no missed elements

+1 Accesses all appropriate elements of `coinBox`. No bounds errors, no missed elements

+1 Accesses elements of `coinBox` in column-major order

+1 Returns correctly filled `coinBox`

Part (c):	fillCoinTypeList	3 points

+1 Loops through `coinBox` at least once in column major order. No bounds errors, no missed elements

+1 Locates `Coin`s of type 1, followed by types 2–6 in the correct order

+1 Instantiates, fills, and returns a correct `ArrayList<Coin>`

Sample Driver:

There are many ways to write these methods. Maybe yours is a bit different from our sample solutions and you are not sure if it works. Here is a sample driver program. Running it will let you see if your code works, and will help you debug it if it does not.

Copy `CoinCollectionToolsDriver` into your IDE along with the complete `Coin` and `CoinCollectionTools` classes (including your solutions). You will also need to add this import statement as the first line in your `CoinCollectionTools` class: `import java.util.ArrayList;`

```java
import java.util.ArrayList;

public class CoinCollectionToolsDriver {

    public static void main(String[] args) {
        CoinCollectionTools tools = new CoinCollectionTools("USA", 3, 4);
        int[] years = { 1920, 1930, 1940, 1940, 1950, 1950,
                1950, 1960, 1970, 1980, 1990 };
        int[] types = { 1, 2, 4, 1, 2, 3, 3, 4, 4, 2, 4 };
        String[] typeNames = { "", "penny", "nickel", "dime", "quarter" };
        Coin[][] coinBox = new Coin[3][4];
        ArrayList<Coin> coins = new ArrayList<Coin>();

        for (int i = 0; i < years.length; i++)
            coins.add(new Coin("USA", years[i], types[i]));

        System.out.println("fillCoinBox test\nExpecting:");
        System.out.println("penny 1920\tpenny 1940\tdime 1950\tnickel 1980"
                + "\nnickel 1930\tnickel 1950\tquarter 1960\tquarter 1990"
                + "\nquarter 1940\tdime 1950\tquarter 1970\t0");

        System.out.println("\nYour answer:");
        coinBox = tools.fillCoinBox(coins);

        for (int row = 0; row < coinBox.length; row++) {
            for (int col = 0; col < coinBox[row].length; col++)
                System.out.print(typeNames[coinBox[row][col].getCoinType()] + " "
                        + coinBox[row][col].getYear() + "\t");
            System.out.println();
        }

        System.out.println("\nfillCoinTypeList test\nExpecting:");
        System.out.println("penny 1920, penny 1940, nickel 1930, "
                + "nickel 1950, nickel 1980, dime 1950, "
                + "\ndime 1950, quarter 1940, quarter 1960, "
                + "quarter 1970, quarter 1990,");
        System.out.println("\nYour answer:");
        coins = tools.fillCoinTypeList();
        for (int i = 0; i < coins.size(); i++) {
            System.out.print(typeNames[coins.get(i).getCoinType()]
                    + " " + coins.get(i).getYear()+ ", ");
            if (i == coins.size() / 2)
                System.out.println();
        }
    }
}
```

STEP **3**

Develop Strategies
for Success

CHAPTER **4** Strategies to Help You Do
Your Best on the Exam

CHAPTER 4

Strategies to Help You Do Your Best on the Exam

IN THIS CHAPTER

Summary: This chapter supplies you with strategies for taking the Multiple-choice and the Free-response sections of the AP Computer Science A Exam. The strategies will help you earn as many points as possible.

Key Ideas

✪ Many questions require you to read and process code. Practice by hand-tracing hundreds of pieces of code.

✪ When you do not know a Multiple-choice answer, eliminate choices you know are incorrect and guess. There is no penalty for guessing.

✪ You need to understand how points are awarded on the Free-response section and when deductions are taken.

✪ You should make an attempt to write some kind of response to every Free-response question, even when you feel you do not understand the question or know the answer. You may earn a point or two even if you do not answer the whole question or get it all right.

✪ On the Multiple-choice section, you must clearly understand the difference between the `System.out.print()` and `System.out.println()` statements and be able to read code that uses each of them. However, on the Free-response questions, it is unlikely that you will need to use a `System.out.print()` or `System.out.println()` statement. If you use one unnecessarily, you could be penalized 1 point.

Strategies for the Multiple-Choice Section

The Multiple-choice section of the exam determines how well you can read someone else's code. There are many problems involving the fundamentals of programming such as `if` and `if-else` statements, looping structures, complex data structures, and boolean logic. Some of the questions have to do with recursion, class design, and inheritance.

Hand-Tracing Code

Hand-tracing code is the act of pretending you are the computer in order to predict the output of some code or the value of a variable. A large number of the questions on the Multiple-choice portion require you to read and process code. You should hand-trace hundreds of sample pieces of code to prepare for the exam.

Do Not Do Too Much in Your Head!
It's very easy to make mental mistakes when hand-tracing code. Write out the current values of all the variables in the white space that is provided on the exam.

When You Do not Know, Guess

There is no penalty for guessing on the Multiple-choice questions. Make sure you eliminate the choices that do not make sense before guessing. If you are running out of time, quickly make guesses for the questions you weren't able to get to.

Read All of the Options Before Selecting Your Answer

Before you fill in the bubble, be sure to look at every one of the options. It's possible that you may have misunderstood the question. Looking at each of the choices could help point you in the right direction. However, some people disagree and say it's a waste of time to read all answer choices. Be mindful of your time and pace and take this advice if you have time to spare.

Input from the User

You will never have to write code that asks for input from the user. Instead, the question will make a generic statement in the form of a comment that shows that they are requesting input from the user as in the example below.

Generic Input from the User
The AP Computer Science A Exam will use a generic reference to show input from the user. When you see this, just assume that the variable receives an appropriate value from a nameless, faceless user.

```
int myValue =  /* call to a method that reads an integer number */
```
or
```
double myValue =  /* read user input */
```

Strategies for the Free-Response Section

The Free-response section of the exam determines how well you can write your own code. Although there are an infinite number of possible questions that could be asked, they will always fall into these four categories:

- Question 1 will require you to implement and call methods. The methods will use control structures like loops and `if` statements, but there will be no data structures involved.
- Question 2 will require you to design and implement a complete class.
- Question 3 will require the use of arrays and/or `ArrayLists`.
- Question 4 will require the use of 2D arrays.

How the Free-Response Questions Are Graded

The Free-response question (FRQ) section is graded by an expert group of high school and college computer science teachers and professors, referred to as "readers." A real person who knows computer science will be reading your code to determine if you have solved the problem correctly. Your written code must be readable by another human being, so do your best to write legibly and use proper formatting for readability.

The Intent of the Question

Every year, the *intent* of each question is explained to the people who are grading the test as part of their training. This is normally a one-line statement that describes the purpose of the question. You should try to predict what the intent of the question is for each of the Free-response questions when you are taking the exam. Thinking about the intent of the question will help you see the big picture and then narrow in on writing the code that solves the problem. If you are oblivious to the intent of the question, then you are likely to go off course and solve a problem that is not the point of the question.

Scoring Guidelines

In order to help the exam readers be consistent when grading tens of thousands of exams, a scoring rubric is used. This rubric dictates how many points are awarded for writing valid code that solves specific components of the problem. The problem is broken down into its most important components and each of these is assigned a point value. The total of all of these components from all sections (a, b, c, etc.) is 9 points.

> **Scoring for the Free-Response Questions**
> You start off with zero points for each Free-response question. As the reader finds valid code that is part of the rubric, you earn points. Each component of the rubric is worth 1 point. Your goal is to earn 9 points, the maximum points awarded for each question.

1-Point Penalty

After your response is graded against the rubric and your maximum score is calculated, the reader decides if points should be deducted from your total. If you break a major rule, then points are subtracted from your total. Any errors in your response will not earn points from the rubric if possible. In certain cases where an error may lose more than one rubric point, a penalty point may be deducted instead. These penalties can change from year to year, but common 1 point penalties include:

- **Array/collection access confusion**
  You must use the correct syntax when accessing elements in arrays (use [ ]) and `ArrayLists` (use the get method).

- **Extraneous code that causes side effects**
  This is a fancy way of saying your code doesn't compile or you have written a `System.out.print()` or `System.out.println()` statement when you weren't asked to print anything. Do not ever print anything to the console unless it is stated in the problem description!

- **Local variables used but none declared**
  Be sure to declare every variable before using it.

- **Destruction of persistent data**
  Anything that is passed to a method or constructor should be left alone. Do not change the argument that is passed. Reassign it to a different variable and only modify that one.

- **Void method or constructor that returns a value**
  Do not ever have a return statement in a void method or constructor.

You Can't Get a Negative Score
- The readers won't deduct points if you haven't earned any points.
- Penalty points can only be deducted in a part of the question that has earned credit so they won't take away points from a different section.
- A penalty can be assessed only once for a question, even if it occurs multiple times or in multiple parts of that question.

Non-Penalized Errors

I feel a little guilty telling you this and as a teacher it goes against my philosophy, but I'm going to tell you anyway. The readers of the exam are told to look the other way when they see certain kinds of errors for which they would normally deduct points in their classroom. Just like penalty points, these can change from year to year, but we commonly see the following:

- Using = instead of = = and vice versa
- Confusing `length` and `size` when using an array, `ArrayList`, or String
- Using a keyword as a variable name
- Confusing [] with () or even <>
- Missing { } where indentation clearly conveys intent

A full list is found in the Appendix.

Now listen up! I'm not telling you to be careless when you write your code or to make those mistakes on purpose. I'm just telling you that, on the AP Computer Science A Exam, the readers will ignore minor syntax mistakes like these.

What Is Valid Code?

Any code that works and satisfies the conditions of the problem will be given credit as valid code. Please remember the readers are humans; so do not go writing crazy, Rube Goldberg–style code to solve a really easy problem. Using unnecessarily complicated code or code that uses libraries outside of the AP Java subset can potentially lead to confusion or unintended errors. When in doubt, approach the problem in the most straightforward, logical way and stick to the AP Computer Science A Java subset.

Fun Fact: Rube Goldberg was a popular cartoonist who depicted gadgets that performed simple tasks in indirect, convoluted ways. He is the inspiration behind the many Rube Goldberg Machine Contests that are held worldwide.

Brute Force Versus Efficiency and Elegance

There are many ways to solve problems in our world. As a programmer, your goal is to find the most *elegant* way to solve any problem. Sometimes that comes easy and other times, not so much.

On the AP Computer Science A Exam, elegance and efficiency are not considered (unless the problem specifically asks for it). When you are asked to write code to solve a problem, try to approach the problem in the most reasonable way first. If you can't think of an efficient way to solve the problem, then use **brute force**. In other words, if the solution doesn't come to you, write the code in a way that works even if it is a really slow way to solve the problem. Be sure your code works for more than one scenario. You should never "hard code" any values from the provided examples into your code.

Answer the Question
Above all else, answer the question. Or at least, make an attempt at it. Do not be afraid to write something down even if you do not have a full solution. Remember that the rubric for every question has components that are pieces of the solution. The one thing that you put down just may be a component that will get you a point or two.

Comments Are Not Graded

Do not spend time writing comments for your Java code. The readers will not read anything that is part of a Java comment.

Cross Out, Do Not Erase

If you think of a new solution, write it out first and then cross out the old one. Because your written responses are scanned and the readers review a scanned copy, code written over erased code can often make your response difficult to read. Do not waste time by erasing the old solution. The readers are trained to ignore anything that is crossed out.

Output to the Console

On the AP Computer Science A Exam, the use of output statements is a little strange. On the Multiple-choice section, you must clearly understand the difference between the `System.out.print()` and `System.out.println()` statements and be able to read code that uses each of them.

However, on the Free-response questions, it is highly *unlikely* that you will be asked to write a `System.out.print()` or `System.out.println()` instruction! You will lose points if the reader reads any kind of output statement in your response to a Free-response question if you weren't asked to do so in the problem description.

Output to the Console!
In general, on the Free response section, it is highly unlikely that you will be asked to write a `System.out.println` statement. So, if they do not ask for it, do not write one. You will get penalized if you write one and they do not ask you to.

STEP 4

Review the Knowledge You Need to Score High

UNIT 0

Background on Software Development

IN THIS UNIT

Summary: This unit will give you background on Java and what a software developer does. You will also learn the purpose of software, and the tools you will use to prepare for the exam.

If you take a bird's eye view of the idea of software development, you can see that it is important for programmers to follow guidelines. The rules that guide programmers help make sure that programs are easily maintainable.

Key Ideas

✪ Java is the programming language of the AP Computer Science A Exam.
✪ Java is an object-oriented programming language.
✪ Software developers design and implement code for countless applications.
✪ An integrated development environment (IDE) is the tool that you will use when you write your Java code.
✪ Program specifications define what a program is supposed to accomplish.
✪ Someone other than the software developer often writes program specifications.
✪ Software engineering is a field that studies how software is designed, developed, and maintained.
✪ Top-down and bottom-up are two approaches to designing class hierarchy.
✪ Procedural abstraction helps make software more modular.
✪ Software developers use testing techniques to verify that their program is working correctly.

What Is Java?

So, you want to learn how to write software for other people. Well, you could write all your programs on paper using a pencil. Then, the users could just read your code and pretend that they're running your program. There's just one minor problem with that: to write software, you need software.

Java is a general-purpose, object-oriented computer programming language that was developed by James Gosling in the mid-1990s when he worked at Sun Microsystems (Sun was later acquired by Oracle). Java is different from other languages in several ways, but the major difference is that it was designed to be **machine-independent**. This means that a Java program could be written on any platform (Windows, Mac, Linux, etc.) and then could be run on any platform. Prior to Java, software was **machine-dependent** which meant that you could only run your program on the same type of machine that you wrote it on.

Here is a simplistic explanation of how Java accomplishes its machine-independent process. Suppose you write a program in Java. The computer can't run the program as you've written it, because it doesn't understand Java. It can only run a program whose instructions are written in **machine code**. A **compiler** is a program that converts your Java program into code called **bytecode**. The compiler checks your program for **syntax errors**, and when all of these errors are eliminated, the compiler generates a new program that is readable by a **Java virtual machine (JVM)**. The JVM is where the Java program actually runs since it translates the bytecode into machine code. The JVM is a part of the **Java Runtime Environment (JRE)** that is provided by Oracle. Oracle writes a JVM for numerous platforms like Windows, which is how a Java program can run on any machine.

It's a Big Java World Out There

Java has thousands of built-in classes that all Java programmers can use. Since the focus of this book is to help you score a 5 on the AP Computer Science A Exam, only the features that are tested on the exam are included in this book.

What Is a Software Developer?

Software developers are the wizards of our technology-based world. They are the people who design and create the programs that run on smartphones, tablets, smart TVs, computers, cars, and so on. It is stunning how many people the software developer affects.

Software developers may work individually, but most of the time, they work as part of a team of developers. It is essential that they write clean, readable code so that others can read and modify it, if needed. Since other developers will often read your code, it is important to insert comments into your code. In the real world of programming, most programmers despise commenting their code, but it is a necessary evil, and every developer appreciates reading code that has been well documented.

One of the most important skills that a programmer needs to have is figuring out how to design and subsequently implement code for a project. The software developer's job can be summarized with this simple graphic:

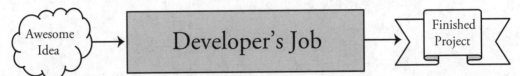

This is the exciting, yet challenging part of the developer's role in project development. Computer programmers get a high level of satisfaction from solving problems, so solving problems is a high priority on the AP Computer Science A Exam.

In many classrooms, students work independently on their programming assignments. This is fine when you are learning how to code; however, few software projects in the work world are like that. Projects can have anywhere from a small handful of programmers to hundreds of programmers. There is a hierarchy among the developers that separates the types of work to be done.

What Is OOP (Object-Oriented Programming)?

Object-oriented programming is an approach to programming that uses the concept of classes and objects. It's a brilliant approach since *we live in an object-oriented world*. Everywhere you look, there are objects (cars, balls, trees, etc). These objects have attributes that make them different from other objects (red 2-door convertible, black 4-door hatchback, youth soccer ball, regulation football). Many of these objects can perform some kind of action, or you can get information from them. In OOP, classes define how an object will be constructed. Then, objects are created from these classes, and you manipulate them in your program. Kind of makes you feel like you rule the world, doesn't it?

Viewing the World Through the Eyes of a Software Developer

Something I challenge all my computer science students to do is to begin viewing the world through the eyes of a software developer. As you learn new concepts, try to relate them to things in your daily life. If you are a gamer, start to analyze the games that you play and see if you can figure out how the developers made the game. My students tell me that their minds "open up" after doing this, and it helps them to be better programmers since they are constantly making connections between the computer science topics and the world that they live in.

For the Good of All Humankind

Let's be honest; in our world, there are good software developers and there are morally challenged software developers. The hackers who live on the dark side will always exist, and our job as noble software developers is to make the world a better place. Integrity is vital to our side and is a badge to be worn with pride. Therefore, we must vow to only write software that is for the good of all humankind and stand up against all morally challenged software developers.

As developers, we strive to:

- Make the best product possible
- Keep our clients' information safe and private
- Honor the intellectual property of others
- Make ethically moral software

Choosing Your IDE

 An Integrated Development Environment, or IDE, is a piece of software that allows you to write software more easily. Professional IDEs, such as Eclipse or IntelliJ, have features that make creating programs easier. Other IDEs are great for introducing a beginner to programming.

There are many excellent IDEs for Java. Your computer science teacher will probably choose the IDE for you. While it is important to learn how to write a program with an IDE, it is also important to remember that *you will not be able to use a computer* on the AP Computer Science A Exam. Many IDEs use autocomplete features that can be helpful when coding, but may not help you learn the exact syntax of Java since you are relying on the IDE to complete or correct your code. It is recommended to turn off the autocomplete feature. Whatever program you use to write your Java code, you *must* learn how to do it without the use of a computer.

> **No Computer!**
> Computers are *not used* on the AP Computer Science A Exam.

HelloWorld

In whatever IDE you choose to write your programs, type in the following code for the HelloWorld program. Compile it and run it. This will get you to the point where you can begin this book.

PROGRAM
```
public class HelloWorld
{
    public static void main(String[] args)
    {
        System.out.println("Hello World.");
    }
}
```

OUTPUT (This is what is displayed on the console screen.)
```
Hello World.
```

Spacing and Indenting in Your Program

Programmers have the freedom to put spacing and indentions in their program in any way they want. Typically, programmers follow spacing guidelines to make it easier to read. The `HelloWorld` example shown on the previous page demonstrates a classic form for spacing and indenting code.

You may also see a `HelloWord` program that looks like the next example. This program will run in exactly the same way as the previous example even though the spacing is different.

```java
public class HelloWorld {
    public static void main(String[] args){
        System.out.println("Hello World.");
    }
}
```

The Software Development Cycle

Program Specifications

When you are in computer science class, your teacher probably gives you assignments that have **program specifications**. This means that in order to receive full credit for the assignment, you have to follow the directions and make sure that your program does what it is supposed to do. When you write your own programs for your own purpose, you make your own specifications.

In the real world of programming, it is common for someone from a design team to give the software developers the program specifications. Specifications are descriptions of what the program should look like and how it should operate. Someone other than the actual programmer writes these **specs**. You may have heard that it is important to be a good communicator. Well, great programmers have good communication skills so that they can talk back and forth with the person who writes the specs to clarify any questions they may have.

Working for Others

Programmers must learn how to write code from specifications. On the Free-response questions section of the AP Computer Science A Exam, you have to write code that matches the specifications that are described in the questions.

Software Engineering

Software engineering is the study of designing, developing, and maintaining software.

Over the years, many different software development models have been designed that help developers create quality software. Here is a brief list.

- Prototyping—an approximation of a final system is built, tested, and reworked until it is acceptable. The complete system is then developed from this prototype.
- Incremental development—The software is designed, implemented, and tested a little bit at a time until the product is finished.
- Rapid application development—the user is actively involved in the evaluation of the product and modifications are made immediately as problems are found. Radical changes in the system are likely at any moment in the process.

- Agile software development—the developers offer frequent releases of the software to the customer and new requirements are generated by the users. Short development cycles are common in this type of development.
- Waterfall model—the progress of development is sequential and flows downward like a waterfall. Steps include conception, initiation, analysis, design, construction, testing, implementation, and maintenance.

 Fun Fact: *Margaret Hamilton, a computer scientist who helped develop the on-board flight software for the Apollo space program, coined the phrase "software engineering." Her code prevented an abort of a moon landing!*

So What's the Best Way?

It depends on the situation. It varies from problem to problem, situation to situation, and even company to company. My belief is that you should view the models of software engineering as tools in a toolbox in which the technique that you apply depends on the project you are working on.

Designing Class Hierarchy

Top-Down Versus Bottom-Up Design

Top-down and **bottom-up** are two ways of approaching class hierarchy design. Top-down is also referred to as **functional decomposition**. The two designs are different only in their approach to the problem. Top-down design starts with the big picture, whereas a bottom-up design starts with the details. They each work toward the other, but where they begin is different.

Top-Down Versus Bottom-Up in Object-Oriented Programming

This concept can be applied to designing a complex class hierarchy. If you start your design by thinking of what would be at the top of the class hierarchy, then you are doing a top-down design. If you start your design by thinking of what would be at the bottom of the class hierarchy, then you are doing a bottom-up design.

For example, suppose you have been given the opportunity to design a video game for the NFL (National Football League). If you approach the design from a bottom-up perspective, you would say, "Let's design the Player class first. We'll determine all the instance variables and methods for the Player. Then we'll move on to the Team class. After we get those done, we'll figure out where to go from there." This approach starts with the lowest level object that could be in your game first (the Player), and then works *up* from there.

If you approach the design from a top-down perspective, you would say, "Let's design the League class first. We'll identify what every League has and what it can do. Then, we'll move onto the Conference class. After we get those done, we'll figure out where to go from there." This approach starts with the highest possible object first (the League), and then works *down* from there.

 Top-Down Versus Bottom-Up
Top-down design begins with the parent classes, while bottom-up starts with the child classes. On the AP Computer Science A Exam, you will need to be able to recognize a top-down versus a bottom-up design.

Procedural Abstraction

When a program is broken down into pieces and each piece has a responsibility, then the program is following **procedural abstraction**. For example, if you write a quest game and have separate methods for hunting, gathering, and collecting, then you are following procedural abstraction. If your hunt method *also* gathers, collects, and slays dragons while eating a peanut butter and jelly sandwich, then you are not following procedural abstraction.

Fun Fact: *The word* procedure *comes from early procedural programming languages like Fortran and Pascal. Procedures are similar to methods in Java. Each procedure has a purpose and does its job when you ask it to.*

Procedural Abstraction
Every method in Java should have a specific job. Complex tasks should be broken down into smaller tasks.

Testing

You may have heard of video game testers whose job it is to find bugs in the software. Talk about a dream job, right? Well, professional programmers test their work to make sure that it does what it's supposed to do before they release it. There are a few standard ways that developers test code.

Unit Testing

Unit tests are typically short methods that test whether or not a specific method is performing its task correctly. Suppose you have a method that performs some kind of mathematical calculation. To test if this method is working correctly, you would write another method, called a **unit test**. The unit test calls the method you want to test to see if it is producing correct answers. To accomplish this, you figure out what the answer is *before* you make the call to the method and compare the method's answer with your answer.

Here are the steps to creating a unit test for a method:

1. Create a method that performs some kind of calculation.
2. Think of an appropriate input for the method and calculate the answer.
3. Create a unit test. The unit test must contain a call to the original method.
4. Run the unit test with your input and compare the result to the answer you calculated.
5. Repeat this process for every possible type of input that you can think of. For example, when creating a unit test method that does a mathematical calculation, you may want to test it with a positive number, a negative number, and zero.
6. If the method produces correct values for every one of your inputs, the method *passes the unit test.*

Example

Create a unit test method for the getArea method of the Circle class. Pass it a value for the radius as well as the known answer for its area to determine if the method is doing its calculation correctly.

```java
public class UnitTestForCircle
{
    public static void main(String[] args)
    {
        testGetArea(new Circle(10), 314.15926); // Supply the correct answers
        testGetArea(new Circle(0), 0.0);
    }

    public static void testGetArea(Circle c, double correctAnswer)
    {
        // Use a tolerance to determine closeness of answer
        double tolerance = 0.0001;

        if (Math.abs(c.getArea() - correctAnswer) <= tolerance)
        {
            System.out.println(c.getRadius() + " passed the test");
        }
        else
        {
            System.out.println(c.getRadius() + " failed the test");
        }
    }
} // End of Circle class
```

```java
public class Circle
{
    /*  Additional implementation not shown */

    public double getArea()
    {
        return Math.PI * Math.pow(radius, 2);
    }
} // End of Circle class
```

```
OUTPUT
10.0 passed the test
0.0 passed the test
```

Integration Testing

Integration testing is used to make sure that connections to outside resources are working correctly. For example, if you are writing software that connects to Snapchat, then you would write a method that tests whether the connection is made correctly.

› Rapid Review

- Java is a general-purpose, object-oriented computer programming language.
- Java source code is translated into bytecode by the compiler.
- Java has thousands of built-in classes that all Java programmers can use.
- A software developer is a person who writes computer programs.
- Software developers must be creative but also pay attention to detail.
- An object-oriented language is a programming model that uses classes and objects.
- To be a better programmer, you should start to view the world through the eyes of a software developer.
- Software developers must keep their clients' information safe, honor the intellectual properties of others, and make ethically moral software.
- An Integrated Development Environment (IDE) is a piece of software that allows you to write software more easily.
- A computer is not used on the AP Computer Science A Exam.
- HelloWorld is traditionally the first computer program that a beginning Java programmer writes.
- Program specifications define what a program is supposed to accomplish.
- Someone other than the software developer often writes program specifications.
- A good software developer has the ability to communicate with others.
- Software engineering is a field that studies how software is designed, developed, and maintained.
- There isn't one correct way to design a computer program. How you write the program depends on the application.
- Top-down and bottom-up are two approaches to designing class hierarchy.
- Top-down design starts with the parent classes and works toward the child classes.
- Bottom-up design starts with the child classes and works toward the parent classes.
- Procedural abstraction helps make software more modular.
- When applying procedural abstraction to a complex task, the developer breaks the complex task down into smaller parts and implements these tasks individually.
- Software developers use testing techniques to verify that their program is working correctly.
- Unit testing is the process of testing a method to make sure that it is working correctly.
- Integration testing is the process of testing connections to outside resources to make sure that they are working correctly.

› Review Questions

1. You are designing a program to simulate the students at your school. Starting with which one of these classes would best demonstrate top-down design?

   (A) The student body
   (B) The senior class
   (C) The girls in the senior class
   (D) The girls taking programming in the senior class
   (E) Mary Zhang, a girl in the programming class

2. If you were designing a unit test for the `isEven` method, which of these methods would you prefer to be working with and why? Note that the two methods both work and return the same result.

Option 1:
```
public boolean isEven(int num)
{
    int digit = num % 10;
    if (digit >= 5)
        if (digit == 6 || digit == 8)
            return true;
        else
            return false;
    else if (digit == 0 || digit == 2 || digit == 4)
        return true;
    else
        return false;
}
```

Option 2:
```
public boolean isEven(int num)
{
    return (num % 2 == 0);
}
```

(A) Option 1 because it doesn't use modulus, so it's easier to understand.
(B) Option 1 because it is longer.
(C) Option 2 because there is only one path through the code, so fewer test cases are needed.
(D) Neither option requires testing because the intent of the method is clear from the name.
(E) It doesn't matter. Testing them would be the same.

3. What is the term used to describe breaking a large program into smaller, well-defined sections that are easier to code and maintain?

(A) Encapsulation
(B) Procedural abstraction
(C) Inheritance
(D) Static design
(E) Polymorphism

› Answers and Explanations

1. The answer is A.

In top-down design, you start by designing the broadest category, and then work your way down. The broadest category here is the student body.

2. The answer is C.

Unit tests have to test every path through the code. The fewer the paths, the shorter the test, the more sure the tester is that the code will work in every case.

3. The answer is B.

This process is called procedural abstraction.

UNIT 1

Primitive Types

2.5-5% AP Exam Weight

IN THIS UNIT

Summary: You will learn the fundamental building blocks that all programmers need to write software. The syntax, which is the technical way of writing the code, will be written in Java; however, all of the structures that you will learn in this concept will apply to any language that you come across in the future. To pass the AP Computer Science A Exam, you must master all of these fundamental concepts.

Learning Objectives

MOD-1.A Call System class methods to generate output to the console.
VAR-1.A Create string literals.
VAR-1.B Identify the most appropriate data type category for a particular specification.
VAR-1.C Declare variables of the correct types to represent primitive data.
CON-1.A Evaluate arithmetic expressions in a program code.
CON-1.B Evaluate what is stored in a variable as a result of an expression with an assignment statement.
CON-1.C Evaluate arithmetic expressions that use casting.

Key Ideas

✪ Variables allow you to store information that is used by the program.
✪ The computer follows the order of operations when performing mathematical calculations.
✪ The console screen is where simple input and output are displayed.
✪ Good software developers can debug their code and the code of others.

Introduction

Do you want to keep track of a score in a game that you want to write? Do you want your program to make choices based on whatever the user wants? Will you be doing any math to get answers for the user? Do you want an easy way to do something a million times? In this unit you will learn the fundamental building blocks that programmers use to write software to do all these things.

Syntax

Syntax is not a fine you have to pay for doing something you're not supposed to do. (Ha, see what I did there?) The syntax of a programming language describes the correct way to type the code so the program will run. An example of a syntax error is forgetting to put a semicolon after an instruction. Another example is not putting a pair of parentheses in the correct place. You have to fix all syntax errors before your program will run. If your program has any syntax errors, the **compiler** will respond with a **compile-time** error. This type of error prevents the compiler from doing its job of turning your Java code into bytecode. As soon as you have eliminated all syntax errors from your program, your program can be compiled and then **run (executed)**. A list of common syntax errors can be found in the Appendix.

> **Inline Comment**
>
> An inline comment is a way for a programmer to tell someone who is reading the code a secret message. The way to make an inline comment is to make two forward slashes, like this: //.
>
> // This is an inline comment.
> // The computer ignores everything after the two forward slashes on the same line.
> // I will use inline comments as a way to give you secret messages throughout this book.

The Console Screen

The **console** screen is the simplest way to input and output information when running a program. The two most common instructions to display information to the screen are **System.out.println()** and **System.out.print()**. A **string literal** is a sequence of characters enclosed in double quotation marks, such as "text goes here". You must enclose the contents of the string literal in quotation marks so the compiler knows you want to *literally* print the string "text goes here".

> **Summary of Console Output**
>
> CASE 1:   To display some text and then move the cursor onto the next line:
> ```
> System.out.println("text goes here");
> ```
> CASE 2:   To display some text and NOT move the cursor onto the next line:
> ```
> System.out.print("text goes here");
> ```
> CASE 3:   To only move the cursor onto the next line:
> ```
> System.out.println();
> ```

Example

The difference between the print() and the println() statements:

Predict the Output of This Code:

```
line 1: System.out.print("Players gonna play, ");
line 2: System.out.println("play, play, play, play");
line 3: System.out.print("Haters gonna hate, hate, hate, ");
line 4: System.out.println("hate, hate");
line 5: System.out.println();
line 6: System.out.println("I shake it off, I shake it off");
```

Output on the Console Screen:

```
Players gonna play, play, play, play, play
Haters gonna hate, hate, hate, hate, hate

I shake it off, I shake it off
```

The Semicolon

The semicolon is a special character that signifies the end of an instruction. Every distinct line of code should end with a semicolon. It tells the compiler that an instruction ends here.

```
System.out.println("some text");   // the semicolon ends the instruction
```

Primitive Variables

Numbers can be stored and retrieved while a program is running if they are given a home. The way that integer and decimal numbers are stored in the computer is by declaring a **variable**. When you declare a variable, the computer sets aside a space for it in the working memory of the computer (RAM) while the program is running. Once that space is declared, the programmer can assign a value to the variable, change the value, or retrieve the value at any time in the program. In other words, if you want to keep track of something in your program, you have to create a home for it, and declaring a variable does just that.

In Java, the kind of number that the programmer wants to store must be decided ahead of time and is called the **data type**. For the AP Computer Science A Exam, you are required to know two primitive data types that store numbers: the **int** and the **double**.

Variable

A variable is a simple data structure that allows the programmer to store a value in the computer. The programmer can retrieve or modify the variable at any time in the program.

The int and double Data Types

Numbers that contain decimals can be stored only in the data type called **double**. Integers can be stored in either the data type called **int** or **double**. Remember that this book is designed for the AP Computer Science A Exam. There are several other data types in Java that can store numbers; however, they are not tested on the AP Computer Science A Exam.

When it is time for you to create a variable, you need to know its data type. It's also a common practice to give the variable a starting value if you know what it should be. This process is called *declaring a variable and initializing it*.

The General Form for Declaring a Variable in Java

```
datatype variableName;
```

The General Form for Declaring a Variable and Then Initializing It

```
datatype variableName = value;
```

Examples

Declaring `int` and `double` primitive variables in Java:

```
int numberOfPokemon = 25;        // numberOfPokemon gets a value of 25
double health = 112.7;           // health gets the value of 112.7
double gpa = 3;                  // a double can receive an int value
double a = 2.4, b = 5.6, c = 4;  // multiple variables on same line
```

The following graphic is intended to give you a visual of how **primitive variables** are stored in the computer's **RAM (random access memory)**. The value of each variable is stored in the computer's memory at a specific **memory address**. The name of the variable and its value are stored together. Whenever you declare a new primitive variable, think of this picture to imagine what is going on inside the computer. The way this process works inside of a computer is a bit more complicated than this, but I hope the diagram helps you imagine how variables are stored in memory.

Memory Address: 0000 numberOfPokemon = 25	*Memory Address: 0001* health = 112.7	*Memory Address: 0002* gpa = 3.0
Memory Address: 0003 a = 2.4	*Memory Address: 0004* b = 5.6	*Memory Address: 0005* c = 4.0
Memory Address: 0006 *<empty>*	*Memory Address: 0007* *<empty>*	*Memory Address: 0008* *<empty>*
Memory Address: 0009 *<empty>*	*Memory Address: 000A* *<empty>*	*Memory Address: 000B* *<empty>*

Naming Convention and Camel Case

The manner in which you choose a variable name should follow the rules of a **naming convention**. A naming convention makes it easy for programmers to recognize and recall variable names.

Obviously, you are familiar with uppercase and lowercase, but let me introduce you to **camel case**, the technique used to create **identifiers** in Java. All primitive variable names start with a lowercase letter; then for each new word in the variable name, the first letter of the new word is assigned an uppercase letter.

All variable names should be descriptive, yet concise. The name should describe exactly what the variable holds and be short enough to not become a pain to write every time you use it. Single-letter variable names should be avoided, as they are not descriptive.

Examples

Mistakes when declaring `int` and `double` primitive variables in Java:

```
double 5dollars = 900.0;        // Error: name cannot begin with a number
int #tickets = 5;               // Error: name cannot start with a # symbol
int theNumberOfPokemonThatAshCaughtDuringHisLifetime = 151;
// the name is valid, but is a terrible choice because it is way too long
```

Constants

A constant is a name for a variable whose value doesn't change during the run of a program. Any attempt to change the value of the constant will generate a compiler error. The Java naming convention is to capitalize each letter of the constant name and to include underscores ("_") when two or more words are combined. This is known as snake case.

The General Form for Declaring a Constant

final datatype VARIABLE_NAME = value;

Examples

Declaring constants in Java:

```
final int INCHES_IN_FOOT = 12;      // INCHES_IN_FOOT gets the value of 12 and
                                    // will remain 12
final double TAX_RATE = 0.06;       // TAX_RATE gets the value of 0.06 and will
                                    // remain 0.06
```

Summary of Variable Names in Java

- Variable names should be meaningful, descriptive, and concise.
- Variable names cannot begin with a number or symbol (the dollar sign and underscore are exceptions to this rule).
- By naming convention, variable names use camel case.
- By naming convention, constant names use snake case.

The `boolean` Data Type

If you want to store a value that is not a number, but rather a **true** or **false** value, then you should choose a **boolean** variable. The `boolean` data type is stored in the computer memory in the same way as `int` and `double`.

Examples

Declaring boolean variables in Java:

```
boolean userHasWon = false;         // userHasWon is false
boolean unicornIsVisible = true;    // unicornIsVisible is true
boolean bananaCount = 5;            // Error: boolean cannot store a number
```

One-Letter Variable Names

On the Free-response section of the AP Computer Science A Exam, you should name your variables in a meaningful way so the reader can understand what you're doing. Declaring all your variable names with single letters that don't explain what is stored is considered bad programming practice.

Keywords in Java

A **keyword** is a reserved word in Java. They are words that the compiler looks for when translating the Java code into bytecode. Examples of keywords are `int`, `double`, `public`, and `boolean`. Keywords can never be used as the names of variables, as it confuses the compiler and therefore causes a syntax error. A full list of Java keywords appears in the Appendix.

Example

The mistake of using a keyword as a variable name:

```
int public = 6;        // Syntax Error: public is a Java keyword
```

Primitive Data Types
- int, double, boolean
- memory associated with a variable holds its actual value

Mathematical Operations

Order of Operations

Java handles all mathematical calculations using the **order of operations** that you were taught in math class (your teacher may have called it PEMDAS). The order of operations does exactly that: it tells you the order to evaluate any expression that may contain parentheses, multiplication, division, addition, subtraction, and so on. The computer will figure out the answers in exactly the same way that you were taught in math class.

Operator	Priority
Parentheses	Top priority
Multiplication, Division, Modulo	Done in order from left to right (equal precedence)
Addition, Subtraction	Done in order from left to right (equal precedence)

Modulo

The **modulus** (or **mod**) operator appears often on the AP Computer Science A Exam. While it is not deliberately taught in most math classes, it is something that you are familiar with.

The mod operator uses the percent symbol, **%**, and produces the remainder after doing a division, and the answer takes the sign of the numerator. Back in grade school, you may have been taught that the answer to 14 divided by 3 was 4 R 2, where the R stood for *remainder*. If this is how you were taught, then mod will be simple for you. The result of 14 % 3 is 2 because there are 2 left over after dividing 14 by 3.

Modulo Example	Answer	Explanation
20 % 7	6	20 divided by 7 is 2 with a remainder of 6
100 % 20	0	100 divided by 20 is 5 with a remainder of 0
4 % 12	4	4 divided by 12 is 0 with a remainder of 4
0 % 2	0	0 divided by 2 is 0 with a remainder of 0
–7 % 5	–2	–7 divided by 5 is –1 with a remainder of –2
7 % –5	2	7 divided by –5 is –1 with a remainder of 2

Using Modulo to Find Even or Odd Numbers

The mod operator is great for determining if a number is even or odd.

If someNumber % 2 == 0, then someNumber is even. Or, if someNumber % 2 == 1, then someNumber is odd.

Furthermore, the mod operator can be used to find a multiple of *any* number. For example, if someNumber % 13 == 0, then someNumber is a multiple of 13.

Division with Integers

When you divide an int by an int in Java, the result is an int. This is referred to as **integer division**. The decimal portion of the answer is ignored. The technical way to say it is that the result is **truncated**, which means that the decimal portion of the answer is dropped.

Arithmetic Operator	Java Symbol	Example	Result	Justification
Addition	+	7 + 3	10	Simple addition
Subtraction	−	7 − 3	4	Simple subtraction
Multiplication	*	7 * 3	21	Simple multiplication
Division	/	7 / 3	2	7 divided by 3 is 2 (remainder is dropped)
Modulo	%	7 % 3	1	7 divided by 3 is 2 with a remainder of 1

Examples

The examples show how division works with int and double values in Java. If either number is a double, you get a double result.

- A double divided by a double is a double.   // example: 10.0 / 4.0 = 2.5
- A double divided by an int is a double.   // example: 10.0 / 4 = 2.5
- An int divided by a double is a double.   // example: 10 / 4.0 = 2.5
- An int divided by an int is an int.   // example: 10 / 4 = 2

ArithmeticException

Any attempt to divide by zero or perform someNumber % 0 will produce a **run-time error** called an **ArithmeticException**. The program crashes when it tries to do this math operation.

Examples

Getting an ArithmeticException error by doing incorrect math:

```
int num1 = 5, num2 = 0;
int num3 = num1 / num2;      // ArithmeticException: division by zero
int num4 = num1 % num2;      // ArithmeticException: division by zero
```

ArithmeticException

Dividing by zero or performing a mod by zero will produce an error called an **ArithmeticException**.

Modifying Number Variables

The Assignment Operator

The equal sign, =, is called an **assignment operator** because you use it when you want to assign a value to a variable. It acts differently from the equal sign in mathematics since the equal sign in math shows that the two sides have the same value. The assignment operator gives the left side the value of whatever is on the right side. The right side of the equal sign is computed first and then the answer is assigned to the variable on the left side.

Assignment statements use the equal sign, =, and are processed from RIGHT to LEFT. The RIGHT side is computed first; then the answer is stored in the variable on the LEFT.

Accumulating

I'm pretty sure that if you were writing some kind of game, you would want to keep track of a score. You may also want a timer. In order to do this, you will need to know how to count and accumulate. When giving a variable a value, the right side of the assignment statement is computed first, and the result is given to the variable on the left side of the statement (even if it is the same variable!). The left side of the assignment statement is replaced by the right side. So, to modify a number variable, you must change it and then store it back on itself.

Example
How to accumulate using the assignment operator:

```
int score = 0;        // create a score variable and initialize it to zero
score = score + 100;  // add 100 to the variable score
```

Step 3: Replace the value of score with the result of the right side.

Step 1: Get the current value of score.

Step 2: Add 100 to the value of score.

```
score = score + 100;
```

Compound Assignment Operators

Java provides another way to modify the value of a variable called a **compound assignment operator**. There is a compound assignment operator for addition, subtraction, multiplication, division, and modulo. It's called a compound assignment operator because you only have to write the variable name one time rather than twice like in the previous explanation.

Examples
How to modify a variable using compound assignment operators:

```
int score = 90;
score += 10;        // adds 10 to score: score is now 100
score -= 25;        // subtracts 25 from score: score is now 75
score *= 10;        // multiplies score by 10: score is now 750
score /= 5;         // divides score by 5: score is now 150
score %= 3;         // score mod 3: score is now 0
```

Incrementing and Decrementing a Variable

To **increment** a variable means to *add* to the value stored in the variable. This is how we can *count up* in Java. There are three common ways to write code to add *one* to a variable. You may see any of these techniques for incrementing by one on the AP Computer Science A Exam.

```
i++;                    // increments i by one
i = i + 1;              // increments i by one
i+=1;                   // increments i by one
```

To **decrement** a variable means to *subtract* from its value. This is how we can *count down* in Java. There are three common ways to subtract *one* from a variable in Java.

```
i--;                    // decrements i by one
i = i - 1;              // decrements i by one
i-=1;                   // decrements i by one
```

Casting a Variable

On the AP Computer Science A Exam, you will be tested on the correct way to **cast** variables. Casting is a way to tell a variable to temporarily become a different data type for the sake of performing some action, such as division. The next example demonstrates why casting is important using division with integers. Observe how the cast uses parentheses.

> **The Most Common Type of Cast**
>
> The most common types of casts are from an `int` to a `double` or a `double` to an `int`.

Example 1

Here is the *correct way* to cast an `int` to a `double`: Make the variable pretend that it is a `double` *before* doing the division.

> Hey `hits`, I know you are an `int`, but could you just temporarily pretend that you are a `double` so that I can give this softball player her correct batting average? If you don't, her average will be 0.0.

```
int atBats = 5;
int hits = 2;
double battingAverage = (double)hits / atBats;      // battingAverage is 0.4
```

Example 2

Here is the *wrong way* to cast an `int` to a `double`. This example does not produce the result we want, because we are casting the *result* of the division between the integers. Remember that 2 divided by 5 is 0 (using integer division).

```
int atBats = 5;
int hits = 2;
double battingAverage = (double)(hits / atBats); // battingAverage is 0.0
```

Manually Rounding a `double`

On the AP Computer Science A Exam, you will have to know how to round a `double` to its nearest whole number. This requires a cast from a `double` to an `int`.

Example 1

Manually rounding a positive decimal number to the nearest integer:

```
double roundMe = 53.6;
int result = (int)(roundMe + 0.5);                        // result is 54
```

Example 2

Manually rounding a negative decimal number to the nearest integer:

```
double roundMe = -53.6;
int result = (int)(roundMe - 0.5);                          // result is -54
```

Arithmetic Overflow

In Java and most other programming languages, integers have a limited range of values. An integer takes up 4 bytes of memory and has a range from `Integer.MIN_VALUE` to `Integer.MAX_VALUE` inclusive. If you attempt to do an assignment or calculation outside of these bounds, arithmetic overflow will occur. The program will still run, but unexpected results will occur.

Example

```
int max = Integer.MAX_VALUE;    // assigns the largest integer that can be stored:
                                // 2,147,483,647
max++;                          // since this value exceeds the largest value, over-
                                // flow occurs
System.out.println(max);        // doesn't cause an error, but an unexpected value
                                // is printed (-2,147,483,648)
```

 Fun Fact: *The value of Integer.MAX_VALUE represents the maximum positive value for a 32-bit signed binary number, which is $2^{31}-1$. In 2014 Psy's music video "Gangnam Style" was on the verge of exceeding the 32-bit integer limit for YouTube video counts. Engineers saw this coming and updated the system to a 64-bit counter.*

The Correct Way to Compare If Two `double` Values Are Equal

It is never a good idea to compare if two `double` values are equal using the `==` sign. Calculations with a double can contain rounding errors. You may have seen this when printing the result of some kind of division and you get something like this as a result: `7.00000000002`.

The correct way to compare if two doubles are equal is to use a *tolerance*. If the difference between the two numbers is less than or equal to the tolerance, then we say that the two numbers are *close enough* to be considered equal. Since we might not know which of the two numbers is bigger, subtract the two numbers and find the absolute value of the result. This way, the difference between the two numbers is always positive.

> **General Form for Comparing If Two `double` Values Are Equal**
>
> ```
> double a =   /*   Some double   */
> double b =   /*   Some double   */
> double tolerance = 0.00001;   // The 0.00001 varies with the application
>
> boolean closeEnough = Math.abs(a - b) <= tolerance;
> ```

Example

Determine if two doubles are "equal" using a very small tolerance:

```
double num1 = 3.99999;
double num2 = 4.0;
double tolerance = 0.0001;
boolean result = Math.abs(num1 - num2) <= tolerance;        // result is true
```

Avoid Using the == Sign When Comparing `double` Values

Rounding errors cause problems when trying to determine if two `double` values are equal. Never use == to compare if two doubles are equal. Instead, determine if the difference between the two doubles is close enough for the two doubles to be considered equal.

Types of Errors

Compile-Time Errors

When you don't use the correct **syntax** in Java, the compiler yells at you. Well, it doesn't actually yell at you, it just won't compile your program and gives you a **compile-time error**. A list of the most common compile-time errors is located in the Appendix.

A brief list of compile-time errors:

- Forgetting a semicolon at the end of an instruction
- Forgetting to put a data type for a variable
- Using a keyword as a variable name
- Forgetting to initialize a variable
- Forgetting a curly brace (curly braces must have partners)

Run-Time Exceptions

If your program crashes while it is running, then you have a **run-time error**. The compiler will display the error and it may have the word **exception** in it.

These are the run-time errors that you are required to understand on the AP Computer Science A Exam:

- `ArithmeticException` (explained in this unit)
- `NullPointerException` (explained in Unit 2: Using Objects)
- `IndexOutOfBoundsException` (explained in Unit 2: Using Objects)
- `ArrayIndexOutOfBoundsException` (explained in Unit 6: Array)
- `ConcurrentModificationException` (explained in Unit 7: ArrayList)

Logic Errors

When your program compiles and runs without crashing, but it doesn't do what you expected it to do, then you have a **logic error**. A logic error is the most challenging type of error to fix because you have to figure out where the problem is in your program. Is your math correct? Are your `if` statements comparing correctly? Does your loop actually do what it's supposed to do? Are any statements out of order or are you missing something? Logic errors require you to read your code very carefully to determine the source of the error.

Logic Errors on the AP Computer Science A Exam

You will have to analyze code in the Multiple-choice section of the exam and find hidden logic errors.

Debugging

The process of removing the errors in your program (compile-time, run-time, and logic) is called **debugging** your program. On the AP Computer Science A Exam, you will be asked to find errors in code.

Fun Fact: *Grace Murray Hopper documented the first actual computer bug on September 9, 1947. It was a moth that got caught in Relay #70 in Panel F of the Harvard Mark II computer.*

`System.out.println` as a Debugging Device

A common way to debug a computer program is to peek inside the computer while it is running and display the current values of variables on the console screen. We aren't actually opening up the computer. We are just displaying the current values of the important variables. By printing the values of the variables at precise moments, you can determine what is going on during the running of the program and hopefully figure out the error.

› Rapid Review

Variables

- Variables store data and must be declared with a data type.
- The `int`, `double`, and `boolean` types are called primitive data types.
- A string literal is enclosed in double quotes.
- Variables may be initialized with a value or be assigned one later in the program.
- Variable names may begin with a letter, dollar sign, or underscore. They cannot begin with a number.
- Camel case is used for all variable names starting with a lowercase letter.
- Choose meaningful names for variables.
- A keyword is a word that has special meaning to the compiler such as `int` or `public`.
- A variable name cannot be the same as a keyword.
- The `int` data type is used to store integer data.
- The `double` data type is used to store decimal data.
- To cast a variable means to temporarily change its data type.
- The most common type of cast is to cast an `int` to a `double`.
- The `boolean` data type is used to store either a true or false value.
- When a variable is declared final, its value cannot be changed once it is initialized.

Math

- The arithmetic operators are +, -, *, /, and %.
- The modulo operator, %, returns the remainder of a division between two integers.
- Java evaluates all mathematical expressions using the order of operations.
- The precedence order for all mathematical calculations is parentheses first, then *, / and % equally from the left to right, then + and - equally from left to right.
- Java uses integer division when dividing an `int` by an `int`. The result is a truncated `int`.
- "Truncating" means dropping (not rounding) the decimal portion of a number.
- The equal sign, =, is called the assignment operator.
- To accumulate means to add (or subtract) a value from a variable.
- Short-cuts for performing mathematical operations are +=, -=, *=, /=, and %=.
- "To increment" means to add one to the value of a number variable.
- "To decrement" means to subtract one from the value of a number variable.
- Avoid comparing double values using the == sign. Instead, use a tolerance.

Miscellaneous

- The `System.out.println()` statement displays information to the console and moves the cursor to the next line.
- The `System.out.print()` statement displays information to the console and does not move the cursor to the next line.
- Programs are documented using comments. There are three different types of comments: inline, multiple line, and Javadoc.
- There are three main types of errors: compile-time, run-time, and logic.
- Compile-time errors are caused by syntax errors.
- *Exception* is another name for error.
- There are many types of run-time exceptions and they are based on the type of error.
- Logic errors are difficult to fix because you have to read the code very carefully to find out what is going wrong.
- Debugging is the process of removing errors from a program.
- Printing variables to the console screen can help you debug your program.

› Review Questions

1. Consider the following code segment.

```
int var = 12;
var = var % 7;
var--;
System.out.println(var);
```

What is printed as a result of executing the code segment?

(A) 0
(B) 1
(C) 2
(D) 4
(E) 5

2. Consider the following code segment.

```
int count = 5;
double multiplier = 2.5;
int answer = (int)(count * multiplier);
answer = (answer * count) % 10;
System.out.println(answer);
```

What is printed as a result of executing the code segment?

(A) 0
(B) 2.5
(C) 6
(D) 12.5
(E) 60

3. Consider the following code segment.

```
double x = 3.6;
double y = 2;
int a = 5, b = 13;
double z = x + y * b / a;
```

What is the value of z after the code segment is executed?

(A) 4.6
(B) 8.6
(C) 8.8
(D) 7.6
(E) 14.56

4. Consider the task of finding the average score in a game.

```
int sum =           // a number representing the sum of all of the scores
int count =         // a number representing the number of games played
```

Which statement will correctly calculate the average score of all the games?

(A) `double average = sum / count;`
(B) `double average = double (sum / count);`
(C) `double average = (double) (sum / count);`
(D) `double average = (double) sum / count;`
(E) `double average = sum / double (count);`

5. Consider the code segment.

```
int a = 16, b = 0;
double c = a/b;
```

The segment compiles but has a run-time error. Which error is generated?

(A) `ArithmeticException`
(B) `DivisionByZeroException`
(C) `IndexOutOfBoundsException`
(D) `NullPointerException`
(E) `TypeMismatchException`

〉 Answers and Explanations

Bullets mark each step in the process of arriving at the correct solution.

1. The answer is D.

   - The value of `var` begins at 12.
   - The operation `var % 7` finds the remainder after `var` is divided by 7. Since 12 / 7 is 1 remainder 5, the value of `var` is now 5.
   - `var--` means subtract 1 from var, so the value of `var` is now 4, and that's what is printed.

2. The answer is A.

   - `count * multiplier` = 12.5
   - When we cast 12.5 to an `int` by putting `(int)` in front of it, we *truncate* (or cut off) the decimals, so the value we assign to answer is 12.
   - `12 * 5 = 60.   60 % 10 = 0` because 60 / 10 has no remainder.
   - So we print 0.

3. The answer is C.

   - After the values of the variables are assigned, the first operation that happens is the multiplication 2.0 * 13, which results in 26.0. Remember, multiplication and division have higher precedence than addition (PEMDAS).
   - The next operation that happens is 26.0 / 5, which results in 5.2.
   - Then finally addition is performed. 3.6 + 5.2 results in 8.8.

4. The answer is D.

   - Since both the `sum` and `count` variables are declared as integers, casting must occur in order for the average to contain a double value.
   - The correct option is to cast either `sum` or `count` as a double and then perform the division, which will result in a double value.
   - Answer E would have been correct if the parentheses were placed around "double" on the right side of the assignment.

5. The answer is A.

   - Division by zero will generate an `ArithmeticException` error.

UNIT 2

Using Objects

5-7.5% AP Exam Weight

IN THIS UNIT

Summary: This chapter introduces you to the most fundamental object-oriented features of Java. It explains the relationship between an object and a class. You will learn how to use objects created from classes that are already defined in Java. More advanced aspects of classes and objects will be discussed in Unit 5. You will learn how letters, words, and even sentences are stored in variables. `String` objects can store alphanumerical data, and the methods from the `String` class can be used to manipulate this data. The Java API (application programming interface) contains a library of thousands of useful classes that you can use to write all kinds of programs. Because the Java API is huge, the AP Computer Science A Exam only tests your knowledge of a subset of these classes. This unit provides practice working with four of those classes: `String`, `Math`, `Integer`, and `Double`.

Learning Objectives

MOD-1.B Explain the relationship between a class and an object.

MOD-1.C Identify, using its signature, the correct constructor being called.

MOD-1.D For creating objects:

   a. Create objects by calling constructors without parameters.

   b. Create objects by calling constructors with parameters.

MOD-1.E Call non-static void methods without parameters.

MOD-1.F Call non-static void methods with parameters.

MOD-1.G Call non-static non-void methods with or without parameters.

MOD-1.H Call static methods.
VAR-1.D Define variables of the correct types to represent reference data.
VAR-1.E For `String` class:
  a. Create `String` objects.
  b. Call `String` methods.
VAR-1.F For wrapper classes:
  a. Create `Integer` objects.
  b. Call `Integer` methods.
  c. Create `Double` objects.
  d. Call `Double` methods.
CON-1.D Evaluate expressions that use the `Math` class methods.

Key Ideas

✪ Java is an object-oriented programming language whose foundation is built on classes and objects.
✪ A class describes the characteristics of any object that is created from it.
✪ An object is a virtual entity that is created using a class as a blueprint.
✪ Objects are created to store and manipulate information in your program.
✪ A method is an action that an object can perform.
✪ The keyword `new` is used to create an object.
✪ A reference variable stores the address of the object, not the object itself.
✪ The Java API contains a library of thousands of classes.
✪ Strings are used to store letters, words, and other special characters.
✪ To concatenate strings means to join them together.
✪ The `String` class has many methods that are useful for manipulating `String` objects.
✪ The `Math` class contains methods for performing mathematical calculations.
✪ The `Integer` class is for creating and manipulating objects that represent integers.
✪ The `Double` class is for creating and manipulating objects that represent decimal numbers.

The Java API and the AP Computer Science A Exam Subset

Want to make a trivia game that poses random questions? Want to flip a coin 1 million times to test the laws of probability? Want to write a program that uses the quadratic formula to do your math homework? If so, you will want to learn about the Java API.

The Java **API**, or **application programming interface**, describes a set of classes and files for building software in Java. The classes in the APIs and libraries are grouped into packages, such as `java.lang`. The documentation for APIs and libraries are essential to understanding the attributes and behaviors of an object of a class. It shows how all the Java features work and interact. Since the Java API is gigantic, only a subset of the Java API is tested on the AP Computer Science A Exam. All of the classes described in this subset are required. The Appendix contains the entire Java subset that is on the exam. The `String`, `Math`, `Integer`, and `Double` classes are part of the `java.lang` package and are available by default.

The `String` Variable

How does X (formerly known as Twitter) know when a post has more than 280 characters? How does the computer know if your username and password are correct? How are Instagram posts stored? We need a way to store letters, characters, words, or even sentences if we want to make programs that are useful to people. The **String** data type helps solve these problems.

When we wanted to store numbers so that we can retrieve them later, we created either an `int` or `double` variable. Now that we want to store letters or words, we need to create **String variables**. A `string` can be a single character or group of characters like a word or a sentence. **String literals** are characters surrounded by double quotation marks.

General Way to Make a `String` Variable and Assign It a Value

```
String nameOfString = "characters that make up a string literal";
```

Examples

Make some `String` variables and assign them values:

```
String myName = "Captain America";    // myName is "Captain America"
String jennysNumber = "867-5309";      // numbers are treated as characters
```

The `String` Object

`String` variables are actually objects. The `String` class is unique because `string` objects can be created by simply declaring a `string` variable like we did above or by using the constructor from the `string` class. The reference variable knows the address of the `string` object. The object is assigned a value of whatever characters make up the String literal.

General Way to Make a `String` Object Using the Constructor from the `String` Class

```
String nameOfString = new String("characters that make a string");
```

Example 1

Make a `String` object and assign it a value:

```
String myName = new String("Captain America"); // myName is Captain America
```

Example 2

Create a `string` object, but don't give it an initial value (use the empty constructor from the `string` class). The `string` object contains an **empty string**, which means that the value exists (it is not null); however, there are no characters in the String literal and it has a length of 0 characters.

```
String yourName = new String();   // yourName contains an empty string
```

Example 3

Create a String reference variable but don't create a `string` object for it. The String reference variable is assigned a value of **null** because there isn't an address of a `string` object for it to hold.

```
String theirName;    // theirName is null
```

> **`null` `String` Versus Empty `String`**
>
> A **null** string is a string that has no value and no length. It does not hold an address of a `String` object.
>
> An **empty** string is a string that has a value of "" and its length is zero. There is no space inside of the double quotation marks, because the string is empty.
>
> It may seem like they are the same thing, but they are not. The difference is subtle. The empty string has a value and the null string does not. It is similar to the idea of 0 and does not exist in math. 0 is a number with no value, whereas does not exist means there is no number. Furthermore, you can perform a method on an empty string, but *you cannot perform a method on a null string.*
>
> Any attempt to execute a method on a null string will result in a run-time error called a **NullPointerException**.

A Visual Representation of a `String` Object

This is a visual representation of what a string looks like in memory. The numbers below the characters are called the **indices** (plural of **index**) of the string. Each index represents the location of where each of the characters lives within the string. Notice that the first index is zero. An example of how we read this is: the character at index 4 of myFavoriteFoodGroup is the character "c". Also, *spaces* count as characters. You can see that the character at index 3 is the space character.

```
String myFavoriteFoodGroup = "ice cream";
```

These numbers represent the index of each character in the `String` object.

`String` Concatenation

Now that you know how to create a string and give it a value, let's make lots of them and string them together (Ha!). The process of joining strings together is called **concatenation**. The + and += signs are used to concatenate strings.

Example 1
Concatenate two strings using +.
```
String firstName = "Harry";
String lastName = "Potter";
String entireName = firstName + lastName;   // entireName is "HarryPotter"
```

Example 2
Concatenate two strings using +=.
```
String firstName = "Harry";
String lastName = "Potter";
lastName += firstName;                       // lastName is "PotterHarry"
```

Example 3

Concatenate a number and a string using +.

```
String firstName = "Harry";
int swords = 8;
String result = firstName + swords;              // result is "Harry8"
```

Example 4

Incorrectly concatenate a string and the sum of two numbers using +. Notice that the sum is not computed since the + operator follows a string variable and is treated as concatenation.

```
String firstName = "Harry";
int swords = 8;
int brooms = 4;
String result = firstName + swords + brooms;      // result is "Harry84"
```

Example 5

Correctly concatenate a string and the sum of two numbers using +. Notice the ( ) are evaluated first which means the + is treated as addition.

```
String firstName = "Harry";
int swords = 8;
int brooms = 4;
String result = firstName + (swords + brooms);    // result is "Harry12"
```

Example 6

Concatenate the sum of two numbers and a string in a different order. Notice that when the numbers come first in the concatenation, the sum is computed.

```
String firstName = "Harry";
int swords = 8;
int brooms = 4;
String result = swords + brooms + firstName;      // result is "12Harry"
```

Concatenation

Strings can be joined together to form a new string using concatenation. The + sign or the += operation may be used to join strings.

You can even join an `int` or a `double` along with a string. These numbers will be rendered useless for any mathematical purpose because they are turned into strings.

The Correct Way to Compare Two `String` Objects

Everyone reading this book has had to log in to a computer at some time. How does the computer know if the user typed the username and password correctly? The answer is that the software uses an operation to compare the input with the information in a database.

In Java, we can determine if two strings are equal to each other. This means that the two strings have exactly the same characters in the same order.

The Correct Way to Compare Two `String` Objects

Use the **equals** method or the **compareTo** method to determine if two `String` variables contain the exact same character sequence.

Important `String` Methods

The `equals` Method

The **equals** method returns a boolean answer of true if the two strings are identical and it returns an answer of false if the two strings differ in any way. The `equals` method is **case-sensitive**, so, for example, the uppercase "A" is different than the lowercase "a". The ! operator can be used in combination with the `equals` method to compare if two strings are not equal.

Example 1

Determine if two strings are equal:

```
String username1 = "Cat Lady";
String username2 = "cat lady";                          // notice the lowercase letters
System.out.println(username1.equals("Cat Lady")); // prints true
System.out.println(username2.equals("Cat Lady")); // prints false
```

Example 2

Determine if two strings are not equal:

```
String pet1 = "Cat";
String pet2 = "Dog";
System.out.println(!pet1.equals(pet2));          // prints true
```

Never Use `==` to Compare Two `String` Objects

We used the double equals (==) to compare if two numbers were the same. However, == does not correctly tell you if two strings are the same. What's worse is that comparing two strings using == does not throw an error; it simply compares whether or not the two String references point to the same object. Even worse is that sometimes it appears to work correctly. Just don't do it!

```
String username = "CatLady";
String first = "Cat";
String last = "Lady";
if (username == first + last)
{
    // Comparison will be false.
    // NEVER USE == TO COMPARE TWO STRINGS!
}
```

The `compareTo` Method

The second way to compare two strings is to use the **compareTo** method. Instead of returning an answer that is a boolean like the `equals` method did, the `compareTo` method returns an integer. The result of the `compareTo` method is a positive number, a negative number, or zero. This integer describes how the two strings are ordered **lexicographically**; a case-sensitive ordering of words similar to a dictionary but using the **UNICODE** codes of each character.

The `compareTo` Method

The `compareTo` method returns an integer that describes how the two strings compare.

```
int result = firstString.compareTo(secondString);
```

The answer is zero if the two strings are exactly the same.
The answer is negative if firstString comes before secondString (lexicographically).
The answer is positive if firstString comes after secondString (lexicographically).

Example 1
The answer is zero if the two strings are exactly the same:
```
String string1 = "Hello";
String string2 = "Hello";
int result = string1.compareTo(string2);     // result is 0
```

Example 2
The answer is negative when the first string comes before the second string (lexicographically):
```
String string1 = "Hello";
String string2 = "World";
int result = string1.compareTo(string2);     // result is negative
```

Example 3
The answer is positive when the first string comes after the second string (lexicographically):
```
String string1 = "Hello";
String string2 = "World";
int result = string2.compareTo(string1);     // result is positive
```

Example 4
Uppercase letters come before their lowercase counterparts. "Hello" comes before "hello" when comparing them using lexicographical order:
```
String string1 = "Hello";
String string2 = "hello";
int result = string1.compareTo(string2);     // result is negative
```

Fun Fact: *Unicode is a worldwide computing standard that assigns a unique number to nearly every possible character (including symbols) for every language. There are more than 120,000 characters listed in the latest version of Unicode. For example, the uppercase letter "A" is 41 (hexadecimal), the lowercase letter "a" is 61 (hexadecimal), and "ñ" is F1 (hexadecimal).*

The `length` Method

The **length** method returns the number of characters in the specified string (including spaces).

Example 1
Find the length of a string:
```
String post = "I'm going to rock this AP CS exam.";
int result = post.length();                   // result is 34
```

Example 2

Find the length of a string that is empty, but not null (it has "" as its value):

```
String pokemonCard = new String();
int result = pokemonCard.length();          // result is 0
```

Example 3

Attempt to find the length of a string that is null:

```
String pokemonCard;                          // no String created
int result = pokemonCard.length();          // error: NullPointerException
```

The `NullPointerException`

Attempting to use a method on a string that has not been initialized will result in a run-time error called a `NullPointerException`. The compiler is basically telling you that there isn't an object to work with, so how can it possibly perform any actions with it?

The `indexOf` Method

To find if a string contains a specific character or group of characters, use the **indexOf** method. It searches the string and if it locates what you are looking for, it returns the index of its location. Remember that the first index of a string is zero and the last index is length -1. If the `indexOf` method doesn't find the string that you are looking for, it returns -1.

Example 1

Find the index of a specific character in a string.

```
String sport = "Soccer";
int result = sport.indexOf("e");            // result is 4
```

Example 2

Find the index of a character in a string when it appears more than once.

```
String sport = "Soccer";
int result = sport.indexOf("c");            // result is 2 (finds only
                                            // the first "c")
```

Example 3

Attempt to find the index when the character is not in the string.

```
String sport = "Team";
int result = sport.indexOf("i");            // result is -1
                                            // there is no "i" in Team (ha)
```

Example 4

Find the index of a string inside a string.

```
String sport = "Soccer";
String findMe = "ce";
int result = sport.indexOf(findMe);         // result is 3 because "ce" begins
                                            // at position 3
```

The `substring` Method

The **substring** method is used to extract a specific character or group of characters from a string. All you have to do is tell the `substring` method where to start extracting and where to stop.

The `substring` method is **overloaded**. This means that there is more than one version of the method.

Overloaded Method	Description
`substring(int index)`	Starts extracting at `index` and stops extracting when it reaches the last character in the string
`substring(int firstIndex, int secondIndex)`	Starts extracting at `firstIndex` and stops extracting at `secondIndex - 1`

Example 1
Extract every character starting at a specified index from a string.
```
String motto = "May the force be with you.";
String result = motto.substring(14);       // result is "be with you."
```

Example 2
Extract one character from a string.
```
String motto = "May the force be with you.";
String result = motto.substring(2,3);       // result is "y"
```

Example 3
Extract two characters from a string.
```
String motto = "May the force be with you.";
String result = motto.substring(5,7);       // result is "he", the letters
                                            // at positions 5 and 6
```

Example 4
Extract the word "force" from a string:
```
String motto = "May the force be with you.";
String result = motto.substring(8,13);    // result is "force"
                                          // the letters at positions 8-12
```

Example 5
Use numbers that don't make any sense:
```
String motto = "May the force be with you.";
String result = motto.substring(72);  //error: StringIndexOutOfBoundsException
```

> **The `StringIndexOutOfBoundsException`**
>
> If you use an index that doesn't make any sense, you will get a run-time error called a **StringIndexOutOfBoundsException**. Using an index that is greater than or equal to the length of the string or an index that is negative will produce this error.

Example 6
Extract the word "the" from the following string by finding and using the first and second spaces in the string:
```
String motto = "May the force be with you.";
int firstSpace = motto.indexOf(" ");
int secondSpace = motto.indexOf(" ",firstSpace + 1);
String word = motto.substring(firstSpace + 1, secondSpace); //word is "the"
```

Helpful Hint for the `substring` Method

To find out how many characters to extract, subtract the first number from the second number.

```
String myString = "I solemnly swear that I am up to no good.";
String result = myString.substring(5,13);        // result is "emnly sw"
```

Since 13 − 5 = 8, the result contains a string that is a total of eight characters.

Note: When the start index and end index are the same number, the `substring` method does not return a character of the string; it returns the empty string `""`.

You will receive a Java Quick Reference sheet to use on the Multiple-choice and Free-response sections, which lists the `String` class methods that may be included in the exam. Make sure you are familiar with it <u>before</u> you take the exam.

Class Constructors and Methods	Explanation
String Class	
`String(String str)`	Constructs a new `String` object that represents the same sequence of characters as `str`
`int length()`	Returns the number of characters in a `String` object
`String substring(int from, int to)`	Returns the substring beginning at index `from` and ending at index `to` -1
`String substring(int from)`	Returns `substring(from, length())`
`int indexOf(String str)`	Returns the index of the first occurrence of `str`; returns -1 if not found
`boolean equals(String other)`	Returns `true` if `this` is equal to `other`; returns `false` otherwise
`int compareTo(String other)`	Returns a value <0 if `this` is less than `other`; returns zero if `this` is equal to `other`; returns a value >0 if `this` is greater than `other`

A `String` Is Immutable

An immutable object is an object whose state cannot be modified after it is created. String objects are immutable, meaning that the String methods do not change the String object. `String` variables are actually references to `String` objects, but they don't operate the same way as normal object reference variables.

Every time you make a change to a `String` variable, Java actually tosses out the old object and creates a new one. You are never actually making changes to the original `String` object and *resaving* the same object with the changes. Java makes the changes to the object and then creates a brand-new `String` object and that is what you end up referencing.

Example

Demonstrate how a `String` variable is immutable through concatenation. Even though it seems like you are modifying the `String` variable, you are not. A completely brand-new `String` object is created and the variable is now referencing it:

```
String str = "CS";    // str references a String object "CS"
str = str + " Rules"; // str now references a new String object "CS Rules"
```

Escape Sequences

How would you put a double quotation mark inside of a string? An error occurs if you try because the double quotes are used to define the start and end of a String literal. The solution is to use an **escape sequence**.

Escape sequences are special codes that are embedded in String literals that are sent to the computer that say, "Hey, watch out, something different is coming." They use a backslash followed by a special character. Escape sequences are commonly used when concatenating strings to create a single string. Here are the most common escape sequences (\t is not tested on the AP Computer Science A exam but is useful for displaying output in columns).

Purpose	Sequence	Example	System.out.print(result)
include a double quote	\"	String result = "\"OMG\"";	"OMG"
tab	\t	String result = "a\tb\tc";	a b c
new line	\n	String result = "a\nb\nc";	a b c
backslash	\\	String result = "I am a backslash: \\";	I am a backslash: \

The `Math` Class

The **Math class** was created to help programmers solve problems that require mathematical computations. Most of these methods can be found on a calculator that you would use in math class. In fact, if you think about how you use your calculator, it will make it easier to understand how the `Math` class methods work. The `Math` class also includes a random number generator to help programmers solve problems that require random events.

Compared to the other classes in the AP Computer Science A subset, the `Math` class is special in that it contains only **static** methods. This means that you don't need to create an object from the class in order to use the methods in the class. All you have to do is use the class name followed by the dot operator and then the method name.

The `Math` Class Doesn't Need an Object

The methods and fields of the `Math` class are accessed by using the class name followed by the method name.

```
Math.methodName();
```

Important `Math` Class Methods

The `Math` class contains dozens of methods for doing mathematical work. The AP Computer Science A exam only requires you to know a small handful of them.

Mathematical Operation	Method Name in Java
Absolute Value	`abs`
Square Root	`sqrt`
Base Raised to a Power	`pow`
Random Number Generator	`random`

Example 1
Demonstrate how to use the absolute value method on an integer:
```
int result = Math.abs(-8);            // result is 8
```

Example 2
Demonstrate how to use the absolute value method on a double:
```
double result = Math.abs(-8.4);       // result is 8.4
```

Example 3
Demonstrate how to use the square root method. The sqrt method will compute the square root of any number that is greater than or equal to 0. The result is always a double, even if the input is a perfect square number.
```
double result = Math.sqrt(49);             // result is 7.0
```

Example 4
Demonstrate how to use the power method. The pow method always returns a double.
```
double result = Math.pow(5,3); // result is 125.0 (5 raised to the 3rd power)
```

Example 5
Demonstrate how to use the random method.
```
double result = Math.random(); // result is a double in the interval [0.0, 1)
```

Example 6
Demonstrate how to access the built-in value of pi from the `Math` class.
```
double result = Math.PI;        // PI is not a method, it is a public field
```

Random Number Generator in the `Math` Class

The random number generator from the `Math` class returns a double value in the range from 0.0 to 1.0, including 0.0, but not including 1.0. Borrowing some notation from math, we say that the method returns a value in the interval [0.0, 1.0).

The word *inclusive* means to include the endpoints of an interval. For example, the interval [3,10] means all of the numbers from 3 to 10, including 3 and 10. Written mathematically, it's the same as $3 \leq x \leq 10$. Finally, you could say you are describing all the numbers between 3 and 10 (inclusive).

Using `Math.random()` to Generate a Random Integer

The `random` method is great for generating a random double, but what if you want to generate a random integer? The secret lies in multiplying the random number by the total number of choices and then casting the result to an integer.

General Form for Generating a Random Integer Between 0 and Some Number

```
int result = (int)(Math.random() * (total # of choices));
```

General Form for Generating a Random Integer Between Two Positive Numbers

```
int high = /*  some number greater than zero  */
int low = /*  some number greater than zero and less than high  */

int result = (int)(Math.random() * (high - low + 1)) + low;
```

Example 1
Generate a random integer between 0 and 12 (inclusive):
```
int result = (int)(Math.random() * 13);          // 13 possible answers
```

Example 2
Generate a random integer between 4 and 20 (inclusive):
```
int result = (int)(Math.random() * 17) + 4;      // 17 possible answers
```

Example 3
Pick a random character from a string. Use the length of the string in the calculation.
```
String quote = "And may the odds be ever in your favor.";
int index = (int)(Math.random() * quote.length());
String result = quote.substring(index, index + 1); //random character
```

Math Class	
`static int abs(int x)`	Returns the absolute value of an `int` value
`static double abs(double x)`	Returns the absolute value of a `double` value
`static double pow(double base, double exponent)`	Returns the value of the first parameter raised to the power of the second parameter
`static double sqrt(double x)`	Returns the positive square root of a `double` value
`static double random()`	Returns a `double` value greater than or equal to 0.0 and less than 1.0

The `Integer` Class

The **Integer** class has the power to turn a primitive `int` into an object. This class is called a **wrapper class** because the class *wraps* the primitive `int` into an object. A major purpose for the `Integer` class will be revealed in Unit 7. Java can convert an `Integer` object back into an `int` using the `intValue` method.

Example 1
Create an `Integer` object from an `int`.
```
int num = 5;
Integer myInteger = new Integer(num); // myInteger is an object, value 5
```

Example 2

Obtain the value of an `Integer` object using the `intValue()` method.

```
Integer myInteger = new Integer(8);    // myInteger is an object, value 8
int result = myInteger.intValue();     // result is a primitive, value 8
```

Example 3

Attempt to create an `Integer` object using a `double` value.

```
double num = 5.67;
Integer myInteger = new Integer(num);    // compile-time error
```

Example 4

Attempt to create an `Integer` object without using a value.

```
Integer myInteger = new Integer();       // compile-time error
```

Fields of the `Integer` Class

MAX_VALUE and **MIN_VALUE** are public **fields** of the `Integer` class. A field is a property of a class (like an instance variable). These two are called **constant** fields and their values cannot be changed during run-time. By naming convention, constants are typed using only uppercase and underscores. Also, they don't have a pair of parentheses, because they are not methods.

Why is there a maximum or minimum integer? Well, Java sets aside 32 bits for every `int`. So, the largest integer that can be stored in 32 bits would look like this: 01111111 11111111 11111111 11111111. Notice that the *leading* bit is 0. That's because the first bit is used to assign the sign (positive or negative value) of the integer. If you do the conversion to decimal, this binary number is equal to 2,147,483,647; the largest integer that can be stored in an `Integer` object. It's also equal to one less than 2 to the 31st power.

If you add one to this maximum number, the result causes an **arithmetic overflow** and the new number is pretty much meaningless. Worse yet, the overflow *does not* cause a run-time error, so your program doesn't crash. Moral of the story: Be careful when you are using extremely large positive or small negative integers.

Example 1

Obtain the maximum value represented by an int or Integer.

```
int result = Integer.MAX_VALUE;        // result is 2147483647 (2³¹ - 1)
```

Example 2

Obtain the minimum value represented by an int or Integer.

```
int result = Integer.MIN_VALUE;        // result is -2147483648 (-2³¹)
```

MAX_VALUE and MIN_VALUE Are Constants

A **constant** in Java is a value that is defined by a programmer and cannot be changed during the running of the program. The two values, MAX_VALUE and MIN_VALUE, are constants of the `Integer` class that were defined by the creators of Java. By naming convention, constants are always typed in uppercase letters and underscores.

Fun Fact: *Java has different data types for storing numbers. The long data type uses 64 bits and the largest number it can store is 9,223,372,036,854,775,807. This is not on the AP Computer Science A exam.*

The `Double` Class

The **Double** class is a wrapper class for primitive doubles. The `Double` class is used to turn a `double` into an object.

Example 1

Create a `Double` object from a `double`.

```
double num = 5.67;
Double myDouble = new Double(num);        // myDouble is an object, value 5.67
```

Example 2

Obtain the value of a `Double` object by using the `doubleValue()` method.

```
Double myDouble = new Double(6.125);
double result = myDouble.doubleValue();   // result is an object, value 6.125
```

Example 3

Create a `Double` object using an `int` value.

```
int num = 9;
Double myDouble = new Double(num);    // myDouble is an object, value is 9.0
```

Example 4

Attempt to create a `Double` object without using a value.

```
Double myDouble = new Double();            // compile-time error
```

 Fun Fact: *The Double class also has a MAX_VALUE and MIN_VALUE, but they are not tested on the AP Computer Science A exam.*

Autoboxing and Unboxing

Conversion between primitive types (`int`, `double`, `boolean`) and the corresponding object wrapper class (`Integer`, `Double`, `Boolean`) is performed automatically by the compiler. This process is called "autoboxing." Conversely, "unboxing" is the automatic conversion from the wrapper class to the primitive type. The reason we need to know this conversion will be relevant in Unit 7.

Example 1

Autobox a `Double` object from a `double`.

```
double num = 7.28;
Double myNum = num;            // myNum is an object, value 7.28
```

Example 2

Unbox an `Integer` object to an integer.

```
int value = new Integer(27);              // value is an integer, value 27
```

Example 3

Multiply the value of a `Double` object by 3 and store its value into a `double`.

```
Double myValue = new Double (2.02);
double triple = 3 * myValue;  // automatically unboxes the object into a
                              // primitive
```

Example 4

Multiply the value of a `Double` object by 3 and store its value into a `double` without using the automatic unboxing feature.

```
Double myValue = new Double (2.02);
double triple = 3 * myValue.doubleValue();
```

Summary of the `Integer` and `Double` Classes

Integer Class	
`Integer(int value)`	Constructs a new `Integer` object that represents the specified `int` value
`Integer.MIN_VALUE`	The minimum value represented by an `int` or `Integer`
`Integer.MAX_VALUE`	The maximum value represented by an `int` or `Integer`
`int intValue()`	Returns the value of this `Integer` as an `int`
Double Class	
`Double(double value)`	Constructs a new `Double` object that represents the specified `double` value
`double doubleValue()`	Returns the value of this `Double` as a `double`

 You will receive a Java Quick Reference sheet to use on the Multiple-choice and Free-response sections, which lists the `Math`, `Integer`, and `Double` class methods that may be included in the exam. Make sure you are familiar with it <u>before</u> you take the exam.

› Rapid Review

Strings

- The `String` class is used to store letters, numbers, or other symbols.
- A String literal is a sequence of characters contained within double quotation marks.
- You can create a `String` variable by declaring it and directly assigning it a value.
- You can create a `String` variable using the keyword `new` along with the String constructor.
- Strings are objects from the `String` class and can utilize methods from the `String` class.
- Strings can be concatenated by using the + or += operators.
- Compare two `String` variables using the `equals` method or the `compareTo` method.
- Strings should never be compared using the == comparator.
- Every character in a string is assigned an index. The first index is zero. The last index is one less than the length of the string.
- Escape sequences are special codes that are embedded in String literals to perform such tasks as issuing a new line or a tab, or printing a double quote or a backslash.
- A null string does not contain any value. It does not reference any object.
- If a string is null, then no methods can be performed on it.
- A `NullPointerException` is thrown if there is any attempt to perform a method on a null string.

- An empty string is not the same as a null string.
- An empty string has a value of "" and a length of zero.

`String` Methods

- The `equals(String other)` method returns true if the two strings that are being compared contain exactly the same characters.
- The `compareTo(String other)` method compares two strings lexicographically.
- Lexicographical order is a way of ordering words based on their Unicode values.
- The `length()` method returns the number of characters in the string.
- The `indexOf(String str)` method finds and returns the index value of the first occurrence of str within the `String` object that called the method. The value of -1 is returned if str is not found.
- The `substring(int index)` method returns a new `String` object that begins with the character at index and extends to the end of the string.
- The `substring(int beginIndex, int endIndex)` method returns a new `String` object that begins at the `beginIndex` and extends to the character at `endIndex - 1`.
- Strings are immutable. A new `String` object is created each time changes are made to the value of a string.
- A `StringIndexOutOfBoundsException` error is thrown for any attempt to access an index that is not in the bounds of the String literal.

Math Class

- The `Math` class has static methods, which means you don't create a `Math` object in order to use the methods or fields from the class.
- The dot operator is used to call the methods from the `Math` class: `Math.methodName()`.
- The `Math.abs(int x)` method returns an `int` that is the absolute value of x.
- The `Math.abs(double x)` method returns a `double` that is the absolute value of x.
- The `Math.sqrt(double x)` method returns a `double` that is the square root of x.
- The `Math.pow(double base, double exponent)` method returns a `double` that is the value of base raised to the power of exponent.
- The `Math.random()` method returns a `double` that is randomly chosen from the interval [0.0, 1.0).
- By casting the result of a `Math.random()` statement, you can generate a random integer.

`Integer` and `Double` Classes

- The `Integer` and `Double` classes are called wrapper classes, since they *wrap* a primitive int or double value into an object.
- An `Integer` object contains a single field whose type is `int`.
- The `Integer(int value)` constructor constructs an `Integer` object using the `int` value.
- The `intValue()` method returns an `int` that is the value of the `Integer` object.
- The `Integer.MAX_VALUE` constant is the largest possible `int` in Java.
- The `Integer.MIN_VALUE` constant is the smallest possible `int` in Java.
- The `Double(double value)` constructor constructs a `Double` object using the `double` value.
- The `doubleValue()` method returns a `double` value that is the value of the `Double` object.

› Review Questions

Basic Level

1. The relationship between a class and an object can be described as:

   (A) The terms *class* and *object* mean the same thing.
   (B) A class is a program, while an object is data.
   (C) A class is the blueprint for an object and objects are instantiated from it.
   (D) An object is the blueprint for a class and classes are instantiated from it.
   (E) A class can be written by anyone, but Java provides all objects.

2. Consider the following code segment.

   ```
   String newString = "Welcome";
   String anotherString = "Home";
   newString = anotherString + "Hello";
   System.out.println(newString);
   ```

   What is printed as a result of executing the code segment?

   (A) `HomeHello`
   (B) `HelloHello`
   (C) `WelcomeHello`
   (D) `Welcome Hello`
   (E) `Home Hello`

3. What is printed as a result of executing the following statement?

   ```
   System.out.println(7 + 8 + (7 + 8) + "Hello" + 7 + 8 + (7 + 8));
   ```

   (A) `7878Hello7878`
   (B) `7815Hello7815`
   (C) `30Hello30`
   (D) `30Hello7815`
   (E) `7815Hello30`

4. Consider the following code segment.

   ```
   String str1 = "presto chango";
   String str2 = "abracadabra";

   int i = str1.indexOf("a");
   System.out.println(str2.substring(i, i + 1) + i);
   ```

   What is printed as a result of executing the code segment?

   (A) `p0`
   (B) `r9`
   (C) `r10`
   (D) `ra9`
   (E) `ra10`

5. Consider the following code segment.

```
String s1 = "avocado";
String s2 = "banana";
System.out.println(s1.compareTo(s2) + " " + s2.compareTo(s1));
```

Which of these could be the result of executing the code segment?

(A) 0 0
(B) -1 -1
(C) -1 1
(D) 1 -1
(E) 1 1

6. Which of the following returns the last character of the string str?

(A) str.substring(0);
(B) str.substring(0, str.length());
(C) str.substring(length(str));
(D) str.substring(str.length() - 1);
(E) str.substring(str.length());

7. Which statement assigns a random integer from 13 to 27 inclusive to the variable rand?

(A) int rand = (int)(Math.random() * 13) + 27;
(B) int rand = (int)(Math.random() * 27) + 13;
(C) int rand = (int)(Math.random() * 15) + 13;
(D) int rand = (int)(Math.random() * 14) + 27;
(E) int rand = (int)(Math.random() * 14) + 13;

8. After executing the code segment, what are the possible values of the variable var?

```
int var = (int) Math.random() * 1 + 10;
```

(A) All integers from 1 to 10
(B) All real numbers from 1 to 10 (not including 10)
(C) 10 and 11
(D) 10
(E) No value. Compile-time error.

9. Which of the following statements generates a random integer between -23 and 8 (inclusive)?

(A) int rand = (int)(Math.random() * 32 - 23);
(B) int rand = (int)(Math.random() * 32 + 8);
(C) int rand = (int)(Math.random() * 31 - 8);
(D) int rand = (int)(Math.random() * 31 - 23);
(E) int rand = (int)(Math.random() * 15 + 23);

10. Consider the following code segment.

```
int r = 100;
int answer = (int)(Math.PI * Math.pow(r, 2));
System.out.println(answer);
```

What is printed as a result of executing the code segment?

(A) `30000`
(B) `31415`
(C) `31416`
(D) `31415.9265359`
(E) Nothing will print. The type conversion will cause an error.

Advanced Level

11. Consider the following code segment.

```
String ex1 = "example";
String ex2 = "elpmaxe";
ex1 = ex1.substring(1, ex1.indexOf("p"));
ex2 = ex2 + ex2.substring(3, ex1.length()) + ex2.substring(3, ex2.length());
String ex3 = ex1.substring(1) + ex2.substring(ex2.indexOf("x"), ex2.length() - 2);
System.out.println(ex3);
```

What is printed as a result of executing the code segment?

(A) `amxem`
(B) `amxema`
(C) `amxepma`
(D) `ampxepm`
(E) The program will terminate with a `StringIndexOutOfBoundsException`.

12. Which print statement will produce the following output?

```
/\what    time
"is it?"//\\
```

(A) `System.out.print("/\\what\ttime\n\"is it?\"//\\\\");`
(B) `System.out.print("//\\what\ttime\n\"is it?\"////\\\\");`
(C) `System.out.print("/\\what\time\n\"is it?\"//\\\\");`
(D) `System.out.print("/\\what\ttime\n"is it?"//\\\\");`
(E) `System.out.print("//\\what\time + \"is it?\"////\\\\");`

13. Consider the following code segment.

```
int rand = (int)(Math.random() * 5 + 3);
rand = (int)(Math.pow(rand, 2));
```

After executing the code segment, what are the possible values for the variable `rand`?

(A) 3, 4, 5, 6, 7
(B) 9, 16, 25, 36, 49
(C) 5, 6, 7
(D) 25, 36, 49
(E) 9

14. Consider the following code segment.

```
int val1 = 10;
int val2 = 7;
val1 = (val1 + val2) % (val1 - val2);
val2 = 3 + val1 * val2;
int val3 = (int)(Math.random() * val2 + val1);
```

After executing the code segment, what is the possible range of values for val3?

(A) All integers from 2 to 17
(B) All integers from 2 to 75
(C) All integers from 75 to 76
(D) All integers from 2 to 74
(E) All integers from 2 to 18

15. Assume `double dnum` has been correctly declared and initialized with a valid value. What is the correct way to find its absolute value, rounded to the nearest integer?

(A) `(int) Math.abs(dnum - 0.5);`
(B) `(int) Math.abs(dnum + 0.5);`
(C) `(int) (Math.abs(dnum) + 0.5);`
(D) `Math.abs((int)dnum - 0.5);`
(E) `Math.abs((int)dnum) - 0.5;`

16. Which of these expressions correctly computes the positive root of a quadratic equation assuming coefficients a, b, c have been correctly declared and initialized with valid values? Remember, the equation is:

$$\frac{-b + \sqrt{b^2 - 4ac}}{2a}$$

(A) `(-b + Math.sqrt (Math.pow(b, 2)) - 4ac) / 2a`
(B) `(-b + Math.sqrt (Math.pow(b, 2) - 4ac)) / 2a`
(C) `(-b + Math.sqrt (Math.pow(b, 2) - 4 * a * c)) / 2 * a`
(D) `(-b + Math.sqrt (Math.pow(b, 2)) - 4 * a * c) / (2 * a)`
(E) `(-b + Math.sqrt (Math.pow(b, 2) - 4 * a * c)) / (2 * a)`

› Answers and Explanations

Bullets mark each step in the process of arriving at the correct solution.

1. The answer is C.

   • A class is a blueprint for constructing objects of the type described by the class definition.

2. The answer is A.

   • When two strings are concatenated (added together), the second one is placed right after the first one (do not add a space).
   ```
   newString = anotherString + "Hello"
             = "Home" + "Hello" = "HomeHello"
   ```

3. The answer is D.

- This question requires that you understand the two uses of the + symbol.
- First, execute what is in the parentheses. Now we have:

```
System.out.println(7 + 8 + 15 + "Hello" + 7 + 8 + 15);
```

- Now do the addition left to right. That's easy until we hit the string:

```
System.out.println(30 + "Hello" + 7 + 8 + 15);
```

- When you add a number and a string in any order, Java turns the number into a string and then concatenates the string:

```
System.out.println("30Hello" + 7 + 8 + 15);
```

- Now every operation we do will have a string and a number, so they all become string concatenations, not number additions.

```
System.out.println("30Hello7815");
```

4. The answer is B.

- The `indexOf` method returns the index location of the parameter.
- The letter "a" has index 9 in "presto chango" (remember to start counting at 0).
- The substring will start at index 9 and stop *before* index 10, meaning it will return only the letter at index 9 in "abracadabra".
- Once again, start counting at 0. Index 9 of "abracadabra" is "r".
- Concatenate that with i which equals 9. Print "r9".

5. The answer is C.

- `compareTo` takes the calling string and compares it to the parameter string. If the calling string comes *before* the parameter string, it returns a negative number. If it comes *after* the parameter string, it returns a positive number. If they are equal, it returns 0.
- The first `compareTo` is "avocado".compareTo("banana") so it returns -1.
- The second `compareTo` switches the order to "banana".compareTo("avocado") so it returns 1.
- Note that although we often only care about whether the answer is positive or negative, the actual number returned has meaning. Because "a" and "b" are one letter apart, 1 (or -1) is returned. If the example had been "avocado" and "cucumber", 2 (or -2) would have been returned.

6. The answer is D.

- Let's take the word "cat" as an example. It has a length of 3, but the indices of its characters are 0, 1, 2, so the last character is at length − 1.
- We need to start our substring at `str.length() - 1`. We could say:

```
str.substring(str.length() - 1, str.length());
```

but since we want the string all the way to the end we can use the single parameter version of substring.

7. The answer is C.

- The basic form for generating a random int between high and low is:

```
int result = (int)(Math.random() * (high - low + 1)) + low;
```

- Our "high" is 27, and our "low" is 13, so the answer is C.
- Be sure to place the parentheses correctly. They can go after the multiplication or after the addition, but not after the `Math.random()`.

8. The answer is D.

- This problem doesn't have the necessary parentheses discussed in the explanation for problem 7.
- As a result, the (int) cast will cast only the value of `Math.random()`. Since `Math.random()` returns a value between 0 and 1 (including 0, not including 1), truncating will *always* give a result of 0.
- Multiplying by 1 still gives us 0, and adding 10 gives us 10.

9. The answer is A.

- This problem is similar to problem 7.
- Fill in (high − low + 1) = (8 − (-23)) + 1 = 32 and low = -23 and the answer becomes `(int)(Math.random() * 32 - 23)`.
- Notice that this time the parentheses were placed around the whole expression, not just the multiplication.

10. The answer is B.

- `(int)(Math.PI * Math.pow(r, 2))`
    - `= (int)(3.1415926... * 10000)`
    - `= (int)(31415.926...)`
    - `= 31415`

11. The answer is B.

- `ex1.substring(1, ex1.indexOf("p"))` starts at the character at index 1 (remember we start counting at 0) and ends before the index of the letter "p". ex1 now equals "xam".
- Let's take this one substring at a time. At the beginning of the statement, ex2 = "elpmaxe".
    - `ex2.substring(3, ex1.length())` The length of ex1 is 3, so this substring starts at the character at index 3 and ends *before* the character at index 3. It stops before it has a chance to begin and returns the empty string. Adding that to the current value of ex2 does not change ex2 at all.
    - `ex2.substring(3, ex2.length())` starts at the character at index 3 and goes to the end of the string, so that's "maxe".
    - Add that to the current value of ex2 and we have "elpmaxemaxe".
- We are going to take two substrings and assign them to ex3.
    - The first one isn't too bad. ex1 = "xam", so `ex1.substring(1)` = "am". Remember that if substring only has 1 parameter, we start there and go to the end of the string.
    - The second substring has two parameters. Let's start by figuring out what the parameters to the substring are equal to.
    - Remember ex2 = "elpmaxemaxe" so indexOf("x") is 5.
    - The second parameter is `ex2.length() - 2`. The length of ex2 = 11, subtract 2 and the second parameter = 9.
    - Now we can take the substring from 5 to 9, or from the first "x" to just before the second "x", which gives us "xema".
    - Add the two substrings together: "amxema".

12. The answer is A.

- Let's take this piece by piece. A forward slash "/" does not require an escape sequence, but a backslash needs to be doubled since "\" is a special character. Our print sequence needs to start: /\\
- The next interesting thing that happens is the tab before "time". The escape sequence for tab is "\t". Our print sequence is now: /\\what\ttime (Don't be confused by the double t. One belongs to "\t" and the other belongs to "time".)
- Now we need to go to the next line. The newline escape sequence is "\n"

- We also need escape sequences for the quote symbols, so now our print sequence is:
  `/\\what\ttime\n\"is it\"`
- Add the last few slashes, remembering to double the "\" and we've got our final result.
  `/\\what\ttime\n\"is it?\"//\\\\`

13. The answer is B.

- This problem is like problem 7 only backwards. If (high − low + 1) = 5 and low = 3, then high = 7. The first line gives us integers from 3 to 7 inclusive.
- The second line squares all those numbers, giving us: 9, 16, 25, 36, 49.

14. The answer is E.

- Taking it line by line, val1 = 10, val2 = 7 so:
  ```
  val1 = (val1 + val2) % (val1 - val2) = 17 % 3 = 2
  val2 = 3 + val1 * val2 = 3 + 2 * 7 = 17
  ```
- The next statement becomes:
  ```
  val3 = (int) (Math.random() * 17 + 2)
  ```
- We know low = 2 and (high − low + 1) = 17, so high = 18.
- val3 will contain integers from 2 to 18 inclusive.

15. The answer is C.

- The easiest way to solve this is to plug in examples. We need to make sure we test both positive and negative numbers, so let's use 2.9 and -2.9. The answer we are looking for in both cases is 3.
- Choice A:
  ```
  (int) Math.abs(2.9 - 0.5) = (int) Math.abs(2.4) = (int) 2.4 = 2
  ```
  NO (but interestingly, this works for -2.9).
- Choice B:
  ```
  (int) Math.abs(2.9 + 0.5) = (int) Math.abs(3.4) = (int) 3.4 = 3
  ```
  YES, but does it work in the negative case?
  ```
  (int) Math.abs(-2.9 + 0.5)= (int) Math.abs(-2.4) = (int) 2.4 = 2
  ```
  NO, keep looking.
- Choice C:
  ```
  (int)(Math.abs(2.9) + 0.5) = (int)(2.9 + 0.5) = (int) 3.4 = 3
  ```
  YES, but does it work in the negative case?
  ```
  int)(Math.abs(-2.9) + 0.5) = (int)(2.9 + 0.5) = (int) 3.4 = 3
  ```
  YES, found it!

16. The answer is E.

- Options A and B are incorrect. They use the math notation 4ac and 2a for multiplication instead of 4 * a * c and 2 * a.
- Solution C is incorrect. This option divides by 2 and then multiplies that entire answer by a, which is not what we want. 2 * a needs to be in parentheses.
- Look carefully at D and E. What's the difference? The only difference is the placement of the closing parenthesis, either after the (b, 2) or after the 4 * a * c. Which should it be? The square root should include both the Math(b, 2) and the 4 * a * c, so the answer is E.

Boolean Expressions and if Statements

15-17% AP Exam Weight

IN THIS UNIT

Summary: Conditional statements allow programs to flow in one or more directions based on the outcome of a Boolean expression. Relational operators and logical operators allow the programmer to construct those conditional statements and act on their result accordingly. The ability to use conditionals is an important concept to master and will be used often in your programs.

Learning Objectives

CON-1.E Evaluate Boolean expressions that use relational operators in program code.

CON-2.A Represent branching logical processes by using conditional statements.

CON-2.B Represent branching logical processes by using nested conditional statements.

CON-1.F Evaluate compound Boolean expressions in program code.

CON-1.G Compare and contrast equivalent Boolean expressions.

CON-1.H Compare object references using Boolean expressions in program code.

Key Ideas

✪ Relational and logical operations are used when decisions occur.
✪ Conditional statements allow for branching in different directions.
✪ An `if` statement is used for one-way selection.

✪ An `if-else` statement is used for two-way selection.

✪ A nested `if` statement is used for multi-way selection.

✪ Short-circuit evaluation can be used to speed up the evaluation of compound conditionals.

✪ Curly braces are used to denote a block of code.

✪ Indentation within a conditional helps the reader know which piece of code gets executed when the condition is evaluated as true and which gets executed when the condition is false.

Introduction

Up to this point, program execution has been sequential. The first statement is executed, then the second statement, then the third statement, and so on. One of the essential features of programs is their ability to execute certain parts of code based on conditions. In this unit you will learn the various types of conditional statements, along with the relational and logical operators that are used.

Relational Operators

Double Equals Versus Single Equals

Java compares numbers the same way that we do in math class, using **relational operators** (like greater than or less than). A **condition** is a comparison of two values using a relational operator. To decide if two numbers are equal in Java, we compare them using the **double equals**, ==. This is different from the **single equals**, =, which is called an **assignment operator** and is used for assigning values to a variable.

The not Operator: !

To compare if two numbers are **not equal** in Java, we use the **not operator**. It uses the exclamation point, **!**, and represents the opposite of something. It is also referred to as a **negation** operator. Some Java developers call it a "bang" operator.

Table of Relational Operators

The following table shows the symbols for comparing numbers using relational operators.

Comparison	Java Symbol
Greater than	>
Less than	<
Greater than or equal to	>=
Less than or equal to	<=
Equal to	==
Not equal to	!=

Examples

Demonstrating relational operators within conditional statements:

```
int a = 6;
System.out.println(a == 10);   // false is printed;  6 is not equal to 10
System.out.println(a < 10);    // true is printed;  6 is less than 10
System.out.println(a >= 10);   // false is printed; 6 is not greater than 10
System.out.println(a != 10);   // true is printed;  6 is not equal to 10
```

The ! as a Toggle Switch

The not operator, !, can be used in a clever way to reverse the value of a boolean.

Example

Using the not operator to toggle player turns for a two-player game:

```
boolean playerOneTurn = true;          // playerOneTurn is true
playerOneTurn = !playerOneTurn;        // playerOneTurn is false
playerOneTurn = !playerOneTurn;        // playerOneTurn is true
```

Logical Operations

Compound Conditionals: Using AND and OR

AND and **OR** are **logical operators**. In Java, the AND operator is typed using two ampersands (&&) while the OR operator uses two vertical bars or pipes (||). These two logical operators are used to form **compound conditional statements**.

Logical Operator	Java Symbol	Compound Conditional	Result with Explanation
AND	&&	condition1 && condition2	True only if both conditions are true. False if either condition is false.
OR	||	condition1 || condition2	True if either condition is true. False only if both conditions are false.

The Truth Table

A **truth table** describes how AND and OR work.

First Operand (A)	Second Operand (B)	A && B	A || B
True	True	True	True
True	False	False	True
False	True	False	True
False	False	False	False

Example 1

Suppose you are writing a game that allows the user to play as long as their score is less than the winning score and they still have time left on the clock. You would want to allow them to play the game as long as *both* of these two conditions are true.

```
boolean continuePlaying = (score < winningScore && timeLeft > 0);
```

Example 2

Computing the results of compound conditionals:

```
int a = 3, b = 4, c = 5;
System.out.println(a <= 3 && b != 4);          // false is printed
System.out.println(b % 2 == 1 || c / 2 == 1);  // false is printed
System.out.println(a > 2 && (b > 5 || c < 6)); // true is printed
```

Explanation: (3 <= 3) && (4 != 4)   → true && false → false
Explanation: (4 % 2 == 1) || (5 / 2 == 1)→ false || false → false
Explanation: (3 > 2) && (4 > 5 || 5 < 6) → true && (false || true)
                                            → true && true → true

 Fun Fact: *The boolean variable is named in honor of George Boole, who founded the field of algebraic logic. His work is at the heart of all computing.*

A truth table lists every possible combination of operand values and the result of the operation for each combination. It is also used to determine if two logical expressions are equivalent.

Example 1

Determine if `!(a && b)` is equivalent to `!a || !b`

Let's set up a truth table for the first expression `!(a && b)`.

a	b	a && b	!(a && b)
True	True	True	False
True	False	False	True
False	True	False	True
False	False	False	True

And set up a truth table for the second expression `!a || !b`.

a	b	!a	!b	!a || !b
True	True	False	False	False
True	False	False	True	True
False	True	True	False	True
False	False	True	True	True

Since the last columns in both tables are the same, we can say that the two expressions are equivalent. They both evaluate to the same value in all cases. This is a proof of the identity known as De Morgan's Law.

Short-Circuit Evaluation

Java uses **short-circuit evaluation** to speed up the evaluation of compound conditionals. As soon as the result of the final evaluation is known, then the result is returned and the remaining evaluations are not even performed.

Find the result of: `(1 < 3 || (a >= c - b % a + (b + a / 7) - (a % b +c)))`

In a *split second,* you can determine that the result is true *because 1 is less than 3.* End of story. The rest is never even evaluated. Short-circuit evaluation is useful when the second half of a compound conditional might cause an error. This is tested on the AP Computer Science A Exam.

Example
Demonstrate how short-circuit evaluation can prevent a division by zero error.

```
int count = 0;
int total = 0;
boolean result = (count != 0 && total/count > 0);  // result is false
```

If the count is equal to zero, the second half of the compound conditional is never evaluated, thereby avoiding a division by zero error.

De Morgan's Law

On the AP Computer Science A Exam, you must be able to evaluate complex compound conditionals. **De Morgan's Law** can help you decipher ones that fit certain criteria.

Compound Conditional	Applying De Morgan's Law
!(a && b)	!a || !b
!(a || b)	!a && !b

An easy way to remember how to apply De Morgan's Law is to think of the distributive property from algebra, but with a twist. Distribute the ! to both of the conditionals and also change the logical operator. Note the use of the parentheses and remember that the law can be applied both forward and backward.

Example
Computing the results of complex logical expressions using De Morgan's Law:

```
int a = 2, b = 3;
boolean result1 = !(b == 3 && a < 1);    // result1 is true
boolean result2 = !(a != 2 || b <= 4);   // result2 is false
```

Explanation for `result1`: De Morgan's Law says that you should *distribute* the negation operator. Therefore, the negation of `b == 3` is `b != 3` and the negation of `a < 1` is `a >= 1`:

!(b == 3 && a < 1) ➜ (b != 3) || (a >= 1) ➜ (3 != 3) || (2 >= 1)
➜ false || true ➜ true

Explanation for `result2`: The negation of `a != 2` is `a == 2` and the negation of `b <= 4` is `b > 4`:

!(a != 2 || b <= 4) ➜ (a == 2) && (b > 4) ➜ (2 == 2) && (3 > 4)
➜ true && false ➜ false

The Negation of a Relational Operator

The negation of *greater than* (>) is *less than or equal to* (<=) and vice versa.
The negation of *less than* (<) is *greater than or equal to* (>=) and vice versa.
The negation of *equal to* (==) is *not equal to* (!=) and vice versa.

Precedence of Java Operators

We already know the precedence of the mathematical operators, but what is the precedence among the logical operators and what if a statement has multiple operators? Luckily Java has well-defined rules for their order. The operation should be applied to the operator in order of precedence from left to right, similar to how we would apply "PEMDAS" in math.

Operation	Symbol	Precedence
Postfix	++, --	1
Unary	+, -,	2
logical NOT	!	2
Multiplication, Division, Modulus	*, /, %	3
Addition, Subtraction	+, -	4
Relational Operators	>, <, >=, <=	6
Equality	==, !=	7
logical AND	&&	11
logical OR	||	12
Assignment	=, +=, -=, *=, /=, %=	14

Conditional Statements

If you want your program to branch out into different directions based on the input from the user or the value of a variable, then you will want to have a **conditional** statement in your program. A conditional statement will interrupt the sequential execution of your program. The conditional statement affects the flow of control by executing different statements based on the value of a Boolean expression.

The if Statement

The **if** statement is a conditional statement. In its simplest form, it allows the program to execute a specific set of instructions if some certain condition is met. If the condition is not met, then the program skips over those instructions. This is also known as a one-way selection.

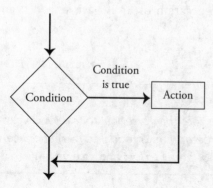

The `if-else` Statement

The **if-else** statement allows the program to execute a specific set of instructions if some certain condition is met and a different set of instructions if the condition is not met. This is also known as a two-way selection. I will sometimes refer to the code that is executed when the condition is true as the *if clause* and the code that follows the else as the *else clause*.

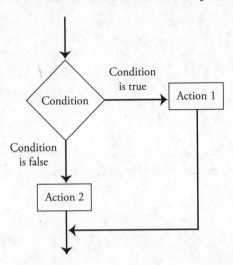

The syntax for `if` and `if-else` statements can be tricky. Pay attention to the use of the curly braces and indentation. The indentation helps the reader (not the compiler) understand what statements are to be executed if the condition is true.

Example 1
The `if` statement for one or more lines of code:

```
if (condition)
{
    // one or more instructions to be performed when condition is true
}
```

Example 2
The `if-else` statement for one or more lines of code for each result:

```
if (condition)
{
    // instructions to be performed when condition is true
}
else
{
    // instructions to be performed when condition is false
}
```

Example 3
The `if-else` statement using a compound conditional:

```
if (condition1 && condition2)
{
    // condition1 and condition2 are both true
}
else
{
    // either condition1 or condition2 is false (or both are false)
}
```

Nested `if` Statements

Instead of using a compound conditional in an `if-else` statement, a nested `if` can be used. This is known as a multi-way selection.

Example

Nested `if-else` statements for one or more lines of code (watch the curly braces!):

```
if (condition1)
{
    // condition1 is true
    if (condition2)
    {
        // condition1 is true and condition2 is true
    }
    else
    {
        // condition1 is true and condition2 is false
    }
}
else
{
    // condition1 is false
    if (condition3)
    {
        // condition1 is false and condition3 is true
    }
    else
    {
        // condition1 is false and condition3 is false
    }
}
```

if-else-if ladder

In an `if-else-if` ladder, conditions are evaluated from the top. Once a condition is found to be true, execution continues to the statement after the ladder. You can have as many conditions that you need in your ladder.

Example

```
if (condition1)
{
    // one or more instructions to be performed when condition1 is true
}
else if (condition2)
{
    // one or more instructions to be performed when condition2 is true
}
else if (condition3)
{
    // one or more instructions to be performed when condition3 is true
}
else
{
    // one or more instructions to be performed when condition3 is false
}
```

Curly Braces

When you want to execute only one line of code when something is true, you don't actually *need* the curly braces. Java will execute the first line of code after the `if` statement if the result is true.

```
if (condition)
    // single instruction to be performed when condition is true
```

The same goes for an `if-else` statement. If you want to execute only one line of code for each value of the condition, then no curly braces are required.

```
if (condition)
    // single instruction to be performed when condition is true
else
    // single instruction to be performed when condition is false
```

Can You Spot the Error in This Program?

```
if (condition);
{
    // instructions to be performed when condition is true
}
```

Answer: Never put a semicolon on the same line as the condition. It ends the `if` statement right there. In general, *never put a semicolon before a curly brace.*

The Dangling `else`

If you don't use curly braces properly within `if-else` statements, you may get a **dangling else**. An `else` attaches itself to the nearest if statement and not necessarily to the one that you may have intended. Use curly braces to avoid a dangling `else` and control which instructions you want executed. The dangling `else` does not cause a compile-time error, but rather it causes a **logic error**. The program doesn't execute in the way that you expected.

Example

The second `else` statement attaches itself to the nearest preceding `if` statement:

```
if (condition1)
    // instruction performed when condition1 is true
    if (condition2)
        // instruction performed when condition1 is true and condition2 is true
    else
        // instruction performed when condition1 is true and condition2 is false
```

Scope of a Variable

The word **scope** refers to the code that knows that a variable exists. Local variables, like the ones we have been declaring, are only known within the block of code in which they are defined. This can be confusing for beginning programmers. Another way to say it is: a variable that is declared inside a pair of curly braces is only known inside that set of curly braces.

Curly Braces and Blocks of Code

Curly braces come in pairs and the code they surround is called a **block of code**.

```
{
    // A group of instructions inside a pair of curly braces
    // is called a "block of code". Variables declared inside a block
    // of code are only known inside that block of code.
}
```

› Rapid Review

Logic

- The relational operators in Java are >, >=, <, <=, ==, and !=.
- A condition is an expression that evaluates to either true or false.
- The logical operator AND is coded using two ampersands, &&.
- The && is true only when both conditions are true.
- The logical operator OR is coded using two vertical bars, ||.
- The || is true when either condition or both are true.
- Programmers use logical operators to write compound conditionals.
- The NOT operator (negation operator) is coded using the exclamation point, !.
- The ! can be used to flip-flop a boolean.
- De Morgan's Law states: !(A && B) = !A || !B and also !(A || B) = !A && !B.
- When evaluating conditionals, the computer uses short-circuit evaluation.

Conditional Statements

- The `if` and the `if-else` are called conditional statements since the flow of the program changes based upon the evaluation of a condition.
- Curly braces come in pairs and the code they contain is called a block of code.
- Curly braces need to be used when more than one instruction is to be executed for `if` and `if-else` statements.
- The scope of a variable refers to the code that knows that the variable exists.
- Variables declared within a conditional are only known within that conditional.

› Review Questions

Basic Level

1. Consider the following code segment.

```
int num1 = 9;
int num2 = 5;
if (num1 > num2)
{
    System.out.print((num1 + num2) % num2);
}
else
{
    System.out.print((num1 - num2) % num2);
}
```

What is printed as a result of executing the code segment?

(A) 0
(B) 2
(C) 4
(D) 9
(E) 14

2. Consider the following code segment.

```
int value = initValue;
if (value > 10)
    if (value > 15)
        value = 0;
else
    value = 1;
System.out.println("value = " + value);
```

Under which of the conditions below will this code segment print value = 1?

(A) initValue = 8;
(B) initValue = 12;
(C) initValue = 20;
(D) Never. value = 0 will always be printed.
(E) Never. Code will not compile.

3. Assume that a, b, and c have been declared and initialized with int values. The expression

```
!(a > b || b <= c)
```

is equivalent to which of the following?

(A) a > b && b <= c
(B) a <= b || b > c
(C) a <= b && b > c
(D) a < b || b >= c
(E) a < b && b >= c

4. Which conditional statement is equivalent to the expression shown below?

```
if ((temp > 80) && !(80 < temp))
```

(A) if (temp == 80)
(B) if (temp != 80)
(C) if ((temp >= 80) || (temp > 80))
(D) false
(E) true

5. A high school class places students in a course based on their average from a previous course. Students that have an average 92 or above are placed in an honors level course. Students that have an average below 74 are placed in a remedial level course. All other students are placed in a regular level course. Which of the following statements correctly places the student based on their average?

```
I.   if (average >= 92)
         level = "honors";
     if (average < 74)
         level = "remedial";
     else
         level = "regular";
```

```
II. if (average >= 92)
        level = "honors";
    else if (average >= 74)
        level = "regular";
    else
        level = "remedial";

III. if (average >= 92)
        level = "honors";
    else if ((average >= 74) && (average < 92))
        level = "regular";
    else
        level = "remedial";
```

(A) I only
(B) II only
(C) III only
(D) I and II only
(E) II and III only

Advanced Level

6. Assume that x, y, and z have been declared as follows:

```
boolean x = true;
boolean y = false;
boolean z = true;
```

Which of the following expressions evaluates to true?

(A) x && y && z
(B) x && y || z && y
(C) !(x && y) || z
(D) !(x || y) && z
(E) x && y || !z

7. Consider the following code segment.

```
int amount = initValue;
if (amount >= 0)
    if (amount <= 10)
        System.out.println("**");
else
    System.out.println("%%");
```

Under what condition will this code segment print %%?

(A) initValue = −5
(B) initValue = 0
(C) initValue = 5
(D) initValue = 10
(E) initValue = 15

8. Which segment of code will correctly print the two Strings name1 and name2 in alphabetical order?

```
I.  if (name1 < name2)
        System.out.println(name1 + " " + name2);
    else
        System.out.println(name2 + " " + name1);
```

II. `if (name1.compareTo(name2))`
      `    System.out.println(name1 + " " + name2);`
      `else`
      `    System.out.println(name2 + " " + name1);`

III. `if (name1.compareTo(name2) < 0)`
      `    System.out.println(name1 + " " + name2);`
      `  else`
      `    System.out.println(name2 + " " + name1);`

(A) I only

(B) II only

(C) III only

(D) II and III only

(E) I, II, and III

› Answers and Explanations

Bullets mark each step in the process of arriving at the correct solution.

1. The answer is C.

- Since 9 > 5, we execute the statements after the if and skip the statements after the else.
- 9 + 5 = 14. 14 % 5 = 4 (since 14 / 5 = 2 remainder 4), so we print 4.

2. The answer is B.

- This is a confusing one. We count on indenting to be correct and we use it to evaluate code, but in this case it is deceiving us. Remember that indenting is for humans; Java doesn't care how we indent our code.
- An else clause always binds to the *closest* available if. That means the else belongs to if (value > 15) not to if (value > 10). The code should be formatted like this:

```
if (value > 10)
   if (value > 15)
      value = 0;
   else
      value = 1;
System.out.println("value = " + value);
```

- This makes it clearer that `value = 1` will be printed if the first condition is true (so value has to be greater than 10) and the second condition is false (so value has to be less than or equal to 15). The only value in the answers that fits those criteria is 12, so initValue =12 is the correct answer.

3. The answer is C.

- We start out by using De Morgan's Law (notice that || becomes && when we distribute the !).

    `!(a > b || b <= c)` → `!(a > b) && !(b <= c)`

- !> is the same as <= (don't forget the =), and !<= is the same as >, so

    `!(a > b) && !(b <= c)` → `a <= b && b > c`

4. The answer is D.

- Changing `!(80 < temp)` to its equivalent expression gives `(80 >= temp)`, which is equivalent to `(temp <= 80)`.
- Substituting that back into the original conditional statement gives if `((temp > 80) && (temp <=80))`, which will always be false.

5. The answer is E.

- The nested if segment II and segment III will correctly assign the level based on the student average.
- Segment I will correctly assign the "honors" after the first if statement, but as soon as the second if statement is evaluated, the condition will be false and fall to the else statement which will incorrectly assign "regular" to students whose average is 92 and above.

6. The answer is C.

- Rewrite the expressions, filling in true or false for x, y, and z. Remember order of operations. && has precedence over ||.
- true && false && true
  - true && false = false, and since false && anything is false, this one is false.
- true && false || true && false
  - Order of operations is && before || so this simplifies to false || false = false.
- !(true && false) || true
  - We don't need to think about the first half because as soon as we see || true, we know this one is true. We've found our answer, but let's keep going so we can explain them all.
- !(true || false) && true
  - true || false is true, !true is false. false && anything is false, so this one is false.
- true && false || !true
  - true and false is false, !true is false, so this is false || false, which is false.

7. The answer is E.

- The code shows an example of a dangling else. The indentation implies that the System.out.println("%%") is reached when a negative amount is encountered, but that is not the case.
- The else System.out.println("%%") statement belongs with the closest unmatched if statement, which is if (amount <=10)

8. The answer is C.

- Relational operators are not defined for Strings, so the syntax in segment I is not correct.
- The compareTo method will return an integer. The expression in the conditional must evaluate to a boolean, so the syntax in segment II is not correct.
- If the compareTo method returns a negative value, that means name1 comes alphabetically before name2, so segment III is correct.

UNIT 4

Iteration

17.5-22.5% AP Exam Weight

IN THIS UNIT

Summary: Iteration causes statements in your program to be repeated more than once. The two common iterative structures are the `for` loop and the `while` loop. Iteration is a fundamental programming structure and is used to solve many common tasks.

Learning Objectives

CON-2.C Represent iterative processes using a `while` loop.

CON-2.D For algorithms in the context of a particular specification that does not require the use of traversals:

Identify standard algorithms.

Modify standard algorithms.

Develop an algorithm.

CON-2.E Represent iterative processes using a `for` loop.

CON-2.F For algorithms in the context of a particular specification that involves `String` objects:

Identify standard algorithms.

Modify standard algorithms.

Develop an algorithm.

CON-2.G Represent nested iterative processes.

CON-2.H Compute statement execution counts and informal run-time comparison of iterative statements.

Key Ideas

✪ Looping structures allow you to repeat instructions many times.
✪ A `for` loop is used to repeat one or more instructions a specific number of times.
✪ A `while` loop is used when you don't know how many times you need to repeat a set of instructions but you know that you want to stop when some condition is met.
✪ Variables declared within a loop are only known within the loop.
✪ An infinite loop is a loop that does not end.
✪ A boundary error occurs when you don't execute a loop the correct number of times.

Introduction

So far each statement in our program has been executed at most one time. There are many situations where we will need to repeat a statement (or several statements) more than once. Repeating a statement more than once is known as iteration. Iteration changes the flow of control by repeating a set of statements zero or more times until a condition is met. There are two types of iterative structures that you need to know for the AP Computer Science A Exam: the `while` loop and the `for` loop.

Looping Statements

The `for` Loop

Suppose your very strict music teacher catches you chewing gum in class and tells you to write out "I will not chew gum while playing the flute" 100 times. You decide to use your computer to do the work for you. How can you write a program to repeat something as many times as you want? The answer is a `loop`. A `for` loop is used when you know ahead of time how many times you want to do a set of instructions. In this case, we know we want to write the phrase 100 times.

> **General Form for Creating a `for` Loop**
>
> ```
> for (initialize loop control variable(LCV);condition using LCV; modify LCV)
> {
>     // instructions to be repeated
> }
> ```

The `for` loop uses a **loop control variable** to repeat its instructions. This loop control variable is typically an `int` and is allowed to have a one-letter name like i, j, k, and so on. This breaks the rule of having meaningful variable names. Yes, the loop control variable is a rebel.

Explanation 1: The `for` loop for those who like to read paragraphs . . .

When a `for` loop starts, its loop control variable is declared and initialized. Then, a comparison is made using the loop control variable. If the result of the comparison is true, the instructions that are to be repeated are executed one time. The loop control variable is then modified in some way (usually incremented or decremented, but not always). Next, the loop control variable is compared again using the same comparison as before. If the result of this comparison is true, the loop performs another **iteration**. The loop control variable is again modified (in the same way that it was before), and this process continues until the comparison of the loop control variable is false. When this happens, the loop ends and we **exit (or terminate) the loop**. The total number of times that the loop repeats the instructions is called the number of iterations.

Explanation 2: The `for` loop for those who like a list of steps . . .

Step 1: Declare and initialize the loop control variable.

Step 2: Compare the loop control variable in some way.

Step 3: If the result of the comparison is true, then execute the instructions one time.
  If the result of the comparison is false, then skip to Step 6.

Step 4: Modify the loop control variable in some way (usually increment or decrement, but not always).

Step 5: Go to Step 2.

Step 6: Exit the loop and move on to the next line of code in the program.

Explanation 3: The `for` loop for those who like pictures . . .

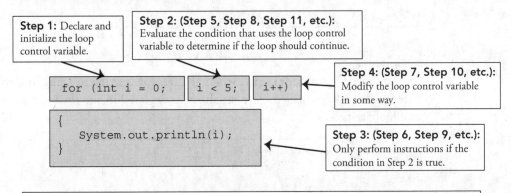

Last step: Exit the loop when the condition in Step 2 becomes false. Move on to the next instruction in the program.

The Loop Control Variable

The most common approach when using a `for` loop is to declare the loop control variable in the `for` loop. If this is the case, then the loop control variable is only known inside the `for` loop. Any attempt to use the loop control variable in an instruction after the loop will get a compile-time error (cannot be resolved to a variable).

However, it is possible to declare a loop control variable prior to the `for` loop code. If this is the case, then the loop control variable is known before the loop, during the loop, and after the loop.

Example 1

A simple example of a `for` loop:

```
for (int i = 0; i < 3; i++)
{
    System.out.println("hello");
}
```

```
OUTPUT
hello
hello
hello
```

Example 2
The loop control variable is often used inside the loop as shown here:

```
for (int j = 9; j > 6; j--)
{
    System.out.print(j + "       ");
    System.out.println(10 - j);
}
```

```
OUTPUT
9       1
8       2
7       3
```

Example 3
In this example, an error occurs when an attempt is made to print the loop control variable after the loop has finished. The variable was declared inside the loop and is not known after the loop exits:

```
for (int k = 1; k <= 4; k++)
{
    System.out.println(k);
}
System.out.println(k*10);
```

```
Compile-time error: k cannot be resolved to a variable
```

Example 4
In this example, the loop control variable is declared in a separate instruction before the loop. This allows the variable to be known before, during, and after the loop:

```
int i;
for (i = 1; i < 12; i +=3)
{
    System.out.println(i);
}
System.out.println(i);
```

```
1
4
7
10
13
```

 Fun Fact: *In an early programming language called Fortran, the letters i, j, and k were reserved for storing integers. To this day, programmers still use these letters for integer variables even though they can be used to store other data types.*

The Nested `for` Loop

A `for` loop that is inside of another `for` loop is called a **nested for loop**. The **outer loop control variable** (OLCV) is used to control the outside loop. The **inner loop control variable** (ILCV) is used to control the inside loop. There is no limit to the number of times you can nest a series of `for` loops.

General Form for a Nested `for` Loop

```
for (initialize OLCV; condition using OLCV; modify OLCV)
{
    for (initialize ILCV; condition using ILCV; modify ILCV)
    {
        // instructions to be repeated
    }
}
```

Execution Count Within a Nested `for` Loop

When a nested `for` loop is executed, the **inner loop** is performed in its entirety for every iteration of the **outer loop**. That means that the number of times that the instructions inside the inner loop are performed is equal to the product of the number of times the outer loop is performed and the number of times the inner loop is performed.

Example

To demonstrate execution count for a nested `for` loop: The outer loop repeats a total of three times (once for i = 0, then for i = 1, and then for i = 2). The inner loop repeats four times (once for j = 1, then for j = 2, then for j = 3, and then for j = 4). The inner loop repeats (starts over) for every iteration of the outer loop. Therefore, the `System.out.println` statement executes a total of 12 times:

```
for (int i = 0; i < 3; i++)              // the outer loop repeats 3 times
{
    for (int j = 1; j < 5; j++)          // the inner loop repeats 4 times
    {
        System.out.println(i + "  " + j); // total of 12 iterations (3 * 4)
    }
}
```

```
OUTPUT
0      1
0      2
0      3
0      4
1      1
1      2
1      3
1      4
2      1
2      2
2      3
2      4
```

Execution Count for a Nested `for` Loop

To find the total number of times that the code inside the inner `for` loop is executed, multiply the number of iterations of the outer loop by the number of iterations of the inner loop.

```
for (int x = 4; x > 0; x--)          // the outer loop repeats 4 times
{
    for (int y = 9; y <= 15; y++)    // the inner loop repeats 7 times
    {
        // some instruction          // total of 28 iterations (4 * 7)
    }
}
```

The `while` Loop

Consider the software that is used to check out customers at a store. The clerk drags each item the customer buys over the scanner until there aren't any more items to be scanned. *Viewing this through the eyes of a programmer,* I can suggest that a **while loop** is used to determine the final cost of all the items. The process repeats until there aren't any more items. Now, in contrast, if the clerk asked you how many items you had in your cart before he started scanning, then I would suggest that a `for` loop is being used to determine the final cost of all the items.

General Form for a `while` Loop

Recommended form: Repeat instructions (using curly braces):

```
while (condition)
{
    // one or more instructions to be repeated
}
```

The `while` loop repeats instructions just like the `for` loop, but it does it differently. Instead of having a loop control variable that is a number like the `for` loop, the `while` loop can use any kind of data type to control when it is to perform another iteration of the loop.

I like to use the phrase *as long as* as a replacement for the word *while* when reading a `while` loop. In other words: *As long as the condition is true, I will continue to repeat the instructions.* It should be noted that a `for` loop can be rewritten into an equivalent `while` loop, and vice versa (but not as easily, so it isn't recommended). If the Boolean expression in the condition evaluates to false initially, then the loop body is not executed at all.

Explanation 1: The `while` loop for those who like to read paragraphs . . .

Declare and initialize some variable of any data type *before* the loop begins. Then compare this variable at the start of the loop. If the result of the comparison is true, the instructions inside the loop get executed one time. Then, modify the variable in some way. Next, compare the variable again in the same way as before. If the result is true, the instructions get executed one more time. This process continues until the result of the comparison is false. At this point, the loop ends and we exit the loop. You must make certain that the variable that is being compared is changed inside of the loop. If you forget to modify this variable, you may end up with a loop that never ends!

Explanation 2: The `while` loop for those who like a list of steps . . .

Step 1: Declare and initialize some variable of any data type.
Step 2: Compare this variable in some way.
Step 3: If the result of the comparison is true, then execute the instructions one time.
       If the result of the comparison is false, then skip to Step 6.
Step 4: Modify the variable that is to be compared.
Step 5: Go to Step 2.
Step 6: Exit the loop and move on to the next line of code in the program.

Example 1

A simple example of a `while` loop:

```java
int count = 0;
while (count < 5)
{
    System.out.println(count);
    count++;
}
```

```
OUTPUT
0
1
2
3
4
```

Example 2

Use a `while` loop to require a user to enter the secret passcode for a vault that contains a million dollars. Do not allow the user to exit the loop until they get it right. If they get it right the first time, do not enter the loop (do not execute any of the instructions inside the loop).

```
System.out.print("Enter the 4-digit secret passcode: ");
int secretPasscode = /* int provided by user */
while (secretPasscode != 1234)
{
    System.out.println("Sorry that is incorrect. Try again: ");
    secretPasscode = /* int provided by user */
}
System.out.println("Congratulations. You have access to the vault.");
```

```
OUTPUT
Enter the secret passcode: 9999
Sorry that is incorrect. Try again: 8888
Sorry that is incorrect. Try again:  1234
Congratulations. You have access to the vault.
```

A Flag in Programming

A **flag** in programming is a virtual way to signal that something has happened. Think of it as, "I'm waving a flag" to tell you that something important just occurred. Normally, `boolean` variables are chosen for flags. They are originally set to false, then when something exciting happens, they are set to true.

Example 3

Use a `while` loop to continue playing a game as long as the game is not over:

```
boolean gameOver = false;
while (!gameOver)
{
    // play the game
    // When a player wins, set gameOver = true
}
```

Strength of the `while` Loop

A strength of the `while` loop is that you don't have to know how many times you will execute the instructions before you begin looping. You just have to know when you want it to end.

The Infinite Loop

If you make a mistake in a looping statement such that the loop never ends, the result is an **infinite loop**. You have to make sure that at some point in the loop body there is a change being made to the Boolean expression to make it false; otherwise, it will always be true and the loop will never end.

A loop must always have an "ITCH": Initialized variable, Tested variable, and CHanged variable.

```
for (initialize; test; change)
{
      // body of loop
}
```

```
initialize
while (test)
{
      // body of loop
      change
}
```

Example 1
Accidentally getting an infinite loop when using a `for` loop:

```
for (int i = 0; i < 10; i--)
{
   i++;
   // i will always revert back to 0 causing an infinite loop
}
```

Example 2
Accidentally getting an infinite loop when using a `while` loop:

```
int i = 0;
while (i < 10)
{
   // do something forever because you forgot to increment i
}
```

Boundary Testing

A very common error when using a `for` loop or a `while` loop is called a **boundary error**. It means that you accidently went one number past or one number short of the right amount. This is known as an "off by one" error, or "obo." *The loop didn't perform the precise number of iterations.* This concept is commonly tested on the AP Computer Science A Exam. The only real way to prevent it is to hand-trace your code very carefully to make sure that your loop is executing the correct number of times.

Goldilocks and the Three Looping Structures
Always test that your `for` loops, nested `for` loops, and `while` loops are executing the correct number of times—not too many, but not too few. Just the right number of times. Hint: If you use:

```
for (int i = 0; i < maximum; i++)
```

then the loop will execute maximum number of times.

Standard Algorithms

Let's take a look at some common tasks that can be done using loops that you might see on the AP Computer Science A Exam. But the tasks shown here are not the only things that you might see on the exam. You are expected to be able to read and/or write any task that involves anything that you have learned so far such as variables, conditionals, and loops for the exam.

Example 1
Find all the factors of an integer.

```java
int number =    /*  some integer value  */
number = Math.abs(number);              // in case the number is negative
for (int i = 1; i <= number; i++)
{
    if (number % i == 0)           // if the remainder is 0, it is a factor
    {
        System.out.println(i + " is a factor");
    }
}
```

Example 2
Find the sum of all the digits in an integer.

```java
int value = /*some integer value*/
int number = Math.abs(value);    // in case the number is negative
int digit, sum = 0;              // you need to initialize the sum to 0
while (number > 0)               // as long as you still have digits left
{
    digit = number % 10;        // mod 10 results in the ones digit
    sum += digit;               // add that digit to the accumulated sum
    number /= 10;               // dividing by 10 removes the ones digit
}
System.out.println("The sum of the digits of " + value + " is " + sum);
```

Example 3
Find the largest value in a list of numbers.

```java
Scanner in = new Scanner(System.in);  // or some other way to get
                                       //       input from the user
System.out.println("Please enter a value. Use -99999 to end");
                                       //    -99999 used as sentinel value
double number = in.nextDouble();       // get the value from the user
double highest = number;               // initialize to the first number
                                       // entered
while (number != -99999)               // as long as the value entered
{                                      //        isn't the sentinel value
    if (number > highest)              // compare the value. If it's higher
    {                                  //        than the current highest
        highest = number;              // replace it
    }
    System.out.println("Please enter a value. Use -99999 to end");
                                       // does the user want to continue?
    number = in.nextDouble();          // get the next value
}
System.out.println("The highest value was  " + highest);
```

Example 4
Find the mean test score in a class of 25 students.

```
Scanner in = new Scanner(System.in);    // or some other way to get
                                         //      input from the user
int grade, sum = 0;                      // initialize the sum to 0
for (int i = 1; i <= 25; i++)
{       // since we know how many times, we can use a for loop
   System.out.print("Please enter student " + i + " test score...");
   grade = in.nextInt();                 // gets the student grade
   sum += grade;                         // adds that grade to the accumulated sum
}

int mean = (int) (sum / 25.0 + 0.5);     // if we want an integer mean,
                                         // double division must be used and
                                         // 0.5 added to it rounds properly

System.out.println("The mean score is " + mean);
```

Example 5
Count the number of spaces that are in a string.

```
String phrase = "AP Computer Science A Rocks!";
int numWords = 1;                           // initialize the count to 1
int posSpace = phrase.indexOf(" ");         // find the first space
while (posSpace != -1)        // as long as there is a space in the phrase
{
   numWords++;                              // increment the word count
   phrase = phrase.substring(posSpace+1);   // the new phrase will be
                                            // everything after the space
   posSpace = phrase.indexOf(" ");          // find the next space
}
System.out.println("The number of words is " + numWords);
```

Example 6
Count the number of punctuation marks in a sentence.

```
String sentence = "A. P. Computer Science, Rocks!";
String punctuation = ".,:;?!";       // or whatever punctuation marks you
                                     //      want to search for
int count = 0;
String letter;
for (int i = 0; i < sentence.length(); i++)    // look through each letter
{
   letter = sentence.substring(i, i+1);        // get one letter at a time
   if (punctuation.indexOf(letter) >= 0) // if the letter is found in the
   {                                     // punctuation string, then add to
     count++;                            //      count
   }
}

System.out.println("The number of punctuation marks is " + count);
```

Example 7

Reverse the order of the characters in a string.

```
String sentence = "AP Computer Science Rocks";
String reverse = "", letter;
for (int i = sentence.length()-1; i >= 0; i--)   // start at the end of
{                                                 //        the sentence
    letter = sentence.substring(i, i+1);    // get one letter at a time
    reverse += letter;                 // concatenate the letter to the end
}

System.out.println("The reverse of " + sentence + " is " + reverse);
```

› Rapid Review

Programming Statements

- Curly braces come in pairs and the code they contain is called a block of code.
- Curly braces need to be used when more than one instruction is to be executed for `for` and `while` statements.
- The scope of a variable refers to the code that knows that the variable exists.
- Variables declared within a loop are only known within that loop.
- The `for` loop is used to repeat one or more instructions a specific number of times.
- The `for` loop is a good choice when you know exactly how many times you want to repeat a set of instructions.
- The `for` loop uses a numeric loop control variable that is compared and also modified during the execution of the loop. When the comparison that includes this variable evaluates to false, the loop exits.
- Variables declared within a `for` loop are only known within that `for` loop.
- A nested for loop is a `for` loop inside of a `for` loop.
- The number of iterations of a nested `for` loop is the product of the number of iterations for each loop.
- The `while` loop does not require a numeric loop control variable.
- The `while` statement must contain a conditional that compares a variable that is modified inside the loop.
- Choose a `while` loop when you don't know how many times you need to repeat a set of instructions but know that you want to stop when some condition is met.
- An infinite loop is a loop that never ends.
- Forgetting to modify the loop control variable or having a condition that will never be satisfied are typical ways to cause infinite loops.
- Variables declared within a `while` loop are only known within the `while` loop.
- A boundary error occurs when you don't execute a loop the correct number of times.

› Review Questions

Basic Level

1. Consider the following code segment.

```
int count = 1;
int value = 31;
while (value >= 10)
{
    value = value - count;
    count = count + 3;
}
System.out.println(value);
```

What is printed as a result of executing the code segment?

(A) 4
(B) 9
(C) 10
(D) 13
(E) 31

2. Consider the following code segment.

```
int count = 5;
for (int i = 3; i < 7; i = i + 2)
{
    count += i;
}
System.out.println(count);
```

What is printed as a result of executing the code segment?

(A) 5
(B) 7
(C) 9
(D) 13
(E) 20

3. Consider the following code segment.

```
int incr = 1;
for (int i = 0; i < 10; i+= incr)
{
    System.out.print(i - incr + "    ");
    incr++;
}
```

What is printed as a result of executing the code segment?

(A) -1   0   2   5
(B) -1   0   3   7
(C) -1   1   4   8
(D) 0   2   5   9
(E) 0   1   3   7

4. Which of the following code segments will print exactly eight "$" symbols?

I.
```
for (int i = 0; i < 8; i++)
{
    System.out.print("$");
}
```

II.
```
int i = 0;
while (i < 8)
{
    System.out.print("$");
    i++;
}
```

III.
```
for (int i = 7; i <= 30 ; i+=3)
{
    System.out.print("$");
}
```

(A) I only
(B) II only
(C) I and II only
(D) I and III only
(E) I, II, and III

5. Consider the following code segment.

```
int a = /* positive value supplied within program */
int b = /* positive value supplied within program */
if (/* missing condition */)
{
    int result = a + b;
}
```

Which of the following should replace /* missing condition */ to ensure that a + b will not be too large to be held correctly in result?

(A) a + b < Integer.MAX_VALUE
(B) a + b <= Integer.MAX_VALUE
(C) Integer.MIN_VALUE + a <= b
(D) Integer.MAX_VALUE - a <= b
(E) Integer.MAX_VALUE - a >= b

Advanced Level

6. Consider the following code segment.

```
for (int j = 0; j < 10; j++)
{
    for (int k = 10; k > j; k--)
    {
        System.out.print("*");
    }
}
```

How many "*" symbols are printed as a result of executing the code segment?

(A) 5

(B) 10

(C) 45

(D) 55

(E) 100

7. Consider the following code segment.

```
boolean b1 = true;
boolean b2 = true;
int x = 7;
while (b1 || b2)
{
    if (x > 4)
    {
        b2 - !b2;
    }
    else
    {
        b1 = !b1;
    }
    x--;
}
System.out.print(x);
```

What is printed as a result of executing the code segment?

(A) 3

(B) 4

(C) 6

(D) 7

(E) Nothing will be printed; infinite loop.

8. Which of the following three code segments will produce the same output?

I.
```
int i = 1;
while (i < 12)
{
    System.out.print(i + " ");
    i *= 2;
}
```

II.
```
for (int i = 4; i > 0; i--)
{
    System.out.print((4 - i) * 2 + 1 + " ");
}
```

III.
```
for (int i = 0; i < 4; i++)
{
    System.out.print((int)Math.pow(2, i) + " ");
}
```

(A) I and II only

(B) II and III only

(C) I and III only

(D) I, II, and III

(E) All three outputs are different.

9. Consider the following code segment.

```
double count = 6.0;
for (int num = 0; num < 5; num++)
{
    if (count != 0 && num / count > 0)
    {
        count -= num;
    }
}
System.out.println(count);
```

What is printed as a result of executing the code segment?

(A) 0.0
(B) -4.0
(C) 5
(D) The program will end successfully, but nothing will be printed.
(E) Nothing will be printed. Run-time error: ArithmeticException.

10. Consider the following code segment.

```
int n = 0;
while (n < 20)
{
    System.out.print(n % 4 + " ");
    if (n % 5 == 2)
    {
        n += 4;
    }
    else
    {
        n += 3;
    }
}
```

What is printed as a result of executing the code segment?

(A) 0 3 2 1 0 0 3
(B) 0 0 3 2 2 1
(C) 0 3 2 1 0 0
(D) 0 0 3 2 2 1 0
(E) Many numbers will be printed; infinite loop.

11. Consider the following code segment.

```
double tabulate = 100.0;
int repeat = 1;
while (tabulate > 20)
{
    tabulate = tabulate - Math.pow(repeat, 2);
    repeat++;
}
System.out.println(tabulate);
```

What is printed as a result of executing the code segment?

(A) 20.0
(B) 6.0
(C) 19.0
(D) 9.0
(E) -40.0

12. During one iteration of the outer loop of the program segment below, how many times is the body of the inner loop executed?

```
for (int i = 1; i <= n-1; i++)
    for (int j = n; j >= i + 1; j--)
        // body of loop
```

(A) i + 1
(B) n − i
(C) n − i + 1
(D) i − n + 1
(E) n(i − 1)

› Answers and Explanations

Bullets mark each step in the process of arriving at the correct solution.

1. The answer is B.

   • The first time we evaluate the while condition, value = 31, which is >= 10, so the loop executes.
     • In the loop, we subtract count from value which becomes 30,
     • and then we add 3 to count, which becomes 4.
   • Then we go back to the top of the while loop and reevaluate the condition. 30 >= 10, so we execute the loop again.
     • This time we subtract 4 from value, since count is now 4. value = 26
     • and count = 7.
   • Back up to the top, 26 >= 10, so on we go.
     • value = 27 − 7 = 19 and count = 10.
   • Since 10 >= 10, we will execute the loop one more time.
     • value = 19 − 10 = 9 and count = 13.
   • This time when we evaluate the condition, it is no longer true, so we exit the loop and print value, which equals 9.

2. The answer is D.

   • When we first enter the for loop count = 5 and i = 3.
   • The first time through the loop, we execute count += i, which makes count = 8, and we increment i by 2, which makes i = 5.
   • i < 7, so we execute the loop again; count = 8 + 5 = 13, and i = i + 2 = 7.
   • This time the condition i < 7 fails and we exit the loop. 13 is printed.

3. The answer is A.

   • The first time through the loop, incr = 1 and i = 0. 0 − 1 = -1, which is printed; then incr is increased to 2. The increment portion of this for loop is a little unusual. Instead of i++ or i = i + 2, it's i = i + incr, so, since incr = 2 and i = 0, i becomes 2.
   • 2 < 10 so we continue. 2 − 2 = 0, which is printed, incr = 3 and i = 2 + 3 = 5.
   • 5 < 10 so we continue. 5 − 3 = 2, which is printed, incr = 4 and i = 5 + 4 = 9.
   • 9 < 10 so we continue. 9 − 4 = 5, which is printed, incr = 5 and i = 9 + 5 = 14.
   • This time we fail the condition, so our loop ends having printed -1 0 2 5

4. The answer is E.

   • The first option is the classic way to write a for loop. If you always start at i = 0 and go until i < n, you know the loop will execute n times without having to think about it (using i++ of course). So this first example prints eight "$".

- The second example is the exact same loop as the first example, except written as a `while` loop instead of a `for` loop. You can see the i = 0, the i < 8, and the i++. So this example also prints eight "$".
- The third example shows why we always stick to the convention used in the first example. Here we have to reason it out: i will equal 7, 10, 13, 16, 19, 22, 25, 28 before finally failing at 31. That's eight different values, which means eight times through the loop. So this example also prints eight "$".

5. The answer is E.

- `Integer.MAX _ VALUE` is a constant that represents the greatest value that can be stored in an `int`. In this problem, we need to make sure that `a + b` is not greater than that value.
- Solution b seems like the logical way to do this, but if a + b is too big to fit in an int, then we can't successfully add them together to test if they are too big. a + b will overflow.
- We need to do some basic algebra and subtract a from both sides giving us:

  `b < Integer.MAX_VALUE - a`

- The left and right sides of the expression have been switched, so we need to flip the inequality. Flipping the < gives us >=.

6. The answer is D.

- The outer loop is going to execute 10 times: j = 0 through j = 9.
- The inner loop is trickier. The number of times it executes depends on j.
  - The first time through, j = 0, so k = 10, 9, 8 . . . 1 (10 times).
  - The second time through, j = 1, so k = 10, 9, 8 . . . 2 (9 times).
  - The third time through, j = 2, so k = 10, 9, 8 . . . 3 (8 times).
  - There's a clear pattern here, so we don't need to write them all out. We do have to be careful that we stop at the right time though.
  - The last time through the loop, j = 9, so k = 10 (1 time).
  - Adding it all together: 10 + 9 + 8 + 7 + 6 + 5 + 4 + 3 + 2 + 1 = 55

7. The answer is A.

- b1 and b2 are both true. The OR (||) in the `while` condition requires that at least one of them be true, so we enter the loop for the first time.
  - 7 > 4 so we execute b2 = ! b2. That's a tricky little statement that is used to flip the value of a `boolean`. Since b2 is true, !b2 is false, and we assign that value back into b2, which becomes false.
  - We skip the `else` clause and subtract one from x.
  - At the bottom of the loop: b1 = true, b2 = false, x = 6.
- The `while` condition now evaluates to (true || false), which is still true, so we execute the loop.
  - 6 > 4 so we flip b2 again. b2 is now true.
  - Skip the `else` clause, subtract one from x.
  - At the bottom of the loop: b1 = true, b2 = true, x = 5.
- The `while` condition now evaluates to (true || true), which is true, so we execute the loop.
  - 5 > 4 so we flip b2 again. b2 is now false.
  - Skip the `else` clause, subtract one from x.
  - At the bottom of the loop: b1 = true, b2 = false, x = 4.
- The `while` condition now evaluates to (true || false), which is still true, so we execute the loop.
  - This time the `if` condition is false, so we execute the `else` clause, which flips the condition of b1 instead of b2. b1 is now false.
  - Subtract one from x.
  - At the bottom of the loop: b1 = false, b2 = false, x = 3.
- Now when we go to evaluate the `while` condition, we have (false || false). Do not execute the loop. Print the value of x, which is 3.

8. The answer is C.

- Option I
  - As we enter the loop for the first time, i = 1, and that's what gets printed. Then we multiply by 2, i = 2.
  - We print 2, multiply by 2, i = 4.
  - We print 4, multiply by 2, i = 8.
  - We print 8, multiply by 2, i = 16, which fails the loop condition so we exit the loop.
  - Final output: 1 2 4 8
- Option II
  - We can see by examining the for loop that we will execute the loop 4 times: i = 4, 3, 2, 1.
  - Each time through the loop we will print $(4 - i) * 2 + 1$.
  - $(4 - 4) * 2 + 1 = 1$
  - $(4 - 3) * 2 + 1 = 3$
  - $(4 - 2) * 2 + 1 = 5$
  - $(4 - 1) * 2 + 1 = 7$
  - Final output: 1 3 5 7
- Option III
  - We can see by examining the for loop that we will execute the loop 4 times: i = 0, 1, 2, 3.
  - Each time through the loop we will print (int)Math.pow(2, i). (Math.pow returns a double, so we cast to an int before printing.)
  - $2^0 = 1$
  - $2^1 = 2$
  - $2^2 = 4$
  - $2^3 = 8$
  - Final output: 1 2 4 8
- Options I and III have the same output.

9. The answer is A.

- The first time through the loop: count = 6.0 and num = 0.
  - Looking at the if condition: 6.0 != 0, but 0 / 6 is 0 → false, so we skip the if clause and go back to the start of the loop.
- Back to the top of the loop: count is still 6.0, but num = 1.
  - Looking at the if condition: 6.0 != 0 && 1 / 6.0 > 0 → true, so we execute the if clause and count = 6.0 − 1 = 5.0.
- Back to the top of the loop: count = 5.0 and num = 2.
  - Looking at the if condition: 5.0 != 0 && 1 / 5.0 > 0 → true, so we execute the if clause and count = 5.0 − 2 = 3.0.
- Back to the top of the loop: count = 3.0 and num = 3.
  - Looking at the if condition: 3.0 != 0 && 3 / 3.0 > 0 → true, so we execute the if clause and count = 3.0 − 3 = 0.0.
- Back to the top of the loop: count = 0.0 and num = 4.
  - Looking at the if condition: Here's where it gets interesting. If we execute 4 / 0.0, we are going to crash our program with an ArithmeticExceptionError, but that's not going to happen. The first part of the condition, count != 0 is false, and Java knows that false AND anything is false, so it doesn't even bother to execute the second part of the condition. That is called short-circuiting, and it is often used for exactly this purpose. The condition is false; the if clause doesn't get executed.
- Back to the top of the loop: count = 0.0 and num = 5, so our loop is complete and we print the value of count, which is 0.0.

10. The answer is A.

   - The only thing we can do is to trace the code carefully line by line until we have the answer.
   - n = 0. Print 0 % 4, which is 0
     - 0 % 5 = 0 so we execute the else, now n = 3.
   - Print 3 % 4, which is 3
     - 3 % 5 = 3 so we execute the else, now n = 6.
   - Print 6 % 4, which is 2
     - 6 % 5 = 1 so we execute the else, now n = 9.
   - Print 9 % 4, which is 1
     - 9 % 5 = 1 so we execute the else, now n = 12.
   - Print 12 % 4, which is 0
     - 12 % 5 = 2 so finally we execute the if, now n = 16.
   - Print 16 % 4, which is 0
     - 16 % 5 = 1 so we execute the else, now n = 19.
   - Print 19 % 4, which is 3
     - 19 % 5 is 4 so we execute the else, now n = 22, which completes the loop.
   - We have printed: 0 3 2 1 0 0 3

11. The answer is D.

   - When we enter the loop, tabulate = 100 and repeat = 1
     - tabulate = 100 − Math.pow(1, 2) = 99; increment repeat to 2
   - 99 > 20 so we enter the loop again
     - tabulate = 99 − Math.pow(2, 2) = 95; increment repeat to 3
   - 95 > 20
     - tabulate = 95 − Math.pow(3, 2) = 86; increment repeat to 4
   - 86 > 20
     - tabulate = 86 − Math.pow(4, 2) = 70; increment repeat to 5
   - 70 > 20
     - tabulate = 70 − Math.pow(5, 2) = 45; increment repeat to 6
   - 45 > 20
     - tabulate = 45 − Math.pow(6, 2) = 9; increment repeat to 7
   - 9 < 20 so we exit the loop and print 9

12. The answer is B.

   - The value can be found by using the starting and stopping values of the index.
   - The inner loop begins at n, ends at i+1, and is incremented by 1.
   - So, the number of times will be n − (i+1) − 1.

UNIT 5

Writing Classes

5-7.5% AP Exam Weight

IN THIS UNIT

Summary: This unit is the continuation of Unit 2, "Using Objects." In this unit you will learn how to design your own classes. Full understanding of designing classes, writing constructors, and writing methods are key to doing well on the AP Computer Science A Exam.

Learning Objectives

MOD-2.A Designate access and visibility constraints to classes, data, constructors, and methods.

MOD-3.A Designate private visibility of instance variables to encapsulate the attributes of an object.

MOD-2.B Define instance variables for the attributes to be initialized through the constructors of a class.

MOD-2.C Describe the functionality and use of program code through comments.

MOD-2.D Define behaviors of an object through non-void methods without parameters written in a class.

MOD-2.E Define behaviors of an object through void methods with or without parameters written in a class.

MOD-2.F Define behaviors of an object through non-void methods with parameters written in a class.

MOD-2.G Define behaviors of a class through static methods.

MOD-2.H Define the static variables that belong to the class.

VAR-1.G Explain where variables can be used in the program code.
VAR-1.H Evaluate object reference expressions that use the keyword `this`.
IOC-1.A Explain the ethical and social implications of computing systems.

Key Ideas

✪ Java is an object-oriented programming language whose foundation is built on classes and objects.

✪ A class describes the characteristics of any object that is created from it.

✪ An object is a virtual entity that is created using a class as a blueprint.

✪ Objects are created to store and manipulate information in your program.

✪ An instance variable is used to store an attribute of an object.

✪ A method is an action that an object can perform.

✪ The keyword `new` is used to create an object.

✪ A reference variable stores the address of the object, not the object itself.

✪ Objects are passed by reference, while primitives are passed by value.

✪ Data encapsulation is a way of hiding object information.

✪ Overloaded constructors have the same name but different parameter lists.

✪ Overloaded methods have the same name but different parameter lists.

✪ Static variables are called class variables and are shared among all objects of the same class.

✪ Static final variables are called class constants and, once given a value, they cannot be changed during the running of the program.

✪ The keyword *this* is used to refer to the current object.

✪ Scope describes the region of the program in which a variable is known.

Overview of the Relationship Between Classes and Objects

The intent of an **object-oriented programming language** is to provide a framework that allows a programmer to manipulate information after storing it in an object. The following paragraphs describe the relationship between many different vocabulary terms that are necessary to understand Java as an object-oriented programming language. The terms are related so they are described all together rather than in separate pieces.

> **Warning: Proceed with Caution**
>
> The next set of paragraphs includes many new terms. You may want to reread this section many times. If you expect to earn a 5 on the exam, you must master everything that follows. Challenge yourself to learn it so well that you can explain this entire chapter to someone else.

Java classes represent things that are nouns (people, places, or things). A **class** is the blueprint for constructing all **objects** that come from it. The **attributes** of the objects from the class are represented using **instance variables**. The values of all of the instance variables determine the **state** of the object. The state of an object changes whenever any of the values of the instance variables change. **Methods** are the virtual actions that the objects can perform. They may either return an answer or provide a service.

Objects are created using the class that holds the blueprint of the object. The class contains a piece of code called a **constructor**, which tells the computer how to build (construct) an object from that class. The keyword **new** is used whenever the programmer wants to create an object from a class. When new is followed by the name of a constructor of a class, a new object is created. The action of constructing an object is also referred to as **instantiating** an object and the object is referred to as an **instance** of the class. In addition to creating the new object, a **reference** to the object is created. The **object reference variable** holds the memory address of the newly created object and is used to call methods that are contained in the object's class.

Writing user-defined classes will be discussed thoroughly in Unit 5. Unit 2 introduces the use of the String, Math, Integer, and Double classes that are available.

The `class` Declaration

When you design your own class, you should create a file that contains the **class declaration**. The name of the class is identified in this declaration. By Java naming convention, a class name should always starts with an uppercase letter and is written in camel case. Classes are designated public so users can create objects from that class.

Example
Create a class called the Circle class:

```
public class Circle                    // Class declaration
{

}
```

Instance Variables

The virtual attributes that describe an object of a class are called its **instance variables**. A class can have as many instance variables of any data type as it wants as long as they describe some characteristic or feature of an object of the class. Unlike local primitive variables, default values are assigned to primitive instance variables when they are created (int variables are 0, doubles are 0.0, booleans are false, and objects are null). The phrase **has-a** refers to the instance variables of a class as in: an objectName has-a instanceVariableName.

Example
Every Circle object has-a radius so create an instance variable called radius:

```
public class Circle                    // Class declaration
{
    private double radius;             // Instance variable
}
```

`private` Versus `public` Visibility

The words **private** and **public** are called **visibility modifiers** (or **access level modifiers**). Access to attributes should be kept internal to the class, so instance variables are designated as `private`. Using the word `private` in an instance variable declaration ensures that other classes do not have access to the data stored in the variable without asking the object to provide it. Using the word `public` in the class declaration ensures that any programmer can make objects from that class.

> **`private` Versus `public`**
>
> On the AP Computer Science A Exam, always give instance variables private access visibility. This ensures that the data in these variables is hidden, and the philosophy of encapsulation is being followed.

Constructors

Constructors are the builders of the virtual objects from a class. They are used in combination with the keyword `new` to create an object from the class. Constructors have the same name as the class and are typically listed near the top of a class. Constructors are designated `public`. Constructors are used to set the initial state of an object, which should include initial values for all of its instance variables.

No-Argument Constructor

The constructor is the code that is called when you create a new object. When you define a new class, there is an implicit **no-argument constructor** in that class. Depending on the IDE that you use, you may or may not see it. It is generally recommended that you write one anyway, especially when you are first learning classes.

> **The No-Argument Constructor**
>
> The no-argument constructor gets its name because no information is passed to this constructor when creating a new object. It is the constructor that allows you to make a generic object from a class.

Parameterized Constructors and Parameters

If you will know some information about an object prior to creating it, then you may want to write a **parameterized constructor** in your class. You use the parameterized constructor to give initial values to the instance variables when creating a brand-new object. The parameters that are defined in the parameterized constructor are placed in a **parameter list** and are on the same line as the declaration of the constructor.

The process of sending the initial values to the constructor is called **passing a parameter** to the constructor. The actual value that is passed to the constructor is called an **argument** (or **actual parameter**) and the variable that receives the value inside the constructor is called the **formal parameter**. You include a line of code in the parameterized constructor that assigns the value of the formal parameter to the instance variable.

If you choose to write a parameterized constructor for a class, then the default, implicit **no-argument constructor** is no longer included in the class. This is why it is generally recommended that you simply write your own.

Example

Write the no-argument constructor and one parameterized constructor for the `Circle` class. The parameterized constructor must have a parameter variable for the radius of a circle.

```
public class Circle                      // Class declaration
{
    private double radius;               // Instance variable

    public Circle()                      // No-argument constructor
    {
        radius = 0.0;
    }

    public Circle(double rad)            // Parameterized constructor
    {
        radius = rad;                    // The radius is set to rad
    }
}
```

Parameters in the Parameter List

A parameter is a variable that is located in a parameter list in the constructor declaration. A pair of parentheses after the name of the constructor encloses the entire parameter list.

For example, the parameterized constructor for the `Circle` class has one parameter variable in its parameter list. The name of the parameter is rad (short for radius) and its data type is a double. The no-argument constructor for the `Circle` class does not have any parameters in its parameter list.

```
public Circle()                     // no parameters in the parameter list
{
    radius = 0.0;
}
public Circle(double rad)           // one parameter in the parameter list
{
    radius = rad;
}
```

Methods

The real power of an object-oriented programming language takes place when you start to manipulate objects. A **method** defines an action that allows you to do these manipulations. A method has two options. It may simply perform a service of some kind, or it may compute a value and give the answer back. The action of giving a value back is called **returning** a value.

Methods that simply perform some action are called **void** methods. Methods that return a value are called **return** (or **non-void**) methods. A method that returns a value must define what data type it will be returning and include a `return` statement in the method. The method can return any kind of data type. In non-void methods, a return expression compatible with the return type is evaluated, and a copy of that value is returned. But if the return expression is a reference to an object, a copy of that reference is returned, not a copy of the object. This is referred to as "return by reference."

Using the word **public** in the **method declaration** ensures that the method is available for other objects from other classes to use. A method declared **private** is only accessible within the class.

> **The `return` Statement on the AP Computer Science A Exam**
>
> Methods that are supposed to return a value must have a reachable `return` statement. Methods that are void do not have a `return` statement. This is a big deal on the Free-response questions of the AP Computer Science A Exam as you could potentially lose points if you include a `return` statement in a `void` method or a constructor.

Accessor and Mutator Methods

When first learning how to write methods for a class, beginning programmers learn two types of methods:

1. Methods that allow you to access the values stored in the instance variables
2. Methods that allow you to modify the values of the instance variables

Methods that return the value of an instance variable are called **accessor** (or **getter**) methods. Methods that change the value of an instance variable are called **mutator** (or **modifier** or **setter**) methods. Methods that don't perform either one of these duties are simply called methods.

> **Is My Carbonated Soft Drink a Soda or a Pop?**
>
> They both refer to the same thing, it just depends on where you live. In a similar way, the methods that retrieve the instance variables of a class can be referred to as accessor or getter methods. The methods that change the value of an instance variable can be called modifier, mutator, or setter methods.

Declaring a Method

Methods are declared using a line of code called a **method declaration** statement. The declaration includes the access modifier, the return type, the name of the method, and the parameter list. The **method signature** only includes the name of the method and the parameter list.

> **General Form of a Method Declaration**
>
> `accessModifier returnType methodName(parameterList)`

> **One-Track Mind**
>
> Methods should have only one goal. The name of the method should clearly describe the purpose of the method.

`toString` Method

It's a good idea to override the `toString()` method that is provided by the `Object` class. By doing this, the class designer (that's you) has control over what is printed each time a user calls the `System.out.println()` and passes an object as the parameter.

The System.out.print() will display a meaningful representation of the attributes rather than simply a reference to the memory location (what good is that?).

In the Circle class below, if the toString() method was not overidden, then the call to System.out.println(myCircle) would print Circle@7852e922 (or some other hexadecimal value referring to the location in memory).

Example

Using the Circle class already written, write an accessor method for the radius, a mutator method for the radius, a method that calculates and returns the area of the circle, and a toString method that returns a string describing the circles attributes.

```java
public class Circle                        // Class declaration
{
    private double radius;                 // Instance variable

    public Circle()                        // No-argument constructor
    {
        radius = 0.0;
    }

    public Circle(double rad)              // Parameterized constructor
    {
        radius = rad;                      // The radius is set to rad
    }

    public double getRadius()              // Accessor method
    {
        return radius;
    }

    public void setRadius(double rad)      // Mutator method
    {
        radius = rad;                      // The radius is set to rad
    }

    public double getArea()                // Method that calculates area
    {
        return 3.14 * radius * radius;     // A simple way to compute area
    }

    public String toString()
    {
        String str;
        str = "The circle has radius " + radius + " and area " + getArea();
        return str;
    }
        // a string is built with all of the information about the circle

}
// End of Circle class
```

Java Ignores Spaces

Java ignores all spacing that isn't relevant. The compiler doesn't care how pretty the code looks in the IDE; it just has to be syntactically correct. On the AP Computer Science A exam, you will sometimes see code that has been streamlined to save space on the page.

For example, the getRadius method for the Circle class could appear like this on the exam:

```java
public double getRadius(){
    return radius;     }
```

Putting It All Together: The `Circle` and `CircleRunner` Classes

We will combine the `Circle` class that we just created with another class to demonstrate how a client class interacts with another class in an object-oriented setting. The `Circle` class defined how to make a `Circle` object. The `CircleRunner` class is where the programmer creates virtual `Circle` objects and then manipulates them. In case you are wondering, the `CircleRunner` class doesn't have to be named that specifically, but it does convey the message that, "You're in a class that runs the program with circles".

Summary of the `Circle` Class

Every circle has-a radius, so the `Circle` class defines an instance variable called radius. The class has two constructors that will build a `Circle` object. The no-argument constructor is used whenever you don't know the radius at the time that you create the `Circle` object. The radius is assigned the default value for a double, which is 0.0. The parameterized constructor is used if you know the radius of the circle at the time you construct the `Circle` object. You pass the radius when you call the parameterized constructor and the constructor assigns the value of its parameter to the instance variable.

The `Circle` class also has four methods:

1. The first method, `getRadius`, returns the radius from that object. Since the method is *getting* the radius for the programmer, it is called an accessor (or getter) method.
2. The second method, `setRadius`, is a `void` method that sets the value of the radius for the object. It is referred to as a modifier (or mutator or setter) method. This method has a parameter, which is a variable that receives a value that is passed to it when the method is called (or invoked) and assigns this value to the instance variable `radius`.
3. The third method, `getArea`, calculates and returns the area of the circle using the object's radius.
4. Finally, the fourth method, `toString` returns a string containing the radius and area of the circle.

Summary of the `CircleRunner` Class

The `Circle` class can't do anything all by itself. To be useful, `Circle` objects are created in a class that is *outside* of the `Circle` class. Each object that is created from a class is called an **instance of the class** and the act of constructing an object is called **instantiating** an object. A class that contains a **main method** is sometimes called a **runner** class. Other times, they are called **client** programs. The main method is the point of entry for a program. That means that when the programmer runs the program, Java finds the main method first and executes it. You will not have to write main methods on the AP Computer Science A exam.

Notice that the `Circle` class does not contain a **public static void main(String[] args)**. The purpose of the `Circle` class is to define how to build and manipulate a `Circle` object; however, `Circle` objects are created and manipulated *in a different class* that contains a main method.

How to Make a New Object from a Class

When you want to make an object from a class, you have to call one of the class's constructors. However, you may have more than one constructor, including the no-argument constructor or one or more parameterized constructors. The computer decides which constructor to call by looking at the parameter list in the declaration of each constructor. Whichever constructor matches the call to the constructor is used to create the object.

Examples

```
// This code uses the no-argument constructor (no parameters)
Circle circle1 = new Circle();

// This code uses the parameterized constructor  (1 parameter)
Circle circle2 = new Circle(4);

// This code causes a compile-time error because there isn't
// a Circle constructor that contains a String in its parameter list
Circle circle3 = new Circle("Fred");
```

Example

Write a runner class that instantiates three Circle objects. Make the first Circle object have a radius of 10, while the second and third Circles will get the default value. Modify the radii of the Circles and print the area of the circle. Call the toString method with each of the three Circle objects to print each circle's radius and area.

```
// This class creates and manipulates three Circle objects
public class CircleRunner
{
    public static void main(String[] args)
    {
        Circle myCircle = new Circle(10); // myCircle's radius = 10.0
        Circle yourCircle = new Circle(); // yourCircle's radius = 0.0
        Circle theirCircle = new Circle(); // theirCircle's radius = 0.0
        System.out.println(myCircle.getArea()); // prints 314.0
        System.out.println(yourCircle.getArea()); // prints 0.0
        yourCircle.setRadius(5); //yourCircle's radius = 5.0
        theirCircle.setRadius(2 * yourCircle.getRadius());
        //theirCircle's radius = 10.0
        System.out.println(yourCircle.getArea()); // prints 78.5
        System.out.println(theirCircle.getArea()); // prints 314.0
        System.out.println(myCircle); // prints radius and area of myCircle
        System.out.println(yourCircle); // prints radius and area of yourCircle
        System.out.println(theirCircle); // prints radius and area of theirCircle
        // notice that the toString method was called by default
        // this is because it overrode the Objects toString method.
    }
}
```

```
OUTPUT
314.0
0.0
78.5
314.0
The circle has radius 10.0 and area 314.0
The circle has radius 5.0 and area 78.5
The circle has radius 10.0 and area 314.0
```

Every Object from the Same Class Is a Different Object

Every object that is constructed from a class has its own instance variables. Two *different* objects can have the same **state**, which means that their instance variables have the same values.

In this example, the `CircleRunner` class creates three different `Circle` objects called `myCircle`, `yourCircle`, and `theirCircle`. Notice that the `myCircle` object has a radius of 10. This is because when the `Circle` object created it, the computer looked for the parameterized constructor and when it found it, assigned the 10 to the parameter `rad` which in turn set the instance variable, radius, to 10.0. For the `yourCircle` and `theirCircle` objects, the no-argument constructor was called and the instance variable, radius, was given the default value of 0.0.

Remember that `myCircle`, `yourCircle`, and `theirCircle` all refer to different objects that were all created from the same `Circle` class and each object has its own radius. When each object calls the `getArea` method, it uses *its own* radius to compute the area.

The Dot Operator

The dot operator is used to call a method of an object. The name of the object's reference variable is followed by a period and then the name of the method.

`objectReference.methodName();`

Understanding the Keyword **new** When Constructing an Object

Beginning Java programmers often have a hard time understanding why the name of the class is used twice when creating an object, such as the `Circle` objects in `CircleRunner`. Let's analyze the following line of code to find out what's really happening.

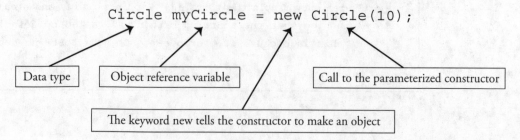

The first use of the word `Circle` is the data type of the variable. It's similar to how we defined an `int` or a `double` variable. The variable `myCircle` is called a **reference variable** of type `Circle`. It's similar to a primitive variable in that it holds a value, but it's *way* different in the fact that it *does not* hold the `Circle` object itself. The value that `myCircle` holds is the memory address of the soon-to-be-created `Circle` object.

The second use of the word `Circle(10)` is a call to the parameterized constructor of the `Circle` class. The keyword **new** tells the computer, "Hey we want to create a new object." The computer looks for a constructor that has a single parameter that matches the data type of the 10. Once it finds this constructor, it gives the 10 to the parameter, `rad`. The code in the constructor assigns the instance variable, `radius`, the value of the parameter `rad`. Then, voilá! The radius of the `Circle` object is 10.

Finally, the computer looks for a place to store the `Circle` object in memory (RAM) and when it finds a location, it records the memory address. The construction of the `Circle` is now complete, and the address of the newly formed `Circle` object is assigned to the reference variable, `myCircle`.

Now, anytime you want to modify the object that is referenced by `myCircle`, such as give it a new radius, you are actually telling `myCircle` to go find the object that it is referencing (also called, *pointing to*), and set the radius for that object.

The Reference Variable

The reference variable does not hold the object itself. It holds the address of where the object is stored in RAM (random access memory).

The Reference Variable Versus the Actual Object

The following diagram is meant to help you visualize the relationship between object reference variables and the objects themselves in the computer's memory. Note: The memory addresses are simulated and only meant to serve as an example of addresses in the computer's memory.

Question 1: What happens after these two lines of code are executed?

```
Circle yourCircle = new Circle(20);
Circle theirCircle = new Circle(15);
```

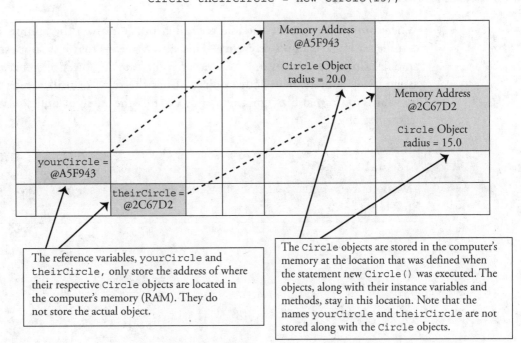

The reference variables, `yourCircle` and `theirCircle`, only store the address of where their respective `Circle` objects are located in the computer's memory (RAM). They do not store the actual object.

The `Circle` objects are stored in the computer's memory at the location that was defined when the statement new `Circle()` was executed. The objects, along with their instance variables and methods, stay in this location. Note that the names `yourCircle` and `theirCircle` are not stored along with the `Circle` objects.

Question 2: What do you suppose happens after this line of code is executed?

```
theirCircle = yourCircle;
```

If you follow the diagram, you will see that `theirCircle` "takes on the value" of the address of the `yourCircle` reference variable. Now, `theirCircle` contains the same address that `yourCircle` contains. This means that both reference variables contain the same address of the same object and are pointing to the same object. The word **alias** is used to describe the situation when two different object reference variables contain the same address of an object.

Look at the object that used to be referenced by `theirCircle`. Nothing is pointing to it. It has been detached from the rest of the world and will be **garbage collected** by Java. This means that Java will delete it when it is good and ready.

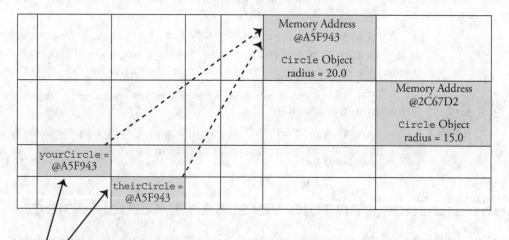

The reference variable, `theirCircle`, now holds the same address that `yourCircle` holds. Both reference variables have the ability to modify the same object. The address of the object that used to be referenced by `theirCircle` is not known by any reference variable anymore and so the object will be garbage collected.

The `null` Reference

When an object reference variable is created but not given the address of an object, it is considered to have a **null reference**. This simply means that it is supposed to know where an object lives, but it does not. Whenever you create an object reference variable and don't assign it the address of an actual object, it has the value of **null**, which means that it has no value. You can also assign a reference variable the value of null to erase its memory of its former object.

The `null` Reference

A reference variable that does not contain the address of any object is called a `null` reference.

Question 3: What do you suppose happens when this statement is executed?

```
yourCircle = null;
```

The reference variable `yourCircle` is now null; it has no value. This means that it does not contain the address of any object. The reference variable `theirCircle` still holds the address of a `Circle` object and so it can access methods of that object.

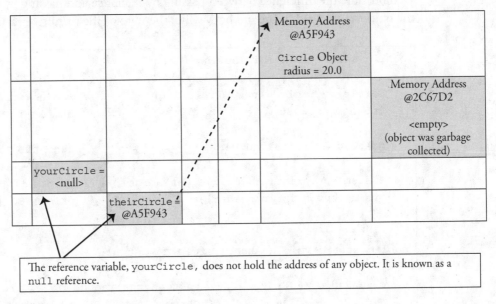

The reference variable, `yourCircle`, does not hold the address of any object. It is known as a `null` reference.

Note: A `null` reference indicates that the object does not exist. This should not be confused with a value of nothing. For example, the empty `String` "" is a `String` that has no characters, whereas `null` indicates that the `String` does not exist. `null` and the empty `String` are not equivalent.

Parameters

Primitives Are Passed by Value

Values that are passed to a method or constructor are called **actual parameters** (or **arguments**), while the variables in the parameter list of the method declaration are called **formal parameters**. When an actual parameter is of a primitive type, its value cannot be changed in the method because only the *value* of the variable is sent to the method.

Said another way, the formal parameter variable becomes a copy of the actual parameter. The method cannot alter the value of the actual parameter variable. The formal parameter variable only receives the *value* of the actual parameter. The method only has the ability to change the value of the formal parameter variable, not the value of the actual parameter.

Objects Are Passed by Reference

Objects are passed by reference. What does that mean?

Simple answer: It means that when an object is passed to a method, the method has the ability to change the state of the object.

Technical answer: When an actual parameter is an object, it is the object reference that is actually the parameter. This means that when the method receives the reference and stores it in a formal parameter variable, the method now has the ability to change the state of the object *because it knows where the object lives*. The formal parameter is now an alias of the actual parameter, so any changes made to the formal parameter variable will affect the actual parameter.

Example

Demonstrate the difference between passing by reference and passing by value. The state of the object is changed in the method, while the state of the primitive variable is unchanged.

```
public static void main(String[] args)
{
    Circle myCircle = new Circle(100);          // radius is 100.0
    int number = 80;                            // number is 80

    goAhead(myCircle, number);                  // send the arguments

    System.out.println(myCircle.getRadius());   // prints 50 (changed)
    System.out.println(number);                 // prints 80 (not changed)
}

public static void goAhead(Circle c, int n)
{
    c.setRadius(50);        // changes the radius of myCircle to 50.0
    n = 20;                 // changes n to 20, but number stays 80
}
```

```
OUTPUT
50
80
```

Comparing Against a `null` Reference

Recall that a `nullPointerException` error occurs if you attempt to perform a method on a reference variable that is null. How can you tell if a reference variable is null so you won't get that error? The answer is to perform a **null check**. Compare the reference variable using the == comparator or != comparator. Just *don't use* the equals method to perform a null check. You'll get a `nullPointerException`!

Example

Demonstrate how to perform a null check using the `Circle` class. If the Circle reference is not null, then compute the area. If the Circle reference is null, then return -1 for the area.

```
public static void main(String[] args)
{
    Circle circle1 = new Circle(10);
    Circle circle2;                             // circle2 is null

    System.out.println(doANullCheck(circle1);   // send a valid reference
    System.out.println(doANullCheck(circle2);   // send a null reference
}

public static double doANullCheck(Circle c)
{
    if (c != null)
        return c.getArea();        // return the area if c is not null
    else
        return -1;                 // return -1 if c is null
}
```

```
OUTPUT
314.15926
-1.0
```

Checking Against null

Never use the equals method to determine if an object reference is null. Only use == or != to check if an object reference variable is null.

Example: if(c.equals(null)) will cause a null pointer error if c is null, because there is an attempt to call a method from an object that does not exist.

Overloaded Constructors

It is possible to have more than one constructor in a class. Constructors are always declared using the name of the class, but their parameter lists can differ. If there are two or more constructors in a class, they are all called **overloaded constructors**. The computer decides which of the overloaded constructors is the correct one to use based on the parameter list.

Overloaded constructors have the same name; however, they must differ by one of these ways:

- a different number of parameters
- the same number of parameters but at least one is a different type
- the same exact parameter types but in a different order

Example

Declare four constructors for a class called Student. The constructors have the same name as the class, but are different because their parameter lists differ.

```
public class Student
{
    private String firstName;
    private String lastName;
    private int age;

    public Student()                      // no-argument constructor
    {
        firstName = lastName = "";
        age = 0;
    }

    public Student(String first)          // constructor has 1 parameter
    {
        firstName = first;
        lastName = "";
        age = 0;
    }

    public Student(String first, String last)    // has 2 parameters
    {
        firstName = first;
        lastName = last;
        age = 0;
    }
    public Student(String first, String last, int yearsOld)   // has 3
    {
        firstName = first;
        lastName = last;
        age = yearsOld;
    }
}
```

Overloaded Methods

Methods that have the same name but different parameter lists are called **overloaded methods**. The computer decides which of the overloaded methods is the correct one to use based on the parameter list.

Overloaded methods must have the same name and may have a different return type; however, they must differ by one of these ways:

- a different number of parameters
- the same number of parameters but at least one is a different type
- the same exact parameter types but in a different order

Example

Declare four overloaded methods. The methods should have the same name, but different parameter lists as described above.

```
public void doSomething(int param)              // has 1 int parameter
{
    // Do something with param
}

public void doSomething(double param)           // has 1 double parameter
{
    // Do something with param
}

public void doSomething(double a, int b)        // has 2 parameters
{
    // Do something with a and b
}

public void doSomething(int a, double b) // has 2 params; different order
{
    // Do something with a and b
}
```

Blast from the Past

Recall that the **substring** method from the `String` class is overloaded. There are two versions of the method, but they are different because their parameter lists are not identical.

static, static, static

static Variables (Class Variables)

There are times when a class needs to have a variable that is shared by all the objects that come from the class. The variable is declared and assigned a value as though it were an instance variable; however, it uses the keyword **static** in its declaration. Static variables are also called **class variables** and can be declared private or public.

`static final` Variables (Class Constants)

Likewise, there are times when a class needs to have a **constant** that is used by all the objects of the class. As the name *constant* suggests, it *cannot* be reassigned a different value at any other place in the program. In fact, a compile-time error will occur if you try to give the constant a different value. Class constants are declared using the keywords `static` and `final` in their declaration and should use all uppercase letters (and underscores, if necessary). These static final variables are also called class constants.

`static` Methods (Class Methods)

If a method is labeled `static`, it can only call other static methods and can only use or modify static variables. Static methods cannot access or change the values of the instance variables or cannot call `non-static` methods in the class. Class methods are associated with methods of the class, not individual objects of the class.

Example

Suppose you are hired by Starbucks to keep track of the total number of stores. You've already decided to have a class called `StarbucksStore`, but how can you keep track of the total number of stores? One solution is to make a static variable, called `storeCount`. Then, each time a store is constructed (pun intended), increment this class variable. Access will be given to the `storeCount` by creating a `static` method called `getStoreCount`. Let's also say that you decide to make a variable that holds the logo for all the stores. You choose to make this variable a constant because every store shares the logo, and none of them should be allowed to change the logo. For this we will make a static final variable called `STARBUCKS_LOGO` and initialize it to "`Mermaid`".

```java
public class StarbucksStore
{
        private double coffeePrice;
        private double totalServed;

        public StarbucksStore(double price)
        {
                coffeePrice = price;
                storeCount++; // increments each time a new store is
                              // constructed
        }

        public double getPrice()
        {
                return coffeePrice;
        }

        public void setPrice(double newPrice)
        {
                coffeePrice = newPrice;
        }

        public double getServed()
        {
                return totalServed;
        }

        public void addServed(double served)
        {
                totalServed += served;
        }

        public double sales()
        {
                return totalServed * coffeePrice;
        }

        // ------------- static variables and methods ----------------
        private static int storeCount = 0;
        public static final String STARBUCKS_LOGO = "Mermaid";

        public static int getStoreCount()
        {
                return storeCount;
        }
}
```

```
public class StoreRunner
{
        public static void main(String[] args)
        {
                StarbucksStore store1 = new StarbucksStore(3.95);
                StarbucksStore store2 = new StarbucksStore(4.95);
                StarbucksStore store3 = new StarbucksStore(5.29);

                System.out.println(StarbucksStore.getStoreCount());
                System.out.println(StarbucksStore.STARBUCKS_LOGO);

                store1.addServed(327);
                store2.addServed(450);
                store3.addServed(678);

                System.out.println(store1.sales());
                System.out.println(store2.sales());
                System.out.println(store3.sales());
        }
}
```

```
OUTPUT
3
Mermaid
1291.65
2227.5
3586.62
```

Did you notice how the class method `getStoreCount()` and constant `STARBUCKS_LOGO` were called from the main program? Since the method and constant belong to the class and not a particular object of that class, they were called by using the class name `StarbucksStore`. Oftentimes, constants are declared as public since there is no risk of a client class modifying the value. Does that look familiar? You've used something like this already when you called `Math.abs()` (a static method from the `Math` class) or `Integer.MAX_VALUE` (a static constant from the `Integer` class).

Data Encapsulation

Information Hiding

Protecting information by restricting its access is important in software development. Since classes are public, all the objects from the class are public. The way that we hide information or **encapsulate data** in Java is to use private access modifiers.

Encapsulated Data

It is expected on the AP Computer Science A Exam that all instance variables of a class are declared private. The only way to gain access to them is to use the accessor or mutator methods provided by the class.

What Happens If I Declare an Instance Variable `public`?

Let's suppose you just want to find out what happens if you declare an instance variable public. The result is that you can use the dot operator to access the instance variables.

Example

Declare the radius instance variable from the `Circle` class as public. Notice that the object has now allowed access to the public variable by anyone using the dot operator. Using the dot operator on a private variable produces a compile-time error.

```
// Suppose this code is in the Circle class
public double radius;  // public instance variable:  Don't ever do this!
```

```
// Suppose this code is in a runner class
Circle myCircle = new Circle(10); // radius is 10.0
myCircle.radius = 5.4;            // radius is easily changed when public
double result = myCircle.radius;  // result is 5.4
```

The Integer Class and Its `public` Fields

Remember how we accessed the largest and smallest Integer? We used the dot operator to just get the value. That's because MAX_VALUE and MIN_VALUE are public constant fields of the Integer class. You don't use an accessor method to get them.

```
int reallyBigInteger = Integer.MAX_VALUE; // MAX_VALUE is a public constant
```

Scope

The scope of a variable refers to the region of the program in which the variable is known. Attempting to use a variable outside of its scope produces a compile-time error.

Different types of variables have different scopes.

- The scope of a **local variable** is within the nearest pair of curly braces that encloses it.
- The scope of a **parameter** is the method or constructor in which it is declared.
- The scope of an **instance variable** is the class in which it is defined.

Documentation

Inline Comments

Inline comments have been used throughout this book and will continue to be used. They begin with two forward slashes, //. All text that comes after the slashes (on the same line) is ignored by the compiler.
```
// This is an example of an inline comment.
```

Multiple-Line Comments

When your comment takes longer than one line, you will want to use a multiple-line comment. These comments begin with /* and end with */. The compiler ignores everything in between these two special character sequences.

```
/*
This is how to write a multiple-line comment. Everything typed here is
ignored by the compiler; even mi mysteaks in spelling, so be particularly
careful of your spelling when you are typing multiple-line comments!
*/
```

Javadoc Comments

You will see **Javadoc comments** (also called **documentation comments**) on the AP Computer Science A Exam, especially in the FRQ section. These comments begin with /** and end with */. The compiler ignores everything in between the two character sequences.

```
/**
* This is an example of a Javadoc comment.
* You will see these "documentation" comments on the AP CS exam.
*/
```

Javadoc

Javadoc is a tool that generates an HTML-formatted document that summarizes a class (including its constructors, instance variables, methods, etc.) in a readable format. Among programmers, this document itself is often referred to as a Javadoc. The summary is called the API (application program interface) for that set of classes and is extremely useful for programmers. You should refer to the Oracle Java website for a list of all Java classes and their methods (but only those listed on the Java Quick Reference will be tested on the AP Computer Science A exam).

Javadoc Tags

Similar to a hashtag, the **@param** is a tag that is used in Javadoc comments. When a programmer uses an @param tag, they state the name of the parameter and provide a brief description of it. Javadoc tags are automatically detected by Javadoc and appear in the API.

The **@return** is also a Javadoc tag. It is only used in return methods, and the programmer identifies the name of the variable being returned and a brief description of it.

Documentation Comments on the AP Computer Science A Exam

You won't have to write any comments on the AP Computer Science A exam. You just need to know how to read them.

Precondition and Postcondition

You know what happens when you assume, right? Well, a **precondition** states what you are allowed to assume about a parameter. It's a statement in the documentation comment before a constructor or method signature that describes the expectations of the parameter passed to the method. There is no expectation that the method will check to ensure preconditions are satisfied. If a method is called and the preconditions haven't been met, then the method most likely won't perform as expected. On the AP Computer Science A Exam, reading the preconditions can help you understand the nature of the parameters and save you from attempting to guard against errors unnecessarily. A **postcondition** is a condition that must always be true after the execution of a section of program code. Postconditions describe the outcome of the execution in terms of what is being returned or the state of an object. Programmers must write method code to satisfy the postconditions when preconditions are met.

Example

This is the same `Circle` class that was created earlier; however, it now includes the Javadoc tags and precondition/postcondition statements as they may appear on the AP Computer Science A Exam. It also includes an improved way to calculate the area using the `Math` class.

```java
public class Circle                      // Class declaration
{
    private double radius;               // Instance variable

    public Circle()                      // The no-argument constructor
    {
        // The radius gets a default value of 0.0
    }

    /**
     *  A parameterized constructor for a Circle
     *  @param r The radius of the Circle
     *         Precondition:  rad > 0
     */
    public Circle(double rad)
    {
        radius = rad;   // The radius gets the value of the parameter, rad
    }

    /**
     *  Accessor method that returns the radius of the Circle object
     *  @return radius of the Circle
     */
    public double getRadius()
    {
        return radius;
    }

    /**
     *  Mutator method that reassigns the radius of the Circle object
     *  @param r The radius of the Circle
     *         Precondition:  rad > 0
     */
    public void setRadius(double rad)
    {
        radius = rad;       // The radius is changed to be the parameter value
    }

    /**
     *  Method that calculates and returns the area of the Circle
     *  @return area of the Circle
     *         Postcondition:  area > 0
     */
    public double getArea()
    {
        return Math.PI * Math.pow(radius, 2); // uses PI for more precision
    }
}  // End of Circle class
```

The Keyword this

The keyword **this** is a reference to the current object, or rather, the object whose method or constructor is being called. It is also referred to as the **implicit** parameter.

Example 1

Pass the implicit parameter **this** to a different method in a class. This usage may be tested on the exam.

```
public static void main(String[] args)
{
    MyClass m1 = new MyClass("Batman");
    m1.doSomething();
}
```

```
public class MyClass
{
    private String name;
    public MyClass(String n)
    {    name = n;    }

    public String getName()
    {    return name;    }

    public void doSomething()
    {
        nowDoSomethingWith(this);          // Pass "this" to another method
    }

    public void nowDoSomethingWith(MyClass myObject) // myObject is m1
    {
        System.out.println("I am " + myObject.getName());
    }
}
```

```
OUTPUT
I am Batman
```

Example 2

A common place to use the keyword this is when the instance variables have the same name as the parameters in a constructor. The keyword this is used on the left side of the assignment statements to assign the instance variables the values of the parameters. The left side is the instance variable; the right side is the parameter variable. Using this here says, "Hey, I understand that we have the same name, so these are my instance variables and not the parameters."

```
public class Whatever
{
    private int a;
    private int b;

    public Whatever(int a, int b)      // Parameters have the same name
    {                                   // as the instance variables.
        this.a = a;                    // Left side are the instance variables
        this.b = b;                    // Right side are the parameters
    }
}
```

› Rapid Review

Classes

- A class contains the blueprint, or design, from which individual objects are created.
- Classes tend to represent things that are nouns.
- A class declaration (or class definition) is the line of code that declares the class.
- By naming convention, class names should begin with an uppercase letter and use camel case.
- The two access modifiers that are tested on the AP Computer Science A Exam are public and private.
- All classes should be declared public.
- A public class means that the class is visible to all classes everywhere.

Instance Variables

- Instance variables (or fields) are properties that all objects from the same class possess. They are the attributes that help distinguish one object from another in the same class.
- All instance variables should be declared private.
- A class can have as many instance variables as is appropriate to describe all the attributes of an object from the class.
- By naming convention, all instance variables begin with a lowercase letter and use camel case.
- All primitive instance variables receive default values. The default value of an int is 0, the default value of a double is 0.0, the default value for a boolean is false, and the default for reference is null.
- The current values of all of the instance variables of an object determine the state of the object.
- The state of the object is changed whenever any of the instance variables are modified.

Constructors

- Every class, by default, comes with a no-argument (or empty) constructor.
- Parameterized constructors should be created if there are values that should be assigned to the instance variables at the moment that an object is created.

- A class can have as many parameterized constructors as is relevant.
- The main reason to have a parameterized constructor is to assign values to the instance variables.
- Other code may be written in the constructor.
- A parameter is a variable that receives values and is declared in a parameter list of a method or constructor.

Methods

- The methods of a class describe the actions that an object can perform.
- Methods tend to represent things that are verbs.
- By naming convention, method names begin with a lowercase letter and use camel case.
- The name of a method should describe the purpose of the method.
- Methods should not be multi-purpose. They should have one goal.
- A method declaration describes pertinent information for the method such as the access modifier, the return type, the name of the method, and the parameter list.
- Methods that don't return a value are called `void` methods.
- Methods that return a value of some data type are called return methods.
- Methods can return any data type.
- return methods must include a reachable return statement.
- Methods that return the value of an instance variable are called accessor (or getter) methods.
- Methods that modify the value of an instance variable are called mutator (or modifier or setter) methods.
- The data type of all parameters must be defined in the parameter list.
- Methods declared as public can be used externally to the class.
- Methods declared as private can be used internally to the class.
- When designing a class programmers make decisions about what data to make accessible and modifiable from an external class.

Objects

- An object from a class is a virtual realization of the class.
- Objects store their own data.
- An instance of a class is the same thing as an object of a class.
- The word "instantiate" is used to describe the action of creating an object. Instantiating is the act of constructing a new object.
- The keyword `new` is used whenever you want to create an object.
- An object reference variable stores the memory address of where the actual object is stored. It can only reference one object.
- The reference variable does not store the object itself.
- Two reference variables are equal only if they refer to the exact same object.
- The word *null* means no value.
- A `null` reference describes a reference variable that does not contain an address of any object.
- You can create as many objects as you want from one class. Each is a different object that is stored in a different location in the computer's memory.

Passing Parameters by Value

- The parameter variables that are passed to a method or constructor are called actual parameters (or arguments).
- The parameter variables that receive the values in a method or constructor are called formal parameters.
- Passing by value means that only the value of the variable is passed.
- Primitive variables are passed by value.
- It is impossible to change the value of actual parameters that are passed by value.

Passing Parameters by Reference

- Passing by reference means that the address of where the object is stored is passed to the method or constructor.
- Objects are passed by reference (including arrays).
- The state of the object can be modified when it is passed by reference.
- It is possible to change the value of actual parameters that are passed by reference.

Overloaded

- Overloaded constructors may have (1) a different number of parameters, (2) the same number of parameters but of a different type, or (3) the same exact parameter types but in a different order.
- Overloaded methods have the same name; however, their method parameter lists are different in some way.
- Overloaded methods may have (1) a different number of parameters, (2) the same number of parameters but of a different type, (3) the same exact parameter types but in a different order.

`static`

- `static` variables are also known as class variables.
- A class variable is a variable that is shared by all instances of a class.
- Changes made to a class variable by any object from the class are reflected in the state of each object for all objects from the class.
- Static final variables are also called class constants.
- Class constants are declared using both the keywords **static** and **final**.
- Constants, by naming convention, use uppercase letters and underscores.
- Constants cannot be modified during run-time.
- If a method is declared static, it can only call other `static` methods and can reference `static` variables.

Scope

- The scope of a variable refers to the area of the program in which it is known.
- The scope of a local variable is in the block of code in which it is defined.
- The scope of an instance variable is the class in which it is defined.
- The scope of a parameter is the method or constructor in which it is defined.

Documentation

- Documentation tags are used by Javadocs.
- The @param tag is used to describe a parameter.
- The @return tag is used to describe what is being returned by a method.
- A precondition describes what can be expected of the values that the parameters receive.
- A postcondition describes the end result criteria for a method.

Miscellaneous

- Data encapsulation is the act of hiding the values of the instance variables from other classes.
- Declaring instance variables as private encapsulates them.
- Use the keyword `this` when you want to refer to the object itself.
- An `IllegalArgumentException` error occurs when a parameter that is passed to a method fails to meet criteria set up by the programmer.

› Review Questions

Basic Level

1. The relationship between a class and an object can be described as:

    (A) The terms *class* and *object* mean the same thing.
    (B) A class is a program, while an object is data.
    (C) A class is the blueprint for an object and objects are instantiated from it.
    (D) An object is the blueprint for a class and classes are instantiated from it.
    (E) A class can be written by anyone, but Java provides all objects.

2. Which of the following is a valid constructor declaration for the `Cube` class?

    ```
    I.   public static Cube()
    II.  public void Cube()
    III. public Cube()
    IV.  public Cube(int side)
    ```

    (A) I only
    (B) II only
    (C) III only
    (D) I and II only
    (E) III and IV only

Questions 3–6 refer to the following class.

```
public class Student
{
    private String name;
    private double gpa;

    public Student(String newName, double newGPA)
    {
        name = newName;
        gpa = newGpa;
    }

    public String getName()
    {
        return name;
    }

    /*  Additional methods not shown  */
}
```

3. Which of the following could be used to instantiate a new Student object called sam?

(A) Student sam = new Student();
(B) sam = new Student();
(C) Student sam = new Student("Sam Smith", 3.5);
(D) new Student sam = ("Sam Smith", 3.5);
(E) new Student(sam);

4. Which of the following could be used in the StudentTester class to print the name associated with the Student object instantiated in problem 3?

(A) System.out.println(getName());
(B) System.out.println(sam.getName());
(C) System.out.println(getName(sam));
(D) System.out.println(Student.name);
(E) System.out.println(getName(Student));

5. Which of the following is the correct way to write a method that changes the value of a Student object's gpa variable?

(A) public double setGpa(double newGpa)
    {
        return gpa;
    }
(B) public double setGpa()
    {
        return gpa;
    }
(C) public void setGpa ()
    {
        gpa++;
    }
(D) public setGpa(double newGpa)
    {
        gpa = newGpa;
    }
(E) public void setGpa(double newGpa)
    {
        gpa = newGpa;
    }

6. Consider the following code segment.

```
Student s1 = new Student("Brody Kai", 3.9);
Student s2 = new Student("Charlie Cole", 3.2);
s2 = s1;
s2.setGpa(4.0);
System.out.println(s1.getGpa());
```

What is printed as a result of executing the code segment?

(A) 3.2
(B) 3.9
(C) 4.0
(D) Nothing will be printed. There will be a compile-time error.
(E) Nothing will be printed. There will be a run-time error.

Questions 7–8 refer to the following information.

Consider the following method.

```
public int calculate(int a, int b)
{
    a = a - b;
    int c = b;
    b = a * a;
    a = b - (a + c);
    return a;
}
```

7. The following code segment appears in another method in the same class.

```
int var = 9;
int count = 2;
System.out.println(calculate(var, count));
```

What is printed as a result of executing the code segment?
(A) 2
(B) 9
(C) 23
(D) 40
(E) 49

8. The following code segment appears in another method in the same class.

```
int a = 9;
int b = 2;
int c = calculate(a, b);
System.out.println(a + " " + b + " " + c);
```

What is printed as a result of executing the code segment?
(A) 40 49 40
(B) 9 2 40
(C) 40 49 49
(D) Run-time error: a and b cannot contain two values at once.
(E) Compile-time error; duplicate variable.

9. Consider the following calculation of the area of a circle.

```
double area = Math.PI * Math.pow(radius, 2);
```

Math.PI can best be described as:
(A) A method in the Math class.
(B) A method in the class containing the given line of code.
(C) A public static final double in the Math class.
(D) A private static final double in the Math class.
(E) A private static final double in the class containing the given line of code.

10. A programmer is designing a BankAccount class. In addition to the usual information needed for a bank account, she would like to have a variable that counts how many BankAccount objects have been instantiated. She asks you how to do this. You tell her:

(A) It cannot be done, since each object has its own variable space.
(B) She should use a class constant.
(C) She should call a mutator method to change the numAccounts variable held in each object.
(D) She should create a static variable and increment it in the constructor as each object is created.
(E) Java automatically keeps a tally. She should reference the variable maintained by Java.

11. Having multiple methods in a class with the same name but with a different number or different types of parameters is called:

(A) abstraction
(B) method overloading
(C) encapsulation
(D) method visibility
(E) parameterization

Advanced Level

12. Consider the following method.

```
public int mystery(int a, int b, int c)
{
    if (a < b && a < c)
    {
        return a;
    }
    if (b < c && b < a)
    {
        return b;
    }
    if (c < a && c < b)
    {
        return c;
    }
}
```

Which statement about this method is true?
(A) mystery returns the smallest of the three integers a, b, and c.
(B) mystery always returns the value of a.
(C) mystery always returns both values a and c.
(D) mystery sometimes returns all three values a, b, and c.
(E) mystery will not compile, because the return statement appears to be unreachable under some conditions.

13. The method from the previous problem is rewritten as shown.

```
public int mystery2(int a, int b, int c)
{
    if (a <= b && a < c)
    {
        return a;
    }
    if (b < c && b < a)
    {
        return b;
    }
    return c;
}
```

Which statement about the method is true?

(A) mystery2 returns the smallest of the three integers a, b, and c.

(B) mystery2 always returns the value of c.

(C) mystery2 returns either the values of both a and c or both b and c.

(D) mystery2 sometimes returns all three values a, b, and c.

(E) mystery2 will not compile, because the return statement appears to be unreachable under some conditions.

14. Consider the following class declaration.

```
public class AnotherClass
{
    private static int val = 31;
    private String data;

    public AnotherClass(String s)
    {
        data = s;
        val /= 2;
    }

    public void join(String s)
    {   data = data + s;   }

    public void setData(String s)
    {   data = s;   }

    public String getData()
    {   return data;   }

    public int getVal()
    {   return val;   }
}
```

The following code segment appears in the main method of another class.

```
AnotherClass word = new AnotherClass("Hello");
word.join("Hello");
AnotherClass sentence = new AnotherClass(word.getData());
sentence.join("Hi");
word.setData(sentence.getData());
word.join("Hello");
sentence.join("Hi");
sentence.setData("Hi");
System.out.println(word.getVal());
```

What is printed as a result of executing the code segment?

(A) `30`

(B) `15`

(C) `7.75`

(D) `7.5`

(E) `7`

15. Consider the following method declaration.

```
public int workaround(int a, double b)
```

Which of these method declarations would correctly overload the given method?

```
I.   public double workaround(int a, double b)
II.  public int workaround(double b, int a)
III. public int workaround(String s, double b)
IV.  public double workaround(int a, double b, String s)
V.   public int workaround(int b, double a)
```

(A) I only

(B) IV only

(C) II and III only

(D) II, III, and IV only

(E) All of the above

16. Free-Response Practice: Dream Vacation Class

Everyone fantasizes about taking a dream vacation.

Write a full `DreamVacation` class that contains the following:

a. An instance variable for the name of the destination

b. An instance variable for the cost of the vacation (dollars and cents)

c. A no-argument constructor

d. A parameterized constructor that takes in both the name of the vacation and the cost

e. Accessor (getter) methods for both instance variables

f. Modifier (setter) methods for both instance variables

17. Free-Response Practice: The `Height` Class

The purpose of the `Height` class is to hold a measurement in feet and inches, facilitate additions to that measurement, and keep the measurement in simplest form (inches < 12). A `Height` object can be instantiated with a measurement in feet and inches, or in total inches.

Write the entire `Height` class that includes the following:

a. Instance variables `int feet` for the number of feet and `int inches` for the number of inches. These instance variables must be updated anytime they are changed so that they hold values in simplest form. That is, inches must *always* be less than 12 (see method described in part C below).

b. Two constructors, one with two parameters representing feet and inches, and one with a single parameter representing inches. The parameters do not necessarily represent the measurement simplest form.

c. A method called `simplify()` that recalculates the number of feet and inches, if necessary, so that the number of inches is less than 12.

d. An `add(int inches)` method that takes the number of inches to add and updates the appropriate instance variables.

e. An `add(Height ht)` method that takes a parameter that is a `Height` object and adds that object's inches and feet to this object's instance variables, updating if necessary.

f. Accessor (getter) methods for the instance variables `inches` and `feet`.

› Answers and Explanations

Bullets mark each step in the process of arriving at the correct solution.

1. The answer is C.

   - A class is a blueprint for constructing objects of the type described by the class definition.

2. The answer is E.

   - The general form of a constructor declaration is:

   ```
   public NameOfClass(optional parameter list)
   ```

   - Notice that there is no return type, not even void.
   - In this example, the name of the class is Cube. III is a correct declaration for a no-argument constructor and IV is a correct declaration for a constructor with one parameter.

3. The answer is C.

   - The general form of an instantiation statement is:

   ```
   Type variableName = new Type(parameter list);
   ```

   - In this example, the type is Student and the variable name is sam.
   - We have to look at the constructor code to see that the parameter list consists of a String followed by a double.
   - The only answer that has the correct form with the parameters in the correct order is:

   ```
   Student sam = new Student("Sam Smith", 3.5);
   ```

4. The answer is B.

   - We do not have direct access to the instance variables of an object, because they are private. We have to ask the object for the data we need with an accessor method. In this case, we need to call the getName method.
   - We need to ask the specific object we are interested in for its name. The general syntax for doing that is:

   ```
   variableName.methodName();
   ```

   - Placing the call in the print statement gives us:

   ```
   System.out.println(sam.getName());
   ```

5. The answer is E.

   - A modifier or setter method has to take a new value for the variable from the caller and assign that value to the variable. The new value is given to the method through the use of a parameter.
   - A modifier method does not return anything. Why would it? The caller has given the value to the method. The method doesn't have to give it back.
   - So we need a void method that has one parameter. It has to change the value of gpa to the value of the parameter. Option E shows the only method that does that.

6. The answer is C.

   - The instantiation statements give us 2 objects: s1 and s2.
   - s1 references (points to) a Student object with the state information: name = "Brody Kai", gpa = 3.9
   - s2 references (points to) a Student object with the state information: name = "Charlie Cole", gpa = 3.2
   - When we execute the statement s2 = s1, s2 changes its reference. It now references the exact same object that s1 references, with the state information: name = "Brody Kai", gpa = 3.9
   - s2.setGpa(4.0); changes the gpa in the object that both s1 and s2 reference, so when s1.getGpa(); is executed, that's the value it retrieves and that's the value that is printed.

7. The answer is D.

- When the method call `calculate(var, count)` is executed, the arguments 9 and 2 are passed by value. That is, their values are copied into the parameters a and b, so a = 9 and b = 2 at the beginning of the method.
- a = 9 − 2 = 7
- int c = 2
- b = 7 * 7 = 49
- a = 49 − (7 + 2) = 40 and that is what will be returned.

8. The answer is B.

- When the method call `calculate(a, b)` is executed, the arguments 9 and 2 are passed by value, that is their values are copied into the parameters a and b. The parameters a and b are completely different variables from the a and b in the calling method and any changes made to a and b inside the method do not affect a and b in the calling method in any way.
- We know from problem #1 that calculate(9, 2) will return 40.
- 9 2 40 will be printed.

9. The answer is C.

- All instance variables in the classes we write must be declared private. In fact, the AP Computer Science A exam readers may deduct points if you do not declare your variables private. However, some built-in Java classes provide us with useful constants by making their fields public.
- We access these fields by using the name of the class followed by a dot, followed by the name of the field. We can tell that it is a constant because its name is written entirely in capital letters. Some other public constants that we use are Integer.MAX_VALUE and Integer.MIN_VALUE.
- Note that we can tell this is not a method call, because the name is not followed by (). The Math.pow(radius, 2) is a method call to a static method of the `Math` class.

10. The answer is D.

- Option A is incorrect. It correctly states that each object has its own variable space, and each object's variables will be different. However, it is not correct about it being impossible.
- Option B is incorrect. It says to use a constant, which doesn't make sense because she wants to be able to update its value as objects are created.
- Option C is incorrect. There is no one mutator method call that will access the instance variables of each object of the class.
- Option D is correct. A `static` variable or class variable is a variable held by the class and accessible to every object of the class.
- Option E is simply not true.

11. The answer is B.

- Method overloading allows us to use the same method name with different parameters.

12. The answer is E.

- The intent of the mystery method is to find and return the smallest of the three integers. We know that all possible conditions are covered by the if statements and one of them has to be true, but the compiler does not know that. The compiler just sees that all of the `return` statements are in if clauses, and so it thinks that if all the conditions are false, the method will not return a value. The compiler generates an error message telling us that the method must return a value.

13. The answer is A.

- The first time a `return` statement is reached, the method returns to the caller. No further code in the method will be executed, so no further returns will be made.

14. The answer is E.

- There are a lot of calls here, but only two that will affect the value of `val`, since the only time val is changed is in the constructor.
- It's important to notice that `val` is a static variable. That means that the class maintains one copy of the variable, rather than the objects each having their own copy. Since there is only one shared copy, changes made to `val` by any object will be seen by all objects.
- The first time the constructor is called is when the word "object" is instantiated. val = 31 when the constructor is called and this call to the constructor changes its value to 15 (integer division).
- The second time the constructor is called is when the sentence object is instantiated. This time val = 15 when the constructor is called and this call to the constructor changes its value to 7 (integer division).

15. The answer is D.

- Options I and V are incorrect. An overloaded method must have a different parameter list so that the compiler knows which version to use.
- Options II, III, and IV are valid declarations for overloaded methods. They can all be distinguished by their parameter lists.

16. On the AP Computer Science A exam, you are often asked to write an entire class, like you were in this question. Check your answer against our version below. The comments are to help you read our solution. Your solution does not need comments.

> **Make Variable Names Meaningful**
>
> It's OK if you use different variable names from what we use in the solutions to the chapter questions. Just be sure that the names are meaningful.

```
public class DreamVacation
{
    // Here are the private instance variables (parts a and b).
    private String destination;
    private double cost;

    // Here is the no-argument constructor (part c).
    public DreamVacation()
    {
    }

    // Here is the parameterized constructor (part d).
    public DreamVacation(String myDestination, double myCost)
    {
        destination = myDestination;
        cost = myCost;
    }

    // Here are the two accessor methods (part e).
    // Their names contain the word "get" since it is standard practice.
    public String getDestination()
```

```
    {
        return destination;
    }

    public double getCost()
    {
        return cost;
    }

    // Here are the two modifier methods (part f).
    // Their names contain the word "set" since it is standard practice.
    public void setDestination(String myDestination)
    {
        destination = myDestination;
    }

    public void setCost(double myCost)
    {
        cost = myCost;
    }
}
```

17. The Height class

```
public class Height
{
    // Part a - remember to simplify when these variables are changed
    private int feet;
    private int inches;

    // Part b - overloaded constructors
    // notice the calls to simplify.
    public Height(int i)
    {
        inches = i;
        simplify();
    }

    public Height(int f, int i)
    {
        feet = f;
        inches = i;
        simplify();
    }

    // Part c - This method puts feet and inches in simplest form
    // see note below for an alternate solution
    public void simplify()
    {
        int totalInches = 12 * feet + inches;
        feet = totalInches / 12;
        inches = totalInches % 12;
    }

    // Parts d and e - overloaded add methods
    // Notice the call to the Height object len passed as a parameter
    public void add(Height ht)
    {
        feet += ht.getFeet();
        inches += ht.getInches();
        simplify();
```

```
    }
    public void add(int in)
    {
        inches += in;
        simplify();
    }

    //Part f - getters for the instance variables inches and feet
    public int getInches()
    {
        return inches;
    }
    public int getFeet()
    {
        return feet;
    }
}
```

Note: There are many ways to write the simplify method. If you aren't sure if yours works, type it into your IDE. Here's one alternate solution:

```
while (inches > 12)
{
    inches -= 12;
    feet++;
}
```

UNIT 6

Array

10-15% AP Exam Weight

IN THIS UNIT

Summary: Sometimes a variable is not enough. To solve certain problems, you need a list of variables or objects. The array, the two-dimensional array, and the `ArrayList` are three complex data structures that are tested on the AP Computer Science A Exam. `ArrayList` and 2D array will be discussed in Units 7 and 8. You must learn the advantages and disadvantages of each of these data structures, know how to work with them, and be able to choose the best one for the job at hand. Programmers use algorithms extensively to write the code that will automate a process in a computer program. The algorithms described in this unit are some of the fundamental algorithms that you should know for the AP Computer Science A Exam.

Learning Objectives

VAR-2.A Represent collections of related primitive or object reference data using one-dimensional (1D) array objects.

VAR-2.B Traverse the elements in a 1D array.

VAR-2.C Traverse the elements in a 1D array object using an enhanced for loop.

CON-2.I For algorithms in the context of a particular specification that requires the use of array traversals:

 Identify standard algorithms.

 Modify standard algorithms.

 Develop an algorithm.

Key Ideas

✪ An array is a data structure that can store a list of variables of the same data type.

✪ An array is not resizable once it is created.

✪ To traverse a data structure means to visit each element in the structure.

✪ The enhanced for loop (`for-each` loop) is a special looping structure that can be used by either arrays or `ArrayLists`.

❮ 215

✪ An algorithm is a set of steps that when followed complete a task.
✪ Pseudocode is a hybrid between an algorithm and actual Java code.
✪ Efficient code performs a task in the fastest way.
✪ The `accumulate` algorithm traverses a list, adding each value to a total.
✪ The `find-highest` algorithm traverses and compares each value in the list to determine which one is the largest.

What Is a Data Structure?

Have you ever dreamed about having the high score in the "Top Scores" of a game? How does Instagram keep track of your followers? How does YouTube know what video to loop next? All of these require the use of a complex data structure.

Simple Data Structure Versus Complex Data Structure

As programmers, we use **data structures** to store information. A primitive variable is an example of a **simple data structure** as it can store a single value to be retrieved later. A variable that can store a list of other variables is called a **complex data structure**.

Simple Data Structure
(can hold one thing)

String myGame
"Mario Kart"

Complex Data Structure
(can hold a list of things)

String[] myGames
"Mario Kart"
"Minecraft"
"Pokemon"
"Tetris"

Thinking of ways to represent physical objects by using virtual objects can be challenging. Really awesome programmers have the ability to visualize complex real-world situations and design data structures to represent these physical objects in a virtual way. In the drawing below, the programmer is trying to figure out a way to represent the choices from the lunch menu in a program by creating a complex data structure.

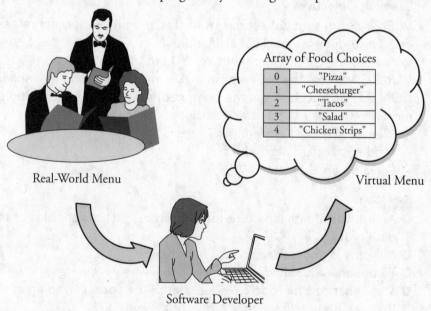

Real-World Menu

Array of Food Choices

0	"Pizza"
1	"Cheeseburger"
2	"Tacos"
3	"Salad"
4	"Chicken Strips"

Virtual Menu

Software Developer

Three Important Complex Data Structures

There are three complex data structures that are tested on the AP Computer Science A Exam:

- The array (or one-dimensional array)
- The 2D array
- The `ArrayList`

The array will be explained in detail later in this unit, `ArrayList` will be explained in Unit 7, and 2D array will be explained in Unit 8, but for now, I want to give you an overview of which data structure would be the best choice for a given situation. You will want to become a master at deciding the best data structure for a particular situation. This normally comes with experience, but here are a few examples as to which one is the best under what circumstances.

Situation	Recommendation	Justification
A program helps an elevator know what floor it is on.	Variable	The current floor the elevator is on should be stored in a variable.
Instagram keeps track of how many followers you have.	`ArrayList`	The number of followers you have on Instagram may increase or decrease. You are allowed to add or remove anyone at any time regardless of where they are in the list.
Your program is going to simulate chess, Candy Crush, or 2048.	2D Array	Each of these games can be simulated on either a square or rectangular grid in which the row and column are used to find out what is in each cell.
A cell phone keeps track of text messages.	`ArrayList`	The number of text messages on a cell phone can increase or decrease. You can even delete all of the messages.
A program keeps track of what classes you have each period of the school day.	Array	The number of class periods in the school day is fixed. Each period is assigned a value (1st hour is math, 2nd hour is science, etc.). You may potentially have a free period and want to represent the gap in your schedule.

The Array

Definition of an Array

The non-programming definition of an array is "an impressive display of a particular thing." We use the word in common language when we say things like, "Wow, look at the wide *array* of phone cases at the mall!" It means that there is a group or list of things that are of the same kind.

An **array** (**one-dimensional array**) in Java is a **complex data structure** because it can store a **list** of primitives or objects. It also stores them in such a way that each of the items in the list can be referenced by an **index**. This means that the array assigns a number to each of the slots that holds each of the values. By doing this, the programmer can easily find the value that is stored in a slot, change it, print it, and so on. The values in the array are called the **elements** of the array. An array can hold any data type, primitive or object.

Declaring an Array and Initializing It Using a Predefined List of Data

There are two common ways to create an array on the AP Computer Science A Exam. The first uses an initializer list. This technique is used when you already know the values that you are going to store in the list and you have no reason to add any more items. **A pair of brackets**, [ ], tells the compiler to create an array, not just a regular variable.

> **General Form for Creating an Array Using a Predefined List of Data**
>
> `dataType[] nameOfArray = {dataValue1, dataValue2, dataValue3, . . . };`
>
> Notice the pair of brackets [ ] after dataType. The brackets signify this variable is a reference to an array object.

Example

Declare an array of `String` variables that represent food choices at a restaurant:

```
String[] foodChoices = {"Pizza", "Cheeseburger", "Tacos", "Salad",
    "Chicken Strips"};
```

The graphic at the right is a visual representation of the foodChoices array. The strings representing the actual food choices are the **elements** in the array (Pizza, Cheeseburger, etc.) and each slot is assigned a number, called the **index** (0, 1, 2, etc.). The index is a number that makes it easy for the programmer to know what element is placed in what slot. The first index is always zero. The last index is always one less than the length of the array.

How to "Speak" Array

When talking about elements of an array, we say things like, "Pizza is the first element in the foodChoices array and its index is zero" or "The element at index 2 of the foodChoices array is Tacos."

The `length` Field

After an array is created and initialized, you can ask it how many slots it has by using the **length** field. Think of the length as an instance variable for an array. Notice that the length does not have a pair of parentheses after it, because it is not a method.

Example

Find the length of the foodChoices array:

```
int result = foodChoices.length;          // result is 5 (not 4!)
```

The `length` of an Array

The `length` field of an array returns the total number of slots that are set aside for that array. It does not return the total number of valid elements in the array. Also, since the first index of an array is always zero, the length of the array is always one more than the last index.

Declaring an Array Using the Keyword `new`

The second technique for creating an array is used when you know the length of the list, but you may not know all of the values that will go in the list. Again, a pair of **brackets**, [ ], is used to tell the compiler that you want to create an array, not just a regular variable.

General Form for Creating an Array Using the Keyword `new`

```
dataType[] nameOfArray = new dataType[numberOfSlots];

dataType nameOfArray [ ] = new dataType[numberOfSlots];
```

The number of slots is fixed and all of the elements in the array get the default value for the data type. You can also declare just an array reference variable and then use the keyword `new` to create the array later.

```
line 1:  dataType[] nameOfArray;                        // no array created
line 2:  nameOfArray = new dataType[numberOfSlots];     // array is created
```

No Resizing an Array

An array cannot be resized after it is created.

Example

Create an array that will represent all of your semester grade point averages for all four years of high school. Let's assume there are two semesters per year. This makes a total of eight semesters. So, let's declare an array to hold eight double values and call the array myGPAs.

```
double[] myGPAs = new double[8];
```

myGPAs	
0	0.0
1	0.0
2	0.0
3	0.0
4	0.0
5	0.0
6	0.0
7	0.0

Ouch, all zeros. That hurts. No worries, we can change that. You see, when an array is created in this manner, all of the elements become whatever the **default value** is for that data type. The default value for a double is 0.0, the default value for an `int` is 0, for `boolean` it is false, and for a reference type (including Strings) it is null.

myGPAs		
0	3.62	} freshman
1	0.0	
2	0.0	} sophomore
3	3.75	
4	0.0	} junior
5	0.0	
6	0.0	} senior
7	0.0	

Now that the array is created, let's put some valid numbers into it. In order to replace a value in an array, you need to know the correct index.

Let's let index 0 represent the first semester of your freshman year and let's suppose you earned a GPA of 3.62.

```
myGPAs[0] = 3.62;  // puts 3.62 in slot 0
```

And, let's suppose you earned a 3.75 for the second semester of your sophomore year.

```
myGPAs[3] = 3.75;  // puts 3.75 in slot 3
```

Smart, but Not So Smart

The computer has no idea that these numbers represent the GPAs for a student in school. As far as it's concerned, it is just storing a bunch of numbers in an array.

Example

Pick a random color from an array of color names:

```
String[] colors = {"Red","Orange","Yellow","Green","Blue","Indigo","Violet"};
String randomColor = colors[(int)(Math.random() * colors.length)];
System.out.println("My favorite color is " + randomColor);
```

OUTPUT

Blue   (Note: The color is chosen randomly and can be different for each run.)

The `ArrayIndexOutOfBoundsException`

The valid index values for an array are 0 through one less than the number of elements in the array, inclusive. If you ever accidently use an index that is too big (greater than or equal to the length of the array) or negative, you will get a run-time error called an **ArrayIndexOutOfBoundsException**.

Example

You declare an array of `Circle` objects and attempt to print the radius of the last circle. But you get an `ArrayIndexOutOfBoundsException` because your index is too large. Note: The length of the array is 6. The index of the last `Circle` object is 5. Then, write it the correct way:

```
Circle[] arr = new Circle[6];
double radius = arr[arr.length].getRadius();        // Run-time error
double result = arr[arr.length - 1].getRadius();     // Correct way
```

Common Error

A common error is to accidentally set the index of an array to be the length of the array. The first index of the array is zero, so the last index of the array is **length − 1**.

```
nameOfArray[nameOfArray.length - 1]    // Last element in an array
nameOfArray[nameOfArray.length]        // ArrayIndexOutOfBoundsException
```

Traversing an Array

To **traverse** an array means to move through each slot in the array, one at a time. The most common way to perform a **traversal** is to start with the first index and end with the last index. But that's not the only way. You could start with the last index and move toward the first. You also could do all of the even indices first and then all of the odds. You get what I'm saying? Traversing an array just means that you visit every element at every index in an array.

Print the Contents of an Array by Traversing It

Example

Print out the names of all your followers on Instagram using a `for` loop. By traversing the array from the first element to the last element, you can print each follower's name.

```
String[] instagramFollowers = {"Sierra", "Ciara", "Siarra", "Ciera"};
for (int i = 0; i < instagramFollowers.length; i++)
{
    System.out.println(instagramFollowers[i]);
}
```

```
OUTPUT
Sierra
Ciara
Siarra
Ciera
```

Off-by-One Error

This is a logic error that every programmer has committed at some point. It means that in a loop of some kind, your index is off by one number. You either went one index too high or one index too low. This will result in an `ArrayIndexOutOfBoundsException` being thrown.

The Enhanced `for` Loop (the `for-each` Loop)

The **enhanced for loop** (aka the **for-each loop**) can also be used to traverse an array. It does not work the same way as the standard `for` loop. The `for-each` loop always starts at the beginning of the array and ends with the last element in the array. As the name indicates, the `for-each` loop iterates through each of the elements in the array, and *for each* element, the temporary variable "takes on" its value. The temporary variable is only a copy of the actual value and any changes to the temporary variable are not reflected in the array.

An enhanced `for` loop is simpler to write than a standard `for` loop since you don't have to keep track of an index. The enhanced `for` loop is also less error-prone because Java automates the setup and processing of the loop control information so you will traverse every element without going out of bounds. However, the enhanced `for` loop cannot be used to move through an array in reverse order, it cannot assign elements to an array, and since it does not have an index, it can't track any position in the array.

General Form for the Enhanced for Loop (the for-each Loop)

```
dataType[] arrayName =  /* array filled in some way */

for (dataType temporaryVariable : arrayName)
{
    // instructions that use temporaryVariable
}
```

There is no loop control variable for the enhanced `for` loop (it is a **black box**). You only have access to the elements in the array, not the index. Also, the data type of the temporary variable **must** be the same as the data type of the array.

Traversing an Array Using the Enhanced `for` Loop

Example
Print out the names of all your followers on Instagram using a `for-each` loop. Note: `follower` is a temporary variable that is of the same data type as the data stored in the array.

```
String[] instagramFollowers = {"Jordan", "Jordin", "Jordyn"};
for (String follower : instagramFollowers)
{
    System.out.println(follower);
}
```

```
OUTPUT
Jordan
Jordin
Jordyn
```

Mistake When Printing the Contents of an Array

Beginning programmers make the mistake of trying to print the contents of an array by printing the array reference variable. The result that is printed appears to be *garbage*. This is because the reference variable only contains the address of where the array is; it does not store the elements of the array.

```
String[] instagramFollowers = {"Jordan", "Jordin", "Jordyn"};
System.out.println(instagramFollowers);  // Don't do this, it doesn't work
```

OUTPUT
```
@1765f32          // This code does not print the contents of the array
```

Note: The best way to print the contents of an array is to traverse the array using either a `for` loop or a `for-each` loop.

How We Use Algorithms

In our daily lives, we develop and use algorithms all the time without realizing that we are doing it. For example, suppose your grandma calls you because she wants to watch *The Crown* using the Nexflix app on her smart TV, but she can't figure out how to do it. You would respond to her by saying, "Hi, Grandma, well, the first thing you have to do is turn your TV on," then yada, yada, yada until finally you say, "Press play."

What you have just done is developed a process for how to solve a problem. Now, if she insists that you write the steps down on a notecard so she can follow it anytime she wants to, then, you will be writing the algorithm for "How to watch *The Crown* on grandma's smart TV."

What if Grandma wants to watch a different show on Netflix? As a programmer, we want to develop algorithms that can solve similar problems instead of a problem with specific parameters.

> Give a man a fish and he will eat for a day; teach a man to fish and he will eat for a lifetime.
> —Chinese proverb

Why Algorithms Are Important

The word **algorithm** can be simply defined as "a process to be followed to solve a problem." Computer programmers use algorithms to teach the computer how to automate a process.

The number of algorithms to learn is infinite, so rather than attempting to learn all possible algorithms, my goal is to teach you *how to write an algorithm*. This will be handy on the AP Computer Science A Exam when you have to either analyze or generate code to accomplish something you've never done before. The two algorithm concepts in this book teach you how to think like a programmer.

> Give developers a line of code and they will smile for a day; teach developers to write their own algorithms and they will smile for a lifetime.
> —Coding proverb

Algorithm Versus Pseudocode Versus Real Java Code

Algorithms are great as directions for how to do something; however, they can't be typed into a computer as a real Java program. The integrated development environment (IDE) needs to have the correct syntax so that the compiler can interpret your code properly. Can you imagine typing in the directions for Grandma as lines of code?

So, to solve this problem, programmers translate algorithms into **pseudocode**, which is a code-like language. This pseudocode is then translated into real code that the computer will understand.

Algorithm ⟶ **Pseudocode** ⟶ **Java code**

This process is really powerful because as programming languages change, the algorithms can stay the same. In the examples that follow, the code is written in Java, but it could've easily been written in C++, Python, etc.

> **Turning Your Ideas into Code**
> Pseudocode is an intermediary step when turning your ideas into code. It is code-like but does not use the syntax of any programming language.

The Swap Algorithm

Swapping is the concept of switching the values that are stored in two different variables. The ability to swap values is essential for sorting algorithms (explained in Unit 7). To complete a swap, you need to use a temporary variable to store one of the values.

> **Problem:** Swap the values inside two integer variables. For example, if a = 6 and b = 8, then make a = 8 and b = 6.

Algorithm:
Step 1: Let a = 6 and b = 8
Step 2: Create a temporary variable called c
Step 3: Assign c the value of a
Step 4: Assign a the value of b
Step 5: Assign b the value of c
Step 6: Now, the value of a is 8 and b is now 6

Pseudocode:
set a = 6
set b = 8
c = a
a = b
b = c

Java Code:

```
int a = 6;
int b = 8;
int c;
c = a;
a = b;
b = c;
```

The Copy Algorithm for the Array

Making a copy of an array means to create a brand-new object that is a duplicate of the original. This is different from creating a new array variable that references the original array. That was called making an alias. It is easy for new programmers to make the mistake of thinking that these two are the same.

> **Problem:** Suppose you have an array of integers. Make a new array object that is a copy of this array. The two arrays should contain the same exact values but not be the same object. In Unit 7 we will modify the code to work with an ArrayList of Integers.

Algorithm:
Step 1: Create an array that is the same length as the original
Step 2: Look at each of the values in the original array one at a time
Step 3: Assign the value in the copy to be the corresponding value in the original
Step 4: Continue until you reach the last index of the original array

Pseudocode:

Create an array called duplicate that has the same length as the original array
for (iterate through each element in the original array)
{
    set duplicate[index] = original[index]
}

Java Code 1: Java code using a for loop

```
int[] original = {23, 51, 14, 50};            // or any random numbers
int[] duplicate = new int[original.length]; // create duplicate array

for (int i = 0; i < original.length; i++)   // iterate through the original
{
    duplicate[i] = original[i];             // copy the values one at a time
}
```

Java Code 2: Java code using a for-each loop

```
int[] original = {23, 51, 14, 50};
int[] duplicate = new int[original.length];
int index = 0;                              // create an index for duplicate array

for (int temp : original)                   // temp is a copy of the actual object
{
    duplicate[index] = temp;                // for-each loop does not use an index
    index++;                                // update index for the duplicate array
}
```

Copying an Array Reference Versus Copying an Array

The following code demonstrates a common mistake when attempting to copy an array.

```
int[] original = {23, 51, 14, 50};
int[] copy = original;
```

This code makes the reference variable copy refer to the same object that original refers to. This means that if you change a value in copy, it also changes the value in the original. This code *does not create a new object* that is a duplicate of the original. This code makes both reference variables refer to the same object (the object that original refers to).

The Accumulate Algorithm

Suppose you have a list of all the baseball players on a team and you want to find the total number of hits that the team had. As humans, we can do this quite easily. Just add them up. But how do you teach a computer to add up all of the hits?

General Problem: Add up all of the hits for a baseball team.

Refined Problem: Write a method that finds the sum of all of the hits in an array of hits.

Final Problem: Write a method called findSum that has one parameter: an int array. The method should return the sum of all of the elements in the array. In Unit 7 we will modify the code to work with an ArrayList of Integer, and in Unit 8 we will modify the code to work with a 2D array of int values.

Algorithm:
Step 1: Create a variable called sum and set it equal to zero
Step 2: Look at each of the elements in the list
Step 3: Add the element to the sum
Step 4: Continue until you reach the end of the list
Step 5: Return the sum

Pseudocode:
set sum = zero
for (iterate through all the elements in the list)
{
    sum = sum + element
}
return sum

Java Code 1: Java code using a for loop

```java
public static int findSum(int[] arr)
{
    int sum = 0;
    for (int i = 0; i < arr.length; i++)
    {
        sum += arr[i];
    }
    return sum;
}
```

Java Code 2: Java code using a for-each loop

```java
public static int findSum(int[] arr)
{
    int sum = 0;                         // initializing the sum to 0
    for (int value : arr)                // for every int in arr
    {
        sum += value;                    // Add the element to the sum
    }
    return sum;                          // return the sum
}
```

The Find-Highest Algorithm

What is the highest score on your favorite video game? As more people play a game, how does the computer figure out what is the highest score in the list?

> **General Problem:** Find the highest score out of all the scores for a video game.
>
> **Refined Problem:** Write a method that finds the highest score in a list of scores.
>
> **Final Problem:** Write a method called findHigh that has one parameter: an `int` array. The method should return the largest value in the array. In Unit 7 we will modify the code to work with an `ArrayList` of `Integer`, and in Unit 8 we will modify the code to work with a 2D array of `int` values.

Solution 1: Let the highest be the first element in the list.

Algorithm:
Step 1: Create a variable called high and set it to the first element in the list
Step 2: Look at each of the scores in the list
Step 3: If the score is greater than the high score, then make it be the new high score
Step 4: Continue until you reach the end of the list
Step 5: Return the high score

Pseudocode:
set high = first score
for (iterate through all the scores in the list)
{
  if (score > high)
  {
    high = score
  }
}
return high

Java Code 1: Java code using a for loop

```java
public static int findHigh(int[] arr)
{
    int high = arr[0];                      // set high = first element
    for (int i = 1; i < arr.length; i++)    // start with the 2nd element
    {
        if (arr[i] > high)                  // if element is greater than
                                            // high
            high = arr[i];                  // set high equal to that
                                            // element
    }
    return high;                            // return the highest in the
                                            // array
}
```

Java Code 2: Java code using a for-each loop

```java
public static int findHigh(int[] arr)
{
    int high = arr[0];
    for (int value : arr)
    {
        if (value > high)
            high = value;
    }
    return high;
}
```

Solution 2: Let the highest be an extremely low value.

There is an alternative solution to the high/low problem that you should know. To execute this alternative, we modify the first step in the previous algorithm.

Step 1: Create a variable called high and set it to *a really, really small number*.

This algorithm works as long as the really, really small number is guaranteed to be smaller than at least one of the numbers in the list. In Java, we can use the public fields from the Integer class to solve this problem.

```
int high = Integer.MIN_VALUE;
```

Likewise, to solve the *find-lowest* problem, you could set the low to be a really, really big number.

```
int low = Integer.MAX_VALUE;
```

Searching for the Smallest Item in a List

If we changed the previous example to find the *lowest* score in the list, then the comparator in the `if` statement would be changed to less than, <, instead of greater than, >. Could you use >= or <=? Sure, it wouldn't change the highest or lowest value if there are duplicates in the list.

Initializing Highest Value to 0

It's not uncommon to initialize the variable used to store the highest value to 0. This, however, makes the assumption that there are no negative values. After the code is run, it is possible that your highest value may incorrectly still be 0.

› Rapid Review

The Array

- An array is a complex data structure that can store a list of data of the same data type.
- An array is also referred to as a one-dimensional (or 1D) array.
- An array can be created by assigning it a predetermined list.
- An array can be created by using the keyword new.
- An array can store either primitive data types or object reference types.
- Even though arrays are objects, they do not have methods.
- An array has one public field, called length.
- The length of the array refers to how many elements can be stored in the array and is decided when the array is created.
- The length of an array cannot be resized once it is declared. That is, an array cannot be made shorter or longer once it is created.
- The length field returns the total number of locations that exist in the array, and not the number of meaningful elements in the array.
- An element of an array refers to the item that is stored in the array.
- The index of an array refers to the position of an element in an array.
- The first index of an array is 0. The last index is its length − 1.
- Unused indices in an array automatically receive the default value for that data type.
- If an array contains objects, their default values are null. You need to instantiate an object for each element of the array before they can be used.
- Using an index that is not in the range of the array will throw an `ArrayIndexOutOfBoundsException`.

Traversing an Array

- Traversing an array refers to the process of visiting every element in the array.
- There are many options for traversing an array; however, the most common way is to start at the beginning and work toward the end.
- Based on the situation, there are times where you may want to traverse an array starting at the end and work toward the beginning.
- Sometimes you may want to traverse only a section of the array.
- When using a `for` loop to traverse an array, be sure to use length − 1 rather than length when accessing the last element in the array.
- The enhanced `for` loop iterates through each element in the array without using an index.
- The enhanced `for` loop is also known as the for-each loop.
- The enhanced `for` loop always starts with the first element and ends with the last.
- Use an enhanced `for` loop when you don't need to know the index for each element and you don't need to change the element in any way.

Algorithms and Pseudocode

- The purpose of this concept is to teach you how to translate an idea into code.
- An algorithm is a sequence of steps that, when followed, produces a specific result.
- Algorithms are an extremely important component of software development since you are teaching the computer how to do something all by itself.
- Pseudocode is a hybrid between an algorithm and real code.
- Pseudocode does not use correct syntax and is not typed into an IDE.
- Pseudocode helps you translate an algorithm into real code since it is code-like and more refined than an algorithm.
- Programmers translate algorithms into pseudocode and then translate pseudocode into real code.

Swap Algorithm

- The swap algorithm allows you to switch the values in two different variables.
- To swap the values in two different variables, you must create a temporary variable to store one of the original variables.

Copy Algorithm

- The copy algorithm is used to create a duplicate version of a data structure.
- It looks at each element in the original list and assigns it to the duplicate list.
- The duplicate is not an alias of the original; it is a new object that contains all of the same values as the original.

Accumulate Algorithm

- The accumulate algorithm finds the sum of all the items in a list.
- It looks at each element in the list one at a time, adding the value to a total.

Find-Highest Algorithm

- The find-highest algorithm finds the largest value in a list.
- It looks at each element in the list one at a time, comparing the value to the current high value.
- Common ways to implement this algorithm include initializing the highest value with the first value in the list or to an extremely small negative number.
- The find-highest algorithm can be modified to find the lowest item in a list.

› Review Questions

Basic Level

1. Consider the following code segment.

```
int number = 13;
int[] values = {0, 1, 2, 3, 4, 5};
for (int val : values)
{
    number += val;
}
System.out.println(number);
```

What is printed as a result of executing the code segment?

(A) 0
(B) 13
(C) 26
(D) 28
(E) 56

2. Consider the following code segment.

```
int total = 3;
int[] values = {8, 6, 4, -2};
total += values[total];
total += values[total];
System.out.println(total);
```

What is printed as a result of executing the code segment?

(A) 0
(B) 1
(C) 3
(D) 7
(E) 16

3. Consider the following code segment.

```
int[] values = {7, 9, 4, 1, 6, 3, 8, 5 };
for (int i = 3; i < values.length; i += 2)
{
    System.out.print(values[i - 2]);
}
```

What is printed as a result of executing the code segment?

(A) 91
(B) 746
(C) 913
(D) 79416385
(E) 416385

4. Which segment of code will correctly count the number of even elements in an array arr?

```
I.  int count = 0;
    for (int i = 0; i < arr.length; i++)
         if (i % 2 == 0)
             count++;

II. int count = 0;
    for (int i = 0; i < arr.length; i++)
        if (arr[i] % 2 == 0)
            count++;

III. int count = 0;
     for (int i = 0; i < arr.length; i+=2)
         if (arr[i] % 2 == 0)
             count++;
```

(A) I only
(B) II only
(C) III only
(D) I and II only
(E) II and III only

5. Consider the following code segment.

```
double [ ] arr = {9.05, 6.13, 4.20, 2.25, 7.28};
for (int i = arr.length - 1; i > 0; i--)
     arr[i] = arr[i - 1];

for (double element : arr)
     System.out.print(element + "  ");
```

What will be printed after the code segment is executed?

(A) 9.05 9.05 6.13 4.2 2.25
(B) 7.28 2.25 4.2 6.13 9.05
(C) 6.13 4.2 2.25 7.28 7.28
(D) 9.05 6.13 4.2 2.25 7.28
(E) Nothing will be printed. An `ArrayIndexOutOfBoundsException` will occur.

Advanced Level

6. Consider the following code segment.

```
int[] nums = {0, 0, 1, 1, 2, 2, 3, 3};
for (int i = 3; i < nums.length - 1; i++)
{
    nums[i + 1] = i;
}
```

What values are stored in array nums after executing the code segment?

(A) `ArrayIndexOutOfBoundsException`
(B) {2, 2, 3, 3, 4, 4, 5, 5}
(C) {0, 0, 1, 3, 5, 7, 9, 11}
(D) {0, 0, 1, 1, 3, 4, 5, 6}
(E) {0, 0, 1, 2, 2, 3, 4, 5}

7. A postcondition of a method is: arr[0] > arr[k] for all k such that 0 < k < arr.length. Which of the following is a correct conclusion?

    (A) All values in the array are identical.
    (B) The array elements are in ascending order.
    (C) The array elements are in descending order.
    (D) The smallest value in the array is arr[0].
    (E) The largest value in the array is arr[0].

8. Consider the following code segment intended to count the number of elements in array `fruits` that contain the letter "e".

```
int count = 0;
for (String element : fruits)
        <statement>
```

Which of the following substitutions for <statement> will cause the segment to work as intended?

```
(A) if (element.equals("e") > 0)
        count++;
(B) if (element.equals("e") >= 0)
        count++;
(C) if (element.indexOf("e") > 0)
        count++;
(D) if (element.indexOf("e") >= 0)
        count++;
(E) if (element.indexOf("e") < 0)
        count++;
```

9. Consider two parallel arrays which contain the names and corresponding scores of players in a trivia game.

```
String [] names = {"Rob", "Pam", "Sandy", "Kelly", "Kim", "J.P."};
int [] scores = {2600, 2420, 1790, 2100, 3100, 3250};
```

Which of the following code segments correctly prints the names and scores of all the players who scored above `high`?

```
(A) for(int element : scores)
        if (element > high)
          System.out.println(names + " " + element);
(B) for(int element : scores)
        if (element >= high)
          System.out.println(names + " " + element);
(C) for(int i = 0; i < scores.length; i++)
        if (scores[i] > high)
          System.out.println(names[i] + " " + scores[i]);
(D) for(int i = 0; i < scores.length; i++)
        if (scores[i] >= high)
          System.out.println(names[i] + " " + scores[i]);
(E) for(int i = 0; i <= scores.length; i++)
        if (scores[i] > high)
          System.out.println(names[i] + " " + scores[i]);
```

10. Count the number of occurrences.

Write a method that counts the number of values in an array that are between a lower bound and an upper bound. The method takes as parameters a double array, and two doubles representing lower and upper respectively. The method should return a count representing the number of elements in the array that are greater than or equal to the upper bound or less than or equal to the lower bound.

For example, if the lower bound is 250.0, the upper bound is 750.0, and the array passed to the method is:

634.5	521.8	786.6	899.0	509.1	235.4	750.0	806.8	142.5	645.3

The method should return the value 6.

```
//  precondition: lower <= upper

public int countBetween(double [ ] values, double lower, double upper)
{
    // Write the implementation
}
```

11. Determine the relative strength index of a stock.

The relative strength index (RSI) of a stock determines if the stock is overpriced or underpriced. The range of the RSI is from 0 to 100 (inclusive). If the value of the RSI is greater than or equal to 70, then the stock is determined to be overpriced and should be sold.

Write a method that takes an array of RSI values for a specific stock and determines when the stock is overpriced. The method has one parameter: a double array. The method should return a new array of the same length as the parameter array. If the value in the RSI array is greater than 70, set the value in the overpriced array to `true`. If the RSI value is less than or equal to 70, set the value in the overpriced array to `false`.

For example, if the RSI array passed to the method is:

55.6	63.2	68.1	70.1	72.4	73.9	71.5	68.3	67.1	66.2

The overpriced array that is returned by the method will be:

false	false	false	true	true	true	true	false	false	false

```
public boolean[] overpriced(double[] rsiValues)
{
    // Write the implementation
}
```

12. Fill an array with even numbers.

Write a method that fills an array with random even numbers. The method takes two parameters: the number of elements in the array and the range of the random numbers (0–number inclusive).

For example:

```
int[] result = onlyEvens(10, 100);  //result contains ten even #'s [0,100]
```

result contains the following (results will change each time program is run):

56	96	88	30	0	92	12	98	4	28

```
public static int[] onlyEvens(int arraySize, int range)
{
    // Write the implementation
}
```

› Answers and Explanations

Bullets mark each step in the process of arriving at the correct solution.

1. The answer is D.

   - This is a `for-each` loop. Read it like this: "For each int (which I will call val) in values. . . ."
   - The loop will go through each element of the array values and add it to number. Notice that number starts at 13.

     `13 + 0 + 1 + 2 + 3 + 4 + 5 = 28`

2. The answer is D.

   - values[total] = values[3] = -2. Remember to start counting at 0.
   - 3 + -2 = 1, now total = 1.
   - values [total] = values[1] = 6.
   - 1 + 6 = 7 and that is what is printed.

3. The answer is C.

   - Let's lay out the array along with its indices.

index	0	1	2	3	4	5	6	7
contents	7	9	4	1	6	3	8	5

   - The first time through the loop, i = 3.
     - values[3−2] = values [1] = 9 Print it.
   - Next time through the loop, i = 5.
     - values [5−2] = values [3] = 1 Print it.
   - Next time through the loop, i = 7.
     - Remember that even though the last index is 7, the length of the array is 8.
     - values [7−2] = values[5] = 3 Print it.
   - We exit the loop having printed "913".

4. The answer is B.

   - Segment I checks if the index of the element is even, not the element itself.
   - Segment II correctly checks if the element is even.
   - Segment III correctly checks if the element is even, but because the increment is +2, it doesn't check each element of the array.

5. The answer is A.

   - The loop will shift each of the elements to the right starting at the second to last element.

6. The answer is D.

   - On entering the loop, nums = {0, 0, 1, 1, 2, 2, 3, 3} and i = 3. Set nums[4] to 3.
   - Now nums = {0, 0, 1, 1, 3, 2, 3, 3} and i = 4. Set nums[5] to 4.
   - Now nums = {0, 0, 1, 1, 3, 4, 3, 3} and i = 5. Set nums[6] to 5.
   - Now nums = {0, 0, 1, 1, 3, 4, 5, 3} and i = 6. Set nums[7] to 6.
   - Now nums = {0, 0, 1, 1, 3, 4, 5, 6} and i = 7. nums.length − 1 = 7, so exit the loop.

7. The answer is E.

   - Since the condition arr[0] > arr[k] holds true for each element, element arr[0] must be the largest.

8. The answer is D.

- The indexOf method returns the index of the first occurrence of the string parameter.
- If the string parameter is not found the value −1 is returned.

9. The answer is C.

- Since we need to access the index of an element a standard for loop must be used, not a for-each loop.
- Only elements that are above high should be printed, so the inequality > must be used.

10. Count the number of occurrences.

Algorithm:
Step 1: Initialize a counter to 0
Step 2: Look at each value in the list
Step 3: If the value is less than or equal to lower, increment the counter
Step 4: If the value is greater than or equal to upper, increment the counter
Step 5: Continue until you reach the end of the list
Step 6: Return the counter

Pseudocode:
```
create and initialize a temporary counter variable
for (iterate through all the values in the array)
{
    if (value <= 250)
        add 1 to counter
    else if (value >= 750)
        add 1 to counter
}
return counter
```

Java code:
```java
public int countBetween(double [ ] values, double lower, double upper)
{
    int count = 0;
    for (double element : values)
    {
        if (element <= lower)
            count ++;
        else if (element >= upper)
            count ++;
    }
    return count;
}
```

11. Determine the relative strength index of a stock.

Algorithm:
Step 1: Create an array called temp that is the same length as the parameter array
Step 2: Look at each of the scores in the array
Step 3: If the score > 70, then set the corresponding element of the temp array to true; otherwise set it to false
Step 4: Continue until you reach the end of the list
Step 5: Return temp

Pseudocode:

create a boolean array called temp that is the same length as the parameter array
for (iterate through all the elements in the parameter array)
{
    if (parameter array[index] > 70)
    {
        temp[index] = true
    }
    else
    {
        temp[index] = false;
    }
}
return temp

Java code:

```java
public boolean[] overpriced(double[] rsiValues)
{
    boolean[] temp = new boolean[rsivalues.length];

    for (int i = 0; i < rsivalues.length; i++)
    {
        if (rsivalues[i] >= 70)
        {
            temp[i] = true;
        }
        else
        {
            temp[i] = false;
        }
    }
    return temp;
}
```

12. Fill an array with randomly chosen even numbers. There are several ways to do this. Here is one.

Algorithm:

Step 1: Create an array called temp that is the same length as the parameter array
Step 2: Loop as many times as the length of the parameter array
Step 3: Generate a random number in the appropriate range
Step 4: While the random number is not even, generate a random number in the appropriate range
Step 5: Put the random number in the array
Step 6: Continue until you complete the correct number of iterations
Step 7: Return temp

Pseudocode:

create an integer array called temp that is the same length as the parameter array
for (iterate as many times as the length of the parameter array)
{
    create a random number in the interval from 0 to parameter range
    while (the newly created random number is not even)
    {
        generate a new random value and assign it to the random number
    }
    temp[index] = random number
}
return temp

Java code:

```java
public int[] onlyEvens(int arraySize, int range)
{
    int[] evens = new int[arraySize];

    for (int i = 0; i < arraySize; i++)
    {
        int number = (int)(Math.random() * (range + 1));
        while (number % 2 != 0)                          // as long as the number is odd
        {
            number = (int)(Math.random() * (range + 1)); // generate a new number
        }
        evens[i] = number;                       // add the even number to the array of evens
    }
    return evens;
}
```

UNIT → 7

ArrayList

2.5-7.5% AP Exam Weight

IN THIS UNIT

Summary: In this unit we will discuss the `ArrayList`, along with some of the methods that are used to access and manipulate its elements. In addition to the array algorithms that were introduced in the previous unit (which can also be done with `ArrayLists`), we will look at searching and sorting algorithms that you need to know for the AP Computer Science A Exam.

Learning Objectives

VAR-2.D Represent collections of related object reference data using ArrayList objects.

VAR-2.E For ArrayList objects:
   a. Traverse using a for or while loop.
   b. Traverse using an enhanced for loop.

CON-2.J For algorithms in the context of a particular specification that requires the use of ArrayList traversals:

   Identify standard algorithms.

   Modify standard algorithms.

   Develop an algorithm.

CON-2.K Apply sequential/linear search algorithms to search for specific information in array or ArrayList objects.

CON-2.L Apply selection sort and insertion sort algorithms to sort the elements of array or ArrayList objects.

CON-2.M Compute statement execution counts and informal run-time comparison of sorting algorithms.

IOC-1.B Explain the risks to privacy from collecting and storing personal data on computer systems.

Key Ideas

✪ An `ArrayList` is a data structure that can store a list of objects from the same class.
✪ An `ArrayList` resizes itself as objects are added to and removed from the list.

- ✪ To traverse a data structure means to visit each element in the structure.
- ✪ The enhanced `for` loop (`for-each` loop) is a special looping structure that can be used by either arrays or `ArrayLists`.
- ✪ The sequential search algorithm finds a value in a list.
- ✪ The Insertion Sort, Selection Sort, and Merge Sort are sorting routines.

The `ArrayList`

Definition of an `ArrayList`

An `ArrayList` is a **complex data structure** that allows you to add or remove objects from a list, changing the size of the list automatically.

Declaring an `ArrayList` Object

An `ArrayList` is an object of the `ArrayList` class. Therefore, to create an `ArrayList`, you need to use the keyword `new` along with the constructor from the `ArrayList` class. You also need to know the data type of the objects that will be stored in the list. The `ArrayList` uses a pair of **angle brackets**, < and >, to enclose the class name of the objects it will store.

Using a raw `ArrayList` (without <>) allows the user to store a different data type in each position of the `ArrayList`, which is not typically done since Java 5.0 arrived in 2004. The `ArrayList <E>` notation is preferred over `ArrayList` because it allows the compiler to find errors that would otherwise be found at run-time. You might see some released AP Computer Science A Exam questions from previous years using this syntax.

General Form for Declaring an `ArrayList`

```
ArrayList <E> nameOfArrayList = new ArrayList<E>();
```
where the generic type E specifies the type of elements that will be stored in the `ArrayList`

The graphic that follows is a visual representation of what the `ArrayList` looks like in memory.

Example

Declare an `ArrayList` of `Circle` objects. Please note that the code refers back to the Circle class from Unit 5 and that the memory address is simulated.

```
ArrayList<Circle> myCircles = new ArrayList<Circle>();
```

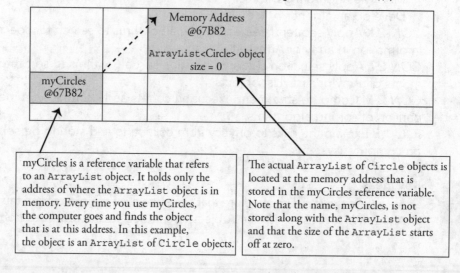

myCircles is a reference variable that refers to an `ArrayList` object. It holds only the address of where the `ArrayList` object is in memory. Every time you use myCircles, the computer goes and finds the object that is at this address. In this example, the object is an `ArrayList` of `Circle` objects.

The actual `ArrayList` of `Circle` objects is located at the memory address that is stored in the myCircles reference variable. Note that the name, myCircles, is not stored along with the `ArrayList` object and that the size of the `ArrayList` starts off at zero.

An `ArrayList` Always Starts Out Empty

When you create an `ArrayList` object, it is empty, meaning that there are no items in the list. It's like when your parent starts to make a "To Do" list and they write the words "To Do" on the top of a piece of paper. The list is created but there is nothing in the list.

Example

```
ArrayList <String> toDoList = new ArrayList <String> ();
// constructs an empty list
```

An `ArrayList` Is Resizable

When your parent writes, "Go grocery shopping" or "Buy awesome video game for favorite child" on their To "Do list", the size of the list grows. As they complete a task on the list, they cross it out and the size of the list shrinks. This is exactly how an `ArrayList` is resized.

> **Automatic Resizing**
>
> A useful feature of the `ArrayList` is its ability to resize itself as elements are added to or removed from the list. The `size()` method (explained later) immediately recalculates how many elements are in the list.

An `ArrayList` Requires an `import` Statement

The `ArrayList` is not part of the built-in Java language package, so you have to let the compiler know that you plan on creating an `ArrayList` by putting an import statement prior to the class declaration.

```
import java.util.ArrayList;
```

You will not see or need to write any import statements on the AP Computer Science A exam.

An `ArrayList` Can Only Store Objects

Unlike the array, which could store primitive variables like an `int` or `double`, as well as objects, like Strings, the `ArrayList` *can only store objects*. If you want to store an `int` or `double` in an `ArrayList`, you must use the `Integer` or `Double` wrapper classes. This is one of the reasons why the wrapper classes were created (refer back to Unit 2 when they were introduced).

Example

Create an `ArrayList` of `Integer` elements. Add an `int` to the `ArrayList` and watch as the `int` is automatically converted to an integer using a secret, Java black box technique called **autoboxing** (also introduced back in Unit 2). It is not necessary to create an `Integer` object to add to the `ArrayList`. Java will convert from an `int` to `Integer` or `Integer` to `int` without any additional code necessary.

```
ArrayList<Integer> myFavoriteIntegers = new ArrayList<Integer>();
int num = 45;
myFavoriteIntegers.add(num);          // The 45 is converted to an Integer
```

Important `ArrayList` Methods

The `ArrayList` class comes with a large array of methods (see my pun). These methods make it easy to work with the objects inside the `ArrayList`. The AP Computer Science A Exam does not require you to know all of the methods from the `ArrayList` class; however, it does require you to know several of them.

The `add` Method

There are two **add** methods for the ArrayList. The **add(E object)** method **appends** the object to the end of the list. It also returns the value true. Although it returns a value, nothing needs to be done with this value, and we can treat a call to add like it is a void method that returns nothing. The size of the `ArrayList` is automatically updated to reflect the addition of the new element.

> **What's with E?**
>
> The data type **E** is known as a **generic type**. It simply means that you can put any kind of data type here. I like to say, "The method takes **E**very kind of data type."

Example

Create an `ArrayList` of `Circle` objects. Add three `Circle` objects to the `ArrayList` where the first has a radius of 8, the second doesn't provide a radius so the radius gets the default value of 0, and finally, the last circle has a radius of 6.5. Note: This example will be used in the explanations for the other `ArrayList` methods.

```
ArrayList<Circle> myCircles = new ArrayList<Circle>();

line 1: myCircles.add(new Circle(8));
line 2: myCircles.add(new Circle());
line 3: myCircles.add(new Circle(6.5));
```

After line 1 is executed: There is one `Circle` object in the `ArrayList`.

index	myCircles
0	Circle with radius 8.0

← A `Circle` object is added to the `ArrayList`.

After line 2 is executed: There are two `Circle` objects in the `ArrayList`.

index	myCircles
0	Circle with radius 8.0
1	Circle with radius 0.0

After line 3 is executed: There are three `Circle` objects in the `ArrayList`.

index	myCircles
0	Circle with radius 8.0
1	Circle with radius 0.0
2	Circle with radius 6.5

Another add Method

The **add(int index, E object)** method inserts the object into the position `index` in the `ArrayList`, shifting the object that was previously at position `index` (and each of the objects after it) over one index. The index for each of the objects affected by the **add** is incremented. The method does not return a value.

An `ArrayList` Is Like the Lunch Line at School

An `ArrayList` can be visualized like the lunch line at school. Imagine there are 10 students in line and they are numbered 0 through 9. Person 0 is the first person in line.

Suppose the unthinkable happens and a student walks up and cuts the line. They have just inserted themselves into the list. If the *cutter* is now the third person in line, then they have just performed an add(2, "cutter"). This action impacts everyone who is in line *after* the cutter. The person who used to be in position 2, is now in position 3. The person who used to be at position 3 is now in position 4, and so on. The index for each person behind the cutter was *incremented by one*.

```
line 4:  myCircles.add(1, new Circle(4));
```

After line 4 is executed: The `Circle` object with a radius of 4 was inserted into the position with an index of 1 (the second position). All of the `Circle` objects after it had to move over one slot.

index	myCircles
0	Circle with radius 8.0
1	Circle with radius 4.0
2	Circle with radius 0.0
3	Circle with radius 6.5

The `add(index, object)` method inserts an object into the list at specific index. All objects after it move over to accommodate it.

The `size` Method

The **size()** method returns the number of elements in the `ArrayList`. Notice that this is different from the **length** field of the array, which tells you how many slots were set aside and not the actual number of valid items stored in the array.

```
line 5: int howManyCircles = myCircles.size();    // howManyCircles is 4
```

IndexOutOfBoundsException

As in the 1D array and the 2D array, you will get an error if you try to access objects outside of the range of the list. The error when doing this with an `ArrayList` is called the `IndexOutOfBoundsException`.

```
myCircles.add(88, new Circle());        //  IndexOutOfBoundsException
```

The index, 88, is not in the range of 0 ≤ index ≤ myCircle.size().

The remove Method

The **remove(int index)** method deletes the object from the list that is at position `index`. Each of the objects after this shifts down one index. The method also returns a reference to the object that was removed from the list.

```
line 6: Circle someCircle = myCircles.remove(2); // someCircle's radius is 0.0
```

After line 6 is executed: the `Circle` object that used to be in the slot at index 2 is removed (the circle with a radius of 0.0). The `Circle` objects that were positioned after it all move down one slot and someCircle now points to the `Circle` object that was removed.

index	myCircles
0	Circle with radius 8.0
1	Circle with radius 4.0
2	Circle with radius 6.5

The `remove(2)` method deleted the object that was at index 2. It returns a reference to the object that used to be at index 2.

The get Method

The **get(int index)** method returns the object that is located in the `ArrayList` at position `index`. It doesn't remove the object; it just returns a copy of the object reference. This way, an alias is created (more than one object reference pointing to the same object). The value of `index` must be greater than or equal to zero and less than the size of the `ArrayList`.

Example

Get the `Circle` object at index 2 and assign it to a different `Circle` reference variable:

```
line 7: Circle someCircle = myCircles.get(2);    // someCircle's radius is 6.5
```

The set Method

The **set(int index, E object)** method replaces the object in the `ArrayList` at position index with object. It returns a reference to the object that was previously at `index`.

Example

Replace the `Circle` object at index 0 with a new `Circle` object with a radius of 20:

```
line 8: Circle c = myCircles.set(0, new Circle(20)); // c's radius is 8.0
```

index	myCircles
0	Circle with radius 20.0
1	Circle with radius 4.0
2	Circle with radius 6.5

The `set(0, Circle(20))` call replaces the object at index 0. It returns a reference to the object that was previously at index 0.

You will receive a Java Quick Reference sheet to use on the Multiple-choice and Free-response sections which lists the `ArrayList` class methods that may be included on the exam. Make sure you are familiar with it *before* you take the exam.

length Versus size() Versus length()

To find the number of slots in an array, use the `length` field.
To find the number of objects in an `ArrayList`, use the `size()` method.
To find the number of characters in a string, use the `length()` method.

Traversing an `ArrayList` Using a for Loop

Traversing is a way of accessing each element in an array or `ArrayList` through the use of iteration. The following code uses a `for` loop to print the area of each of the `Circle` objects in the `ArrayList`. The `get` method is used to retrieve each `Circle` object and subsequently the `getArea` method is used on each of these `Circle` objects.

```
// print the area of each circle in the ArrayList using a for loop
for (int i = 0; i < myCircles.size(); i++)
{
    Circle temp = myCircles.get(i);
    System.out.println(temp.getArea());            // print each area
}
```

```
OUTPUT
1256.636
50.265
132.732
```

Traversing an `ArrayList` Using the Enhanced for Loop

The enhanced `for` loop (`for-each` loop) can be used with an `ArrayList`. The following code prints the area of each of the `Circle` objects in the `ArrayList`. Notice that the temporary variable, element, is the same data type as the objects in the `ArrayList`. In contrast to the general `for` loop shown above, the enhanced `for` loop does not use a loop control variable. Therefore, there is *no need for the get(i)* method since the variable element is a copy of each of the `Circle` objects, one at a time and the `getArea` method can be used directly with circle.

```
// print the area of each circle in the ArrayList using a for-each loop
for (Circle element : myCircles)
{
    System.out.println(element.getArea()); // no index used in for-each loop
}
```

```
OUTPUT
1256.636
50.265
132.732
```

Printing the Contents of an `ArrayList`

Unlike an array, the contents of an `ArrayList` can be displayed to the console by printing the reference variable. The contents are enclosed in brackets and separated by commas.

```
ArrayList<Double> myDoubles = new ArrayList<Double>();
myDoubles.add(23.5);
myDoubles.add(50.1);
myDoubles.add(7.5);
System.out.println(myDoubles);    // print the contents of the ArrayList
```

OUTPUT

`[23.5, 50.1, 7.5]`

Note: If you want to format the output when printing the contents of an `ArrayList`, you should traverse the `ArrayList`.

Do Not Use `remove()` in the Enhanced `for` Loop

Deleting elements during a traversal requires special techniques to avoid skipping elements. Never use the enhanced `for` loop (`for-each`) loop to remove an item from an `ArrayList`. You need the index to perform this process and the `for-each` loop doesn't use one.

If you have to perform a remove, use an index variable with a `while` loop. Increment the index to get to the next element in the `ArrayList`. But, if you perform a remove, then don't increment the index.

```
int index = 0;
while (index < myCircles.size())
{
    if (myCircles.get(index).getRadius() <= 0)
        myCircles.remove(index);      // remove any circle whose radius <= 0
    else
        index++;            // only increment index when not removing a circle
}
```

You can alternatively use a for loop if you increment the index only in the case where you have not removed an element. You can achieve this by decrementing the index when you remove the element so it will negate the increment of the variable update.

```
for(int i = 0; i < myCircles.size(); i++)
{
    if(myCircles.get(i).getRadius() <= 0)
    {
        myCircles.remove(i);
        i--;
    }
}
```

Avoid Run-time Exceptions

Since the indices for an `ArrayList` start at 0 and end at the number of elements - 1, accessing an index value outside of this range will result in an `ArrayIndexOutOfBoundsException` being thrown.

Changing the size of an `ArrayList` while traversing it using an enhanced `for` loop can result in a `ConcurrentModifcationException` being thrown. Therefore, when using an enhanced `for` loop to traverse an `ArrayList`, you should not add or remove elements.

 You will receive a Java Quick Reference sheet to use on the Multiple-choice and Free-response sections, which lists the `String` class methods that may be included in the exam. Make sure you are familiar with it <u>before</u> you take the exam.

ArrayList Class	
`int size()`	Returns the number of elements in the list
`boolean add(E obj)`	Appends `obj` to end of list; returns `true`
`void add(int index, E obj)`	Inserts `obj` at position `index`(0 <= `index` <= `size`), moving elements at position `index` and higher to the right (adds 1 to their indices) and adds 1 to size
`E get(int index)`	Returns the element at position `index` in the list
`E set(int index, E obj)`	Replaces the element at position `index` with `obj`; returns the element formerly at position `index`
`E remove(int index)`	Removes element from position `index`, moving elements at position `index` +1 and higher to the left (subtracts 1 from their indices) and subtracts 1 from size; returns the elements formerly at position `index`

array vs ArrayList

Both an array and an ArrayList hold collections of data, so you just have to choose which one you want to use in your code (it's great to have choices, am I right?). Both have some limitations. The size of an array needs to be established when declaring and cannot be changed, whereas an ArrayList grows and shrinks as needed. An ArrayList can only have elements that are objects (such as String, Circle, Integer) but an array can have either primitive (int, double, boolean) or objects. To add or remove elements from an ArrayList a method needs to be called, but with an array you have to write (in most cases) a loop to shift all of the elements to accommodate the change.

Here is a summary of the differences between an array and an ArrayList.

Task	array	ArrayList
Declaring	`int [] arr = new int[100];`	`ArrayList<Integer> list = new ArrayList <Integer>();`
Length needs to be defined when created?	yes	no
Type of elements	primitive or reference	reference (objects)
Number of elements	`arr.length`	`list.size()`
Size can change?	no	yes
Accessing an element	`int value = arr[5];`	`int value = list.get(5);`
Assigning an element	`arr[5] = 16;`	`list.add(5,16);` or `list.add(16);`
Change a value	`arr[5] = 21;`	`list.set(5,21);`
Remove an element	user must write code	`list.remove(3);`

Note: notice that there are only []s used in the array column and only ()s and <>s used in the ArrayList column.

The Accumulate Advanced Algorithm

You have been hired by the high school baseball team to write a program that calculates statistics for the players on the team. You decide to have a class called `BaseballPlayer`. Every `BaseballPlayer` has a name, a numberOfHits, and a numberOfAtBats. `BaseballRunner` has an array of `BaseballPlayer` objects called roster. Your goal is to find the team batting average.

```
public class BaseballPlayer
{
    private String name;
    private int hits;
    private int atBats;
    public BaseballPlayer(String name, int hits, int atBats)
    {
     this.name = name;
     this.hits = hits;
     this.atBats = atBats;
    }
    public String getName()
    {    return name;    }

    public int getHits()
    {    return hits;    }

    public int getAtBats()
    {    return atBats;    }

    public double getBattingAverage()
    {    return (double) atBats / hits;    }

    /*  Additional implementation not shown   */
}
```

General Problem: Given a roster of baseball players, find the team's batting average.

Refined Problem: You are given a list of baseball players. Every baseball player knows his number of hits and number of at-bats. The team average is found by first computing the sum of the at-bats and the sum of the hits and then dividing the total hits by the total at-bats. Write a method that computes the team batting average.

Final Problem: Write a method called `findTeamAverage` that has one parameter: a `BaseballPlayer` array. The method should return a double that is the team's batting average. Compute the team average by dividing the total hits by the total at-bats. Make sure a player exists before processing him. Also, perform a check against zero before computing the team average. If the team total at-bats is 0, return a team batting average of 0.0. Finally, adapt your algorithm to work with an `ArrayList` of `BaseballPlayer` objects.

Algorithm:

Step 1: Create a variable called totalHits and set it equal to 0
Step 2: Create a variable called totalAtBats and set it equal to 0
Step 3: Look at each player on the roster
Step 4: Get the number of hits for the player and add it to totalHits
Step 5: Get the number of atBats for the player and add it to totalAtBats
Step 6: Continue until you reach the end of the list
Step 7: Compute the teamBattingAverage by dividing the totalHits by the totalAtBats
Step 8: Return the teamBattingAverage

Pseudocode:

```
set totalHits = 0
set totalAtBats = 0
for (iterate through all the players in the roster)
{
        totalHits = totalHits + player's hits
        totalAtBats = totalAtBats + player's at-bats
}
if (totalAtBats = 0)
{
    return 0
}
else
{
    return totalHits / totalAtBats
}
```

Java Code 1: Java code using an `ArrayList` (for loop)

```java
public static double findTeamAverage(ArrayList<BaseballPlayer> arr)
{
    int totalHits = 0;
    int totalAtBats = 0;

    for (int i = 0; i < arr.size(); i++)
    {
      totalHits += arr.get(i).getHits();
      totalAtBats += arr.get(i).getAtBats();
    }

    if (totalAtBats == 0)
        return 0;
    else
        return (double)totalHits / totalAtBats;
}
```

Java Code 2: Java code using an `ArrayList` (for-each loop)

```java
public static double findTeamAverage(ArrayList<BaseballPlayer> arr)
{
    int totalHits = 0;
    int totalAtBats = 0;

    for (BaseballPlayer player : arr)
    {
        totalHits += player.getHits();
        totalAtBats += player.getAtBats();
    }

    if (totalAtBats == 0)
        return 0;
    else
        return (double)totalHits / totalAtBats;
}
```

```java
import java.util.ArrayList;
public class BaseballRunner
{
    public static void main(String[] args)
    {
ArrayList <BaseballPlayer> roster = new ArrayList <BaseballPlayer> ( );

        roster.add(new BaseballPlayer("Doug", 2, 4));
        roster.add(new BaseballPlayer("Sam", 3, 4));
        roster.add(new BaseballPlayer("Chase", 2, 4));
        roster.add(new BaseballPlayer("Brody", 3, 4));
        roster.add(new BaseballPlayer("Tom", 1, 3));
        roster.add(new BaseballPlayer("Triston", 2, 3));
        roster.add(new BaseballPlayer("Larry", 1, 3));
        roster.add(new BaseballPlayer("Charlie", 1, 3));
        roster.add(new BaseballPlayer("Chaser", 2, 3));

        System.out.println("Team average:  " + findTeamAverage(roster));
    }

    public static double findTeamAverage (ArrayList <BaseballPlayer> arr)
    {
        /* implementation is either Code 1 or Code 2 described above */
    }
}
```

```
OUTPUT
Team average:  0.5483870967741935
```

The Find-Highest Advanced Algorithm

General Problem: Given a roster of baseball players, find the name of the player that has the highest batting average.

Refined Problem: You are given a list of baseball players. Every baseball player has a name and knows how to calculate his batting average. Write a method that gets the batting average for every player in the list, and find the name of the player that has the highest batting average.

Final Problem: Write a method called findBestPlayer that has one parameter: a `BaseballPlayer` array. The method should return a string that is the name of the player that has the highest batting average. Make sure a player exists before processing him. If two players have the same high average, only select the first player. Also, adapt your algorithm to work with an ArrayList of BaseballPlayer objects.

Note: We will use the BaseballPlayer class from the previous example.

Algorithm:

Step 1: Create a variable called highestAverage and assign it a really small number

Step 2: Create a variable called bestPlayer and assign it the empty string

Step 3: Look at each of the players in the roster

Step 4: If the batting average of the player is greater than highestAverage, then set the highestAverage to be that player's average and set bestPlayer to be the name of the player

Step 5: Continue until you reach the end of the list

Step 6: Return the name of bestPlayer

Pseudocode:

```
set highestAverage = the smallest available number in Java
set bestPlayer = ""
for (iterate through all the players in the list)
{
    if (current player's batting average > highestAverage)
    {
        set highestAverage = current player's batting average
        set bestPlayer = name of current player
    }
}
return bestPlayer
```

Java Code 1: Returning one player with highest score

```java
public static String findBestPlayer(ArrayList <BaseballPlayer>
players)
{
  double highestAverage = Integer.MIN_VALUE;
  double battingAverage;
  String bestPlayer = "";
  for (BaseballPlayer player : players)
  {
      battingAverage = player.getBattingAverage();
      if (battingAverage > highestAverage)
      {
          highestAverage = battingAverage;
          bestPlayer = player.getName();
      }

  }
  return bestPlayer;
}
```

Java Code 2: Returns each player with highest score

```java
public static String findBestPlayer(ArrayList <BaseballPlayer> players)
{
  double highestAverage = Integer.MIN_VALUE;
  double battingAverage;
  String bestPlayer = "";
  for (BaseballPlayer player : players)
  {
      battingAverage = player.getBattingAverage();
      if (battingAverage > highestAverage)
      {
          highestAverage = battingAverage;
      }
  }
  for (BaseballPlayer player : players)
  {
      battingAverage = player.getBattingAverage();
      if (battingAverage == highestAverage)
      {
          bestPlayer += player.getName() + " ";
      }
  }
  return bestPlayer;
}
```

Example: Runner Program

```java
import java.util.ArrayList;
public class BaseballRunner
{
    public static void main(String[] args)
    {
        ArrayList <BaseballPlayer> roster = new ArrayList <BaseballPlayer> ( );

        roster.add(new BaseballPlayer("Doug", 2, 4));
        roster.add(new BaseballPlayer("Sam", 3, 4));
        roster.add(new BaseballPlayer("Chase", 2, 4));
        roster.add(new BaseballPlayer("Brody", 3, 4));
        roster.add(new BaseballPlayer("Tom", 1, 3));
        roster.add(new BaseballPlayer("Triston", 2, 3));
        roster.add(new BaseballPlayer("Larry", 1, 3));
        roster.add(new BaseballPlayer("Charlie", 1, 3));
        roster.add(new BaseballPlayer("Chaser", 2, 3));

        System.out.println("Best Player:  " + findBestPlayer(roster));
    }

public static String findBestPlayer(ArrayList <BaseballPlayer> players)
    {
        /* implementation is either Code 1 or Code 2 described above  */
    }
}
```

```
OUTPUT Code 1
Best Player: Sam

OUTPUT Code 2
Best Player: Sam   Brody
```

The X-Sentiment-Analysis Advanced Algorithm

X (formerly known as Twitter) is very popular and X Sentiment Analysis has grown in popularity. The idea behind X Sentiment is to pull emotions and/or draw conclusions from the posts. A large collection of posts can be used to make general conclusions of how people feel about something. The important words in the post are analyzed against a library of words to give a post a sentiment score.

One of the first steps in processing a post is to remove all of the words that don't add any real value to the post. These words are called **stop words,** and this step is typically part of a phase called **preprocessing**. For this problem, your job is to remove all the stop words from the post. There are many different ways to find meaningless words, but for our example, the stop words will be all words that are three characters long or less.

General Problem: Given a post, remove all of the meaningless words.

Refined Problem: You are given a post as a list of words. Find all of the words in the list that are greater than three characters and add them to a new list. Leave the original post unchanged. The new list will contain all the words that are not stop words.

Final Problem: Write a method called `removeStopWords` that has one parameter: an `ArrayList` of Strings. The method should return a new `ArrayList` of Strings that contains only the words from the original list that are greater than three characters long. Do not modify the original `ArrayList`. Also, modify the code to work on a `String` array.

Solution 1: Using an `ArrayList`

Algorithm 1:
Step 1: Create a list called longWords
Step 2: Look at each word in the original list
Step 3: If the word is greater than three characters, add that word to longWords
Step 4: Continue until you reach the end of the original list
Step 5: Return longWords

Pseudocode 1:
create a list called longWords
for (every word in the original list)
{
    if (word length > 3)
    {
        add the word to longWords
    }
}
return longWords

Java Code 1: Using an `ArrayList` (`for-each` loop)

```java
public static ArrayList<String> removeStopWords(ArrayList<String> words)
{
    ArrayList<String> longWords = new ArrayList<String>();
    for (String word : words)
    {
        if (word.length() > 3)
        {
            longWords.add(word);
        }
    }
    return longWords;
}
```

Solution 2: Using an Array

This solution requires more work than the `ArrayList` solution. Since we don't know how big to make the array, we need to count how many words are greater than three characters before creating it.

Algorithm 2:

Step 1: Create a counter and set it to zero
Step 2: Look at each word in the original list
Step 3: If the length of the word is greater than three characters, add one to the counter
Step 4: Continue until you reach the end of the list
Step 5: Create an array called longWords that has a length of counter
Step 6: Create a variable that will be used as an index for longWords and set it to zero
Step 7: Look at each word in the original list
Step 8: If the length of the word is greater than three characters, add the word to longWords
        and also add one to the index that is used for longWords
Step 9: Continue until you reach the end of the list
Step 10: Return the longWords array

Pseudocode 2:

```
set counter = 0
for (iterate through every word in the original list)
{
    if (word length > 3)
    {
        counter = counter + 1
    }
}
create an array called longWords whose length is the same as counter
set index = 0
for (iterate through every word in the original list)
{
    if (word length > 3)
    {
        add the word to longWords using index
        set index = index + 1
    }
}
return longWords
```

Java Code 2: Using an array (using a `for-each` loop and a `for` loop)

```java
public static String[] removeStopWords(String[] words)
{
    int count = 0;
    for (String word : words)
    {
        if (word.length() > 3)
        {
            count++;
        }
    }
    String[] longWords = new String[count];
    index = 0;
    for (int i = 0; i < words.length; i++)
    {
        if (words[i].length() > 3)
        {
            longWords[index] = words[i];
            index++;
        }
    }
    return longWords;
}
```

Example

Using an `ArrayList`:

```java
public class PostSentimentRunner
{
    public static void main(String[] args)
    {
        ArrayList<String> post = new ArrayList<String>();

        post.add("If");
        post.add("only");
        post.add("Bradley's");
        post.add("arm");
        post.add("was");
        post.add("longer");
        post.add("best");
        post.add("photo");
        post.add("ever");

        ArrayList<String> processedPost = removeStopWords(post);

        System.out.println(processedPost);        // print the ArrayList
    }

    public static ArrayList<String> removeStopWords(ArrayList<String> arr)
    {
        /*  implementation is described above Java code 1 */
    }
}
```

```
OUTPUT
[only, Bradley's, longer, best, photo, ever]
```

The Sequential (or Linear) Search Algorithm

When you search Spotify for a song, how does it actually find what you are looking for? It may use a sequential search to find the name of a song. A **sequential (or linear) search** is the process of looking at each of the elements in a list, one at a time, until you find what you are looking for. Sequential (or linear) search is one standard algorithm for searching. Another search algorithm, the binary search, will be discussed in Unit 10.

General Problem: Search for "Sweet Melissa" in a list of song titles.

Refined Problem: Write a method that allows you to search an array of song titles for a specific song title.

Final Problem: Write a method called searchForTitle that has two parameters: a string array and a string that represents the search target. The method should return the index of the target string if it is found and -1 if it does not find the target string. Note: Two solutions are provided to solve this problem and their efficiencies are compared afterward.

The Search Target

When you search for a specific item in a list, the item you are looking for is often referred to as the search target. If the target is not found, a value of -1 is often returned.

Solution 1: Look at every item in the list.

Algorithm 1:
Step 1: Create a variable called foundIndex and set it equal to -1
Step 2: Look at each of the titles in the array one at a time
Step 3: Compare each title to the target title
Step 4: If the title is equal to the target title, then assign foundIndex to value of the current index
Step 5: Continue looking until you reach the end of the list
Step 6: Return the value of foundIndex

Pseudocode 1:
```
set foundIndex = -1
for (iterate through every element in the list)
{
  if (title = target title)
  {
    set foundIndex = current index
  }
}
return the value of foundIndex
```

Java Code

```java
public static int searchForTitle(ArrayList <String> titles, String target)
{
    int foundIndex = -1;
    for (int i = 0; i < titles.size(); i++)
    {
        if (titles.get(i).equals(target))
        {
            foundIndex = i;                      // remember this index
        }
    }
    return foundIndex;                           // returns the foundIndex
}
```

Did you notice that the example used a for loop? That was intentional. Remember, if you need to access the index of an element in an array or `ArrayList`, then a for-each loop cannot be used.

Solution 2: Stop looking if you find the search target.

Algorithm 2:
Step 1: Look at each of the titles in the array one at a time
Step 2: Compare the target title to each of the titles
Step 3: If the title is equal to the target title, then stop looking and return the current index
Step 4: Continue looking until you reach the end of the list
Step 5: Return -1

Pseudocode 2:
index = 0
while (not at the end of the list)
{
  if (title = target title)
  {
    return index
  }
  index++
}
return -1

Java Code

```
public static int searchForTitle(ArrayList <String> titles, String target)
{
    int index = 0;
    while (index < titles.size())
    {
        if (titles.get(index).equals(target))
        {
            return index;              // target was found
        }
        index ++;                      // target was not found yet
    }
    return -1;  // after searching entire list, the target was not found
}
```

Efficiency

Analyze the two solutions that searched for the title of a song.

The second algorithm is *more efficient* than the first because the method stops looking for the title as soon as it finds it. The first algorithm is *less efficient* than the second because it continues to compare each of the titles in the list against the search target even though it may have already found the search target.

Efficiency

An efficient algorithm does its job in the fastest way it can. Efficient programs are optimized to reduce CPU (central processing unit) time and memory usage.

Sorting Data

The idea of sorting is quite easy for humans to understand. In contrast, teaching a computer to sort items all by itself can be a challenge. Through the years, hundreds of sorting algorithms have been developed, and they have all been critiqued for their efficiency and memory usage. The AP Computer Science A Exam expects you to be able to read and analyze code that uses three basic sorts: the Insertion Sort, the Selection Sort, and the Merge Sort (to be discussed in Unit 10).

The most important thing to remember is different sorting algorithms are good for different things. Some are easy to code, some use the CPU efficiently, some use memory efficiently, some are good at adding an element to a pre-sorted list, some don't care whether the list is pre-sorted or not, and so on. Of our three algorithms, Merge Sort is the fastest, but it uses the most memory.

The Swap Algorithm

Recall the swapping algorithm that you learned in Unit 6: Array. It is used in some of the sorting algorithms in this concept.

Sorting Algorithms on the AP Computer Science A Exam

You will not have to write the full code for any of the sorting routines described in this unit in the Free-Response Section. You should, however, understand how each works because they might appear in the Multiple-Choice Section and it would be advantageous to quickly identify the sorting algorithm based on the given code.

Insertion Sort

The **Insertion Sort** algorithm is similar to the natural way that people sort a list of numbers if they are given the numbers one at a time. For example, if you gave a person a series of number cards one at a time, the person could easily sort the numbers "on the fly" by inserting the card where it belonged as soon as the card was received. Insertion Sort is considered to be a relatively simple sort and works best on very small data sets.

To write the code that can automate this process on a list of numbers requires an algorithm that does a lot of comparing. Let's do an example of how Insertion Sort sorts a list of numbers from smallest to largest.

Insertion Sort	1st number	2nd number	3rd number	4th number	5th number	6th number
Original list	67	23	12	54	35	18
After 1st pass	23	67	12	54	35	18
After 2nd pass	12	23	67	54	35	18
After 3rd pass	12	23	54	67	35	18
After 4th pass	12	23	35	54	67	18
After 5th pass	12	18	23	35	54	67

This algorithm uses a temporary variable that we will call temp. The first step is to put the number that is in the second position into the temporary variable (temp). Compare temp with the number in the first position. If temp is less than the number in the first position, then move the number that is in the first position to the second position and put temp in the first position. Now, the first pass is completed and the first two numbers are sorted from smallest to largest.

Next, put the number in the third position in temp. Compare temp to the number in the second position in the list. If temp is less than the second number, move the second number into the third position and compare temp to the number in the first position. If temp is less than the number in the first position, move the number in the first position to the second position, and move temp to the first position. Now, the second pass is completed and the first three numbers in the list are sorted. Continue this process until the last number is compared against all of the other numbers and inserted where it belongs.

Making a Pass

A **pass** in programming is one iteration of a process. Each of these sorts makes a series of passes before it completes the sort. An efficient algorithm uses the smallest number of passes that it can.

Implementation

The following class contains a method that sorts an array of integers from smallest to greatest using the Insertion Sort algorithm. Note, an `ArrayList` could have also been used. Also important to note is that any type could be stored in an array/ArrayList. The examples that follow use the int type.

```
public class InsertionSort
{
    public static void main(String[] args)
    {
        int[] myArray = {67, 23, 12, 54, 35, 18};
        insertionSort(myArray);
        for (int i : myArray)
        {
            System.out.print(i + "\t");
        }
    }


    /**
     * This method sorts an int array using Insertion Sort.
     *
     * @param element the array containing the items to be sorted
     *
     * Postcondition:  arr contains the original elements and
     *                 elements are sorted in ascending order
     */
    public static void insertionSort(int[] arr)
    {
        for (int j = 1; j < arr.length; j++)
        {
            int temp = arr[j];
            int index = j;
            while (index > 0 && temp < arr[index - 1])
            {
                arr[index] = arr[index - 1];
                index--;
            }
            arr[index] = temp;
        }
    }
}
```

```
OUTPUT
12    18    23    35    54    67
```

Selection Sort

The **Selection Sort** algorithm forms a sorted list by repeatedly finding and selecting the smallest item in a list and putting it in its proper place.

Selection Sort	1st number	2nd number	3rd number	4th number	5th number	6th number
Original list	67	23	12	54	35	18
After 1st pass	12	23	67	54	35	18
After 2nd pass	12	18	67	54	35	23
After 3rd pass	12	18	23	54	35	67
After 4th pass	12	18	23	35	54	67
After 5th pass	12	18	23	35	54	67
After 6th pass	12	18	23	35	54	67

To sort a list of numbers from smallest to largest using Selection Sort, search the entire list for the smallest item, select it, and swap it with the first item in the list (the two numbers change positions). This completes the first pass. Next, search for the smallest item in the remaining list (not including the first item), select it, and swap it with the item in the second position. This completes the second pass. Then, search for the smallest item in the remaining list (not including the first or second items), select it, and swap it with the item in the third position. Repeat this process until the last item in the list becomes (automatically) the largest item in the list.

Implementation

The following class contains a method that sorts an array of integers from smallest to greatest using the Selection Sort algorithm. Note, an `ArrayList` could have also been used. Also important to note when applying a sort, any Comparable type could be stored in an array/ArrayList. The examples that follow use the int type.

```
public class SelectionSort
{
    public static void main(String[] args)
    {
        int[] myArray = {67, 23, 12, 54, 35, 18};
        selectionSort(myArray);
        for (int i : myArray)
        {
            System.out.print(i + "\t");
        }
    }
    /**
      * This method sorts an int array using Selection Sort.
      *
      * @param arr   the array to be sorted
      *
      * Postcondition:  arr contains the original elements and
      *                 elements are sorted in ascending order
      */
    public static void selectionSort(int[] arr)
    {
        for (int j = 0; j < arr.length - 1; j++)
        {
            int index = j; // index of smallest element
            for (int k = j + 1; k < arr.length; k++)
            {
                if (arr[k] < arr[index]) // current element is smaller
                index = k;                    // the new smallest index

            }

          // swap the two elements
          int temp = arr[j];
          arr[j] = arr[index];
          arr[index] = temp;
        }
    }
}
```

```
OUTPUT
12    18    23    35    54    67
```

› Rapid Review

The ArrayList

- The ArrayList is a complex data structure that can store a list of objects.
- The two general forms for declaring an ArrayList are:
  ```
  ArrayList <ClassName> generic = new ArrayList <ClassName> ( );
  ArrayList raw = new ArrayList ( );
  ```
- An ArrayList can only hold a list of objects; it cannot hold a list of primitive data.
- Use the Integer or Double classes to make an ArrayList of int or double values.

- The initial size of an `ArrayList` is 0.
- The `add(E object)` method appends the object to the end of the `ArrayList`. It also returns true.
- To append means to add on to the end of a list.
- The `add(int index, E object)` method inserts object at position index (Note: index must be in the interval: [0,size]). As a result of this insertion, the elements at position index and higher move 1 index farther from the 0 index.
- The `get(int index)` method returns a reference to the object that is at index.
- The `set(int index, E object)` method replaces the element at position index with object and returns the element that was formerly at index.
- The `remove(int index)` method removes the element at position index, and subsequently subtracts one from the indices of the elements at positions index + 1 and greater. It also returns the element that was removed.
- The `size()` method returns an int that represents the number of elements that are currently in the `ArrayList`.
- The size of the `ArrayList` grows and shrinks by either adding or removing elements.
- The `size()` method adjusts accordingly as elements are added or removed.
- Using an index that is not in the range of the `ArrayList` will throw an `IndexOutOfBoundsException`.
- The `ArrayList` requires an import statement since it is not in the standard library, but this will never be required on the AP Computer Science A exam.

Traversing an `ArrayList`

- To traverse an `ArrayList` means to visit each of the elements in the list.
- There are many ways to traverse an `ArrayList`, but the most common way is to start at the beginning and work toward the end.
- If a `for` loop is used to traverse an `ArrayList`, then the `get()` method will be required to gain access to each of the elements in the `ArrayList`.
- If an enhanced `for` loop is used to traverse an `ArrayList`, then the `get()` method is not required to gain access to each of the elements in the `ArrayList`, since each object is automatically retrieved by the loop, one at a time.
- If you need to remove elements from an `ArrayList`, you may consider starting at the end of the list and working toward the beginning.

Sequential (or Linear) Search Algorithm

- The sequential search algorithm searches a list to find a search target.
- It looks at each element in the list one at a time comparing the element to the search target.
- If the element is found, the index is returned.
- If the element is not found, -1 is usually returned.

Insertion Sort

- Insertion Sort uses an algorithm that repeatedly compares the next number in the list to the previously sorted numbers in the list and inserts it where it belongs.

Selection Sort

- Selection Sort uses an algorithm that repeatedly selects the smallest number in a list and swaps it with the current element in the list.

» Review Questions

Basic Level

1. Assume that cities is an `ArrayList<String>` that has been correctly constructed and populated with the following items.

   ```
   ["Oakland", "Chicago", "Milwaukee", "Seattle", "Denver", "Boston"]
   ```

   Consider the following code segment.

   ```
   cities.remove(2);
   cities.add("Detroit");
   cities.remove(4);
   cities.add("Cleveland");
   ```

   What items does `cities` contain after executing the code segment?

   (A) `["Cleveland", "Detroit", "Oakland", "Chicago", "Seattle", "Denver", "Boston"]`
   (B) `["Oakland", "Milwaukee", "Seattle", "Boston", "Detroit", "Cleveland"]`
   (C) `["Oakland", "Chicago", "Seattle", "Boston", "Detroit", "Cleveland"]`
   (D) `["Oakland", "Milwaukee", "Denver", "Boston", "Detroit", "Cleveland"]`
   (E) `["Oakland", "Chicago", "Seattle", "Denver", "Detroit", "Cleveland"]`

2. Consider the following code segment.

   ```
   ArrayList<String> subjects = new ArrayList<String>();
   subjects.add("French");
   subjects.add("History");
   subjects.set(1, "English");
   subjects.add("Art");
   subjects.remove(1);
   subjects.set(2, "Math");
   subjects.add("Biology");
   System.out.println(subjects);
   ```

   What is printed as a result of executing the code segment?

   (A) `[French, English, Math, Biology]`
   (B) `[French, Art, Biology]`
   (C) `[French, English, Art, Math, Biology]`
   (D) `[French, Math, Biology]`
   (E) `IndexOutOfBoundsException`

Questions 3-6 refer to the following information.

Array `arr` has been defined and initialized as follows

```
int[] arr = {5, 3, 8, 1, 6, 4, 2, 7};
```

3. Which of the following shows the elements of the array in the correct order after the first pass through the outer loop of the Insertion Sort algorithm?

   (A) 1 5 3 8 6 4 2 7
   (B) 1 3 8 5 6 4 2 7
   (C) 5 3 7 1 6 4 2 8
   (D) 3 5 8 1 6 4 2 7
   (E) 1 2 3 4 5 6 7 8

4. Which of the following shows the elements of the array in the correct order after the fourth pass through the outer loop of the Insertion Sort algorithm?

(A) 1 3 5 6 8 4 2 7
(B) 1 2 3 4 6 5 8 7
(C) 1 2 3 4 5 6 7 8
(D) 3 5 8 1 6 4 2 7
(E) 1 2 3 4 5 6 8 7

5. Which of the following shows the elements of the array in the correct order after the first pass through the outer loop of the Selection Sort algorithm?

(A) 1 2 3 5 6 4 8 7
(B) 1 3 8 5 6 4 2 7
(C) 1 3 5 8 6 4 2 7
(D) 1 5 3 8 6 4 2 7
(E) 5 3 1 6 4 2 7 8

6. Which of the following shows the elements of the array in the correct order after the fourth pass through the outer loop of the Selection Sort algorithm?

(A) 3 1 4 2 5 6 7 8
(B) 3 1 4 2 5 8 6 7
(C) 1 2 3 4 5 6 7 8
(D) 1 2 3 4 5 8 6 7
(E) 1 2 3 4 6 5 8 7

Advanced Level

7. Consider the following code segment.

```
int total = 3;
ArrayList<Integer> integerList = new ArrayList<Integer>();
for (int k = 7; k < 11; k++)
{
    integerList.add(k + 3);
}
for (Integer i : integerList)
{
    total += i;
    if (total % 2 == 1)
    {
        total -= 1;
    }
}
System.out.println(total);
```

What is printed as a result of executing the code segment?

(A) 34
(B) 37
(C) 46
(D) 47
(E) 49

8. Assume that `msg` is an `ArrayList<String>` that has been correctly constructed and populated with the following items.

```
["can", "i", "delete", "words", "starting", "with", "letters",
        "between", "n", "and", "z"]
```

Which code segment removes all `String` objects starting with a letter from the second half of the alphabet (n–z) from the `ArrayList`?

　　Precondition: all `String` objects will be lowercase

　　Postcondition: msg will contain only `String` objects from the first half of the alphabet (a–m)

I.
```
for (int i = 0; i < msg.size(); i++)
{
    if (msg.get(i).compareTo("n") >= 0)
    {
        msg.remove(i);
    }
}
```

II.
```
for (int i = msg.size() - 1; i >= 0; i--)
{
    if (msg.get(i).compareTo("n") >= 0)
    {
        msg.remove(i);
    }
}
```

III.
```
int i = 0;
while (i < msg.size())
{
    if (msg.get(i).compareTo("n") >= 0)
    {
        msg.remove(i);
    }
    else
    {
        i++;
    }
}
```

(A) I only

(B) I and II only

(C) II and III only

(D) I and III only

(E) I, II, and III

9. Consider the following code segment that implements the Insertion Sort algorithm.

```
public void insertionSort(int[] arr)
{
    for (int i = 1; i < arr.length; i++)
    {
        int key = arr[i];
        int j = i - 1;
        while (j >= 0 && /* condition */)
        {
            arr[j + 1] = arr[j];
            j--;
        }
        arr[j + 1] = key;
    }
}
```

Which of the following can be used to replace /* condition */ so that insertionSort will work as intended?

(A) arr[i] > key

(B) arr[j] > key

(C) arr[i + 1] > key

(D) arr[j + 1] > key

(E) arr[i - 1] > key

10. Determine if the numbers in an ArrayList are always increasing.

Write a method that determines if the values in an ArrayList are always increasing. The method takes one parameter: an ArrayList of Integer. The method returns true if the elements in the array are continually increasing and false if the elements are not continually increasing.

```
ArrayList<Integer> listOfIntegers = /* contains values from table below  */
boolean result = isIncreasing(listOfIntegers);    // result is true
```

For example, if the ArrayList passed to the method is:

34	35	36	37	38	40	42	43	51	52

then the value true is returned

```
public boolean isIncreasing(ArrayList<Integer> arr)
{
    // Write the implementation
}
```

11. Determine if the rate is increasing.

If a stock price is increasing, that means the value of it is going up. If the *rate* that the stock price is increasing is increasing, it means that the price is rising at a faster rate than it was the day before. Write a method that determines if the rate at which a stock price increases is increasing. The method has one parameter: an ArrayList of Double values that represent the stock prices. Return true if the rate that the stock is increasing is increasing, and false if the rate is not increasing.

```
ArrayList<Double> prices = /* contains the values from the table below  */
boolean result = rateIsIncreasing(prices);    // result is true
```

For example, if stockPrices contains the following:

10.1	12.2	15.3	20.4	28.5	40.6	61.7	85.8

then the value true is returned

```
public boolean rateIsIncreasing(ArrayList<Double> stockPrices)
{
    // Write the implementation
}
```

12. Count the empty lockers.

A high school has a specific number of lockers so students can store their belongings. The office staff wants to know how many of the lockers are empty so they can assign these lockers to new students. Consider the following classes and complete the implementation for the `countEmptyLockers` method.

```
public class Locker
{
    private boolean inUse;

    public boolean isInUse()
    {    return inUse;    }

    public void setInUse(boolean isInUse)
    {    inUse = isInUse;    }
}

public class School
{
    private ArrayList <Locker> lockerlist;

    /*    Additional implementation not shown    */

    /**
     * This method counts the number of empty lockers in the list of lockers.
     * @param lockers the list of Locker objects
     * @return the number of empty lockers
     * PRECONDITION:  No object in the list lockers is null
     *                (every locker has a true/false value)
     */
    public static int countEmptyLockers(ArrayList <Locker> lockers)
    {
        /* to be implemented */
    }
}
```

› Answers and Explanations

Bullets mark each step in the process of arriving at the correct solution.

1. The answer is E.

- Let's picture the contents of our `ArrayList` in a table:

0	1	2	3	4	5
Oakland	Chicago	Milwaukee	Seattle	Denver	Boston

- After the remove at index 2, we have this (notice how the indices have changed):

0	1	2	3	4
Oakland	Chicago	Seattle	Denver	Boston

- After adding Detroit, we have:

0	1	2	3	4	5
Oakland	Chicago	Seattle	Denver	Boston	Detroit

- After the remove at index 4, we have:

0	1	2	3	4
Oakland	Chicago	Seattle	Denver	Detroit

- And then we add Cleveland:

0	1	2	3	4	5
Oakland	Chicago	Seattle	Denver	Detroit	Cleveland

2. **The answer is E.**

- Let's make tables to represent what happens as each statement is executed.
  ```
  subjects.add("French");
  ```

0
French

  ```
  subjects.add("History");
  ```

0	1
French	History

  ```
  subjects.set(1, "English");
  ```

0	1
French	English

  ```
  subjects.add("Art");
  ```

0	1	2
French	English	Art

  ```
  subjects.remove(1);
  ```

0	1
French	Art

  ```
  subjects.set(2, "Math");
  ```
  Oops! Can't do it. Trying will generate an `IndexOutOfBoundsException`.

3. **The answer is D.**

- Our array starts as:

5	3	8	1	6	4	2	7

- The 5 is bigger than everything to its left (which is nothing), so let it be. Our algorithm starts with the 3.
- Take out the 3 and store it in a variable: tempKey = 3. Now we have a gap.

5		8	1	6	4	2	7

- Is 3 < 5? Yes, so move the 5 to the right.

	5	8	1	6	4	2	7

- There's nothing more to check, so pop the 3 into the open space the 5 left behind.

3	5	8	1	6	4	2	7

- That's the order after the first pass through the loop (question 3).

4. The answer is A.

- We start where we left off at the end of question 3.

3	5	8	1	6	4	2	7

- Now for the second pass. The 3 and 5 are in order; tempKey = 8, leaving a gap.

3	5		1	6	4	2	7

- Since 5 < 8, we put the 8 back into its original spot.

3	5	8	1	6	4	2	7

- Now for the third pass: 3, 5, 8 are sorted; tempKey = 1, leaving a gap.

3	5	8		6	4	2	7

- 1 < 8, move 8 into the space 1 left behind. 1 < 5, move 5 over. 1 < 3, move 3 over, and put 1 in the first spot.

1	3	5	8	6	4	2	7

- Now for the fourth pass: 1, 3, 5, 8 are sorted; tempKey = 6, leaving a gap.

1	3	5	8		4	2	7

- 6 < 8, move the 8 into the space 6 left behind. 5 < 6, so we've found the spot for 6 and we pop it in.

1	3	5	6	8	4	2	7

- Giving us the answer to question 4.
- Note: One thing to look for in the answers when trying to recognize Insertion Sort—the end of the array doesn't change until it is ready to be sorted. So the 4 2 7 in our example are in the same order that they were in at the beginning.

5. The answer is B.

- Our array starts as:

5	3	8	1	6	4	2	7

- We scan the array to find the smallest element: 1.
- Now swap the 1 and the 5.

1	3	8	5	6	4	2	7

- That's the order after the first pass through the loop (question 5).

6. The answer is E.

- We start where we left off at the end of question 5.
- Now for the second pass. Leave the 1 alone and scan for the smallest remaining item: 2.

1	3	8	5	6	4	2	7

- The 3 is in the spot the 2 needs to go into, so swap the 3 and the 2.

1	2	8	5	6	4	3	7

- The third pass swaps the 8 and the 3.

1	2	3	5	6	4	8	7

- The fourth pass swaps the 5 and the 4.

1	2	3	4	6	5	8	7

- This gives us the answer to question 6.

7. The answer is C.

- After the initial for loop, the contents of the `ArrayList` are: [10, 11, 12, 13].
- Let's consider what the `for-each` loop is doing. For each `Integer` (called i) in integerList
  - add it to total (notice that total starts at 3).
  - (total % 2 == 1) is a way of determining if a number is odd. If total is odd, subtract 1 from it.
- Executing the `for-each` loop gives us:
  - total = 3 + 10 = 13 . . . odd → 12
  - total = 12 + 11 = 23 . . . odd → 22
  - total = 22 + 12 = 34 . . . even!
  - total = 34 + 13 = 47 . . . odd → 46 and our final answer.

8. The answer is C.

- Using a loop to remove items from an `ArrayList` can be very tricky because when you remove an item, all the items after the removed item change indices. That's why option I does not work. When item 3 "words" is removed, "starting" shifts over and becomes item 3, but the loop marches on to item 4 (now "with") and so "starting" is never considered and never removed.
- Working backward through a loop works very well when removing items from an `ArrayList` because only items after the removed item will change indices, and you will have already looked at those items. Option II works and is the simplest solution.
- Option III also works because it only increments the loop counter when an item is not removed. If an item is removed, the loop counter remains the same, so the item that gets shifted down ("starting" in the example above) is not skipped. Option III uses a `while` loop because it changes the loop index i, and it is bad programming style to mess with the loop index inside a `for` loop.

9. The answer is B.

- There are many small alterations possible when writing any algorithm. Do you go from 1 to length or from 0 to length -1, for example. This algorithm makes those kinds of alterations to the version given in the text. But in all cases, the general approach is:
  - The outer loop goes through the array. Everything to the left of the outer loop index (i in this case) is sorted.
  - Take the next element and put it into a temporary variable (key in this case).
  - Look at the element to the left of the element you are working on. If it is larger than the element to be sorted, move it over. Keep doing that until you find an element that is smaller than the element to be sorted (this is the condition we need).
  - Now you've found where our element needs to go. Exit inner loop and pop the element into place.
- So the condition we are looking for reflects *keep doing that until we find an element that is smaller than the element to be sorted*, or, phrasing it like a `while` loop ("as long as" instead of "until"), *keep going as long as the element we are looking at is larger than our key*. In code, we want to keep going as long as arr[j] > key, so that's our condition.

10. Determine if the numbers in an `ArrayList` are always increasing.

Algorithm:
Step 1: Look at each of the numbers in the list starting at the second element
Step 2: If the first number is greater than or equal to the second number, then return false
Step 3: Advance to the next element and continue until you reach the end of the list
Step 4: Return true

Pseudocode:
```
for (iterate through all the numbers in the original list starting at the second element)
{
    if (list[index]<= list[index - 1])
    {
      return false
    }
}
return true
```

Java code:
```java
public static boolean isIncreasing(ArrayList<Integer> arr)
{
    for (int i = 1; i < arr.size(); i++)
    {
       if (arr.get(i) <= arr.get(i - 1))      // if current <= previous
       {
          return false;                       // list is not increasing
       }
    }
    return true;
}
```

11. Determine if the rate is increasing.

Algorithm:
Step 1: Iterate through the parameter array starting at the third element
Step 2: If (the third element minus the second element) is less than or equal to the (second element minus the first element), then return false
Step 3: Move onto the next element and go to Step 2 (and adjust the elements #s)
Step 4: If you get this far without returning, return true

Pseudocode:
```
for (iterate through the parameter array starting with the third element (index 2))
{
    if ((list[index] − list[index − 1]) <= (list[index − 1] − list[index − 2]))
    {
      return false
    }
}
return true
```

Java code:

```java
public static boolean rateIsIncreasing(ArrayList<Double> stockPrices)
{
    for (int i = 2; i < stockPrices.size(); i++) // start with the 3rd element
    {
        if ((stockPrices.get(i) - stockPrices.get(i - 1)) <=
            (stockPrices.get(i - 1) - stockPrices.get(i - 2)))
        {
            return false;
        }
    }
    return true;                // the rate is increasing
}
```

12. Count the empty lockers.

Algorithm:

Step 1: Create a variable called total and set it to zero
Step 2: Look at each of the lockers in the list
Step 3: If the locker is not in use, increment the total
Step 4: Continue until you reach the end of the list
Step 5: Return the total

Pseudocode:

set total = 0
for (iterate through all the lockers in the list)
{
    if (the locker is not in use)
    {
        total = total + 1
    }
}
return total

Java Code:

```java
public static int countEmptyLockers(ArrayList <Locker> lockers)
{
    int total = 0;
    for  (Locker element : lockers)
    {
        if (!element.isInUse())
        {
            total++;
        }
    }
    return total;
}
```

2D Array

7.5-10% AP Exam Weight

IN THIS UNIT

Summary: The data structures that we've worked with so far have all been one-dimensional arrays because they stored a simple list of data values. Sometimes using an array or `ArrayList` is not enough. A two-dimensional array stores values in rows and columns like in a table. In this unit we will discuss 2D arrays. We will also look back at some of the code that we already wrote and modify it to work with a 2D array.

Learning Objectives

VAR-2.F Represent collections of related primitive or object reference data using two-dimensional (2D) array objects.

VAR-2.G For 2D array objects:

Traverse using nested `for` loops.

Traverse using nested enhanced for loops.

CON-2.N For algorithms in the context of a particular specification that requires the use of 2D array traversals:

Identify standard algorithms.

Modify standard algorithms.

Develop an algorithm.

Key Ideas
- ✪ A two-dimensional (2D) array is a data structure that is an array of arrays.
- ✪ The 2D array simulates a rectangular grid with coordinates for each location based on the row and the column.
- ✪ 2D arrays can be traversed using row-major or column-major order.
- ✪ All standard array or `ArrayList` algorithms can be applied to 2D arrays.

The 2D Array

Definition of a 2D Array

A **two-dimensional (2D) array** is a complex data structure that can be visualized as a rectangular **grid** made up of **rows** and **columns**. Technically, it is **an array of arrays**. It can store any kind of data in its slots; however, each piece of data has to be of the same data type.

Two-dimensional arrays are actually fun to work with and are very practical when creating grid-style games. Many board games are based on a grid: checkers, chess, Scrabble, etc. Many apps are based on grids too: CandyCrush, 2048, Ruzzle. I'm sure you can think of others.

Declaring a 2D Array and Initializing It Using a Predefined List of Data

When you know the values that you want to store in the 2D array, you can declare the array and store the values in it immediately. This operation is just like what we did for the one-dimensional array. **Two pairs of brackets**, [ ][ ], are used to tell the computer that it is not a regular variable.

General Form for Creating a 2D Array Using an Initializer List

```
dataType[][] nameOf2DArray = { {value1, value2, value3},
                               {value4, value5, value6},
                               {. . ., . . ., . . .} };
```

value1	value2	value3
value4	value5	value6
. . .	. . .	. . .

Note: Pairs of curly braces are used to wrap the first row, then the second row, and so on. If you look closely at this visual, you will see how a 2D array is really an array of arrays.

Example

Declare a 2D array that represents a CandyCrush board with four rows and three columns. Notice that the four rows are numbered 0 through 3 and the three columns are numbered 0 through 2.

```
String[][] candyBoard = {{"Jelly Bean", "Lozenge", "Lemon Drop"},
                         {"Gum Square", "Lollipop Head", "Jujube Cluster"},
                         {"Lozenge", "Lollipop Head", "Lemon Drop"},
                         {"Jelly Bean", "Lollipop Head", "Lozenge"}};
```

This is the visual representation of what the candyBoard array looks like inside the computer.

	0	1	2
0	"Jelly Bean"	"Lozenge"	"Lemon Drop"
1	"Gum Square"	"Lollipop Head"	"Jujube Cluster"
2	"Lozenge"	"Lollipop Head"	"Lemon Drop"
3	"Jelly Bean"	"Lollipop Head"	"Lozenge"

Rows and Columns of the 2D Array

Every cell in a 2D array is assigned a pair of coordinates that are based on the row number and the column number on the AP exam. The first pair of brackets represents the row number and the second pair of brackets represents the column number. The rows and columns both begin at zero and end with one less than the number of rows or columns, just like they did with arrays and ArrayLists.

It is possible to have the first pair of brackets represent columns and the second pair of brackets represent rows as long as this order is consistent when referring to the element by index. These index numbers are simply treated like an ordered pair coordinate by the compiler.

Example
Change the "Lozenge" in row 2 and column 0 to be a "Lemon Drop".

```
candyBoard[2][0] = "Lemon Drop";
```

	0	1	2
0	"Jelly Bean"	"Lozenge"	"Lemon Drop"
1	"Gum Square"	"Lollipop Head"	"Jujube Cluster"
2	"Lemon Drop"	"Lollipop Head"	"Lemon Drop"
3	"Jelly Bean"	"Lollipop Head"	"Lozenge"

Declaring a 2D Array Using the Keyword new

A 2D array object can be created using the keyword **new**. Every cell in the 2D array is filled with the default value for its data type.

General Form for Creating a 2D Array Using the Keyword new

```
dataType[][] nameOfArray = new dataType[numberOfRows][numberOfColumns];
```

Example
Declare a 2D array that represents a Sudoku Board that has nine rows and nine columns. Put the number 6 in row 2, column 7:

```
int[][] mySudokuBoard = new int[9][9]; // the order is always [rows][columns]
mySudokuBoard[2][7] = 6;               // puts a 6 in row 2, column 7
```

---

9 Columns

	0	1	2	3	4	5	6	7	8
0	0	0	0	0	0	0	0	0	0
1	0	0	0	0	0	0	0	0	0
2	0	0	0	0	0	0	0	6	0
3	0	0	0	0	0	0	0	0	0
4	0	0	0	0	0	0	0	0	0
5	0	0	0	0	0	0	0	0	0
6	0	0	0	0	0	0	0	0	0
7	0	0	0	0	0	0	0	0	0
8	0	0	0	0	0	0	0	0	0

9 Rows

How to Refer to the Rows and Columns in a 2D Array

The position, `myBoard[0][5]`, is read as *row 0, column 5*.
The position, `myBoard[3][0]`, is read as *row 3, column 0*.

Using the `length` Field to Find the Number of Rows and Columns

The number of rows in a 2D array is found by accessing the `length` field. The number of columns in a 2D array is found by accessing the `length` field using the name of the array *along with one of the rows* (it doesn't matter which row on the AP exam as all 2D arrays are assumed to be rectangular).

Example 1
Retrieve the number of rows from a 2D array:

```
double[][] myBoard = new double[8][3];
int result = myBoard.length;        // result is 8 (number of rows)
```

Example 2
Retrieve the number of columns from a 2D array:

```
double[][] myBoard = new double[8][3];
int result1 = myBoard[0].length;    // result1 is 3 (number of columns)
int result2 = myBoard[5].length;    // result2 is also 3
```

Accessing a 1-D Array from Within the 2D Array

Consider this 2D array declaration:

```
double[][] myBoard = new double[8][3];
```

`myBoard[0]` is a 1-D array that consists of the row with index 0.
`myBoard[5]` is a 1-D array that consists of the row with index 5.

Traversing a 2D Array in Row-Major Order

Traversing a 2D array means to visit every cell in the grid. This can be done in many different ways, but for the AP Computer Science A exam, you need to know two specific ways.

Row-Major order is the process of traversing a 2D array in the manner that English-speaking people read a book. Start at the top left cell and move toward the right along the first row until you reach the end of the row. Then start at the next row at the left-most cell, and then move along to the right until you reach the end of that row. Repeat this process until you have visited every cell in the grid and finish with the bottom-right cell.

Example

Traverse an array in Row-Major order. Start with row 0 and end with the last row. For each row, start with column 0 and end with the last column.

Java Code 1: Using a nested for loop

```
String[][] myGrid =  /* 2D array provided by the user */
for (int row = 0; row < myGrid.length; row++)                // every row
{
   for (int column = 0; column < myGrid[0].length; column++)   // every column
   {
     System.out.print(myGrid[row][column] + " ");              // every cell
   }
   System.out.println( );                              // so it prints like a grid
}
```

Java Code 2: Using enhanced for loop

```
String[][] myGrid =    /* 2D array provided by the user */
for (String [] arr : myGrid)          // put each row into an array
{
    for (String element : arr)            // traverse one single row
    {
        System.out.print(element + " ");     // one cell
    }
    System.out.println( );                // so it prints like a grid
}
```

Example

Traverse an array in reverse row-major order, starting with the last row and last column and moving toward the first column before traversing the next row.

```
String [][] myGrid = /* 2D array provided by the user */
for(int row = myGrid.length - 1; row >= 0; row--)
{
    for(int column = myGrid[row].length; column >= 0; column--)
    {
        System.out.print(myGrid[row][column] + " ");
    }
    System.out.println();
}
```

Traversing a 2D Array in Column-Major Order

Column-Major order is the process of traversing a 2D array by starting at the top-left cell and moving downward until you reach the bottom of the first column. Then start at the top of the next column and work your way down until you reach the bottom of that column. Repeat this until you have visited every cell in the grid and finish with the bottom-right cell.

Example

Traverse an array in column-major order using a nested `for` loop. Start with column 0 and end with the last column. For each column, start with row 0 and end with the last row.

```java
String[][] myGrid =  /* 2D array provided by the user */
for (int column = 0; column < myGrid[0].length; column++) // every column
{
    for (int row = 0; row < myGrid.length; row++)          // every row
    {
        System.out.println(myGrid[row][column]);           // every cell
    }
}
```

Example

Traverse an array in reverse column-major order, starting with the last row and last column and moving towards the first row before traversing the next column.

```java
String [][] myGrid = /* 2D array provided by the user */
for(int column = myGrid[0].length - 1; columns >= 0; column--)
{
    for(int row = myGrid.length; row >= 0; row--)
    {
        System.out.print(myGrid[row][column] + " ");
    }
    System.out.println();
}
```

> **ArrayIndexOutOfBoundsException**
>
> As with a 1-D array, if you use an index that is not within the 2D array, you will get an `ArrayIndexOutOfBoundsException`.

 Fun Fact: *Java provides support for multi-dimensional arrays, such as 3D arrays; however, the AP Computer Science A Exam does not require you to know about them.*

More Algorithms

All standard array/`ArrayList` algorithms can be applied to 2D arrays. Let's revisit a few of them from units 6 and 7.

The Accumulate Algorithm

Remember the baseball scenario from unit 6 where we found the total number of hits the team had? We are going to make modifications so instead of finding the total hits from one game (1D array) we will find the total number of hits for all the games in the season (2D array).

General Problem: Add up all of the hits for a baseball team.

Refined Problem: Write a method that finds the sum of all of the hits in an 2D array of hits.

Final Problem: Write a method called findSum that has one parameter: a 2D array of ints. The method should return the sum of all of the elements in the array.

Algorithm:

Step 1: Create a variable called sum and set it equal to zero
Step 2: Look at each of the elements in the list
Step 3: Add the element to the sum
Step 4: Continue until you reach the end of the list
Step 5: Return the sum

Pseudocode:

set sum = zero
for (iterate through all the elements in the list)
{
    sum = sum + element
}
return sum

Java code using a 2D array (Row-Major order)

```java
public static int findSum(int[][] arr)
{
    int sum = 0;                                 // initialize sum to 0
    for (int row = 0; row < arr.length; row++)   // do every row
    {
        for (int col = 0; col < arr[row].length; col++)
        {                                        // do every column in the row
            sum += arr[row][col];                // add value in cell to sum
        }
    }
    return sum;                                  // return sum
}
```

The Find-Highest Algorithm

What is the highest score on your favorite video game? As more people play a game, how does the computer figure out what is the highest score in the list?

> **General Problem:** Find the highest score out of all the scores for a video game.
>
> **Refined Problem:** Write a method that finds the highest score in a list of scores.
>
> **Final Problem:** Write a method called `findHigh` that has one parameter: a 2D array. The method should return the largest value in the array.

Solution: Let the highest be the first element in the list.

Algorithm:

Step 1: Create a variable called high and set it to the first element in the list
Step 2: Look at each of the scores in the list
Step 3: If the score is greater than the high score, then make it be the new high score
Step 4: Continue until you reach the end of the list
Step 5: Return the high score

Pseudocode:

set high = first score
for (iterate through all the scores in the list)
{
  if (score > high)
  {
    high = score
  }
}
return high

Java code using a 2D array (Row-Major order)

```java
public static int findHigh(int[][] arr)
{
    int high = arr[0][0];      // first element
    for (int row = 0; row < arr.length; row++)
    {
        for (int col = 0; col < arr[row].length; col++)
        {
            if (arr[row][col] > high)
            {
                high = arr[row][col];
            }
        }
    }
    return high;
}
```

The Connect-Four Advanced Algorithm

Connect Four is a two-player game played on a grid of six rows and seven columns. Players take turns inserting disks into the grid in hopes of connecting four disks in a row to win the game. You have been hired to work on the app version of the game, and it is your responsibility to determine whether a player has won the game.

General Problem: Determine if a player has won the game of Connect Four.

Refined Problem: The Connect Four app version uses a 2D array that is 6 × 7. After a player makes a move, determine if he or she has won by checking all possible ways to win. If four of the same color disks are found in a line, then the game is over. Decide who won the game (player one or player two). A way to win can be vertical, horizontal, diagonally downward, or diagonally upward.

Final Problem: Write a method called `checkForWinner` that has one parameter: a 2D array of `int`. The 2D array consists of 1s and 2s to represent a move by player one or player two. Cells that do not contain a move have a value of 0. This method checks all four directions to win (vertical, horizontal, diagonally downward, and diagonally upward). The method should return the number of the player who won or return 0 if nobody has won.

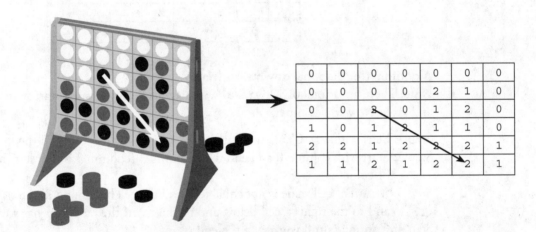

Algorithm (for vertical win):

Note: There are a total of 21 ways to win vertically. Start with the top left cell and move in Row-Major order.

Step 1: Start with row 0 and end with row 2 (row 2 is four less than the number of rows)
Step 2: Start with column 0 and end with column 6 (use every column)
Step 3: If current cell value is not equal to 0 and the current cell = cell below it = cell below it = cell below it, then a player has won
Step 4: Continue until you reach the end of row 2
Step 5: Return the player who won or zero

Pseudocode (for vertical win):

```
for (start with row 0 and end with row 2)
{
    for (start with column 0 and end with column 6)
    {
        if (current cell != 0 && current cell = cell below it = cell below it = cell below it)
        {
            return current cell value
        }
    }
}
return 0 (no winning player is found)
```

	0	1	2	3	4	5	6
0	0	0	0	0	0	0	0
1	0	0	0	0	2	1	0
2	0	0	2	0	1	2	0
3	1	0	1	2	1	1	0
4	2	2	1	2	2	2	1
5	1	1	2	1	2	2	1

Algorithm (for diagonal downward win):

Note: There are a total of 12 ways to win diagonally downward. Start with the top left cell and go in Row-Major order.

Step 1: Start with row 0 and end with row 2 (row 2 is four less than the number of rows)

Step 2: Start with column 0 and end with column 3 (column 3 is four less than the number of columns)

Step 3: If current cell value is not equal to 0 and the cell below and to the right = cell below and to the right = cell below and to the right, then a player has won

Step 4: Continue until you reach the end of row 2

Step 5: Return the player who won or zero

Pseudocode (for diagonal downward win):

```
for (start with row 0 and end with row 2)
{
  for (start with column 0 and end with column 3)
  {
    if (current cell != 0 && current cell = cell below/right = cell below/right
        = cell below/right)
    {
        return current cell value
    }
  }
}
return 0
```

Note: I have provided the algorithm and pseudocode for only the vertical win and the diagonal downward win. The code for these, as well as the horizontal win and the diagonal upward win, are provided in the Java code that follows.

**Java Code: Using a 2D array and nested for loops
(includes all four ways to win):**

```java
public static int checkForWinner(int[][] board)
{
    // Check for Vertical Win
    for (int r = 0; r <= board.length - 4; r++)
    {
        for (int c = 0; c < board[0].length; c++)
        {
            if (board[r][c] != 0 &&
                board[r][c] == board[r+1][c] &&
                board[r+1][c] == board[r+2][c] &&
                board[r+2][c] == board[r+3][c])
            return board[r][c];
        }
    }


    // Check for Diagonal Downward Win
    for (int r = 0; r <= board.length - 4; r++)
    {
        for (int c = 0; c <= board[0].length - 4; c++)
        {
            if (board[r][c] != 0 &&
                board[r][c] == board[r+1][c+1] &&
                board[r+1][c+1] == board[r+2][c+2] &&
                board[r+2][c+2] == board[r+3][c+3])
            return board[r][c];
        }
    }


    // Check for Horizontal Win
    for (int r = 0; r < board.length; r++)
    {
        for (int c = 0; c <= board[0].length - 4; c++)
        {
            if (board[r][c] != 0 &&
                board[r][c] == board[r][c+1] &&
                board[r][c+1] == board[r][c+2] &&
                board[r][c+2] == board[r][c+3])
            return board[r][c];
        }
    }

    // Check for Diagonal Upward Win
    for (int r = 3; r < board.length; r++)
    {
        for (int c = 0; c <= board[0].length - 4; c++)
        {
            if (board[r][c] != 0 &&
                board[r][c] == board[r-1][c+1] &&
                board[r-1][c+1] == board[r-2][c+2] &&
                board[r-2][c+2] == board[r-3][c+3])
```

```
            return board[r][c];
        }
    }


    // No winner was found after checking all 4 ways to win
    return 0;
}
```

```
public class ConnectFourRunner
{
    public static void main(String[] args)
    {
        int[][] board = {{0,0,0,0,0,0,0},
                         {0,0,0,0,2,1,0},
                         {0,0,2,0,1,2,0},
                         {1,0,1,2,1,1,0},
                         {2,2,1,2,2,2,1},
                         {1,1,2,1,2,2,1} };

        System.out.println("Winner:  " + checkForWinner(board));
    }

    public static int checkForWinner(int[][] arr)
    {
        /*  implementation is described above  */
    }
}
```

```
OUTPUT
Winner:  2
```

› Rapid Review

The 2D Array

- A 2D array is a complex data structure that can store a grid of data of the same type.
- The 2D array is actually an array of arrays.
- The rows and columns are numbered starting with zero.
- The top row is row zero. The left-most column is column zero.
- The access to each cell in the 2D array is always [row][column].
- The indices of the top-left cell are [0][0].
- The index of the bottom-right cell is [numberOfRows − 1][numberOfColumns − 1].
- Two-dimensional arrays can store primitive data or object data.
- To store a value in a 2D array: arrayName[rowNumber][columnNumber] = value;
- To retrieve the number of rows in a 2D array, use arrayName.length.
- To retrieve the number of columns in a rectangular 2D array, use arrayName[0].length. Note: Any valid row number works instead of 0.
- Using an index that is not in the range of the 2D array will throw an ArrayIndexOutOfBoundsException.

Traversing a 2D Array

- To traverse a 2D array means to visit each element in every row and column.
- The most common way to traverse a 2D array is called Row-Major order.
- Row-Major order starts in the upper-left location [0][0], and travels to the right until the end of the row is reached. Then the next move is to the next row [1][0]. The process is repeated until the right-most column in the bottom row is reached.
- The second most common way to traverse a 2D array is called Column-Major order.
- Column-Major order also starts in the upper-left location [0][0]; however, it travels down until the end of the first column is reached. Then, the next move is to the top of the next column [0][1]. The process is repeated until the bottom row in the right-most column is reached.
- All of the 2D arrays on the AP Computer Science A Exam will be rectangular.

Accumulate Algorithm

- The accumulate algorithm finds the sum of all the items in a list.
- It looks at each element in the list one at a time, adding the value to a total.

Find-Highest Algorithm

- The find-highest algorithm finds the largest value in a list.
- It looks at each element in the list one at a time, comparing the value to the current high value.
- Common ways to implement this algorithm include initializing the highest value with the first value in the list or to an extremely small negative number.
- The find-highest algorithm can be modified to find the lowest item in a list.

› Review Questions

Basic Level

1. Consider the following code segment.

```
int n = // some positive integer
int [ ][ ] table = new int[n][n];
//  input values into table

int sum = 0;
for (int row = 0; row < table.length; row++)
    sum += table[table.length - row - 1][row];

System.out.println(sum);
```

What value will sum contain after the code segment is executed?

(A) The sum of all the values in the table
(B) The sum of all the values in the major diagonal (top left to bottom right)
(C) The sum of all the values in the minor diagonal (top right to bottom left)
(D) The sum of all the values in both diagonals
(E) The sum of all the values in the last row

2. Consider the following code segment.

```
int m = // some positive integer
int n = // some positive integer
int [ ] [ ] table = new int [m] [n];
//  input values into table

for (int row = 0; row < table.length; row++)
    for (int col = 0; col < table[0].length; col++)
        if(table[row][col] < 0)
            table[row][col] = - table[row][col];
```

Which of the following best describes the result of executing the code segment?

(A) Each element in the two-dimensional array table contains the value 0.

(B) Each element in the two-dimensional array table contains a nonnegative value.

(C) Each element in the two-dimensional array table contains a nonpositive value.

(D) Each element in the two-dimensional array table contains the opposite value from when it was initialized.

(E) Each element in the two-dimensional array table contains the value row – col.

3. Consider the following incomplete method.

```
public static double findRowSum(double [] [] mat, int n)
{
    double sum = 0;
    // missing code

    return sum;
}
```

Method findRowSum is intended to return the sum of elements in parameter mat that are in row n, also passed as a parameter. Which of the following code segments could be used to replace // missing code so that findRowSum will work as intended?

```
(A) for (int i = 0; i < table.length; i++)
        sum += mat[i][n];
(B) for (int i = 0; i < table[0].length; i++)
        sum += mat[i][n];
(C) for (int i = 0; i < table.length; i++)
        sum += mat[n][i];
(D) for (int i = 0; i < table[0].length; i++)
        sum += mat[n][i];
(E) for (int i = 0; i < table[0].length; i++)
        sum += mat[n][n];
```

Advanced Level

4. Consider the following definition and code segment.

```
int [] [] table =  new int [5] [5];

for (int row = 0; row < table.length-1; row++)
    for (int col = 0; col < table[0].length-1; col++)
    {
        table[row][col] = row * col;
    }
```

What values will `table` contain after the code segment is executed?

(A)

0	0	0	0	0
0	1	2	3	4
0	2	4	6	8
0	3	6	9	12
0	4	8	12	16

(D)

0	0	0	0	0
0	1	2	3	0
0	2	4	6	0
0	3	6	9	0
0	0	0	0	0

(B)

0	1	2	3	4
1	2	3	4	5
2	3	4	5	6
3	4	5	6	7
4	5	6	7	8

(E)

0	0	0	0	0
0	3	6	9	0
0	2	4	6	0
0	1	2	3	0
0	0	0	0	0

(C)

0	1	2	3	0
1	2	3	4	0
2	3	4	5	0
3	4	5	6	0
0	0	0	0	0

5. Modifying a 2D array

Write a method that takes a 2D array as a parameter and returns a new 2D array.
The even rows of the new array should be exactly the same as the array passed in.
The odd rows of the new array should be replaced by the contents of the row above.

For example, if the input array is:

1	5	4	8	7	3
2	4	3	5	7	6
2	4	3	3	6	0
9	8	9	9	4	1

Then the returned array should be:

1	5	4	8	7	3
1	5	4	8	7	3
2	4	3	3	6	0
2	4	3	3	6	0

Here is the declaration for your method.
```
public int[][] modify(int[][] arr)
```

6. Filling a 2D array

Write a method that will fill in a 2D `boolean` array with a checkerboard pattern of alternating `true` and
`false`. The upper-left corner (0, 0) should always be `true`.
Given a grid size of 3 × 4, the method should return:

true	false	true	false
false	true	false	true
true	false	true	false

The method will take the number of rows and columns as parameters and return the completed array. Here is the method declaration and the array declaration:

```
public static boolean[][] makeGrid(int rows, int cols)
{
    boolean[][] grid;


    /* to be implemented */
}
```

7. Find all the songs that contain the word "Love" in the title.

One of the most popular themes in music lyrics is love. Suppose a compilation of thousands of songs is stored in a grid. Count the number of songs that contain the word "Love" in the title.

Write a method that counts the number of song titles that contains a certain string in the title. The method has two parameters: a 2D array of `string` objects and a target string. The method should return an integer that represents the number of strings in the 2D array that contains the target string.

```
String[][] songs = /*  2D array fill with the values in the table below  */
int result = findCount(songs, "Love");                  // result is 5
```

The 2D array passed to the method:

"We Are the Champions"	"You Shook Me All Night Long"	"We Found Love"
"Bleeding Love"	"Stairway to Heaven"	"Won't Get Fooled Again"
"I'd Do Anything for Love"	"Stupid Crazy Love"	"Love in This Club"
"Since U Been Gone"	"One More Time"	"Walk This Way"

```
public int findCount(String[][] arr, String target)
{
    // Write the implementation
}
```

› Answers and Explanations

1. The answer is C.

   • This is not a nested `for` loop, which means each element of the 2D array will not be accessed.
   • The first element that is accessed would be the last row, 1st column, table [length - 0 - 1] [0].
   • The second element that is accessed would be the next to last row and the 2nd column. Table[length - 1 - 1] [1].
   • The loop will continue moving upwards along the minor diagonal until all elements are accessed and added to sum.

2. The answer is B

   • This uses a nested `for` loop with both loop control variables starting at 0 and ending at the length of the row or column, which means each element of the 2D array is potentially accessed.
   • It tests each element against 0. If that element is negative (< 0), it will be changed to the opposite, which is positive.
   • After the loops are complete, each element in the table will be nonnegative (positive or 0).

3. The answer is D.

   • Only one row needs to be summed, so a single `for` loop is appropriate.

- Since row n is the row to be summed, this value needs to remain unchanged throughout the loop.
- Choice D correctly accesses each element in the correct row in `mat`.

4. The answer is D.

- Choice A would be the result if both loops ended at the length of the table instead of length-1.
- Choice B would be the result if both loops ended at the length of the table instead of length-1 and the operation was addition (+) and not multiplication (*).
- Choice C would be the result if the operation was addition (+) and not multiplication (*).
- Choice E would be the result if the loop started at the last row.

5. We can find the even rows by using the condition (row % 2 == 0). In other words, if I can divide the row number by 2 and not have a remainder, it's an even row. Even rows just get copied as is. Odd rows get copied from the row above [row − 1].

Here is the completed method.

```
public int[][] modify(int[][] arr) {

    int[][] newArr = new int[arr.length][arr[0].length];

    for (int row = 0; row < arr.length; row++)
    {
        for (int col = 0; col < arr[row].length; col++)
        {
            if (row % 2 == 0)
            {
                newArr[row][col] = arr[row][col];        // even row
            }
            else
            {
                newArr[row][col] = arr[row - 1][col];    // odd row
            }
        }
    }
    return newArr;
}
```

6. There are many ways to solve this problem. This implementation uses the fact that grid[row][col] is true when row + col is even.

```
public static boolean[][] makeGrid(int rows, int cols)
{
    boolean[][] grid;
    grid = new boolean[rows][cols];        //initializes all elements to false
    for (int r = 0; r < rows; r++)
    {
        for (int c = 0; c < cols; c++)
        {
            if ((r + c) % 2 == 0)          // r + c is even
            {
                grid[r][c] = true;
            }
        }
    }
    return grid;
}
```

Here is a tester class so you can see if the way you wrote the method was also correct. Copy in your code. Try it with all shapes and sizes of grid to test it thoroughly.

```
public class GridBuilder
{
    public static void main(String[] args)
    {
        boolean[][] grid = makeGrid(3, 4); //change (3,4) to test
        for (int r = 0; r < grid.length; r++)
        {
            for (int c = 0; c < grid[0].length; c++)
            {
                System.out.print(grid[r][c] + "\t");
            }
            System.out.println();
        }
    }

    public static boolean[][] makeGrid(int rows, int cols)
    {
        boolean[][] grid;
        //put your code in here
    }
}
```

7. Find all the songs that contain the word "Love" in the title.

Algorithm:

Step 1: Initialize a count variable to zero
Step 2: Look at each of the scores in the 2D array (using Row-Major order)
Step 3: If the song title contains the target String, then increment the count
Step 4: Continue until you reach the end of the list
Step 5: Return count

Pseudocode:

```
for (iterate through all the rows in the 2D array)
{
    for (iterate through all the columns in the 2D array)
    {
        if (list[row][column] contains target String)
        {
            count = count + 1
        }
    }
}
return count
```

Java code:

```
public static int findCount(String[][] arr, String target)
{
    int count = 0;
    for (int r = 0; r < arr.length; r++)
    {
        for (int c = 0; c < arr[r].length; c++)
        {
            if (arr[r][c].indexOf(target) != -1)        // target is in title
            {
                count++;
            }
        }
    }
    return count;
}
```

UNIT 9

Inheritance

5-10% AP Exam Weight

IN THIS UNIT

Summary: In order to take advantage of everything an object-oriented language has to offer, you must learn about its ability to handle inheritance. This unit explains how superclasses and subclasses are related within a class hierarchy. It also explains what polymorphism is and how objects within a class hierarchy may act independently of each other.

Learning Objectives

MOD-3.B Create an inheritance relationship from a subclass to the superclass.
MOD-3.C Define reference variables of a superclass to be assigned to an object of a subclass in the same hierarchy.
MOD-3.D Call methods in an inheritance relationship.
MOD-3.E Call `Object` class methods through inheritance.

Key Ideas

✪ A class hierarchy describes the relationship between classes.
✪ Inheritance allows objects to use features that are not defined in their own class.
✪ A subclass extends a superclass (a child class extends a parent class).
✪ Child classes do not have direct access to their parent's private instance variables.
✪ A child class can override the parent class methods by simply redefining the method.

✪ Polymorphism is what happens when objects from child classes are allowed to act in a different way than objects from their parent classes.
✪ The `Object` class is the parent of all classes (the mother of all classes).

Inheritance

Sorry, this inheritance is not about a large sum of money that your crazy, rich uncle has left you. It is, however, a feature of Java that is immensely valuable. It allows objects from one class to inherit the features of another class to take advantage of code reusability and to save you the trouble of copy and pasting methods from one class to another.

Class Hierarchy

One of the most powerful features of Java is the ability to create a **class hierarchy**. A hierarchy allows a class to inherit the attributes of another class, making the code **reusable**. This means that the classes on the lower end of the hierarchy inherit features (like methods and instance variables) without having to define them in their own class.

In biology, animals are ranked with classifications such as species, genus, family, class, kingdom, and so on. Any given rank **inherits** the traits and features from the rank above it.

Example

Demonstrate the hierarchy of cats, dogs, horses, and elephants. Note that all German shepherds are dogs, and all dogs are mammals, so all German shepherds are mammals.

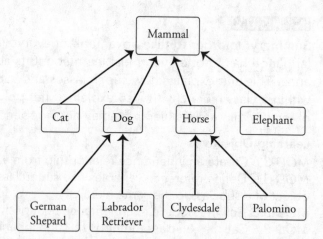

Parent Versus Child Classes (Superclass Versus Subclass)

So what does this have to do with computer programming? Well, in Java, a class has the ability to extend another class. That is, a **child** class (**subclass**) has the ability to extend a **parent** class (**superclass**). When a child class extends a parent class, it inherits the instance variables and methods of the parent class. This means that even though the child class doesn't define these instance variables or methods on its own, it has them. This is a powerful way to reuse code without having to rewrite it.

Note: The methods from a parent class are inherited and can be used by the child class. However, the child class gets its *own set* of instance variables that are separate from the parent class. The instance variables for the parent and the instance variables for the child are two different sets of instance variables. The child class can only access the private instance variables of the parent by using the accessor and mutator methods from the parent class.

Something for Nothing
Child classes inherit the methods of their parent class. This means that the child objects automatically get these methods without having to define them for themselves.

The Keyword extends

The words **superclass** and **parent** are interchangeable as are **subclass** and **child**. We say, "a child class **extends** a parent class" or "a subclass is derived from a superclass." The phrase **is-a** refers to class hierarchy. So when we refer to classes such as Dog or Mammal, we say "a Dog is-a Mammal" or even "a GermanShepherd is-a Mammal."

A class can extend *at most one other class*; however, there is no limit to how many classes can exist in a class hierarchy.

The Keyword extends
The keyword extends is used to identify that inheritance is taking place. A child class can only extend one parent class.

Example
Simulate class hierarchy and inheritance using the Mammal hierarchy. Each subclass inherits the traits of its superclass and can add additional traits of its own.

```
public class Mammal
{
    // All mammals are warm blooded
    // All mammals have lungs to breathe air

}
```

```
public class Dog extends Mammal
{
    // The Dog Class is a child class of the Mammal Class
    // A Dog is-a Mammal
    // All Dogs are warm blooded (inherited)
    // All Dogs have lungs to breathe air (inherited)
    // Dogs are domesticated (unique trait of a Dog)

}
```

```
public class LabradorRetriever extends Dog
{
    // The LabradorRetriever Class is a direct child class of the Dog Class
    // A LabradorRetriever is-a Dog
    // A LabradorRetriver is-a Mammal
    // LabradorRetrievers are warm blooded (inherited)
    // LabradorRetrievers have lungs to breathe air (inherited)
    // LabradorRetrievers are domesticated (inherited)
    // LabradorRetrievers are cute (unique trait of LabradorRetrievers)

}
```

Be Your Own Class
Child classes are allowed to define additional methods of their own. The total number of methods that the child class has is a combination of both the parent class and child class methods.

Constructors and the Keyword super

Constructors in a subclass are not inherited from their superclass. When you make an object from a child class, the child class constructor automatically calls the no-argument constructor of the parent class using the **super()** call (some integrated development environments, or IDEs, display this instruction). However, if you want to call a parent constructor with arguments from the child class constructor, you need to put that in your code explicitly as the first line of code in the child class constructor using the **super(arguments)** instruction. The child is then making a call to a parameterized constructor of the parent class. The actual parameters (arguments) passed in the call to the superclass constructor provide values that the constructor can use to initialize the object's instance variables. Regardless of whether the superclass constructor is called implicitly or explicitly, the process of calling superclass constructors continues until the Object constructor is called. At this point, all of the constructors within the hierarchy execute beginning with the Object constructor.

Example

Demonstrate a child class that has two constructors. The no-parameter constructor makes a call to the parent's no-parameter constructor. The parameterized constructor makes a call to the parent's parameterized constructor. Note: The super() call *must* be the first line of code in each of the child's constructors.

```
public class Mammal
{
    private boolean vertebrate;      // instance variable for a Mammal
    private boolean milkProducer;    // instance variable for a Mammal
    private String hairColor;        // instance variable for a Mammal

    public Mammal()                  // No parameter Mammal constructor
    {
        vertebrate = true;           // mammals are vertebrates
        milkProducer = true;         // mammals produce milk
    }

    public Mammal(String color)      // One parameter Mammal constructor
    {
        vertebrate = true;
        milkProducer = true;
        hairColor = color;           // Assign the hair color
    }

    /**  Assume accessor methods are defined  */
}
```

```
public class Dog extends Mammal
{
    private String name;            // every Dog has a name

    public Dog()
    {
        super();            // This call is made with or without typing it
    }

    public Dog(String hairColor, String nameOfDog)
    {
        super(hairColor);    // the call to the parent must come first!

        name = nameOfDog;    // assign the Dog's name in the Dog constructor
    }

    /**  Assume accessor methods are defined  */
}
```

```
public static void main(String[] args)
{
    Dog myDog1 = new Dog();
    System.out.println(myDog1.getName());        // will not have a name
    System.out.println(myDog1.getHairColor());   // will not have hair color
    System.out.println(myDog1.isVertebrate());   // will be true
    System.out.println(myDog1.isMilkProducer()); // will be true
    System.out.println();

    Dog myDog2 = new Dog("Brown", "Bella");
    System.out.println(myDog2.getName());        // the name is Bella
    System.out.println(myDog2.getHairColor());   // the color is Brown
    System.out.println(myDog2.isVertebrate());   // will be true
    System.out.println(myDog2.isMilkProducer()); // will be true
}
```

```
OUTPUT
null
null
true
true

Bella
Brown
true
true
```

Data Encapsulation Within Class Hierarchy

A subclass can only access or modify the private instance variables of its parent class *by using the accessor and modifier methods* of the parent class.

> **Children Don't Have Direct Access to Their Parent's `private` Instance Variables**
> Parent and child classes may both contain instance variables. These instance variables should be declared private. This is data encapsulation. Children have to use the accessor and modifier methods of the parent class to access their parent's private instance variables.

Polymorphism

"Sometimes children want to act in a different way from their parents."

Overriding a Method of the Parent Class

In Java, a child class is allowed to **override** a method of a parent class. This means that even though the child inherited a certain way to do something from its parent, it can do it in a different way if it wants to. This is an example of **polymorphism**.

The way to make a child override a parent method is to redefine a method (signature/ method header) and change what is done in the method. When an object from the child class calls the method, it will perform the action that is found in the child class rather than the method of the parent class.

Example

All objects from the `FamilyMember` class drink from a cup and eat with a fork. However, objects from the `Baby` class drink from a cup and eat with their hands. All objects from the `SporkUser` class drink from a cup and eat with a spork. In this case, the eat method of the `FamilyMember` class is overridden by both the `Baby` class and the `SporkUser` class. Therefore, even though the name of the method is the same, the objects from `Baby` class and `SporkUser` class eat in a different way than objects from the `FamilyMember` class. The decision of when to use the overridden method by all objects that extend a superclass is made when the program is compiled and this process is called **static binding**.

Any method that is called must be defined within its own class or its superclass. A subclass is usually designed to have modified (overridden) or additional methods or instance variables. A subclass will inherit all public methods from the superclass; these methods remain public in the subclass.

```
public class FamilyMember // This is the superclass
{
   public String drink()
   {
      return "cup";        // the way that all FamilyMember objects drink
   }

   public String eat()
   {
      return "fork";       // the default way that all FamilyMembers eat
   }
}
```

```
public class Baby extends FamilyMember
{
   public String eat()      // Baby is overriding the eat() method
   {
      return "hands";       // all Baby objects eat with their hands
   }
}
```

```
public class SporkUser extends FamilyMember
{
   public String eat()  // SporkUser is overriding the eat() method
   {
      return "spork";    // all SporkUser objects eat with a spork
   }
}
```

```
public static void main(String[] args)
{
   FamilyMember mom = new FamilyMember();
   Baby junior = new Baby();
   SporkUser auntSue = new SporkUser();

   System.out.println(mom.drink());        // mom drinks with a cup
   System.out.println(junior.drink());     // junior drinks with a cup
   System.out.println(auntSue.drink());    // auntSue drinks with a cup

   System.out.println(mom.eat());          // mom eats with a fork
   System.out.println(junior.eat());       // junior eats with his hands
   System.out.println(auntSue.eat());      // auntSue eats with a spork
}
```

```
OUTPUT
cup
cup
cup
fork
hands
spork
```

Polymorphism
Java uses the term **polymorphism** to describe how different child classes of the same parent class can act differently. This is accomplished by having the child class override the methods of the parent class.

Dynamic Binding

A problem arises when we want to make a list of family members. *To make an array or* `ArrayList` *of people in the family, they all have to be of the same type!* To solve this problem, we make the reference variables all of the *parent* type.

Example
Create a FamilyMember `ArrayList` to demonstrate dynamic binding. Make the reference variables all the same type (the name of the parent class) and make the objects from the child classes. Allow each object to eat and drink the way they were designed to eat and drink. The decision of how each `FamilyMember` object eats is decided while the program is running (known as **run-time**) and this process is called **dynamic binding**. It's pretty cool!

```java
public static void main(String[] args)
{
    FamilyMember mom = new FamilyMember();
    FamilyMember junior = new Baby();
    FamilyMember auntSue = new SporkUser();

    // Make a list of family members
    ArrayList<FamilyMember> family = new ArrayList<FamilyMember>();

    family.add(mom);
    family.add(junior);
    family.add(auntSue);

    // Demonstrate polymorphism by allowing everyone to eat their way
    for (FamilyMember member : family)
    {
        System.out.println(member.drink()); // everyone drinks with a cup
        System.out.println(member.eat());    // everyone eats their way
        System.out.println();
    }
}
```

```
OUTPUT
cup
fork

cup
hands

cup
spork
```

Reference Variables and Hierarchy

The reference variable *can* be the parent of a child object.

```
FamilyMember somebody = new Baby();    // Legal
```

The reference variable *cannot* be a child of a parent object.

```
Baby somebody = new FamilyMember();    // Illegal:  Type Mismatch error
```

Using super from a Child Method

Even if a child class overrides a method from the parent class, an object from a child class can call its parent's method if it wants to; however, it must do it from the overriding method and pass the appropriate parameters. By using the keyword **super**, a child can make a call to the parent method that it has already overridden. We say, "The child can invoke the parent's method if it wants to."

Example

Revise the Baby class so that if a baby is older than three years, it eats with either its hands or a fork; otherwise it eats with its hands. Use the keyword **super** to make a call to the parent's eat method. Also, add an instance variable for the age.

```
public class Baby extends FamilyMember
{
    private int age;        // every Baby has an age

    public Baby(int myAge)
    {
        age = myAge;        // assign the age to the Baby
    }

    public String eat()
    {
        if (age > 3)        // older baby may eat with hands or a fork
            return "hands or a " + super.eat();
        else
            return "hands";
    }
}
```

```
public static void main(String[] args)
{
   Baby youngBaby = new Baby(2);          // youngBaby is 2 years old
   Baby olderBaby = new Baby(4);          // olderBaby is 4 years old

   System.out.println(youngBaby.eat());   // youngBaby uses only hands
   System.out.println(olderBaby.eat());   // olderBaby uses hands or a fork
}
```

```
OUTPUT
hands
hands or a fork
```

Beware When Using a Parent Reference Variable for a Child Object

A child object has the ability to perform all the public methods of its parent class. However, a parent does not have the ability to do what the child does if the child action is original. Also, if a child object has a parent reference variable, the child *does not* have the ability to perform any of the unique methods that are defined in its own class.

Example

Demonstrate that a parent reference variable cannot perform any of the methods that are unique to a child class. A FamilyMember object does not know how to throwTantrum. Only a Baby object knows how to throwTantrum. Note: Even though babyCousin is a Baby object, the FamilyMember reference variable prevents it from being able to throwTantrum.

```
public class Baby extends FamilyMember
{
   public String throwTantrum()       // A Baby's impressive new ability
   {
      return "scream loudly";
   }

   /*  all other implementation is not shown  */
}
```

```
public static void main(String[] args)
{
   Baby junior = new Baby();                  // reference is a Baby
   FamilyMember babyCousin = new Baby(); // reference is a FamilyMember

   System.out.println(junior.throwTantrum());       // legal
   System.out.println(babyCousin.throwTantrum());   // illegal
}
```

```
COMPILE TIME ERROR:  the method, throwTantrum is undefined for FamilyMember
```

Downcasting

The problem described in the previous example can be solved using a technique called **downcasting**. This is similar to—but not exactly the same as—casting an int to a double. A parent object reference variable is cast to the object type of the object that it references.

> **Downcasting**
> You can downcast a parent reference variable to a child object as long as the object it is referring to is that child.
>
> ```
> FamilyMember somebody = new Baby();  // Parent reference and child object
> ((Baby) somebody).uniqueMethodForBaby(); // Correct way to downcast
> ```

Example 1

Demonstrate downcasting by allowing the parent reference variable to perform a method that is unique to a child class. The parent reference variable is cast as a child and must refer to the child object. Pay close attention to the parentheses when casting.

```
public static void main(String[] args)
{
   Baby junior = new Baby();              // reference is a Baby
   FamilyMember babyCousin = new Baby(); // reference is a FamilyMember

   System.out.println(junior.throwTantrum());              // legal
   System.out.println(((Baby) babyCousin).throwTantrum()); // legal
}
```

```
OUTPUT
scream loudly
scream loudly
```

Example 2

You *are not allowed* to cast a parent reference object to a child if the object is a parent. In this example, mom is a FamilyMember reference variable that refers to a FamilyMember object. Attempting to cast mom as a Baby results in an error.

```
FamilyMember mom = new FamilyMember();
((Baby) mom).eat(); // ClassCastException:FamilyMember cannot be cast to Baby
```

The Object Class

The **Object class** is the mother of all classes. It is part of the java.lang package. Every class, even the ones you write, is a descendent of the Object class. The extends is *implied*, so you don't have to write, "extends Object", in your own classes. The Object class does not have any instance variables, but it does have several methods that every descendent inherits.

Two of these methods, the **toString** and the **equals**, are tested on the AP Computer Science A Exam and are included on the Java Quick Reference sheet. Subclasses of Object often override the equals and toString methods with class-specific implementation. You must be able to implement the toString method; however, you only need to know how to use the equals method (like we do when we compare String objects).

 You will receive a Java Quick Reference sheet to use on the Multiple-choice and Free-response sections, which lists the String class methods that may be included in the exam. Make sure you are familiar with it <u>before</u> you take the exam.

Object Class	
`boolean equals(Object other)`	
`String toString()`	

Overriding the toString Method

The **toString** method is inherited from the Object class and was created to describe the object in some way, typically by referencing its instance variables. The Object class's toString method doesn't give you anything valuable (it returns the hex value of the object's address). Most of the time, when creating your own classes, you will override the toString method so it returns a String that describes the object in a meaningful way.

Example

We overrode the toString method for the Circle class in Unit 5 so the method gives a description of the Circle object that calls it. The String that is returned should include the radius of the circle and its area.

```
public class Circle
{
    /*  All other implementation not shown  */

    public String toString()            // Override the toString method
    {
        return "The circle has radius " + radius + " and area " +
            getArea();
    }
}
```

```
public static void main(String[] args)
{
    Circle circle = new Circle(5);          // Circle with a radius of 5
    System.out.println(circle);             // call the toString() method
}
```

Overriding the `toString` Method
All classes extend the Object class. When you design your own classes, *be sure to override the toString() method* of the Object class so that it describes objects from your class in a unique way using its own instance variables.

Casting an `Object`

If a method's parameter list contains an `Object` reference variable, then you will have to downcast the reference before using it. You must make sure that the object that you are casting `is-a` object from the class.

Example

Demonstrate how to handle an `Object` reference parameter. In this example, when the `FamilyMember` object, `uncleDon`, gets passed to the `timeToEat` method, he is sent as a `FamilyMember` reference variable. When he is received by the `timeToEat` method, he is renamed as `hungryMember` and is now an `Object` reference. Finally, he is cast to a `FamilyMember` and is then able to eat.

```
public static void main(String[] args)
{
    FamilyMember uncleDon = new FamilyMember();
    timeToEat(uncleDon);
}

public static void timeToEat(Object hungryMember)
{
    ((FamilyMember) hungryMember).eat();  // casting Object to FamilyMember

    // Even though uncleDon is an Object reference, he can eat like a
    // FamilyMember because he was downcast to a FamilyMember
}
```

OUTPUT
fork

› Rapid Review

Hierarchy and Inheritance

- One major advantage of an object-oriented language is the ability to create a hierarchy of classes that allows objects from one class to inherit the features from another class.
- A class hierarchy is formed when one class extends another class.
- A class that extends another class is called the child or subclass.
- The class that is extended is called the parent or superclass.
- A class can only extend one other class.
- A class hierarchy can extend as many times as you want. That is, a child can extend a parent, then the parent can extend another parent, and so on.
- When a class hierarchy gets extended to more than just one parent and one child, the lower ends of the hierarchy inherit the features of each of the parent classes above it.
- The phrase "is-a" helps describe what parent classes a child class belongs to.
- If you want a child class to modify a parent class's method, then you override the parent class's method. To do this, you simply redefine the method in the child class (using the exact same method declaration and replace the code with what you want the child to do).
- The word "super" can be used to refer to either a parent's constructor or methods.
- To purposefully call the no-argument super constructor, you must put super() as the first line of code in the child's constructor. Other instructions are placed after the super() call.
- To call the parameterized super constructor, you must put super(arguments) as the first line of code in the child's parameterized constructor. Other instructions are placed after the super() call.
- If you write a method that overrides the parent class's method, you can still call the original parent's method if you want to. Example: `super.parentMethod()`.
- A reference variable can be a parent class type if the object being created is its child class type.
- A reference variable cannot be a child class type if the object being created is its parent class type.
- A reference variable that is of a parent data type can be cast to a child data type as long as the object that it is referencing is a child object of that type.

Polymorphism

- Polymorphism is when more than one child class extends the same parent class and each child object is allowed to act in a different way than its parent and even its siblings.
- If several child classes extend the same parent class and each child class overrides the same method of the parent class in its own unique way, then each child will act differently for that method.
- Static binding is the process of deciding which method the child reference variable will perform during compile-time.
- Dynamic binding is the process of deciding which method the parent reference will perform during run-time.
- The `Object` class is the mother of all classes in Java since it is the root of the class hierarchy and every class has `Object` as a superclass.
- The Object class contains two methods that are tested on the AP Computer Science A exam: equals and toString.
- The public boolean `equals(Object other)` method returns true if the object reference variable that calls it is referencing the same exact object as other. It returns false if the object reference variables are not referencing the same object.

- It is common to override the `equals` method when you want to determine if two objects from a class are the same.
- The public String `toString()` method returns a String representation of the object.
- It is very common to override the `toString()` method when generating your own classes.
- Downcasting is casting a reference variable of a parent class to one of its child classes.
- Downcasting is commonly used when an `Object` is in a parameter list or `ArrayList`.
- A major problem with downcasting is that the compiler will not catch any errors, and if the cast is made incorrectly, a run-time error will be thrown.

› Review Questions

Basic Level

1. Assuming all classes are defined in a manner appropriate to their names, which of the following statements will cause a compile-time error?

   (A) `Object obj = new Lunch();`
   (B) `Lunch lunch = new Lunch();`
   (C) `Lunch sandwich = new Sandwich();`
   (D) `Lunch lunch = new Object();`
   (E) `Sandwich sandwich = new Sandwich();`

Questions 2–5 refer to the following classes.

```
public class Student
{
    private int gradYear;
    private double gpa;

    /*  other implementation not shown  */
}

public class UnderClassman extends Student
{
    private int homeRoomNum;
    private String counselor;

    /*  other implementation not shown  */
}

public class Freshman extends UnderClassman
{
    private int middleSchoolCode;

    /*  other implementation not shown  */
}
```

2. Which of the following is true with respect to the classes defined above?

   I.   `Freshman` is a subclass of `UnderClassman` and `UnderClassman` is a subclass of `Student`
   II. `Student` is a superclass of both `UnderClassman` and `Freshman`
   III. `UnderClassman` is a superclass of `Freshman` and a subclass of `Student`

   (A) I only
   (B) II only
   (C) I and II only
   (D) II and III only
   (E) I, II, and III

3. Which of the following lists of instance data contains only variables that are directly accessible to a Freshman class object?

(A) middleSchoolCode
(B) gradYear, gpa
(C) homeRoomNum, counselor
(D) middleSchoolCode, homeRoomNum, counselor
(E) middleSchoolCode, homeRoomNum, counselor, gradYear, gpa

4. Assume that all three classes contain parameterized constructors with the following declarations and that all variables are logically named.

```
public Student (int gradYear, double gpa)

public UnderClassman (int gradYear, double gpa, int homeRoomNum, String counselor)

public Freshman (int gradYear, double gpa, int homeRoomNum, String counselor,
        int middleSchoolCode)
```

Which of the following calls to super would appear in the constructor for the Freshman class?
(A) super(gradYear, gpa, homeRoomNum, counselor, middleSchoolCode);
(B) super(gradYear, gpa, homeRoomNum, counselor);
(C) super(homeRoomNum, counselor);
(D) super(gradYear, gpa);
(E) super();

5. Consider the following method in the Student class.

```
public void attendClass(int roomNumber, String subject)
{
    /* implementation not shown */
}
```

A Freshman object must attendClass like a Student object, but also have the teacher initial his/her homework planner (using the initialPlanner method, not shown).

Which of the following shows a possible implementation of the Freshman attendClass method?
(A)
```
public void attendClass extends Student(int roomNumber, String subject)
{
    super.attendClass(int roomNumber, String subject);
    initialPlanner();
}
```

(B)
```
public void attendClass extends Student(int roomNumber, String subject)
{
    super.attendClass();
    initialPlanner();
}
```

(C)
```
public void attendClass(int roomNumber, String  subject)
{
    super(int roomNumber, String subject);
    initialPlanner();
}
```

(D)
```
public void attendClass(int roomNumber, String  subject)
    {
        super(roomNumber, subject);
        initialPlanner();
    }
```

(E)
```
public void attendClass(int roomNumber, String  subject)
    {
        super.roomNumber = roomNumber;
        super.subject = subject;
        initialPlanner();
    }
```

Advanced Level

Questions 6–7 refer to the following classes.

```
public class Club
{
    private ArrayList<String> members;

    public Club() {   }

    public Club(ArrayList<String> theMembers)
    {  members = theMembers;   }

    /* Additional implementation not shown */
}

public class SchoolClub extends Club
{
    private String advisor;

    public SchoolClub(String theAdvisor, ArrayList<String> theMembers)
    {
        /* missing code */
    }

    /* Additional implementation not shown */
}
```

6. Assume `ArrayList<String> members_1` and `ArrayList<String> members_2` have been properly instantiated and initialized with a non-zero number of appropriate elements.

   Which of the following declarations is NOT valid?
   (A) `Club[] clubs = new SchoolClub[7];`
   (B) `Club[] clubs = {new Club(members_1), new Club()};`
   (C) `SchoolClub[] clubs = {new SchoolClub("Mr. Johnson", members_1),`
   `        new Club(members_2)};`
   (D) `SchoolClub[] clubs = {new SchoolClub("Ms. Paymer", members_1),`
   `           new SchoolClub("Mr. Johnson", members_2)};`
   (E) All of the above are valid.

7. Which of the following could replace /* missing code */ in the SchoolClub constructor to ensure that all instance variables are initialized correctly?

(A) `super(theMembers);`
`advisor = theAdvisor;`

(B) `super(new Club(theMembers));`
`advisor = theAdvisor;`

(C) `this.SchoolClub = new Club(members);`
`advisor = theAdvisor;`

(D) `advisor = theAdvisor;`

(E) `advisor = theAdvisor;`
`super(theMembers);`

Questions 8–9 refer to the following classes.

```java
public class Present
{
    private String contents;

    public Present(String theContents)
    {   contents = theContents;   }

    public String getContents()
    {   return contents;   }

    public void setContents(String theContents)
    {   contents = theContents;   }

    public String toString()
    {   return "contains " + getContents();   }
}

public class KidsPresent extends Present
{
    private int age;

    public KidsPresent(String contents, int theAge)
    {
        super(contents);
        age = theAge;
    }

    public int getAge()
    {   return age;   }

    public String toString()
    {   return super.toString() + " for a child age " + getAge();   }
}
```

8. Consider the following code segment.

```
Present p = new KidsPresent("kazoo", 4);
System.out.println(p);
```

What is printed as a result of executing the code segment?
(A) `contains kazoo`
(B) `kazoo`
(C) `contains kazoo for a child age 4`
(D) Nothing is printed. Compile-time error: illegal cast
(E) Nothing is printed. Run-time error: illegal cast

9. Consider the following code segment.

```
Present p = new KidsPresent("kazoo", 4);
p.setContents("blocks");
System.out.println(p);
```

What is printed as a result of executing the code segment?
(A) `contains blocks`
(B) `contains blocks for a child age 4`
(C) `contains kazoo for a child age 4`
(D) Nothing is printed. Compile-time error: there is no `setContents` method in the `KidsPresent` class
(E) Nothing is printed. Run-time error: there is no `setContents` method in the `KidsPresent` class

10. Point3D Class

Consider the following class:

```
public class Point
{
    private int x;
    private int y;

    public Point(int newX, int newY)
    {
        x = newX;
        y = newY;
    }

    public int getX()
    {   return x;  }

    public int getY()
    {   return y;  }
}
```

Write the class `Point3D` that extends this class to represent a three-dimensional point with x, y, and z coordinates. Be sure to use appropriate inheritance. Do not duplicate code.

You will need to write:
a. A constructor that takes three `int` values representing the x, y, and z coordinates
b. Appropriate mutator and accessor methods (setters and getters)

› Answers and Explanations

Bullets mark each step in the process of arriving at the correct solution.

1. The answer is D.

   - When you instantiate an object, you tell the compiler what type it is (left side of the equal sign) and then you call the constructor for a specific type (right side of the equal sign). Here's where you can put is-a to good use. You can construct an object as long as it is-a version of the type you have declared. You can say, "Make me a sandwich, and I'll say thanks for lunch," and you will always be right, but you can't say, "Make me lunch and I'll say thanks for the sandwich." What if I made soup?
   - Option A is correct, since Lunch *is-a* Object.
   - Options B and E are correct since Lunch *is-a* Lunch, and Sandwich *is-a* Sandwich. (Don't confuse the variable name sandwich with the type Lunch. It's a bad programming choice, since a reader expects that a variable named sandwich is an object of the class Sandwich, but it's legal.)
   - Option C is correct since Sandwich *is-a* Lunch.
   - Option D is incorrect. Object is not a Lunch. It's not reversible. The one on the right has to have an *is-a* relationship to the one on the left in that order. Option D will not compile.

2. The answer is E.

   - Superclass refers to grandparents as well as parents, all the way up the inheritance line, and subclass refers to grandchildren as well as children, all the way down the inheritance line, so all three relationships are true.

3. The answer is A.

   - A Freshman object will have direct access to its own private variables.
   - The instance variables for UnderClassman and Student are private and can only be accessed within that class.
   - Please note that it is considered a violation of encapsulation to declare instance variables public, and points will be taken off on the AP Computer Science A exam if you do so!

4. The answer is B.

   - Since the super call must be the first thing in the constructor, the Freshman constructor will hang on to the parameter middleSchoolCode and use the super call to pass the remaining parameters to the constructor for Underclassman. It will then set its own instance variable to the middleSchoolCode parameter. (It's worth noting that the Underclassman constructor will set its own two variables and pass the remaining variables to its super constructor.)

5. The answer is D.

   - Options A and B are incorrect. They show an incorrect usage of "extends". The keyword extends belongs on the class declaration, not the method declaration.
   - Option C is incorrect. It puts data types next to the arguments (actual parameters) in the super method call. Types only appear next to the formal parameters in the method declaration.
   - Option D is correct. It has fixed both of the above errors. The method with the same name in the superclass is called using the super.methodName notation, and it is passed the two parameters it is expecting. Then the initialPlanner method is called.
   - Option E is incorrect. It attempts to assign the parameters directly to their corresponding variables in the Student class. The variables in the parent class should be private, so the child doesn't know if they exist, and can't access them even if they do. Also, the child class shouldn't assume that assigning variables is all the parent class method does. Surely attendClass involves more than that!

6. The answer is C.

- Option A is valid. It instantiates an array of `Club` objects. The right side of the instantiation specifies that there will be two entries, but it does not instantiate those entries. This is a valid statement, but note that the entries in this array are null.
- Option B is valid. It uses an initialization list to instantiate the array of `Club` objects. `Club` has overloaded constructors. There is a constructor that takes an `ArrayList<String>` as an argument, so the first entry is correct, and there is a no-argument constructor, so the second entry is correct.
- Option C is not valid. It uses an initialization list to instantiate an array of `SchoolClub` objects, but the list includes not only a `SchoolClub` object, but also a `Club` object. We could make a `Club[]` and include `SchoolClub` objects, but not the other way around. Remember the *is-a* designation. A `Club` is not a `SchoolClub`.
- Option D is valid. It instantiates an array of `SchoolClub` objects by giving an initialization list of correctly instantiated `SchoolClub` objects.

7. The answer is A.

- The first statement in the constructor of an extended class is a super call to the constructor of the parent class. This may be an implicit call to the no-argument constructor (not explicitly written by you) or it may be an explicit call to any of the superclass's constructors.
- Option B is incorrect. It calls the super constructor but passes a parameter of the wrong type.
- Option C is incorrect. `this.SchoolClub` has no meaning.
- Option D is incorrect. This option is syntactically correct. The no-argument constructor will be called implicitly, but the members `ArrayList` instance variable will not be set.
- Option E is incorrect. The super call must be the first statement in the constructor.

8. The answer is C.

- First of all, remember that when an object is printed, Java looks for that object's `toString` method to find out how to print the object. (If there is no `toString` method, the memory address of the object is printed, which is not what you want!)
- Variable p is of type Present. That's what the compiler knows. But when we instantiate variable p, we make is a KidsPresent. That's what the runtime environment knows. So when the runtime environment looks for a toString method, it looks in the KidsPresent class. The KidsPresent toString prints both the contents and the appropriate age.

9. The answer is B.

- Since p is declared as a Present, and the Present class has a `setContents` method, the compiler is fine with this sequence.
- When `setContents` is called, the run-time environment will look first in the KidsPresent class and it will not find a `setContents` method. But it doesn't give up! Next it looks in the parent class, which is Present and there it is. So the run-time environment happily uses the Present class's `setContents` method and successfully sets the Present class's contents variable to "blocks".
- When the KidsPresent `toString` is called, the first thing it does is call `super.toString()`, which accesses the value of the contents variable. Since that variable now equals "blocks", the code segment works as you might hope it would and prints "contains blocks for a child age 4".

10. On the AP Computer Science A exam, you are often asked to extend a class, as you were in this question. Check your answer against my version below. A few things to notice:

- The constructor takes x, y, and z but then immediately passes x and y to the Point class constructor through the super(x, y) call.
- x and y, their setters and getters are in the Point class; they don't need to be duplicated here. Only variable z, setZ and getZ need to be added.

```java
public class Point3D extends Point
{
    private int z;

    // Part a
    public Point3D(int myX, int myY, int myZ)
    {
        super(myX, myY);
        z = myZ;
    }

    // Part b
    public void setZ(int myZ)
    {
        z = myZ;
    }

    public int getZ()
    {
        return z;
    }
}
```

Recursion

5-7.5% AP Exam Weight

IN THIS UNIT

Summary: This unit defines and explains recursion. It also shows how to read and trace a recursive method. You will also learn how to implement recursive algorithms for searching and sorting.

Learning Objectives

CON-2.O Determine the result of executing recursive methods.

CON-2.P Apply recursive search algorithms to information in `String`, 1D array, or `ArrayList` objects.

CON-2.Q Apply recursive algorithms to sort elements of array or `ArrayList` objects.

Key Ideas

✪ A recursive method is a method that calls itself.

✪ Recursion is not the same as nested `for` loops or `while` loops.

✪ A recursive method must have a base case that tells the method to stop calling itself and a recursive call.

✪ The Binary Search is an efficient way to search for a target in a sorted list.

✪ The Merge Sort is a recursive sorting routine.

✪ You will need to know how to trace recursive methods on the AP Computer Science A Exam. You will not have to write recursive methods.

Recursion Versus Looping

The `for` loop and the `while` loop allow the programmer to repeat a set of instructions. **Recursion** is the process of repeating instructions too, but in a **self-similar** way. I know that's kind of weird. Let me explain by using the following example.

Example 1

Imagine you are standing in a really long line and you want to know how many people are in line in front of you, but you can't see everyone. If you ask the person in front of you how many people are in front of him, and he turns to the person in front of him and asks the person in front of him how many people are in front of him, and so on, eventually this chain reaction will reach the first person in line. This person will turn to the person behind him and say, "No one." Then something fun happens. The second person in line will turn to the third person and say, "One." The third person will turn to the fourth person and say, "Two," and so on, until finally the person in front of you will respond with the number of people who are in front of him. This creative solution to the problem is an example of how a recursive algorithm works.

A **recursive** method is a method that calls itself. Recursion is a programming technique that can be used to solve a problem in which a solution to the problem can be found by making subsequently smaller iterations of the same problem. When used correctly, it can be an extremely elegant solution to a problem. And by the way, a recursive solution can be written by using iteration, but we still need to know it because it does make some problems much easier to write and understand.

We know that one method can call another method, right? What if the method called itself? If you stop and think about that, after the method was **invoked** the first time, the program would never end because the method would continue to call itself forever (think of the movie *Inception*).

Example 2

Here's an example of a really bad recursive method.

```
public static void IAmABadRecursiveMethod()
{
    IAmABadRecursiveMethod();   // This method never stops calling itself
}
```

However, if the method had some kind of trigger that told it when to stop calling itself, then it would be a good recursive method.

General Form for a Recursive Method

```
public static returnType goodRecursiveMethod(parameterList)
{
    if ( /* base case is true */)
        return something;
    else
        return goodRecursiveMethod(argumentList);
}
```

Note: All recursive methods must have a base case and a recursive call.

The Base Case

The **base case** of a recursive method is a comparison between a parameter of the method and a predefined value strategically chosen by the programmer. The base case comparison determines whether or not the method should call itself again. Referring back to the example in the introduction of this concept, the response by the first person in line of "no one" is the base case. It is the answer that reverses the recursive process.

Each time the recursive method calls itself and the base case is not satisfied, the method temporarily sets that call aside before making a new call to itself. This continues until the base case is satisfied. When there is finally a call to the method that makes the base case true (the base case is satisfied), the method stops calling itself and starts the process of returning a value for each of the previous method calls. Since the calls are placed on a **stack**, the returns are executed in the reverse order of how they were placed. This order is known as last-in, first-out (LIFO), which means that the last recursive call made is the first one to return a value.

Furthermore, each successive call of the method should bring the value of the parameter *closer and closer to making the base case true*. This means that with each call to the method, the value of the parameter should be *closing in* on making the base case true rather than moving farther away from it being true.

If a recursive method does not contain a valid base case comparison, then it may continue to call itself into oblivion. That would be bad.

What do I mean by bad? Remember that every time a recursive method is called, it has to set that call aside temporarily until the base case is satisfied. This process is called *putting the call on the stack* and the computer stores this stack in its RAM. If the base case is *never* satisfied, then the method calls pile up and the computer eventually runs out of memory. This will cause a **stack overflow error** and it occurs when you have an **infinite recursion.**

The Base Case
The base case is a comparison between a parameter of the method and some specific predefined value chosen by the programmer. When the base case is true, the method stops calling itself and starts the process of returning values. Every recursive method needs a valid base case or else it will continue to call itself indefinitely (infinite recursion) and cause an out-of-memory error, called a stack overflow error.

Example: The Factorial Recursive Method

A very popular problem to solve using recursion is the factorial calculation. The factorial of a number uses the notation **n!** and is calculated by multiplying the integer n by each of the integers that precede it all the way down to 1. Factorial is useful for computing combinations and permutations when doing probability and statistics.

Example
Find the answer to 4! and 10!

4! = 4 * 3 * 2 * 1 = 24. Therefore 4! is 24.
10! = 10 * 9 * 8 * 7 * 6 * 5 * 4 * 3 * 2 * 1 = 3628800. Therefore, 10! is 3628800.

Why the Factorial Calculation Is a Good Recursive Example

The definition of a factorial can be written recursively. This means that the factorial of the number, n, can use the factorial of the previous number, n − 1, in its computation.

$$n! = n * (n - 1)! \qquad \text{where 1! is defined as 1}$$

Example

Write 4! recursively using math.

When you start to compute 4! using the definition of factorial, you see that 4! is 4 times 3! This means that in order to compute 4!, you need to figure out what 3! is. But 3! is 3 times 2! so we have to figure out what 2! is. And 2! is 2 times 1!, and 1! is 1.

Do you see how we had to put our calculations on hold until we got to 1!? Once we got a final answer of 1 for 1!, we were able to compute 4! by working backward.

1! = 1
so 2! = 2 * 1! = 2 * 1 = 2
so 3! = 3 * 2! = 3 * 2 = 6
so 4! = 4 * 3! = 4 * 6 = 24

Now that I know that 1! is 1,
I can work backward to find 4!

Implementation of the Factorial Recursive Method

```java
public class Factorial
{
    public static void main(String[] args)
    {
        System.out.println(factorial(5));    // find factorial(5)
    }

    /**
     * This is a recursive method that computes the
     * factorial of a number.
     *
     * @param n the number we are finding the factorial of
     * @return the answer to the factorial of n
     *
     * PRECONDITION:  n >= 1
     * POSTCONDITION:  The result of the recursive call
     *                 is the factorial of the original argument
     */
    public static int factorial(int n)
    {
        if (n == 1)                          // base case comparison
            return 1;
        else
            return n * factorial(n - 1);     // move closer to base case
    }
}
```

```
OUTPUT
120
```

Hand-Tracing the Factorial Recursive Method

This is kind of tricky, so read it over very carefully. When tracing a recursive method call, write out each call to the method including its parameter. When the base case is reached, replace the result from each method call with its result, one at a time. This process will force you to calculate the return values in the reverse order from the way that the calls were made.

Goal: Compute the value of factorial(5) using the process of recursion.

Step 1: This problem is similar to the "find the number of people in line" example. The answer to a factorial requires knowledge of the factorial preceding it.

Suppose I ask the number 5, "Hey what's your factorial?" 5 responds with, "I don't know. I need to ask 4 what its factorial is before I can find out my own." Then 4 asks 3 what its factorial is. Then 3 asks 2 what its factorial is. Then 2 asks 1 what its factorial is. Then 1 says, "1".

Step 2: After 1 says, "1", the process reverses itself and each number answers the question that was asked of it. The answer of "1" is the base case.

1 says, "My factorial is 1."

2 then says, "My factorial is 2 because 2 * 1 is 2."

3 then says, "My factorial is 6 because 3 * 2 is 6."

4 then says, "My factorial is 24 because 4 * 6 is 24."

And finally, 5 turns to me and says, "My factorial is 120, because 5 * 24 is 120."

```
factorial(1) = 1
factorial(2) = 2 * factorial(1) = 2 * 1 = 2
factorial(3) = 3 * factorial(2) = 3 * 2 = 6
factorial(4) = 4 * factorial(3) = 4 * 6 = 24
factorial(5) = 5 * factorial(4) = 5 * 24 = 120
```

Conclusion: factorial(5) = 120

A Visual Representation of Computing a Recursive Value

Example

Explain how to compute the value of factorial(5) for the visual learner. As you trace through this problem, think of the original example of the people in the long line.

Each recursive call has its own set of local variables, including the formal parameters. In the example above a new formal parameter n gets created with each call to the factorial method. The parameter values capture the progress of a recursive process, much like loop control variables capture the progress of the loop. Once the parameter n reaches the value 1, the recursion reaches the base case and ends.

Example: The Fibonacci Recursive Method

On the AP Computer Science A exam, you will need to be able to hand-trace recursive method calls that have either multiple parameters or make multiple calls within the return statement. The following example shows a recursive method that has multiple calls to the recursive method within its return statement.

The Fibonacci Sequence

This popular sequence is often covered in math class as it has some interesting applications. In the Fibonacci sequence, the first two terms are 1, and then each term starting with the third term is equal to the sum of the two previous terms.

1, 1, 2, 3, 5, 8, 13, 21, 34, 55 . . .

The Java code that is provided below is a recursive method that returns the value of the nth term in a Fibonacci sequence. **Example:** fibonacci(6) is 8. The value of the sixth term is 8.

```
public class AdvancedRecursiveProblem
{
    public static void main(String[] args)
    {
        System.out.println(fibonacci(6));              // find fibonacci(6)
    }

    /**
     * This is a recursive method that has multiple base cases and
     * uses two recursive calls within the return statement.
     *
     * @param n The fibonacci term to be calculated
     * @return The nth term of the fibonacci sequence
     */
    public static int fibonacci(int n)
    {
        if (n == 1 || n == 2)
            return 1;
        else
            return fibonacci(n - 1) + fibonacci(n - 2);
    }
}
```

```
OUTPUT
8
```

Hand-Tracing the Fibonacci Recursive Method

This is harder to follow than the factorial recursive method because the return statement includes two calls to the recursive method. Also, there are two base cases.

Goal: Compute the value of fibonacci(6).

Step 1: In a manner similar to the previous example, I ask 6, "What's your fibonacci?" 6 responds by saying, "I don't know right now, I need to ask both 5 and 4 what their fibonaccis are." In response, 5 says, "I need to ask both 4 and 3 what their fibonaccis are." And, 4 says, "I need to ask both 3 and 2 what their fibonaccis are." This continues until 2 and 1 are asked what their fibonaccis are.

Step 2: Ultimately, 2 and 1 will respond with "1" and "1" and each number can then answer the question that was asked of them. The 2 and 1 are the base cases for this problem.

fibonacci(1) = 1
fibonacci(2) = 1
fibonacci(3) = fibonacci(2) + fibonacci(1) = 1 + 1 = 2
fibonacci(4) = fibonacci(3) + fibonacci(2) = 2 + 1 = 3
fibonacci(5) = fibonacci(4) + fibonacci(3) = 3 + 2 = 5
fibonacci(6) = fibonacci(5) + fibonacci(4) = 5 + 3 = 8

Conclusion: fibonacci(6) is 8

Merge Sort

The **Merge Sort** is called a "divide and conquer" algorithm and uses recursion. The Merge Sort algorithm repeatedly divides the list into two groups until it can't do it anymore (that's where the recursion comes in). Next, the algorithm merges the smaller groups together and sorts them as it joins them. This process repeats until all the groups form one sorted group.

Merge Sort is a relatively fast sort and is much more efficient on large data sets than Insertion Sort or Selection Sort. Although it seems like Merge Sort is the best of these three sorts, its downside is that it requires more memory to execute.

Example
Sort a group of numbers using the Merge Sort algorithm.

Goal: Sort these numbers from smallest to largest: 8, 5, 2, 6, 9, 1, 3, 4

Step 1: Split the group of numbers into two groups: 8, 5, 2, 6 and 9, 1, 3, 4
Step 2: Split each of these groups into two groups: 8, 5 and 2, 6 and 9, 1 and 3, 4
Step 3: Repeat until you can't anymore: 8 and 5 and 2 and 6 and 9 and 1 and 3 and 4
Step 4: Combine two groups, sorting as you group them: 5, 8 and 2, 6 and 1, 9 and 3, 4
Step 5: Combine two groups, sorting as you group them: 2, 5, 6, 8 and 1, 3, 4, 9
Step 6: Repeat the previous step until you have one sorted group: 1, 2, 3, 4, 5, 6, 8, 9

Implementation
The following class contains three interdependent methods that sort a list of integers from smallest to greatest using the Merge Sort algorithm. The method setUpMerge is a recursive method.

```java
public class MergeSort
{
    private static int[] myArray;
    private static int[] tempArray;

    public static void main(String[] args)
    {
        int[] inputArray = {8, 5, 2, 6, 9, 1, 3, 4};
        mergeSort(inputArray);
        for (int i: inputArray)
        {
            System.out.print(i + "\t");
        }
    }

    /**
     * This method starts the process of the Merge Sort.
     *
     * @param arr  the array to be sorted
     */
    private static void mergeSort(int arr[])
    {
        myArray = arr;
        int length = arr.length;
```

```java
        tempArray = new int[length];
        setUpMerge(0, length - 1);
    }


    /**
     * This method is called recursively to divide the array
     * into each of the groups to be sorted.
     *
     * @param lower   the lower index of the subgroup
     * @param higher  the higher index of the subgroup
     */
    private static void setUpMerge(int lower, int higher)
    {
        if (lower < higher)
        {
            int middle = lower + (higher - lower) / 2;
            setUpMerge(lower, middle);
            setUpMerge(middle + 1, higher);
            doTheMerge(lower, middle, higher);
        }
    }


    /**
     * This method merges the elements in two subgroups
     * ([start, middle] and [middle + 1, end]) in ascending order.
     * @param lower the index of the lower element
     * @param middle the index of the  middle element
     * @param higher the index of the higher element
     */
    private static void doTheMerge(int lower, int middle, int higher)
    {
        for (int i = lower; i <= higher; i++)
        {
            tempArray[i] = myArray[i];
        }
        int i = lower;
        int j = middle + 1;
        int k = lower;
        while (i <= middle && j <= higher)
        {
            if (tempArray[i] <= tempArray[j])
            {
                myArray[k] = tempArray[i];
                i++;
            }
            else
            {
                myArray[k] = tempArray[j];
                j++;
            }
            k++;
        }
```

```
        while (i <= middle)
        {
            myArray[k] = tempArray[i];
            k++;
            i++;
        }
    }
}
```

```
OUTPUT
1   2   3   4   5   6   8   9
```

Binary Search

So far, the only algorithm we know to search for a target in a list is the Sequential Search. It starts at one end of a list and works toward the other end, comparing each element to the target. Although it works, it's not very efficient. The **Binary Search** algorithm is the most efficient way to search for a target item *provided the list is already sorted*. The binary search algorithm starts at the middle of a sorted array or `ArrayList` and eliminates half of the array or `ArrayList` in each iteration (either the "low" side of the array or the "high" side of the array) until the desired value is found or all elements have been eliminated.

 Sorted Data
The Binary Search only works on sorted data. Performing a Binary Search on unsorted data produces invalid results.

Example
The "Guess My Number" game consists of someone saying something like, "I'm thinking of a number between 1 and 100. Try to guess it. I will tell you if your guess is too high or too low."

Solution 1: Terrible way to win the "Guess My Number" game

First guess:	1	Response: Too Low
Second guess:	2	Response: Too Low
Third guess:	3	Response: Too Low
and so on		
and so on		

Solution 2: Fastest way to win the "Guess My Number" game
(the Binary Search algorithm)

Guess halfway between 1 and 100	First Guess: 50	Response: Too Low
Guess halfway between 51 and 100	Second Guess: 75	Response: Too High
Guess halfway between 51 and 74	Third Guess: 62	Response: Too Low
Guess halfway between 63 and 74	Fourth Guess: 68	Response: Too Low
Guess halfway between 69 and 74	Fifth Guess: 71	Response: Too High
Guess halfway between 69 and 70	Sixth Guess: 70	Response: YOU GOT IT!

Visual description of the "Guess My Number" game using the Binary Search algorithm:

A list of sorted numbers from 1 to 100

First Guess: 50
Second Guess: 75
Third Guess: 62
Fourth Guess: 68
Fifth Guess: 71
Sixth Guess: 70

Iterative Implementation

The following class contains a method that searches an array of integers for a target value using the Binary Search algorithm. Notice that the main method makes a method call to sort the array prior to calling the binarySearch method.

```java
public class BinarySearch
{
    public static void main(String[] args)
    {
        int[] myArray = {23, 146, 57, 467, 69, 36, 184, 492, 100};
        int searchTarget = 57;
        insertionSort(myArray);              // Any sorting method can be used

        System.out.println(binarySearch(myArray, searchTarget));
    }


    /**
     * This method performs a Binary Search on a sorted array of integers.
     *
     * @param target the value that you are searching for
     * @param data the array you are searching
     * @return the result of the search. True if found, False if not found.
     *
     * Precondition:  The data is already sorted from smallest to largest
     */
    public static boolean binarySearch(int [] data, int target)
    {
        int low = 0;
        int high = data.length;

        while(high >= low)
        {
            int middle = (low + high) / 2;
            if (data[middle] == target)
            {
                return true;
            }
```

```
            if (data[middle] < target)
            {
               low = middle + 1;
            }
            if (data[middle] > target)
            {
               high = middle - 1;
            }
         }
         return false;
      }
}
```

```
OUTPUT
true
```

Recursive Implementation

The following is the recursive version of the Binary Search algorithm. This solution assumes the array is already sorted and it returns the index of the target.

```java
public class BinarySearch
{
    public static void main(String[] args)
    {
       int[] myArray = {-230, -146, 25, 58, 179, 316, 384, 492, 500};
       int target = 25;
       int foundIndex = recursiveBinarySearch(myArray,target,0,
                                     myArray.length-1);
       if (foundIndex == -1)
          System.out.println(target + " was not found);
       else
          System.out.println(target + " was found at position " +
                       foundIndex);
}

/**
 *This method performs a Binary Search on a sorted array of integers.
 *
 *@param target the value that you are searching for
 *@param data the array you are searching
 *@return the position the target was found.
 *
 *Precondition: The data is already sorted from smallest to largest
 */
public static int recursiveBinarySearch(int[] array, int target,
                                     int start, int end)
{
  int middle = (start + end)/2;
  if (target == array[middle])   // base case: check middle element
     return middle;
  else if (start > end) // base case: check if we've run out of elements
     return -1;                  // not found
```

```
else if (target < array[middle]) // recursive call: search start to middle
    return recursiveBinarySearch(array, target, start, middle - 1);


 else if (target > array[middle]) // recursive call: search middle to end
     return recursiveBinarySearch(array, target, middle + 1, end);
  return -1;         // not found
  }
}
```

```
OUTPUT
25 was found at position 2
```

❯ Rapid Review

- Recursive methods are methods that call themselves.
- Choose recursion rather than looping when the problem you are trying to solve can be solved by repeatedly shrinking the problem down to a single, final simple problem.
- Recursive methods usually have a return type (rather than void) and must take a parameter.
- The re-calling of the method should bring you closer to the base case.
- Many problems can be solved without recursion; however, if done properly, recursion can be an extremely elegant way to solve a problem.
- Once the recursive process has started, the only way to end it is to satisfy the base case.
- The base case is a comparison that is done in the method. When this comparison becomes true, the method returns a value that begins the return process.
- If you write a recursive method and forget to put in a base case, or your subsequent calls to the method do not get you closer to the base case, you will probably cause infinite recursion, which will result in a stack overflow error.
- To trace a recursive call, write out each call of the method with the value of the parameter. When the base case is reached, replace each method call with its result. This will happen in reverse order.

Merge Sort

- Merge Sort uses an algorithm that repeatedly divides the data into two groups until it can divide no longer. The algorithm joins the smaller groups together and sorts them as it joins them. This process repeats until all the groups are joined to form one sorted group.
- Merge Sort uses a divide and conquer algorithm and recursion.
- Merge Sort is more efficient than Selection Sort and Insertion Sort.
- Merge Sort requires more internal memory (RAM) than Selection Sort and Insertion Sort.

Binary Search

- A Binary Search algorithm is the most efficient way to search for a target value in a sorted list.
- A Binary Search algorithm requires that the list be sorted prior to searching.
- A Binary Search algorithm eliminates half of the search list with each pass.

› Review Questions

Basic Level

1. Consider the following recursive method.

```
public int puzzle(int num)
{
    if (num <= 1)
        return 1;
    else
        return num + puzzle(num / 2);
}
```

What value is returned when puzzle(10) is called?

(A) 18
(B) 15
(C) 11
(D) 1
(E) Nothing is returned. Infinite recursion causes a stack overflow error.

2. Consider the following recursive method.

```
public int mystery(int k)
{
    if (k == 0)
    {
        return 1;
    }
    return 2 * k + mystery(k - 2);
}
```

What value is returned when mystery(11) is called?

(A) 1
(B) 49
(C) 73
(D) 665280
(E) Nothing is returned. Infinite recursion causes a stack overflow error.

3. Consider the following recursive method.

```
public int enigma(int n)
{
    if (n < 3)
        return 2;
    if (n < 5)
        return 2 + enigma(n - 1);
    return 3 + enigma(n - 2);
}
```

What value is returned when enigma(9) is called?

(A) 7
(B) 10
(C) 13
(D) 15
(E) 16

4. Consider the following recursive method.

```java
public void printStars(int n)
{
    if (n == 1)
    {
        System.out.println("*");
    }
    else
    {
        System.out.print("*");
        printStars(n - 1);
    }
}
```

What will be printed when `printStars(15)` is called?

(A) `***************`

(B) `*`

(C) Nothing is printed. Method will not compile. Recursive methods cannot print.

(D) Nothing is printed. Method returns successfully.

(E) Many stars are printed. Infinite recursion causes a stack overflow error.

5. Consider the following method.

```java
public String weird(String s)
{
    if (s.length() >= 10)
    {
        return s;
    }
    return weird(s + s.substring(s.indexOf("lo")));
}
```

What value is returned when `weird("Hello")` is called?

(A) `"Hello"`

(B) `"Hellolo"`

(C) `"Hellolololo"`

(D) `"Hellolololololololo"`

(E) Nothing is returned. Infinite recursion causes a stack overflow error.

6. Array `arr2` has been defined and initialized as follows.

```java
int[] arr2 = {1, 2, 3, 4, 5, 6, 7, 8, 9, 10, 11};
```

If the array is being searched for the number 4, which sequence of numbers is still in the area to be searched after two passes through the `while` loop of the Binary Search algorithm?

(A) 1   2   3   4   5

(B) 2   3   4

(C) 4   5   6

(D) 4   5

(E) The number has been found in the second pass. Nothing is left to be searched.

Advanced Level

Questions 7–8 refer to the following methods.

```
public int factors(int number)
{
    return factors(number, number - 1, 0);
}

public int factors(int number, int check, int count)
{
    if (number % check == 0)
    {
        count++;
    }
    check--;
    if (check == 1)
    {
        return count;
    }
    return factors(number, check, count);
}
```

7. What value is returned when `factors(10)` is called?

   (A) 0
   (B) 1
   (C) 2
   (D) 3
   (E) 4

8. Which of the following statements will execute successfully?

   I.   `int answer = factors(0);`
   II. `int answer = factors(2);`
   III. `int answer = factors(12, 2, 5);`

   (A) I only
   (B) II only
   (C) III only
   (D) I and II only
   (E) I, II, and III

9. Consider the following recursive method.

```
public int function(int x, int y)
{
    if (x <= y)
        return x + y;
    else
        return function(x - y, y + 1) + 2;
}
```

What value is returned when `function(24, 3)` is called?
   (A) 13
   (B) 21
   (C) 25
   (D) 27
   (E) Nothing is returned. Infinite recursion causes a stack overflow error.

10. Consider this recursive problem.

In elementary school, we learned that if you add up the digits of a number and get a sum of 9, then that number is divisible by 9. If your answer is less than 9, then that number is not divisible by 9. For example,

- 81 → 8 + 1 = 9, divisible by 9.
- 71 → 7 + 1 = 8, not divisible by 9.

The trouble is, if you add up the digits of a big number, you get a sum that is greater than 9, for example, 999 → 9 + 9 + 9 = 27. We can fix this by using the same trick on that sum: 27 → 2 + 7 = 9, divisible by 9.

Here's another example:

- 457829 → 4 + 5 + 7 + 8 + 2 + 9 = 35, keep going,
- 35 → 3 + 5 = 8, not divisible by 9.

If your number is big enough, you may have to repeat the process three, four, five, or even more times, but eventually, you will get a sum that is <= 9 and that will let you determine whether your number is divisible by 9.

Your client code will call method `divisible`, passing a number and expecting a `boolean` result, and `divisible` will call the recursive method `sumUp` to do the repeated addition.

Consider the class below that implements a solution to the problem.

```
public class Div9
{
    public boolean divisible (int dividend)
    {
        return sumUp(dividend) == 9;
    }

    public int sumUp(int dividend)
    {
        int sum = 0;

        // This loop adds the digits of dividend into the sum variable
        while (dividend > 0)
        {
            sum += dividend % 10;
            dividend = dividend /10;
        }

        if ( /* condition */ )
            return sum;
        else
            return sumUp( /* argument */ );
    }
}
```

Which of the following can be used to replace /* `condition` */ and /* `argument` */ so that `sumUp` will work as intended?

(A) condition: `sum <= 9`   argument: `sum`
(B) condition: `sum = 9`   argument: `dividend`
(C) condition: `sum <= 9`   argument: `dividend`
(D) condition: `sum < 9`   argument: `sum`
(E) condition: `sum < 9`   argument: `dividend / sum`

11. Consider the following method.

```java
public static int mystery (int[] array, int a)
{
    int low = 0;
    int high = array.length - 1;
    while (low <= high)
    {
        int mid = (high + low) / 2;
        if (a < array[mid])
            high = mid - 1;
        else if (a > array[mid])
            low = mid + 1;
        else
            return mid;
    }
    return -1;
}
```

The algorithm implemented by the method can best be described as:
(A) Insertion Sort
(B) Selection Sort
(C) Binary Search
(D) Merge Sort
(E) Sequential Sort

› Answers and Explanations

Bullets mark each step in the process of arriving at the correct solution.

1. The answer is A.

- Let's trace the calls. The parts in *italics* were filled in on the way back up. That is, the calls in the plain type were written top to bottom until the base case returned 1. Then the answers were filled in *bottom to top*.

    puzzle(10) = num + puzzle(num/2) = 10 + puzzle(5) = 10 + *8* = **18**
    puzzle(5) = num + puzzle(num/2) = 5 + puzzle(2) = 5 + *3* = *8*
    puzzle(2) = num + puzzle(num/2) = 2 + puzzle(1) = 2 + *1* = *3*
    puzzle(1) = base case! return 1

- Don't forget to do integer division.

2. The answer is E.

- Let's trace the calls just like we did in problem 1.

    mystery(11) = 2 * 11 + mystery(9)
    mystery(9) = 2 * 9 + mystery(7)
    mystery(7) = 2 * 7 + mystery(5)
    mystery(5) = 2 * 5 + mystery(3)
    mystery(3) = 2 * 3 + mystery(1)
    mystery(1) = 2 * 1 + mystery(-1)

    Uh oh—the parameter skipped right over 0, and it's only going to get smaller. This example will recurse until there is a stack overflow error.

- You might be confused by the fact that sometimes people leave out else when writing code like this. Let's take a look at the code again:

```
if (k == 0)
    return 1;
return 2 * k + mystery(k - 2);
```

Why doesn't this have to say *else* return 2 * k + mystery(k − 2)? The purpose of an else clause is to tell the flow of control to skip that section when the if part is executed. So *either* the if clause or the else clause is executed. In this case, the if clause contains a return. Once a return is executed, nothing further in the method will be read and control returns to the calling method. We don't have to tell it to skip the else clause, because it has already gone off to execute code in another method. It doesn't matter whether you choose to write your code like this or to include the else, but don't be confused if you see it on the exam.

3. The answer is C.

- Here we go again!

  enigma(9) = 3 + enigma(7) = 3 + *10* = **13**
  enigma(7) = 3 + enigma(5) = 3 + *7* = *10*
  enigma(5) = 3 + enigma(3) = 3 + *4* = *7*
  enigma(3) = 2 + enigma(2) = 2 + *2* = *4*
  ...the base case!
  enigma(2) = 2...and up we go!

4. The answer is A.

- We don't really want to trace 15 calls of the printStars method, so let's see if we can just figure it after a few calls.

  printStars(15): prints one * and calls printStars(14)
  printStars(14): prints one * and calls printStars(13)
  . . .
  . . .
  printStars(1): prints one * and returns (remember, void methods also return, they just don't return a value).

- Without tracing every single call, we can see the pattern. 15 stars will be printed.
- This recursive method is a little different because it is not a return method. That's allowed, but it is not very common.

5. The answer is C.

- This time with Strings!

  weird("Hello") = weird("Hello" + "lo") = weird("Hellolo") = ***"Hellolololo"***
  weird("Hellolo") = weird("Hellolo" + "lo") = weird("Hellololo") = *"Hellolololo"*
  weird("Hellololo") = weird("Hellololo" + "lo") = weird("Hellolololo") = *"Hellolololo"*
  . . . that has a length >10, so we just start returning s.

- This one is a little different because there is no computation on the "return trip."

6. The answer is D.

- The Binary Search algorithm looks at the element in the middle of the array, sees if it is the right answer, and then decides if the target item is higher or lower than that element. At that point, it knows which half of the array the target item is in. Then it looks at the middle element of that half, and so on.

- Here's our array:

1	2	3	4	5	6	7	8	9	10	11

- First pass: The middle element is 6. We are looking for 4. 4 < 6, so eliminate the right half of the array (and the 6). Now we are considering:

1	2	3	4	5	6	7	8	9	10	11

- Second pass: The middle element is 3. 4 > 3, so we eliminate the left half of the section we are considering (and the 3). Now we are considering:

1	2	3	4	5	6	7	8	9	10	11

- You can see that we will find the 4 on our next round, but the answer to the question is 4 5.
- Good to know: In this example, there always *was* a middle element when we needed one. If there is an even number of elements, the middle will be halfway in between two elements. The algorithm will just decide whether to round up or down in those cases (usually down, as integer division makes that easy).

7. The answer is C.

- Instead of tracing the code, this time we are going to reason out what the method is doing.
- Notice that factors is an overloaded method. Our first call has one int parameter, but the remaining calls all have three. Our first call, factors(10), will result in the call factors(10, 9, 0).
- Looking at the factors method with three parameters, we can see that each time through, we subtract one from check, and the base case is check == 1. We start with check = 9 and call the method eight more times before returning count. Count begins at 0 and will be incremented when number % check == 0. Since number is 10, and check will equal all the numbers between 1 and 9, that will happen twice, at 10 % 5 and at 10 % 2. When the return statement is reached, count = 2.

8. The answer is C.

- Option I is incorrect. factors(0) will call factors(0, -1, 0). Since check is decremented each time, we will move further and further from the base case of 1. Infinite recursion will result in a stack overflow exception.
- Option II is incorrect. factors(2) will call factors(2, 1, 0). Since check is decremented to 0 before checking for the base case, once again we have infinite recursion resulting in a stack overflow error.
- Option III is correct. factors(12, 2, 5) will increment count (12 % 2 == 0), decrement check to 1, and then check for the base case and return count.

9. The answer is B.

- Let's trace.

    function(24, 3) = function(21, 4) + 2 = *19 + 2 = **21***
    function(21, 4) = function(17, 5) + 2 = *17 + 2 = 19*
    function(17, 5) = function(12, 6) + 2 = *15 + 2 = 17*
    function(12, 6) = function(6, 7) + 2 = *13 + 2 = 15*
    function(6, 7) = 6 + 7 = 13 (base case!)

10. The answer is A.

- The if statement we are completing represents the base case and the recursive call.
- We need to keep going if sum > 9, so the base case, the case that says we are done, occurs at sum <= 9. That is the *condition*. If sum <= 9, all we need to do is return sum.

- If sum >= 9, we need to add the digits up again, but the question is, the digits of *what*? If you go back to the examples in the description, 999, for example, the `while` loop will add 9 + 9 + 9 and put the result in sum, which now = 27. Then the next step is to add 2 + 7. Since 27 is held in the variable sum, that's what we need to pass to the next round of recursion. The *argument* is sum.
- You don't need to understand the `while` loop to answer the question, but it is a pretty cool loop, so let's explain it here anyway.
  - dividend % 10 gives you the last digit of dividend
  - dividend / 10 gets rid of the last digit of dividend (because it is integer division)
  - Here's an example, using the number 365.

    365 / 10 = 36 remainder 5 (mod will give us 5, add it to sum)
    36 / 10 = 3 remainder 6 (mod will give us 6, add it to sum)
    3 / 10 = 0 remainder 3 (mod will give us 3, add it to sum)
    0 will cause the loop to terminate.

11. The answer is C.

- Binary Search works like this:
  - We look at the midpoint of a list, compare it to the element to be found (let's call it the key) and decide if our key is >, <, or = that midpoint element.
  - If our key = midpoint element, we have found our key in the list.
  - If our key > midpoint element, we want to reset the list so that we will search just the top half of the current list.
  - If our key < midpoint element, we want to reset the list so that we will search just the bottom half of the current list.
- Look at the given code. We can see those comparisons, and we can see the high and low ends of the list being changed to match the answers to those comparisons. This code implements Binary Search.

STEP 5

Building Your Test-Taking Confidence

AP Computer Science A Practice Exam 1

AP Computer Science A Practice Exam 2

AP Computer Science A
Practice Exam 1

Multiple-Choice Questions

ANSWER SHEET

1 (A) (B) (C) (D) (E)
2 (A) (B) (C) (D) (E)
3 (A) (B) (C) (D) (E)
4 (A) (B) (C) (D) (E)
5 (A) (B) (C) (D) (E)
6 (A) (B) (C) (D) (E)
7 (A) (B) (C) (D) (E)
8 (A) (B) (C) (D) (E)
9 (A) (B) (C) (D) (E)
10 (A) (B) (C) (D) (E)
11 (A) (B) (C) (D) (E)
12 (A) (B) (C) (D) (E)
13 (A) (B) (C) (D) (E)
14 (A) (B) (C) (D) (E)
15 (A) (B) (C) (D) (E)
16 (A) (B) (C) (D) (E)
17 (A) (B) (C) (D) (E)
18 (A) (B) (C) (D) (E)
19 (A) (B) (C) (D) (E)
20 (A) (B) (C) (D) (E)

21 (A) (B) (C) (D) (E)
22 (A) (B) (C) (D) (E)
23 (A) (B) (C) (D) (E)
24 (A) (B) (C) (D) (E)
25 (A) (B) (C) (D) (E)
26 (A) (B) (C) (D) (E)
27 (A) (B) (C) (D) (E)
28 (A) (B) (C) (D) (E)
29 (A) (B) (C) (D) (E)
30 (A) (B) (C) (D) (E)
31 (A) (B) (C) (D) (E)
32 (A) (B) (C) (D) (E)
33 (A) (B) (C) (D) (E)
34 (A) (B) (C) (D) (E)
35 (A) (B) (C) (D) (E)
36 (A) (B) (C) (D) (E)
37 (A) (B) (C) (D) (E)
38 (A) (B) (C) (D) (E)
39 (A) (B) (C) (D) (E)
40 (A) (B) (C) (D) (E)

AP Computer Science A
Practice Exam 1

Part I (Multiple Choice)

Time: 90 minutes
Number of questions: 40
Percent of total score: 50

Directions: Choose the best answer for each problem. Use available space for scratch work and hand tracing. Some problems take longer than others. Consider how much time you have left before spending too much time on any one problem.

Notes:
- You may assume all import statements have been included where they are needed.
- You may assume that the parameters in method calls are not null and the methods are called when their preconditions are met.
- You may assume that declarations of variables and methods appear within the context of an enclosing class.
- You may refer to the Java Quick Reference sheet as needed.

GO ON TO THE NEXT PAGE

1. Consider the following code segment.

```
int myValue = 17;
int multiplier = 3;
int answer = myValue % multiplier + myValue / multiplier;
answer = answer * multiplier;
System.out.println(answer);
```

What is printed as a result of executing the code segment?
(A) 9
(B) 10
(C) 7
(D) 30
(E) 21

2. Assume that a, b, and c have been declared and correctly initialized with int values. Consider the following expression.

```
boolean bool = !(a < b || b <= c) && !(a < c || b >= a);
```

Under what conditions does bool evaluate to true?
(A) a = 1, b = 2, c = 3
(B) a = 3, b = 2, c = 1
(C) a = 3, b = 1, c = 2
(D) All conditions; bool is always true.
(E) No conditions; bool is always false.

3. Consider the following code segment.

```
int[] myArray = {2, 3, 4, 1, 7, 6, 8};
int index = 0;
while (myArray[index] < 7)
{
    myArray[index] += 3;
    index++;
}
```

What values are stored in myArray after executing the code segment?
(A) {2, 3, 4, 1, 7, 6, 8}
(B) {2, 3, 4, 1, 7, 9, 11}
(C) {5, 6, 7, 4, 7, 9, 8}
(D) {5, 6, 7, 4, 7, 6, 8}
(E) {5, 6, 7, 4, 0, 9, 11}

GO ON TO THE NEXT PAGE

4. Consider the following class used by a company to represent the items it has available for online purchase.

```
public class OnlinePurchaseItem

{

        public double getPrice()        // implementation not shown

        public String getItem()         // implementation not shown

        public String getMonth()        // implementation not shown

                                        // instance variables, constructors, and
                                        // other methods not shown

}
```

The company bills at the end of the quarter. Until then, it uses an `ArrayList` of `OnlinePurchaseItem` objects to track a customer's purchases.

```
private ArrayList<OnlinePurchaseItem> items;
```

The company decides to offer a 20-percent-off promotion on all items purchased in September. Which of the following code segments properly calculates the correct total price at the end of the quarter?

```
I.   double total = 0.0;
     for (int i = 0; i < items.size(); i++)
     {
         if (items.get(i).getMonth().equals("September"))
             total += 0.80 * items.get(i).getPrice();
         else
             total += items.get(i).getPrice();
     }


II.  double total = 0.0;
     for (OnlinePurchaseItem purchase : items)
     {
         if (purchase.get(i).getMonth().equals("September"))
             total = total + 0.80 * purchase.getPrice();
         else
             total += items.get(i).getPrice();

     }


III. double total = 0.0;
     for (int i = items.size(); i >= 0; i--)
     {
         if (items.get(i).getMonth().equals("September"))
             total = total + 0.80 * items.get(i).getPrice();
         else
             total += items.get(i).getPrice();
     }
```

(A) I only
(B) II only
(C) I and II only
(D) II and III only
(E) I, II, and III

5. Consider the following method.

```
public int mystery(int n)
{
    if (n <= 1)
        return 1;
    return 2 + mystery(n - 1);
}
```

What value is returned by the call `mystery(5)`?

(A) 1
(B) 7
(C) 8
(D) 9
(E) 10

6. Consider the following code segment.

```
String myString = "H";
int index = 0;
while (index < 4)
{
    for (int i = 0; i < index; i++)
        myString = "A" + myString + "A";
    index ++;
}
```

What is the value of `myString` after executing the code segment?

(A) `"H"`
(B) `"AHA"`
(C) `"AAAHAAA"`
(D) `"AAAAHAAAA"`
(E) `"AAAAAAHAAAAAA"`

7. Consider the following statement.

```
int var = (int)(Math.random() * 50) + 10;
```

What are the possible values of `var` after executing the statement?
(A) All integers from 1 to 59 (inclusive)
(B) All integers from 10 to 59 (inclusive)
(C) All integers from 10 to 60 (inclusive)
(D) All real numbers from 50 to 60 (not including 60)
(E) All real numbers from 10 to 60 (not including 60)

8. Consider the following statement.

```
System.out.print(13 + 6 + "APCSA" + (9 - 5) + 4);
```

What is printed as a result of executing the statement?
(A) `136APCSA(9 - 5)4`
(B) `19APCSA8`
(C) `19APCSA44`
(D) `136APCSA8`
(E) `136APCSA44`

GO ON TO THE NEXT PAGE

9. Assume truth1 and truth2 are boolean variables that have been properly declared and initialized.

Consider this expression.

```
(truth1 && truth2) || ((!truth1) && (!truth2))
```

Which expression below is its logical equivalent?

(A) truth1 != truth2
(B) truth1 || truth2
(C) truth1 && truth2
(D) !truth1 && !truth2
(E) truth1 == truth2

10. Consider the following method.

```
/** Precondition: numbers.size() > 0
 */
public int totalValue(ArrayList<Integer> numbers)
{
    int total = 0;
    for (Integer val : numbers)
    {
        if (val > 1 && numbers.size() - 3 > val)
            total += val;
    }
    return total;
}
```

Assume that the ArrayList passed as a parameter contains the following Integer values.

```
[0, 1, 2, 3, 4, 5, 6, 7, 8, 9]
```

What value is returned by the call totalValue?

(A) 20
(B) 21
(C) 27
(D) 44
(E) 45

GO ON TO THE NEXT PAGE

Questions 11–14 refer to the following class definition.

```
public class Depot
{
    private String city;
    private String state;
    private String country = "USA";
    private boolean active = true;

    public Depot(String myCity, String myState, String myCountry, boolean myActive)
    {
        city = myCity;
        state = myState;
        country = myCountry;
        active = myActive;
    }

    public Depot(String myState, String myCity)
    {
        state = myState;
        city = myCity;
    }

    public Depot(String myCity, String myState, boolean myActive)
    {
        city = myCity;
        state = myState;
        active = myActive;
    }

    public String toString()
    {
        return city + ", " + state + " " + country + " " + active;
    }

    /* Additional implementation not shown */
}
```

11. The Depot class has three constructors. Which of the following is the correct term for this practice?

(A) Overriding
(B) Procedural abstraction
(C) Encapsulation
(D) Polymorphism
(E) Overloading

12. Consider the following code segment in another class.

```
Depot station = new Depot("Oakland", "California");
System.out.println(station);
```

What is printed as a result of executing the code segment?

(A) `California, Oakland USA true`
(B) `California, Oakland USA active`
(C) `USA, California USA true`
(D) `Oakland, California USA active`
(E) `Oakland, California USA true`

GO ON TO THE NEXT PAGE

13. Consider the following class definition.

```
public class WhistleStop extends Depot
```

Which of the following constructors compiles without error?

I.
```
public WhistleStop()
{
    super();
}
```

II.
```
public WhistleStop()
{
    super("Waubaushene", "Ontario", "Canada", true);
}
```

III.
```
public WhistleStop(String city, String province)
{
    super(city, province);
}
```

(A) I only
(B) II only
(C) III only
(D) II and III only
(E) I, II, and III

14. Assume a correct no-argument constructor has been added to the `WhistleStop` class.

Which of the following code segments compiles without error?

I.
```
ArrayList<Depot> stations = new ArrayList<Depot>();
stations.add(new WhistleStop());
stations.add(new Depot("Mansonville", "Quebec", "Canada", false));
```

II.
```
ArrayList<WhistleStop> stations = new ArrayList<Depot>();
stations.add(new WhistleStop());
stations.add(new Depot("Orinda", "California", true));
```

III.
```
ArrayList<WhistleStop> stations = new ArrayList<WhistleStop>();
stations.add(new WhistleStop());
stations.add(new Depot("Needham", "Massachusetts", true));
```

(A) I only
(B) I and II only
(C) I and III only
(D) II and III only
(E) I, II, and III

15. Consider the following code segment.

```
String crazyString = "crazy";
ArrayList<String> crazyList = new ArrayList<String>();
crazyList.add("weird");
crazyList.add("enigma");
for (String s : crazyList)
{
    crazyString = s.substring(1, 3) + crazyString.substring(0, 4);
}
System.out.println(crazyString);
```

What is printed as a result of executing the code segment?

(A) `nicraz`

(B) `nieicr`

(C) `nieicraz`

(D) `einicraz`

(E) `weienicraz`

16. Consider the following method.

```
public int pathways(int n)
{
    int ans;
    if (n < -5)
        ans = 1;
    else if (n < 0)
        ans = 2;
    else if (n > 10)
        ans = 3;
    else
        ans = 4;
    return ans;
}
```

Which of the following sets of data tests every possible path through the code?

(A) `-6, -1, 15, 12`

(B) `-5, -3, 12, 15`

(C) `-8, -5, 8, 10`

(D) `-6, 0, 20, 7`

(E) `-10, -5, 10, 12`

GO ON TO THE NEXT PAGE

Questions 17–18 refer to the following scenario.

A resort wants to recommend activities for its guests, based on the temperature (degrees F) as follows:

76° and above	go swimming
61°–75°	go hiking
46°–60°	go horseback riding
45° and below	play ping pong

17. Consider the following method.

```
public String chooseActivity(int temperature)
{
    String activity;
    if (temperature > 75)
        activity = "go swimming";
    if (temperature > 60)
        activity = "go hiking";
    if (temperature > 45)
        activity = "go horseback riding";
    else
        activity = "play ping pong";
    return activity;
}
```

Consider the following statement.

```
System.out.println("We recommend that you " + chooseActivity(temperature));
```

For which temperature range is the correct suggestion printed (as defined above)?

(A) `temperature > 75`

(B) `temperature > 60`

(C) `temperature > 45`

(D) `temperature <= 60`

(E) Never correct

18. After discovering that the method did not work correctly, it was rewritten as follows.

```
public String chooseActivity(int temperature)
{
    String activity;
    if (temperature > 45)
        activity = "go horseback riding";
    else if (temperature > 60)
        activity = "go hiking";
    else if (temperature > 75)
        activity = "go swimming";
    else
        activity = "play ping pong";
    return activity;
}
```

Consider the following statement.

```
System.out.println("We recommend that you " + chooseActivity(temperature));
```

What is the largest temperature range for which the correct suggestion is printed (as defined above)?

(A) Always correct

(B) Never correct

(C) `temperature <= 75`

(D) `temperature <= 60`

(E) `temperature <= 45`

GO ON TO THE NEXT PAGE

19. Assume `int[] arr` has been correctly instantiated and is of sufficient size. Which of these code segments results in identical arrays?

    I.
    ```
    int i = 1;
    while (i < 6)
    {
        arr[i / 2] = i;
        i += 2;
    }
    ```

    II.
    ```
    for (int i = 0; i < 3; i++)
    {
        arr[i] = 2 * i + 1;
    }
    ```

    III.
    ```
    for (int i = 6; i > 0; i = i - 2)
    {
        arr[(6 - i) / 2] = 6 - i;
    }
    ```

    (A) I and II only
    (B) II and III only
    (C) I and III only
    (D) I, II, and III
    (E) All three arrays are different.

20. Consider the following code segment.
    ```
    ArrayList<String> nations = new ArrayList<String>();
    nations.add("Argentina");
    nations.add("Canada");
    nations.add("Australia");
    nations.add("Cambodia");
    nations.add("Russia");
    nations.add("France");
    for (int i = 0; i < nations.size(); i++)
    {
        if (nations.get(i).length() >= 7)
            nations.remove(0);
    }
    System.out.println(nations);
    ```

    What is printed as a result of executing the code segment?
    (A) `[Canada, Russia, France]`
    (B) `[Cambodia, Russia, France]`
    (C) `[Australia, Cambodia, Russia, France]`
    (D) `[Canada, Cambodia, Russia, France]`
    (E) Nothing is printed. `IndexOutOfBoundsException`

21. Consider the following class used to represent a student.

```
public class Student
{
    private String name;
    private int year;

    public Student()
    {
        name = "name";
        year = 0;
    }

    public Student(String myName, int myYear)
    {
        name = myName;
        year = myYear;
    }
}
```

Consider the ExchangeStudent class that extends the Student class.

```
public class ExchangeStudent extends Student
{
    private String country;
    private String language;

    public ExchangeStudent(String myName, int myYear,
                           String myCountry, String myLanguage)
    {
        super(myName, myYear);
        country = myCountry;
        language = myLanguage;
    }
}
```

Which of the following constructors could also be included in the ExchangeStudent class without generating a compile-time error?

```
I.   public ExchangeStudent(String myName, int myYear, String myCountry)
     {
         super(myName, myYear);
         country = myCountry;
         language = "English";
     }
II.  public ExchangeStudent(String myCountry, String myLanguage)
     {
         super("name", "2015");
         country = myCountry;
         language = myLanguage;
     }
III. public ExchangeStudent()
     {
     }
```

(A) I only
(B) II only
(C) III only
(D) I and III only
(E) I, II, and III

22. Consider the following method.

```
public int countLetters(String word, String letter)
{
    int count = 0;
    for (int index = 0; index < word.length(); index++)
    {
        if ( /*  missing code  */ )
            count++;
    }
    return count;
}
```

What could replace /* *missing code* */ to allow the method to return the number of times `letter` appears in `word`?

(A) `word.substring(index).equals(letter)`

(B) `word.substring(index, index + 1) == letter`

(C) `word.indexOf(letter) == letter.indexOf(letter)`

(D) `word.substring(index, index + 1).equals(letter)`

(E) `letter.equals(word.substring(index).indexOf(letter))`

23. Assume `obscureAnimals` is an `ArrayList<String>` that has been correctly constructed and populated with the following items.

```
["okapi", "aye-aye", "cassowary", "echidna", "sugar glider", "jerboa"]
```

Consider the following code segment.

```
for (int i = 0; i < obscureAnimals.size(); i++)
{
    if (obscureAnimals.get(i).compareTo("pink fairy armadillo") < 0)
        obscureAnimals.remove(i);
}
System.out.print(animals);
```

What will be printed as a result of executing the code segment?

(A) `[]`

(B) `[sugar glider]`

(C) `[aye-aye, echidna, sugar glider]`

(D) `[aye-aye, echidna, sugar glider, jerboa]`

(E) Nothing will be printed. There is an `ArrayListIndexOutOfBoundsException`.

GO ON TO THE NEXT PAGE

24. Consider the following method.

```
public boolean whatDoesItDo(String st)
{
    for (int i = 0; i < st.length() / 2; i++)
    {
        String sub1 = st.substring(i, i + 1);
        String sub2 = st.substring(st.length() - i - 1, st.length() - i);
        if (!sub1.equals(sub2))
        {
            return false;
        }
    }
    return true;
}
```

What is the purpose of the method whatDoesItDo?

(A) The method returns true if st has an even length, false if it has an odd length.

(B) The method returns true if st contains any character more than once.

(C) The method returns true if st is a palindrome (spelled the same backward and forward), false if it is not a palindrome.

(D) The method returns true if st begins and ends with the same letter.

(E) The method returns true if the second half of st contains the same sequence of letters as the first half, false if it does not.

25. Consider the following code segment.

```
int value = 33;
boolean calculate = true;
while (value > 5 || calculate)
{
    if (value % 3 == 0)
        value = value - 2;
    if (value / 4 < 3)
        calculate = false;
}
System.out.print(value);
```

What is printed as a result of executing the code segment?

(A) 0

(B) 1

(C) 8

(D) 33

(E) Nothing will be printed. It is an infinite loop.

Questions 26–28 refer to the following classes.

```java
public class Person
{
    private String firstName;
    private String lastName;

    public Person(String fName, String lName)
    {
        firstName = fName;
        lastName = lName;
    }

    public String getName()
    {
        return firstName + " " + lastName;
    }
}

public class Adult extends Person
{
    private String title;

    public Adult(String fname, String lName, String myTitle)
    {
        super(fname, lName);
        title = myTitle;
    }

    /*  toString method to be implemented in question 27  */
}

public class Child extends Person
{
    private int age;

    /*  Constructor to be implemented in question 26  */
}
```

GO ON TO THE NEXT PAGE

26. Which of the following is a correct implementation of a `Child` class constructor?

   (A)
   ```
   public Child(String first, String last, String t, int a)
   {
       super(first, last, t);
       age = a;
   }
   ```
   (B)
   ```
   public Child()
   {
       super();
   }
   ```
   (C)
   ```
   public Child(String first, String last, int a)
   {
       super(first, last);
       age = a;
   }
   ```
   (D)
   ```
   public Child extends Adult (String first, String last, String t, int a)
   {
       super(first, last, t);
       age = a;
   }
   ```
   (E)
   ```
   public Child extends Person(String first, String last, int a)
   {
       super(first, last);
       age = a;
   }
   ```

27. Which of the following is a correct implementation of the `Adult` class `toString` method?

   (A)
   ```
   public String toString()
   {
       System.out.println(title + " " + super.toString());
   }
   ```
   (B)
   ```
   public String toString()
   {
       return title + " " + super.toString();
   }
   ```
   (C)
   ```
   public String toString()
   {
       return title + " " + firstName + " " + lastName;
   }
   ```
   (D)
   ```
   public void toString()
   {
       System.out.println(title + " " + super.getName());
   }
   ```
   (E)
   ```
   public String toString()
   {
       return title + " " + super.getName();
   }
   ```

GO ON TO THE NEXT PAGE

28. Consider the following method declaration in a different class.

```
public void findSomeone(Adult someone)
```

Assume the following variables have been correctly instantiated and initialized with appropriate values.

```
Person p;
Adult a;
Child c;
```

Which of the following method calls compiles without error?

I.   `findSomeone(p);`
II. `findSomeone(a);`
III. `findSomeone(c);`
IV. `findSomeone((Adult) p);`
V.   `findSomeone((Adult) c);`

(A) II only
(B) I and II only
(C) II and IV only
(D) II, IV, and V only
(E) II, III, and IV only

29. Consider the following method. The method is intended to return `true` if the value `val` raised to the power `power` is within the tolerance `tolerance` of the target value `target`, and `false` otherwise.

```
public boolean similar(double val, double power, double target, double tolerance)
{
    /* missing code */
}
```

Which code segment below can replace `/* missing code */` to make the method work as intended?
```
(A) double answer = Math.pow(val, power);
    if (answer - tolerance >= target)
       return true;
    return false;
(B) return (Math.abs(Math.pow(val, power))) - target <= tolerance;
(C) double answer = Math.pow(Math.abs(val), power);
    return answer - target <= tolerance;
(D) double answer = Math.pow(val, power) - target;
    boolean within = answer - tolerance >= 0;
    return within;
(E) return (Math.abs(Math.pow(val, power) - target) <= tolerance);
```

30. Consider the following method.

```
public int changeEm(int num1, int num2, int[] values)
{
    num1 = values[num2];
    values[num1] = num2;
    num2++;
    return num2;
}
```

Consider the following code segment.

```
int[] values = {1, 2, 3, 4, 5};
int num1 = 2;
int num2 = 3;
num2 = changeEm(num1, num2, values);
System.out.println("num1 = " + num1 + "  values[" + num2 + "] = " + values[num2]);
```

What is printed as a result of executing the code segment?

(A) num1 = 2   values[4] = 4
(B) num1 = 2   values[4] = 5
(C) num1 = 2   values[4] = 3
(D) num1 = 4   values[3] = 3
(E) num1 = 4   values[3] = 4

31. Consider the following method.

```
public int firstLetterIndex(String s2)
{
    String s1 = "abcdefghijklmnopqrstuvwxyz";
    return s1.indexOf(s2.substring(s2.length() - 2));
}
```

What is returned as a result of the call firstLetterIndex("on your side")?

(A) -1
(B) 0
(C) 3
(D) 4
(E) 5

GO ON TO THE NEXT PAGE

32. The following code segment appears in the main method of another class.

```
AnotherClass[] acArray = new AnotherClass[10];
acArray[2] = new AnotherClass("two");
acArray[3] = new AnotherClass("three");
for (int i = 0; i < acArray.length; i++)
{
    /* missing condition */
    {
        System.out.println(acArray[i].getData());
    }
}
```

Which of the following statements should be used to replace /* missing condition */ so that the code segment will not terminate with a NullPointerException?

(A) if (acArray[i] != null)

(B) if (acArray.get(i) != null)

(C) if (acArray.getData() != null)

(D) if (acArray.getData().equals("two") || acArray.getData().equals("three"))

(E) Since not all of acArray's entries contain an AnotherClass object, there is no way to loop through the array without a NullPointerException.

33. A programmer intends to apply the standard Binary Search algorithm on the following array of integers. The standard Binary Search algorithm returns the index of the search target if it is found and -1 if the target is not found. What is returned by the algorithm when a search for 50 is executed?

```
int[] array = {9, 100, 11, 45, 76, 100, 50, 1, 0, 55, 99};
```

(A) -1

(B) 0

(C) 5

(D) 6

(E) 7

34. Consider the following code segment.

```
int[][] nums = { {0, 1, 2}, {3, 4, 5}, {6, 7, 8} };

for (int x = 0; x < nums.length; x++)
{
    int temp = nums[x][0];
    nums[x][0] = nums[x][2];
    nums[x][2] = temp;
}
```

What are the values in array nums after the code segment is executed?

(A) { {0, 1, 0}, {3, 4, 3}, {6, 7, 6} }

(B) { {0, 0, 0}, {3, 3, 3}, {6, 6, 6} }

(C) { {2, 1, 0}, {5, 4, 3}, {8, 7, 6} }

(D) { {0, 1, 2}, {3, 4, 5}, {6, 7, 8} }

(E) { {8, 7, 6}, {5, 4, 3}, {2, 1, 0} }

GO ON TO THE NEXT PAGE

35. Consider the following code segment.

```
ArrayList<Integer> newList = new ArrayList<Integer>();
Integer[] list = {2, 4, 3, 3, 2, 5, 1};
newList.add(list[0]);

for (int i = 1; i < list.length; i++)
{
    if (list[i] > newList.get(newList.size() - 1))
        newList.add(list[i]);
}

System.out.println(newList);
```

What is printed as a result of executing the code segment?

(A) `[2, 4, 5]`

(B) `[2, 2, 1]`

(C) `[2, 4, 3, 5, 1]`

(D) `[1, 2, 3, 3, 4, 5]`

(E) `[2, 4, 3, 3, 5, 1]`

36. Consider the following code segment.

```
int[][] a = new int[5][5];

for (int r = 0; r < a.length; r++)
    for (int c = r + 1; c < a[0].length; c++)
        a[r][c] = 9;

for (int d = 0; d < a.length; d++)
    a[d][d] = d;

System.out.println(a[1][2] + " " + a[3][3] + " " + a[4][3]);
```

What is printed as a result of executing the code segment?

(A) `9 9 9`

(B) `0 0 0`

(C) `0 3 9`

(D) `9 3 9`

(E) `9 3 0`

37. Consider the following sorting method.

```
public void mysterySort(int[] arr)
{
    for (int j = 1; j < arr.length; j++)
    {
        int temp = arr[j];
        int index = j;
        while (index > 0 && temp < arr[index - 1])
        {
            arr[index] = arr[index - 1];
            index--;
        }
        arr[index] = temp;
    }
}
```

Consider the following code segment.

```
int[] values = {9, 1, 3, 0, 2};
mysterySort(values);
```

Which of the following shows the elements of the array in the correct order after the second pass through the outer loop of the sorting algorithm?

(A) {0, 1, 2, 9, 3}
(B) {0, 1, 3, 9, 2}
(C) {0, 1, 9, 3, 2}
(D) {1, 3, 9, 0, 2}
(E) {1, 3, 0, 2, 9}

38. Consider the following method.

```
public int puzzle(int m, int n)
{
    if (n == 1)
        return m;
    return m * puzzle(m, n - 1);
}
```

What is returned by the method call `puzzle(3, 4)`?

(A) 9
(B) 64
(C) 81
(D) 128
(E) Nothing is returned. Infinite recursion causes a stack overflow error.

GO ON TO THE NEXT PAGE

39. Consider the following code segment.

```
int[][] table = new int[5][6];
int val = 0;
for (int k = 0; k < table[0].length; k++)
{
    for (int j = table.length - 1; j >= 0; j--)
    {
        table[j][k] = val;
        val = val + 2;
    }
}
```

What is the value of `table[3][4]` after executing the code segment?

(A) 22

(B) 30

(C) 34

(D) 42

(E) 46

40. Consider the following method.

```
public void selectionSort(String[] arr)
{
    for (int i = 0; i < arr.length; i++)
    {
        int small = i;
        for (int j = i; j < arr.length; j++)
        {
            /*  missing code */
            small = j;
        }
        String temp = arr[small];
        arr[small] = arr[i];
        arr[i] = temp;
    }
}
```

Assume `String[]` ray has been properly instantiated and populated with `String` objects.

Which line of code should replace /* *missing code* */ so that the method call `selectionSort(ray)` results in an array whose elements are sorted from least to greatest?

(A) `if (arr[j].equals(arr[small]))`

(B) `if (arr[j] > arr[small])`

(C) `if (arr[j] < arr[small])`

(D) `if (arr[j].compareTo(arr[small]) > 0)`

(E) `if (arr[j].compareTo(arr[small]) < 0)`

STOP. End of Part I.

AP Computer Science A
Practice Exam 1

Part II (Free Response)

Time: 90 minutes
Number of questions: 4
Percent of total score: 50

Directions: Write all of your code in Java. Show all your work.

Notes:
- You may assume all import statements have been included where they are needed.
- You may assume that all preconditions are met when making calls to methods.
- You may assume that all parameters within method calls are not null.
- Be aware that you should, when possible, use methods that are defined in the classes provided as opposed to duplicating them by writing your own code. Doing so you will not receive full credit.
- You may use the Java Quick Reference sheet as needed.

GO ON TO THE NEXT PAGE

1. A `Password` class contains methods used to determine information about passwords. You will write two methods of the class.

```
public class Password
{
    private String upper = "ABCDEFGHIJKLMNOPQRSTUVWXYZ";
    private String lower = "abcdefghijklmnopqrstuvwxyz";
    private String symbols = "!@#$%^&*";
    private int minLength;
    private int maxLength;

    public Password(int min, int max)
    {
        /* implementation not shown   */
    }

    public boolean isValid(String password)
    {
        /* implemented in part (a)    */
    }

    public String generatePassword()
    {
        /* implemented in part (b)    */
    }

    // There may be instance variables, constructors, and other methods not shown.

}
```

(a) Write the method `isValid`, which returns true if a password is valid and false otherwise. A password is considered valid if
- Its length is a valid length. The length must be at least `minLength` number of characters and at most `maxLength` number of characters, inclusive.
- It contains at least one character from `upper`, `lower`, and `symbols`.
- It does NOT contain any characters that are not in `upper`, `lower`, or `symbols`.

Statement	Value Returned	Comment
`Password p1 = new Password(3,15);`		Passwords can be any length between 3 and 15 inclusive.
`p1.isValid("HelloWorld!");`	true	Password has length 11, contains at least 1 uppercase letter, 1 lowercase letter, and 1 symbol.
`p1.isValid("Aloha")`	false	Password does not include a symbol
`p1.isValid("#APComputerScience Rocks");`	false	Password has length 24

Complete method `isValid` below.

```
public boolean isValid(String password)
```

GO ON TO THE NEXT PAGE

(b) Write the method `generatePassword`, which returns a `String` representing a valid password. In writing `generatePassword` you must call `isValid`. Assume `isValid` works correctly regardless of what you wrote in part (a).

The `generatePassword` method must randomly choose the length of the password and randomly choose characters from the uppercase, lowercase, and symbol strings.

Statement	Value Returned	Comment
`Password p2 = new Password(4,10);`		Passwords can be any length between 4 and 10 inclusive.
`p2.generatePassword();`	Bkb@mHI	Password has length 7, contains at least 1 uppercase letter, 1 lowercase letter, and 1 symbol.
`p2.generatePassword();`	k&iHBe	Password has length 6, contains at least 1 uppercase letter, 1 lowercase letter, and 1 symbol.
`p2.generatePassword();`	hY*G	Password has length 4, contains at least 1 uppercase letter, 1 lowercase letter, and 1 symbol.

Complete method `generatePassword` below.

```
public String generatePassword()
```

GO ON TO THE NEXT PAGE

2. An ISBN (International Standard Book Number) is a numeric book identifier that is assigned to each published book. Prior to 2007, the ISBN numbers were 10 digits in length. The ISBN number is broken down into sections (group, publisher, title, and check digit). The last digit, or check digit, is used for error detection.

To generate a valid check digit, the first nine digits in the ISBN is multiplied by a weight. Each weight is multiplied by the corresponding digit, and then the products are added together.

ISBN with no check digit	1	2	6	0	4	5	4	9	1
Weight	10	9	8	7	6	5	4	3	2
Product	10	18	48	0	24	25	16	27	2
Sum	$10 + 18 + 48 + 0 + 24 + 25 + 16 + 27 + 2 = 170$							
Check Digit	$11 - (sum \% 11) = 11 - (170 \% 11) = 6$							

ISBN with no check digit	0	3	0	6	4	0	6	1	1
Weight	10	9	8	7	6	5	4	3	2
Product	0	27	0	42	24	0	24	3	2
Sum	$0 + 27 + 0 + 42 + 24 + 0 + 24 + 3 + 2 = 122$							
Check Digit	$11 - (sum \% 11) = 11 - (122 \% 11) = 10 = X$							

If the value of the check digit is 10, then the check digit becomes "X".

An ISBN object is created with a parameter that contains a nine-digit ISBN number. The ISBN class provides two methods: calculateCheckDigit and generateNumber.

- calculateCheckDigit will perform the calculations described above to determine the check digit.
- generateNumber will join together the nine-digit number and the check digit generated from the method defined above.

For example, consider the following code that is in a class other than the ISBN class.

```
ISBN book1 = new ISBN(126045491);
String check1 = book1.calculateCheckDigit();      //  "6" will be returned
String isbnNumber1 = book1.generateNumber();      // "126045491-6" will be returned

ISBN book2 = new ISBN(030640611);
String check2 = book2.calculateCheckDigit();      //  "X" will be returned
String isbnNumber2 = book2.generateNumber();      // "030640611-X" will be returned
```

Write the complete ISBN class, including the constructor and any required instance variables and methods. Your implementation must meet all specifications to confirm to the example.

GO ON TO THE NEXT PAGE

3. A train is composed of an engine and any number of train cars. The engine is rated to pull up to a maximum weight, based on its power. The weight of all the train cars combined, including the engine, must be below this maximum weight or the engine will not be able to move the train.

Trains are represented by the `Train` class and contain an engine followed by any number of cars. An `ArrayList` will be used to store the weight of the engine (in element 0), and the weights of each of the cars (in elements 1, 2, 3, etc.).

The weight of a `Train` object is calculated by adding the weight of the engine to the weight of each of the objects in the `trainCars` ArrayList [to be completed in part (a)].

Trains need to be checked to make sure that their weight can be pulled by their engine. If the train is overweight, train operators must remove train cars from the end of the train until the train is within the acceptable weight range [to be completed in part (b)].

```
public class Train
{
    private double maxWeight;
    private ArrayList <Double> trainCars;

    public Train(Double max, ArrayList <Double> tc)
    {
        maxWeight = max;
        trainCars = tc;
    }

    public double getMaximumWeight()
    /*        implementation not shown    */

    /** Finds the total weight of the train.
     *
     *    @return double value containing the sum of the weights of the train
     */
    public double getTotalWeight()
    {     /*      To be implemented in part (a)     */     }


    /** Removes Double objects from the end of the train
     *     until the train can be pulled by the Engine.
     *
     *     @return ArrayList<Double> containing the removed cars in
     *              the order they were removed (the last car is
     *              item 0, etc.). If no cars are removed, the returned
     *              list will be empty.
     */
    public ArrayList<Double> removeExcessTrainCars()
    {     /*      To be implemented in part (b)    */     }

    /* Additional implementation not shown */
}
```

(a) Write the `getTotalWeight` method that will calculate the total weight of the train by adding the weight of each of the train cars to the weight of the engine (element 0).

```
/** Finds the total weight of the train.
 *
 * @return double value containing the sum of the weights of the train cars
 */
public double getTotalWeight()
{  /*      To be implemented in part (a)      */     }
```

GO ON TO THE NEXT PAGE

(b) Write the removeExcessTrainCars method of the Train class that removes Double objects one at a time from the end of the train until the train weight is less than or equal to the maximum weight allowed as given by the getMaximumWeight method of the Train object. The removed train cars are added to the end of an ArrayList of Double objects as they are removed. This ArrayList of removed Double objects is returned by the method. If no Double objects need to be removed, an empty ArrayList is returned. You may assume what you wrote for part (a) works as intended.

Example:

A train is composed of the cars listed below. The engine has a maximum weight rating of 475,000 pounds.

Car	Weight
Engine/ trainCars[0]	200,000
trainCars[1]	100,000
trainCars[2]	140,000
trainCars[3]	50,000
trainCars[4]	100,000
trainCars[5]	60,000

In the example, the train initially weighs 650,000 pounds. Train cars need to be removed one by one from the end of the train until the total weight is under the maximum allowed weight of 475,000.

- Removing the train car from index 5 lowers the weight to 590,000
- Removing the train car from index 4 lowers the weight to 490,000
- Removing the train car from index 3 lowers the weight to 440,000

At 440,000 pounds, the train is now in the acceptable weight range. The following ArrayList is returned by the method:

```
[60000.0, 100000.0, 50000.0]
```

Complete the removeExcessTrainCars method.

```
/** Removes TrainCar objects from the end of the train
 *   until the train can be pulled by the Engine.
 *
 *   @return ArrayList<TrainCar> containing the removed cars in
 *           the order they were removed (the first car removed is
 *           item 0, etc.) If no cars are removed, the returned
 *           list will be empty.
 */
public ArrayList <Double> removeExcessTrainCars()
```

4. The colors of the pixels on a TV or computer screen are made by combining different quantities of red, green, and blue light. Each of the three colors is represented by a value between 0 and 255, where 0 means none of that color light and 255 means as much of that color as there can be. This way of representing colors is referred to as RGB, for red-green-blue, and the color values are written in ordered triples like this (80, 144, 240). That particular combination means red at a value of 80, green at a value of 144, and blue at a value of 240. The resulting color is a kind of medium blue. The combination (0, 0, 0) produces black and (255, 255, 255) produces white.

Pixels can be modeled by the `Pixel` class shown below.

```java
public class Pixel
{
    private int red;
    private int green;
    private int blue;

    public Pixel(int myRed, int myGreen, int myBlue)
    {
        red = myRed;
        green = myGreen;
        blue = myBlue;
    }
    public String toString()
    {
        return "(" + red + ", " + green + ", "  + blue + ")";
    }
}
```

An artist wants to manipulate the pixels on a large computer display. She begins by creating three two-dimensional arrays the size of the screen, `rows` by `columns`. One array contains the red value of each pixel, one contains the blue value of each pixel, and one contains the green value of each pixel. She then calls methods of the `AlterImage` class to generate and then manipulate the data.

```java
public class AlterImage
{
    /** Converts 3 arrays of color values into one array
     *  of Pixel objects
     *
     *  @param reds the red color values
     *  @param greens the green color values
     *  @param blues the blue color values
     *  @return the Pixel array generated with information
     *          in the red, green and blue arrays
     *
     *  Precondition:  The three color arrays are all the same
     *                 size and contain int values in the range 0-255.
     *  Postcondition: The returned array is the same size as the
     *                 3 color arrays.
     */
    public Pixel[][] generatePixelArray(int[][] reds, int[][] greens, int[][] blues)
    {  /* to be implemented in part (a) */  }
```

GO ON TO THE NEXT PAGE

```
/** Flips a 2D array of Pixel objects either
 *  horizontally or vertically
 *
 *  @param image the 2D array of Pixel objects to be processed
 *  @param horiz true: flip horizontally, false: flip vertically
 *  @return the processed image
 */
public Pixel[][] flipImage(Pixel[][] image, boolean horiz)
{   /* to be implemened in part (b) */   }

/* Additional implementation not shown */

}
```

(a) Given the three arrays reds, greens, and blues, and the Pixel and AlterImage classes, implement the generatePixelArray method that converts the raw information in the three color arrays into a rows by columns array of Pixel objects.

Precondition: The three color arrays are all the same size and contain int values in the range 0–255.
Postcondition: The returned array is the same size as the three color arrays.

```
/** Converts 3 arrays of color values into one array
 *  of Pixel objects
 *
 *  @param reds the red color values
 *  @param greens the green color values
 *  @param blues the blue color values
 *  @return the Pixel array generated with information
 *          from the red, green and blue arrays
 *
 *  Precondition:   The three color arrays are all the same
 *                  size and contain int values in the range 0-255.
 *  Postcondition:  The returned array is the same size as the
 *                  3 color arrays.
 */
public Pixel[][] generatePixelArray(int[][] reds, int[][] greens, int[][] blues)
```

GO ON TO THE NEXT PAGE

(b) The artist uses various techniques to modify the image displayed on the screen. One of these techniques is to flip the image, either horizontally (along the *x*-axis, top-to-bottom) or vertically (along the *y*-axis, left-to-right), so that a mirror image is produced as shown below.

In this example, the data in the cells are the RGB values stored in the `Pixel` objects. To make the example clearer, red is set to the original row number, green is set to the original column number, and blue is constant at 100.

Original array:

0, 0, 100	0, 1, 100	0, 2, 100	0, 3, 100
1, 0, 100	1, 1, 100	1, 2, 100	1, 3, 100
2, 0, 100	2, 1, 100	2, 2, 100	2, 3, 100
3, 0, 100	3, 1, 100	3, 2, 100	3, 3, 100

Flipped horizontally:

3, 0, 100	3, 1, 100	3, 2, 100	3, 3, 100
2, 0, 100	2, 1, 100	2, 2, 100	2, 3, 100
1, 0, 100	1, 1, 100	1, 2, 100	1, 3, 100
0, 0, 100	0, 1, 100	0, 2, 100	0, 3, 100

Flipped vertically:

0, 3, 100	0, 2, 100	0, 1, 100	0, 0, 100
1, 3, 100	1, 2, 100	1, 1, 100	1, 0, 100
2, 3, 100	2, 2, 100	2, 1, 100	2, 0, 100
3, 3, 100	3, 2, 100	3, 1, 100	3, 0, 100

Write the `flipImage` method, which takes as parameters a 2D array of `Pixel` objects and a `boolean` direction to flip, where true means horizontally and false means vertically. The method returns the flipped image as a 2D array of `Pixel` objects.

```
/** Flips a 2D array of Pixel objects either
 *   horizontally or vertically
 *
 *   @param image the 2D array of Pixel objects to be processed
 *   @param horiz true: flip horizontally, false: flip vertically
 *   @return the processed image
 */
public Pixel[][] flipImage(Pixel[][] image, boolean horiz)
```

STOP. End of Part II.

Practice Exam 1
Answers and Explanations

Part I (Multiple Choice)
Answers and Explanations

Bullets mark each step in the process of arriving at the correct solution.

1. The answer is E.

   - Lines 1 and 2 give us: myValue = 17 and multiplier = 3
   - Line 3: answer = 17 % 3 + 17 / 3
     - Using integer division: 17 / 3 = 5 remainder 2, giving us:
     - 17 / 3 = 5
     - 17 % 3 = 2
     - The expression simplifies to answer = 2 + 5 = 7 (remember order of operations)
   - Line 4: answer = 7 * 3 = 21

2. The answer is B.

   - Let's use De Morgan's theorem to simplify the expression.

     `!(a < b || b <= c) && !(a < c || b >= a)`

   - Distribute the first !. Remember to change `||` to `&&`. This gives:

     `!(a < b) && !(b <= c)`

   - Distribute the second ! This gives:

     `!(a < c) && !(b >= a)`

   - It's easy to simplify all those !s. Remember that !< → >= and !<= → > (the same with > and >=).

     `(a >= b) && (b > c) && (a >= c) && (b < a)`

   - Since these are all &&s, all four conditions must be true. The first condition says a >= b and the fourth condition says b < a. No problem there. Options B and C both have a > b. Option A can be eliminated.
   - The second condition says b > c. That's true in option B. Option C can be eliminated.
   - The third condition says b < a. Still true in option B, so that's the answer.
   - You could also solve this problem with guess and check by plugging in the given values, but all those ands and ors and nots tend to get pretty confusing. Simplifying at least a little will help, even if you are going to ultimately plug and chug.

3. The answer is D.

   - The `while` loop condition is (myArray[index] < 7). If you did not read carefully, you may have assumed that the condition was (index < 7), which, along with the index++ is the way you would write it if you wanted to access every element in the array.
   - Because the condition is (myArray[index] < 7), we will start at element 0 and continue until we come to an element that is greater than or equal to 7. At that point we will exit the loop and no more elements will be processed.
   - Every element before the 7 in the array will have 3 added to its value.

4. **The answer is A.**

   - Option I correctly accesses and processes every element in the `ArrayList`.
   - Option II uses a `for-each` loop. That is an excellent option for this problem, since we need to process each element in exactly the same way, but option II does not access the element correctly. Read the `for-each` loop like this: "For each OnlinePurchaseItem (which I will call purchase) in items. . . ." The variable purchase already holds the needed element. Using get(i) to get the element is unnecessary and there is no variable i.
   - Option III uses a `for` loop and processes the elements in reverse order. That is acceptable. Since we need to process every item, it doesn't matter what order we do it in. However, option III starts at i = items.size(), which will cause an `IndexOutOfBoundsException`. Remember that the last element in an `ArrayList` is list.size() − 1 (just like a String or an array).

5. **The answer is D.**

   - This is a recursive method. Let's trace the calls. The parts in *italics* were filled in on the way back up. That is, the calls in the plain type were written top to bottom until the base case returned a value. Then the answers were filled in *bottom to top*.
     - mystery(5) = 2 + mystery(4) = 2 + *7* = **9** which gives us our final answer.
     - mystery(4) = 2 + mystery(3) = 2 + *5* = *7*
     - mystery(3) = 2 + mystery(2) = 2 + *3* = *5*
     - mystery(2) = 2 + mystery(1) = 2 + *1* = *3*
     - mystery(1) Base Case! return 1

6. **The answer is E.**

   - The outer loop will execute three times, starting at index = 0 and continuing as long as index < 4, increasing by one each time through. So index will equal 0, 1, 2, 3 in successive iterations through the loop.
   - The only statement inside the outer loop is the inner loop. Let's look at what the inner loop does in general terms.
   - The inner loop executes from i = 0 to i < index, so it will execute index times.
   - Each time through it puts an "A" in front of and after myString.
   - Putting it all together:
     - The first iteration of the outer loop, index = 0, the inner loop executes 0 times, myString does not change.
     - The second iteration of the outer loop, index = 1, the inner loop executes one time, adding an "A" in front of and after myString. myString = "AHA"
     - The third iteration of the outer loop, index = 2, the inner loop executes two times, adding two "A"s in front of and after myString. myString = "AAAHAAA"
     - The fourth (and last) iteration of the outer loop, index = 3, the inner loop executes three times, adding three more "A"s in front of and after myString. myString = "AAAAAAHAAAAAA"
   - Putting it another way, when index = 1, we add one "A"; when index = 2, we add two "A"s; when index = 3, we add three "A"s. That's six "A"s all together added to the beginning and end of "H" ➜ "AAAAAAHAAAAAA"

7. The answer is B.

- The general form for generating a random number between *high* and *low* is:

  ```
  (int)(Math.random() * (high - low + 1)) + low
  ```

- high − low + 1 = 50, low = 10, so high = 59
- The correct answer is integers between 10 and 59 inclusive

8. The answer is C.

- This question requires that you understand the two uses of the + symbol.
- First, we execute what is in the parentheses. Now we have:

  ```
  13 + 6 + "APCSA" + 4 + 4
  ```

- Now do the addition left to right. That's easy until we hit the string:

  ```
  19 + "APCSA" + 4 + 4
  ```

- When you add a number and a string in any order, Java turns the number into a string and then concatenates the strings:

  ```
  "19APCSA" + 4 + 4
  ```

- Now every operation we do will have a string and a number, so they all become string concatenations, not number additions.

  ```
  "19APCSA44"
  ```

9. The answer is E.

- Let's consider what the expression is telling us.

  ```
  (truth1 && truth2) || ((!truth1) && (!truth2))
  ```

- The expression is true if both truth1 and truth2 are true OR if both truth1 and truth2 are false.
- Therefore, the expression is true as long as truth1 == truth2.

10. The answer is A.

- The for-each loop looks at every item in the ArrayList and adds it to sum if:
  - the value of the item > 1 (all values except 0 and 1) AND
  - the size of the list − 3 > the value of the item. Since the list has 10 elements, we can rewrite this as the value of the item < 7, which is true for all elements 6 and below.
  - Both conditions are true for 2, 3, 4, 5, 6; so the sum is 20.

11. The answer is E.

- Methods or constructors with the same name (and return type, in the case of methods) may have different parameter lists. The parameters may differ in type or number. This is called *overloading*.

12. The answer is A.

- We can eliminate options B and D immediately by noticing that active is a `boolean` and will therefore print as either "true" or "false" and not as "active" even though that is more informative.
- We would expect option E to be correct by reading the code, but the constructor was called incorrectly. The overloaded constructor that is being called is the two-parameter constructor, and that constructor is going to assign its first parameter to state and its second parameter to city. Since we passed city, state, in that order, the city name and the state name have been assigned incorrectly and will therefore be printed incorrectly.
- Note that this is a confusing way to write an overloaded constructor! The order of the variables changes for no reason.

13. The answer is D.

- Option I is incorrect. Most classes have a no-argument constructor; either the default constructor provided automatically if no other constructor is provided, or one written by the programmer. However, the Depot class does not. The super call causes a compile-time error.
- Option II is correct. It implements a no-argument constructor in the `WhistleStop` class, which passes the needed parameters to the Depot constructor.
- Option III is also correct. It takes two parameters and correctly passes them to the Depot constructor via the call to super. However, this code will probably not give you the result you are expecting. Just like in question 12, the order of the city and province has been switched.

14. The answer is A.

- Option I is correct. The `ArrayList` is correctly instantiated as an `ArrayList` of Depot objects. Since a `WhistleStop` object *is-a* Depot object, a `WhistleStop` object may be added to the `ArrayList`. `WhistleStop` contains a no-argument constructor, and the Depot constructor is called correctly as well.
- Option II is incorrect. A `WhistleStop` *is-a* Depot, but not the other way around. We cannot put Depot objects into an `ArrayList` that is declared to hold `WhistleStop` objects. The `ArrayList` declaration will generate a compile-time error.
- Option III is incorrect. The `ArrayList` is correctly instantiated as an `ArrayList` of `WhistleStop` objects. We can add `WhistleStop` objects to this `ArrayList`, but we cannot add Depot objects. The second add will generate a compile-time error.

15. The answer is B.

- When we start the `for-each` loop, the variable crazyString = "crazy" and the `ArrayList` crazyList has two elements ["weird," "enigma"].
- You can read the `for-each` like this: "For each String (which I am going to call s) in crazyList. . . ."
- So for each String s in crazyList we execute the assignment statement:

```
crazyString = s.substring(1, 3) + crazyString.substring(0, 4);
```

which takes two characters starting at index 1 from s and concatenates the first four characters of crazyString.

- The first time through the loop, s = "weird" and crazyString = "crazy" so the assignment becomes:

  ```
  crazyString = "ei" + "craz" = "eicraz"
  ```

  Remember that substring starts at the first parameter and ends *before* the second parameter, and remember that we start counting the first letter at 0.
- The second time through the loop, s = "enigma" and crazyString = "eicraz" so the assignment becomes:

  ```
  crazyString = "ni" + "eicr" = "nieicr"
  ```

16. The answer is E.

- There are four possible paths through the code. We need one data element that will pass through each path.
    - The first path is executed if n < –5.
    - The second path is executed if –5 ≤ n < 0 (because if n < –5, the first path is executed and we will not reach the second path).
    - The third path is executed if n > 10.
    - The fourth path is executed in all other cases.
- We need to be sure that we have at least one piece of data for all four of those cases.
- Option A does not test the fourth path, because 12 and 15 are both > 10.
- Option B does not test the first path, because it doesn't have a number that is < –5.
- Option C does not test the third path, because it doesn't have a number that is > 10.
- Option D does not test the second path, because 0 is not less than 0.
- Option E tests all four paths.

17. The answer is D.

- This statement should be written with if-else ladder. When the clause associated with a true condition is executed, the rest of the statements should be skipped. Unfortunately, that is not how it is written. For example, if the parameter temperature = 80, the first if is evaluated and found to be true and activity = "go swimming"; however, since there is no else, the second if is also evaluated and found to be true, so activity = "go hiking". Then the third if is evaluated and found to be true, so activity = "go horseback riding". The else clause is skipped and "go horseback riding" is returned (incorrectly).
- All temperatures that are true for multiple if statements will cause activity to be set incorrectly. Only the values of temperature that will execute the last if or the else clause will return the correct answer.
- In order for this code to function as intended, all ifs except the first one should be preceded with *else*.

18. The answer is D.

- This time, there is an if-else ladder, but they are in the wrong order. It is important to write the most restrictive case first. Let's test this code by using 80 as an example. 80 > 75, and that is the condition we intend to execute, but unfortunately, it is also > 45, which is the first condition in the code, so that is the if clause that is executed and activity is set to "go horseback riding". Since the code is written as an if-else ladder, no more conditions are evaluated and flow of control jumps to the return statement.
- Two sets of values give the right answer:
    - Values that execute the first if clause correctly—that is, values that are greater than 45, but less than or equal to 60.
    - Values that fail all the if conditions and execute the else clause—that is, values that are less than or equal to 45.
- Those two conditions can be combined into temperatures <= 60.
- In order for this code to function as intended, the order of the conditions needs to be reversed.

19. The answer is A.

- Let's look at the three code segments one by one.
- Option I:
  - When we enter the loop, i = 1.
  - arr[1 / 2] = arr[0] = 1 (don't forget integer division)
  - i = i + 2 = 3, 3 < 6 so we enter the loop again.
  - arr [3 / 2] = arr[1] = 3
  - i = i + 2 = 5, 5 < 6 so we enter the loop again.
  - arr[5 / 2] = arr[2] = 5
  - i = i + 2 = 7, 7 is not < 6 so we exit the loop.
  - The array arr = [1, 3, 5]
- Option II:
  - When we enter the loop, i = 0.
  - arr[0] = 2 * 0 + 1 = 1
  - increment i to 1, 1 < 3 so we enter the loop again.
  - arr[1] = 2 * 1 + 1 = 3
  - increment i to 2, 2 < 3 so we enter the loop again.
  - arr[2] = 2 * 2 + 1 = 5
  - increment i to 3, 3 is not < 3 so we exit the loop.
  - The array arr = [1, 3, 5]
- Option III:
  - When we enter the loop, i = 6.
  - arr[(6 − 6) / 2] = arr[0] = 6 − 6 = 0
  - Since we know the first element should be 1, not 0, we can stop here and eliminate this option.
- Options I and II produce the same results.

20. The answer is C.

- Let's picture our `ArrayList` as a table. After the add statements, `ArrayList` nations looks like this:

Argentina	Canada	Australia	Cambodia	Russia	France

- It looks like perhaps the loop is intended to remove all elements whose length is greater than or equal to 7, but that is not what this loop does. Let's walk through it.
- i = 0. nations.size() = 6, 0 < 6 so we enter the loop.
  - nations.get(0).length() gives us the length of "Argentina" = 9.
  - 9 >= 7, so we remove the element at location 0. Now our `ArrayList` looks like this:

Canada	Australia	Cambodia	Russia	France

- increment i to 1. nations.size() = 5, 1 < 5, so we enter the loop.
  - nations.get(1).length() gives us the length of "Australia" = 9. (We skipped over "Canada" because it moved into position 0 when "Argentina" was removed.)
  - 9 >= 7, so we remove the element at location 0. Now our `ArrayList` looks like this:

Australia	Cambodia	Russia	France

- increment i to 2. nations.size() = 4, 2 < 4 so we enter the loop.
  - nations.get(2).length() gives us the length of "Russia" = 6.
  - 6 is not >= 7 so we skip the if clause.
- increment i to 3. nations.size() = 4, 3 < 4 so we enter the loop.
  - nations.get(3).length() gives us the length of "France" = 6.
  - 6 is not >= 7 so we skip the if clause.
- increment i to 4. nations.size() = 4, 4 is not < 4 so we exit the loop with the ArrayList:

Australia	Cambodia	Russia	France

- Note: You have to be really careful when you remove items from an ArrayList in the context of a loop. Keep in mind that when you remove an item, the items with higher indices don't stay put. They all shift over one, changing their indices. If you just keep counting up, you will skip items. Also, unlike an array, the size of the ArrayList will change as you delete items.

21. The answer is D.

- Option I is correct. It calls the super constructor, correctly passing on 2 parameters, and then sets its own instance variables, one to the passed parameter, one to a default value.
- Option II is incorrect. It attempts to call the student class 2 parameter constructor, passing default values, but the year is being passed as a String, not as an int.
- Option III is correct. There will be an implicit call to Student's no-argument constructor.

22. The answer is D.

- index starts at 0 and goes to the end of the String. We want a condition that will look at the letter in word at index, compare it to the letter parameter, and count it if it is the same.
- Option A is incorrect. The one-parameter substring includes everything from the starting index to the end of the word. We need one letter only.
- Option B is incorrect. We cannot compare Strings with ==.
- Option C is incorrect. indexOf will tell us whether a letter appears in a word and where it appears, but not how many times. It is possible to count the occurrences of letter using indexOf, but not this way. Option C does not change the if condition each time through the loop. It just asks the same question over and over.
- Option D is correct. It selects one letter at index and compares it to letter using the equals method, incrementing count if they match.
- Option E is incorrect. It will not compile. It tries to compare letter to the int returned by indexOf.

23. The answer is C.

- You might expect that the loop will remove any animal whose name comes before pink fairy armadillo lexicographically, but removing elements from an ArrayList in the context of a loop is tricky. Let's walk through it.
- We start with:

okapi	aye-aye	cassowary	echidna	sugar glider	jerboa

- The `for` loop begins, i = 0. Compare "okapi" with "pink fairy armadillo", and since "o" comes before "p", remove "okapi".

aye-aye	cassowary	echidna	sugar glider	jerboa

- The next iteration begins with i = 1. The remove operation has caused all the elements' index numbers to change. We skip "aye-aye", which is now element 0, and look at "cassowary", which we remove.

aye-aye	echidna	sugar glider	jerboa

- The next iteration begins with i = 2. Again the elements have shifted, so we skip "echidna", compare to "sugar glider" but that comes after "pink fairy armadillo" so it stays put leaving the ArrayList unchanged.

aye-aye	echidna	sugar glider	jerboa

- The next iteration begins with i = 3. Remove "jerboa".

aye-aye	echidna	sugar glider

- i = 4, which is not < animals.size(). We exit the loop and print the ArrayList.
- Remember that if you are going to remove elements from an ArrayList in a loop, you have to adjust the index when an element is removed so that no elements are skipped.
- Note that if we used the loop condition i < 6 (the size of the original ArrayList), then there would have been an `IndexOutOfBoundsException`, but because we used animals.size(), the value changed each time we removed an element.

24. The answer is C.

- This method takes a String parameter and loops through the first half of the letters in the string.
- The first substring statement assigns the letter at index i to sub1. You may have to run through an example by hand to discover what the second substring does.
- If our string is "quest":
  - the first time through the loop, i = 0, so sub1 = "q" and sub2 = st.substring(5 − 0 − 1, 5 − 0) = "t",
  - the second time, i = 1, so sub1 = "u" and sub2 = st.substring(5 − 1 − 1, 5 − 1) = "s".
- This loop is comparing the first letter to the last, the second to the second to last, and so on, which will tell us if the string is a palindrome.

25. The answer is E.

- The loop will continue to execute until either value <= 5 or calculate = false.
- When we enter the loop, value = 33, calculate = true.
  - Since 33 % 3 = 0 we execute the first if clause and set value = 31.
  - 31 / 4 = 7, which is not < 3, so we do not execute the second if clause.
- The second iteration of the loop begins with value = 31 and calculate = true.
  - Since 31 % 3 != 0, we do not execute the first if clause.
  - Since 31 / 4 = 7, which is not < 3, we do not execute the second if clause.
- At this point, we notice that nothing is ever going to change. Value will always be equal to 31 and calculate will always be true. This is an infinite loop.

26. The answer is C.

- Option A is incorrect. If Child extended Adult, this would be the correct constructor, but Child extends Person. The Person constructor does not take a title, only a first name and last name.
- Option B is incorrect because Person does not have a no-argument constructor. The call to super() will cause a compile time error.
- Options D and E are incorrect because of the "extends" phrase. The keyword `extends` is used in the class declaration, not the constructor declaration.
- Option C is the correctly written constructor.

27. The answer is E.

- Options A and D are incorrect because they print information to the console rather than returning it as a string. Option A also calls super.toString, which does not exist.
- Option B is incorrect because, like option A, it calls super.toString, which does not exist.
- Option C is incorrect because firstName and lastName are private instance variables of the `Person` class and cannot be accessed by the `Adult` class.
- Option E is a correctly written `toString` method.

28. The answer is C.

- Method findSomeone is expecting a parameter of type Adult. The question is, which of the options correctly provides a parameter of type Adult?
- Option I is incorrect. Here, the parameter is of type Person. Adult extends Person, not the other way around, so a Person is not an Adult.
- Option II is correct. The parameter is of type Adult.
- Option III is incorrect. Here, the parameter is of type Child. Child extends Person, not Adult, so a Child is not an Adult.
- Option IV is correct. A Person reference variable can be downcast to an Adult since Adult extends Person. At run-time, if the reference variable does not reference an Adult object as promised by the cast, the program will crash with a run-time error.
- Option V is incorrect. Child is not a superclass of Adult. Child cannot be downcast to Adult.

29. The answer is E.

- The basic formula for tolerance is:

```
Math.abs(a - b) <= tolerance;
```

- In our case, a is val^{power}, or Math.pow(val, power), and b is target, so the equation becomes:

```
Math.abs(Math.pow(val, power) - target) <= tolerance;
```

- That evaluates to a `boolean`. We could assign it to a `boolean` variable and return the variable, but we can also just return the expression as in option E.

30. The answer is C.

- This problem requires you to understand that primitives are passed by value and objects are passed by reference.
- When a primitive argument (or actual parameter) is passed to a method, its value is copied into the formal parameter. Changing the formal parameter inside the method has no effect on the value of the variable passed in. The caller's num1 will not be changed by the method.
- The caller's num2 is not changed when the num2++ is executed inside the method. That new value, however, is returned by the method, and the caller uses the returned value to reset num2. The value of num2 will change.

- When an object is passed to a method, its reference is copied into the formal parameter. The actual and formal parameters become aliases of each other; that is, they both point to the same object. Therefore, when the object is changed inside the method, those changes will be seen outside of the method. Changes to array values inside the method will be seen in array values outside of the method.
- num1 remains equal to 2, even though the method's num1 variable is changed to 4. num2 is reset to 4, because the method returns that value, and values[4] is set to 3.

31. The answer is C.

- Let's figure this out step by step. The length of "on your side" is 12 (don't forget to count spaces), so `s1.indexOf(s2.substring(s2.length() - 2))` simplifies to `s1.indexOf(s2.substring(10))`
- That gives us the last two letters of s2, so our statement becomes `s1.indexOf("de")`
- Can we find "de" in s1? Yes. It starts at index 3 and that is what is returned.

32. The answer is A.

- acArray is an array of objects. Initially, all the entries in the array are null. That is, they do not reference anything. If a program tries to use one of these entries as if it were an object, the program will terminate with a `NullPointerException`.
- To avoid the `NullPointerException`, we must not attempt to use a null entry as if it contained a reference to an object.
- Option B is incorrect. It uses `ArrayList` syntax, not array syntax, so it will not even compile.
- Options C and D are incorrect. They attempt to call getData() on a null entry and so will terminate with a `NullPointerException`.
- Option A is correct. It checks to see whether the array entry is null before allowing the System.out.println statement to treat it as an object.

33. The answer is A.

- The Binary Search algorithm should not be applied to this array! Binary Search only works on a sorted array. However, the algorithm will run; it just won't return reasonable results. Let's take a look at what it will do.
- First look at the middle element. That's 100. 50 < 100, so eliminate the second half of the array.

9	100	11	45	76	~~100~~	~~50~~	~~1~~	~~0~~	~~55~~	~~99~~

- Look at the middle element of the remaining part; 50 > 11, so eliminate the lower half.

~~9~~	~~100~~	~~11~~	45	76	~~100~~	~~50~~	~~1~~	~~0~~	~~55~~	~~99~~

- 50 does not appear in the remaining elements, return -1 (incorrectly, as it turns out).

34. The answer is C.

- After the array is instantiated, it looks like this:

0	1	2
3	4	5
6	7	8

- The `for` loop will execute three times: x = 0, x = 1, and x = 2.
- You should recognize that the code in the loop is a simple swap algorithm that swaps the value at nums[x][0] with the value at nums[x][2].
- The result is that in each row, element 0 and element 2 will be swapped.
- Our final answer is:

2	1	0
5	4	3
8	7	6

35. The answer is A.

- Let's trace the loop and see what happens. On entry we have:

list (which will not change):   newList:

2	4	3	3	2	5	1

2

- i = 1. In pseudocode, the `if` statement says "if (element 1 of list > the last element in newList) add it to newList". Since 4 > 2, add 4 to newList, which becomes:

2	4

- i = 2. "if (element 2 of list > the last element in newList) add it to newList" 3 is not > 4 so we do not add it.
- i = 3. "if (element 3 of list > the last element in newList) add it to newList" 3 is not > 4, we do not add it. (By this point, you may recognize what the code is doing and you may be able to complete newList without tracing the remaining iterations of the loop.)
- i = 4 "if (element 4 of list > the last element in newList) add it to newList" 2 is not > 4, we do not add it.
- i = 5. "if (element 5 of list > the last element in newList) add it to newList" 5 > 4, add 5 to newList which becomes:

2	4	5

- i = 6. "if (element 6 of list > the last element in newList) add it to newList" 1 is not > 5, so we do not add it.
- We have completed the loop; we exit and print newList.

36. The answer is E.

- After the array is instantiated, it is filled with 0s because that is the default value for an int, so anything we don't overwrite will be a 0.
- Let's look at the first loop. r goes from 0 to 4, so all rows are affected. c starts at r+1 and goes to 4, so not all columns are affected. When r = 0, c will = 1,2,3,4; when r = 1, c will = 2,3,4; when r = 2, c will = 3,4; when r = 3, c will = 4. That will assign 9 to the upper-right corner of the grid like this.

0	9	9	9	9
0	0	9	9	9
0	0	0	9	9
0	0	0	0	9
0	0	0	0	0

- In the second loop, d goes from 0 to 4, so all rows are affected, and c always equals r, so the diagonals are filled in with their row/column number.

0	9	9	9	9
0	1	9	9	9
0	0	2	9	9
0	0	0	3	9
0	0	0	0	4

- Now we just have to look for the three cells specified in the problem.

37. The answer is D.

- The first thing to do is to identify the sorting algorithm implemented by mysterySort.
- We can tell it's not Merge Sort, because it is not recursive.
- There are several things we can look for to identify whether a sort is Insertion Sort or Selection Sort. Some easy things to look for:
  - In the inner loop, Insertion Sort shifts items over one slot.
  - After the loops are complete, Selection Sort swaps two elements.
- We can see items being shifted over and we can't see a swap, so this is Insertion Sort.
- Let's look at the state of the array in table form. Before the sort begins, we have this. The sort starts by saying that 9 (all by itself) is already sorted.

9	1	3	0	2

- The first iteration through the loop puts the first two elements in sorted order.

1	9	3	0	2

- The second iteration through the loop puts the first three elements in sorted order.

1	3	9	0	2

- Notice that in Insertion Sort, the elements at the end of the array are never touched until it is their turn to be "inserted." Selection Sort will change elements all through the array.

38. The answer is C.

- This is a recursive method. Let's trace the calls. The parts in *italics* were filled in on the way back up. That is, the calls in the plain type were written top to bottom until the base case returned a value. Then the answers were filled in *bottom to top*.
  - puzzle (3, 4) = 3 * puzzle (3, 3) = 3 * *27* = ***81*** which gives us our final answer
  - puzzle (3, 3) = 3 * puzzle (3, 2) = 3 * *9* = *27*
  - puzzle (3, 2) = 3 * puzzle (3, 1) = 3 * *3* = *9*
  - puzzle (3, 1) Base Case! return 3
- It is interesting to notice that this recursive method finds the first parameter raised to the power of the second parameter.

39. The answer is D.

- This nested `for` loop is traversing the array in column major order. I can tell this is the case because the outer loop, the one that is changing more slowly, is controlling the column variable. For every time the column variable changes, the row variable goes through the entire row.
- In addition, although the outer loop is traversing the columns from least to greatest, the inner loop is working backward through the rows.
- Since we increase val by 2 each time, values are being filled in like this:

8	18	28	38	48	58
6	16	26	36	46	56
4	14	24	34	44	54
2	12	22	32	42	52
0	10	20	30	40	50

- You probably didn't need to fill in the whole table to figure out that table[3][4] = 42.

40. The answer is E.

- Since this is a Selection Sort algorithm, we know that the inner loop is looking for the smallest element.
- small is storing the index of the smallest element we have found so far. We need to find out if the current element being examined is smaller than the element at index small, or, in other words, if arr[j] is less than arr[small].
- Option C would be correct if we were sorting an array of ints, but < doesn't work with strings. We have to use the method `compareTo`. `compareTo` returns a negative value if the calling element is before the parameter value. We need:

```
if (arr[j].compareTo(arr[small] < 0))
```

Part II (Free Response)
Answers and Explanations

Please keep in mind that there are multiple ways to write the solution to a Free-response question, but the general and refined statements of the problem should be pretty much the same for everyone. Look at the algorithms and coded solutions, and determine if yours accomplishes the same task.

General Penalties (assessed only once per problem):
-1 using a local variable without first declaring it
-1 returning a value from a void method or constructor
-1 confusing array/ArrayList access
-1 overwriting information passed as a parameter
-1 including unnecessary code that causes a side effect such as a compile error or console output

1. Password

   (a) **General Problem:** Write the `isValid` method for the `Password` class.
   Refined Problem: Determine if a password is valid by checking if the password has the correct length and the correct combination of letters and symbols.

   Algorithm:
   - Determine the length of the password.
   - If the length is not between the minimum length and the maximum length, then return false. Otherwise, continue checking.
   - Initialize counters for the number of uppercase letters, lowercase letters, and symbols to zero.
   - For each character in the password increment the appropriate counter.
   - If the counter for each isn't zero (meaning there was at least one occurrence) and the sum of all three counters equal the length of the password (meaning there were no symbols outside those that are acceptable), then it is a valid password.
   - Return the result.

Java Code:

```java
public boolean isValid(String password)
{
if (password.length() < minLength || password.length() > maxLength)
    return false;
int countUpper =0, countLower = 0, countSymbol = 0;
for (int i = 0; i < password.length(); i++)
{
    String letter = password.substring(i, i+1);
    if (upper.indexOf(letter) > -1)
       countUpper++;
    else if (lower.indexOf(letter) > -1)
        countLower++;
    else if (symbols.indexOf(letter) > -1)
        countSymbol++;
}
return (countUpper > 0) && (countLower > 0) && (countSymbol > 0)
      && (countUpper + countLower + countSymbol == password.length());
}
```

Common Errors:
- Not taking into account that there might be characters other than letters or acceptable symbols.
- Not checking for the length of the password.
- Not initializing or declaring the necessary variables.

(b) **General Problem:** Write the `generatePassword` method for the `Password` class.
Refined Problem: Use the random number generator to choose upper case, lower case, and symbols from the given strings. Determine if the generated password is valid by using the method written in part (a).

Algorithm:
- Concatenate the upper case, lower case and symbol strings.
- Determine if a valid password has been generated.
  - Use the random number generator to choose a valid length of the password.
  - Use the random number generator to randomly choose a letter from the concatenated upper/lower/symbol string.
  - Continue randomly choosing letters until the string has reached the desired length.
  - Test to see if the password is valid.
- If the password is not valid, start the process again until a valid password has been generated.
- Return the generated password string.

Java Code:

```java
public String generatePassword()
{
    String password = "";
    String allPossible = upper + lower + symbols;
    int position;
    while (!isValid(password))
    {
      password = "";
      int length = (int) (Math.random() * (maxLength - minLength + 1)) + 1;
      for (int i = 1; i <= length; i++)
      {
          position = (int) (Math.random() * allPossible.length());
          password += allPossible.substring(position, position+1);
      }
    }
    return password;
}
```

Common Errors:
- Not checking to see if the generated password is valid.
- Not randomly choosing a length for the new password.
- Not initializing or declaring necessary variables.
- Not returning the generated password.

Scoring Guidelines: Password

Part (a)	isValid	5 points

+1 Determine if the password has a valid length

+1 Examine each character of the password one at a time

+1 Determine if the password has upper case, lower case, and valid symbols

+1 Ensure there are no other characters besides upper case, lower case, and valid symbols

+1 Return the appropriate value

Part (b)	generatePassword	4 points

+1 Calls the `isValid` method correctly

+1 Randomly chooses a length of the password

+1 Randomly choose upper case, lower case, and valid symbols

+1 Returns the generated password

Sample Driver:

There are many ways to write these methods. Maybe yours is a bit different from our sample solutions and you are not sure if it works. Here is a sample driver program. Running it will let you see if your code works, and will help you debug it if it does not.

Copy PasswordDriver into your IDE along with the complete `Password` class (including your solutions).

```
public class PasswordDriver
{
    public static void main(String[] args)
    {
        Password pass1 = new Password(3,15);
        String pass = "HelloWorld!";
        boolean valid = pass1.isValid(pass);
        System.out.println(pass + " is valid: " + valid);
        pass = pass1.generatePassword();
        System.out.println(pass);

        Password pass2 = new Password(3,15);
        pass = "#APComputerScienceRocks";
        valid = pass2.isValid(pass);
        System.out.println(pass + " is valid: " + valid);
        pass = pass2.generatePassword();
        System.out.println(pass);

    }
}
```

2. ISBN

General Problem: Write an ISBN class.
Refined Problem: Define necessary instance variables, a constructor with one integer parameter, and two methods.

Algorithm:
- Declare a private instance variable to hold the 9-digit ISBN number.
- Define a constructor with one integer parameter and assign the value of the parameter to the instance variable.
- Write a calculateCheckDigit method that returns a string containing the check digit.
  - For each of the 9 digits in the ISBN number, find the product of digit and the weighted value.
  - Maintain a sum of those products.
  - Determine the check digit by using the formula given.
- Write a generateNumber method that concatenates the instance variable with the result of the call to the calculateCheckDigit method.

Java Code:
```java
public class ISBN
{
    private int isbnNumber;

    public ISBN(int number)
    {
        isbnNumber = number;
    }

    public String calculateCheckDigit()
    {
        int temp = isbnNumber;
        int digit, product;
        int multiple = 2;
        int sum = 0;
        for (int i = 1; i <= 9; i++)
        {
            digit = temp % 10;
            temp /= 10;
            product = digit * multiple;
            sum += product;
            multiple++;
        }
        int check = 11 - sum % 11;
        if (check == 10)
            return "X";
        return "" + check;
    }

    public String generateNumber()
    {
        return isbnNumber + "-" + calculateCheckDigit();
    }
}
```

Scoring Guidelines: ISBN

ISBN class	1 point

+1 Complete, correct header for ISBN

state maintenance	1 point

+1 Declares a private instance variable capable of maintaining the 9-digit ISBN number

ISBN Constructor	2 points

+1 Correctly formed header
+1 Sets appropriate state variables based on parameter

calculateCheckDigit	3 points

+1 Correctly formed header
+1 Finds the sum of the products of digits and weighted values
+1 Returns correct check digit

generateNumber	2 points

+1 Correctly formed header
+1 Returns 10-digit ISBN number

Sample Driver:

There are many ways to write these methods. Maybe yours is a bit different from our sample solutions and you are not sure if it works. Here is a sample driver program. Running it will let you see if your code works, and will help you debug it if it does not.

Copy ISBNDriver into your IDE along with the complete ISBN class (including your solutions).

```
public class ISBN Driver
{
    public static void main(String [] args)
    {
        ISBN book1 = new ISBN(126045491);
        String check1 = book1.calculateCheckDigit();    //  "6" will be returned
        String isbnNumber1 = book1.generateNumber();     // "126045491-6" will be
                                                         // returned


        ISBN book2 = new ISBN(030640611);
        String check2 = book2.calculateCheckDigit();    //  "X" will be returned
        String isbnNumber2 = book2.generateNumber();     // "030640611-X" will be
                                                         //  returned

    }
}
```

3. Train

(a) **General Problem:** Write the `getTotalWeight` method to find the total weight of the engine and train.

Refined Problem: The method should loop through each element of the `ArrayList` and add it to a sum variable.

Algorithm:
- Initialize a sum variable to 0.
- Loop through each element of the `ArrayList`.
  - Add the value of the current element to the accumulated sum.
- Return the accumulated sum.

Java Code:

```java
public double getTotalWeight()
{
    double weight = 0;
    for (Double car : trainCars)
        weight += car;
    return weight;
}
```

Common Errors:
- Not initializing the sum to 0.
- Not accessing each element of the `ArrayList`.
- Not returning the sum.

Java Code Alternate Solution:
```java
public double getTotalWeight()
{
    double weight = 0;
    for (int i = 0; i < trainCars.size(); i++)
        weight += trainCars.get(i);
    return weight;
}
```

(b) **General Problem:** Write the `removeExcessTrainCars` method of the `Train` class that removes cars from the train until the train is light enough to be pulled by the engine.

Refined Problem: Calculate the initial weight of the train. If the weight exceeds the weight limit, TrainCars are removed from the end of the train until the weight is in the acceptable range. All train cars that are removed are returned in an `ArrayList` in the order they are removed from the train.

Algorithm:
- Create an `ArrayList` of Double to hold the removed cars.
- While the total weight is greater than the Engine's maximum weight,
  - Remove a train car from the end of the train
  - Add it to the `ArrayList` to be returned
- Return the `ArrayList` of removed cars (which may be empty).

Java Code:

```java
public ArrayList<Double> removeExcessTrainCars()
{
   if (getTotalWeight() < getMaximumWeight())
     return null;
  ArrayList<Double> removed = new ArrayList<Double>();

   while (getTotalWeight() > getMaximumWeight())
   {
      Double removedCar = trainCars.remove(trainCars.size() - 1);
      removed.add(removedCar);
   }
   return removed;
}
```

Common Errors:
- Not creating a temporary `ArrayList` when needed.
- Remember that remove also returns the removed element. You do not need a `get` followed by a `remove`.
- Not returning the temporary `ArrayList`.

Scoring Guidelines: Train

Part (a)	getTotalWeight	4 points

+1 Declare and initialize a weight variable
+1 Accesses the weight of every element of the `ArrayList`; no bounds errors, no missed elements
+1 Calculates the total weight of the train
+1 Returns the accumulated weight

Part (b)	removeExcessTrainCars	5 points

+1 Declares and instantiates an `ArrayList` for the removed values
+3 Removes necessary cars from the train
    +1 Writes a loop with an appropriate terminating condition
    +1 Removes a car from the end of the train
    +1 Adds the car to the end of the declared `ArrayList`
+1 Returns the correctly generated `ArrayList`

Sample Driver:

There are many ways to write these methods. Maybe yours is a bit different from our sample solutions and you are not sure if it works. Here is a sample driver program. Running it will let you see if your code works, and will help you debug it if it does not.

Copy TrainDriver and the complete `Train` class into your IDE. Add your `getTotalWeight` and `removeExcessTrainCars` methods to the bottom of the `TrainDriver` class.

```java
import java.util.ArrayList;

public class TrainDriver
{
    public static void main(String[] args)
    {
        ArrayList <Double> trainCars = new ArrayList <Double>();
        trainCars.add(200000.0);
        trainCars.add(100000.0);
        trainCars.add(140000.0);
        trainCars.add(50000.0);
```

```
                        trainCars.add(100000.0);
                        trainCars.add(60000.0);

                Train t = new Train(475000, trainCars);
                double weight = t.getTotalWeight();
                System.out.println("The total weight is " + weight);
                ArrayList <Double> removed = t.removeExcessTrainCars();
                System.out.println("The removed train cars are " + removed);
        }
}

import java.util.ArrayList;

public class Train
{
     private double maxWeight;
     private ArrayList <Double> trainCars;

     public Train (Double max, ArrayList<Double> tc)
     {
      maxWeight = max;
      trainCars = tc;
     }

     public double getMaximumWeight()
     {
      return maxWeight;
     }


/* insert your code here */

}
```

4. Pixels

(a) **General Problem:** Write the generatePixelArray method to convert three 2-D int arrays into a 2-D array of Pixel objects.

Refined Problem: Use a nested for loop to instantiate a Pixel object for each element of the Pixel object array. Use the corresponding values in the red, green, and blue arrays as parameters to the Pixel constructor. When the loops are complete, return the completed array.

Algorithm:
- Create a 2-D array of type Pixel to hold the new Pixel objects. The dimensions of this array are the same as any of the color arrays because there is a precondition saying all the arrays must be the same size.
- Write a for loop that goes through all the rows of the new array.
  - Nested in that for loop, write a for loop that goes through all the columns of the new array. (These can be switched. Row-major order is more common, but column-major order will also work here.)
    - Instantiate a new Pixel object, passing the values in the red, green, and blue arrays at the position given by the two loop counters, and assign it to the element of the Pixel array given by the two loop counters.
- When the loops are complete and every element has been processed, return the completed Pixel array.

Java Code:

```
public static Pixel[][] generatePixelArray(int[][] reds, int[][] greens, int[][] blues)
{
    Pixel[][] pix = new Pixel[reds.length][reds[0].length];
    for (int r = 0; r < pix.length; r++)
        for (int c = 0; c < pix[r].length; c++)
            pix[r][c] = new Pixel(reds[r][c], greens[r][c], blues[r][c]);
    return pix;
}
```

(b) **General Problem:** Write a `flipImage` method that takes a 2-D array of `Pixel` objects and flips it into a mirror image, either vertically or horizontally.

Refined Problem: Create a new array to hold the altered image. Determine whether to flip the image horizontally or vertically. Write a nested `for` loop to move all the Pixels to their mirror-image location in the new array, either horizontally or vertically. When the loops are complete, return the new array.

Algorithm:

- Instantiate a 2-D Pixel array that has the same dimensions as the array passed as a parameter. This array will hold the altered image.
- Create an `if-else` statement with one clause for a horizontal flip and one for a vertical flip.
- If the flip is horizontal, write a nested `for` loop that goes through the array in row-major order.
  - For each iteration of the loop, an entire row is moved into its new "flipped" place in the altered array.
- Otherwise, the flip is vertical. Write a nested `for` loop that goes through the array in column-major order.
  - For each iteration of the loop, an entire column is moved into its new "flipped" place in the altered array.
- Return the altered array.

Java Code:

```java
public static Pixel[][] flipImage(Pixel[][] image, boolean horiz)
{
    Pixel[][] flipped = new Pixel[image.length][image[0].length];
    if (horiz)
        for (int r = 0; r < image.length; r++)
            for (int c = 0; c < image[0].length; c++)
                flipped[r][c] = image[image.length - 1 - r][c];
    else
        for (int c = 0; c < image[0].length; c++)
            for (int r = 0; r <image.length; r++)
                flipped[r][c] = image[r][image[0].length - 1 - c];
    return flipped;
}
```

Or, alternatively:

```java
public static Pixel [][] flipImage(Pixel[][] image, boolean horiz)
{
    Pixel[][] flipped = new Pixel[image.length][image[0].length];
    for(int r = 0; r < image.length; r++)
    {
        for(int c = 0; c < image[r].length; c++)
        {
            if(horiz)
                flipped[r][c] = image[image.length - 1 - r][c];
            else
                flipped[r][c] = image[r][image[0].length - 1 - c];
        }
    }
    return flipped;
}
```

Common Errors:

- Watch off-by-one errors. Always think: do I want length or length − 1? Using variables, like in the alternate solution, can help you be consistent.
- Be sure you understand the difference between row-major and column-major order.
- Check your answer with both even and odd numbers of rows and columns.
- Create a new array to hold the "flipped" version. Do not overwrite the array that is passed in. This is called *destruction of persistent data* and incurs a penalty.

Java Code Alternate Solution:
- This solution only loops halfway through the array. It flips a pair of lines on each iteration.

  This solution also uses a few extra variables to keep things easier to read. This is not necessary but it reduces the amount of typing and the chance of an off-by-one error with length, as opposed to length − 1.

```java
public static Pixel[][] flipImage(Pixel[][] image, boolean horiz)
{
    Pixel[][] flipped = new Pixel[image.length][image[0].length];
    int maxR = image.length - 1;
    int maxC = image[0].length - 1;
    if (horiz)
    {
        for (int r = 0; r <= maxR / 2; r++)
        {
            for (int c = 0; c <= maxC; c++)
            {
                flipped[r][c] = image[maxR - r][c];
                flipped[maxR - r][c] = image[r][c];
            }
        }
    }
    else
    {
        for (int c = 0; c <= maxC / 2; c++)
        {
            for (int r = 0; r <= maxR; r++)
            {
                flipped[r][c] = image[r][maxC - c];
                flipped[r][maxC - c] = image[r][c];
            }
        }
    }
    return flipped;
}
```

Scoring Guidelines: Pixels

Part (a)　　　　　　　　　**generatePixelArray**　　　　　　　　　**3 points**

+1　Instantiates a 2-D array of `Pixel` objects with the correct dimensions

+1　Instantiates a new `Pixel` object with the corresponding elements of the red, green, and blue arrays for every element of the array; no bounds errors, no missed elements

+1　Returns the properly constructed and filled array

Part (b)　　　　　　　　　**flipImage**　　　　　　　　　**6 points**

+1　Correctly determines whether the image should be flipped vertically or horizontally

+2　Flips the array horizontally

　　+1　Correctly repositions at least one element

　　+1　Correctly repositions all elements

+2　Flips the array vertically

　　+1　Correctly repositions at least one element

　　+1　Correctly repositions all elements

+1　Returns the correctly generated flipped array

Sample Driver:

There are many ways to write these methods. Maybe yours is a bit different from our sample solutions and you are not sure if it works. Here is a sample driver program. Running it will let you see if your code works, and will help you debug it if it does not.

Copy PixelDriver and the complete Pixel class into your IDE. Add your generatePixelArray and flipImage methods to the bottom of the PixelDriver class.

```java
public class PixelDriver {

    public static void main(String[] args) {
        int[][] red = { { 0, 0, 0, 0 }, { 1, 1, 1, 1 }, { 2, 2, 2, 2 },
                        { 3, 3, 3, 3 } };
        int[][] green = { { 0, 1, 2, 3 }, { 0, 1, 2, 3 }, { 0, 1, 2, 3 },
                        { 0, 1, 2, 3 } };
        int[][] blue = { { 100, 100, 100, 100 }, { 100, 100, 100, 100 },
                        { 100, 100, 100, 100 }, { 100, 100, 100, 100 } };
        System.out.println("generatePixelArray test");
        System.out.println("Expecting:");
        for (int r = 0; r < red.length; r++) {
            for (int c = 0; c < red[r].length; c++)
                System.out.print("(" + red[r][c] + ", " + green[r][c] +
                        ", " + blue[r][c] + ") ");
            System.out.println();
        }
        Pixel[][] pix = generatePixelArray(red, green, blue);
        System.out.println("\nYour Answer:");
        printIt(pix);

        final boolean HORIZ = true;
        final boolean VERT = !HORIZ;
        System.out.println("\nflipImage - Horizontal test");
        System.out.println("Expecting:");
        for (int r = red.length-1; r >=0; r--) {
            for (int c = 0; c < red[r].length; c++)
                System.out.print("(" + red[r][c] + ", " + green[r][c] +
                        ", " + blue[r][c] + ") ");
            System.out.println();
        }
        System.out.println("\nYour Answer:");
        Pixel[][] pix2 = flipImage(pix, HORIZ);
        printIt(pix2);

        System.out.println("\nflipImage - Vertical test");
        System.out.println("Expecting:");
        for (int r = 0; r < red.length; r++) {
            for (int c = red[r].length - 1; c >= 0; c--)
                System.out.print("(" + red[r][c] + ", " + green[r][c] +
                        ", " + blue[r][c] + ") ");
            System.out.println();
        }
        System.out.println("\nYour Answer:");
        Pixel[][] pix3 = flipImage(pix, VERT);
        printIt(pix3);
    }

    public static void printIt(Pixel[][] pix) {
        for (int r = 0; r < pix.length; r++) {
            for (int c = 0; c < pix[r].length; c++) {
                System.out.print(pix[r][c] + " ");
            }
            System.out.println();
        }
    }
}
    // Enter your generatePixelArray and flipImage methods here
}
```

Scoring Worksheet

This worksheet will help you to approximate your performance on Practice Exam 1 in terms of an AP score of 1–5.

Part I (Multiple Choice)

Number right (out of 40 questions)   = _____

Part II (Short Answer)
See the scoring guidelines included with the explanations for each of the questions and award yourself points based on those guidelines.

Question 1: Points Obtained (out of 9 possible)   _____

Question 2: Points Obtained (out of 9 possible)   _____

Question 3: Points Obtained (out of 9 possible)   _____

Question 4: Points Obtained (out of 9 possible)   _____

Add the points and multiply by 1.1111   _____ × 1.1111   = _____

Add your totals from both parts of the test   Total Raw Score _____
(round to nearest whole number)

Approximate conversion from raw score to AP score

Raw Score Range	AP Score	Interpretation
62–80	5	Extremely Well Qualified
44–61	4	Well Qualified
31–43	3	Qualified
25–30	2	Possibly Qualified
0–24	1	No Recommendation

AP Computer Science A
Practice Exam 2

Multiple-Choice Questions
ANSWER SHEET

1 (A) (B) (C) (D) (E)
2 (A) (B) (C) (D) (E)
3 (A) (B) (C) (D) (E)
4 (A) (B) (C) (D) (E)
5 (A) (B) (C) (D) (E)
6 (A) (B) (C) (D) (E)
7 (A) (B) (C) (D) (E)
8 (A) (B) (C) (D) (E)
9 (A) (B) (C) (D) (E)
10 (A) (B) (C) (D) (E)
11 (A) (B) (C) (D) (E)
12 (A) (B) (C) (D) (E)
13 (A) (B) (C) (D) (E)
14 (A) (B) (C) (D) (E)
15 (A) (B) (C) (D) (E)
16 (A) (B) (C) (D) (E)
17 (A) (B) (C) (D) (E)
18 (A) (B) (C) (D) (E)
19 (A) (B) (C) (D) (E)
20 (A) (B) (C) (D) (E)

21 (A) (B) (C) (D) (E)
22 (A) (B) (C) (D) (E)
23 (A) (B) (C) (D) (E)
24 (A) (B) (C) (D) (E)
25 (A) (B) (C) (D) (E)
26 (A) (B) (C) (D) (E)
27 (A) (B) (C) (D) (E)
28 (A) (B) (C) (D) (E)
29 (A) (B) (C) (D) (E)
30 (A) (B) (C) (D) (E)
31 (A) (B) (C) (D) (E)
32 (A) (B) (C) (D) (E)
33 (A) (B) (C) (D) (E)
34 (A) (B) (C) (D) (E)
35 (A) (B) (C) (D) (E)
36 (A) (B) (C) (D) (E)
37 (A) (B) (C) (D) (E)
38 (A) (B) (C) (D) (E)
39 (A) (B) (C) (D) (E)
40 (A) (B) (C) (D) (E)

AP Computer Science A
Practice Exam 2

Part I (Multiple Choice)

Time: 90 minutes
Number of questions: 40
Percent of total score: 50

Directions: Choose the best answer for each problem. Use available space for scratch work and hand tracing. Some problems take longer than others. Consider how much time you have left before spending too much time on any one problem.

Notes:
- You may assume all import statements have been included where they are needed.
- You may assume that the parameters in method calls are not null and the methods are called when their preconditions are met.
- You may assume that declarations of variables and methods appear within the context of an enclosing class.
- You may refer to the Java Quick Reference sheet as needed.

GO ON TO THE NEXT PAGE

1. Consider the following code segment.

```
for (int h = 5; h >= 0; h = h - 2)
{
    for (int k = 0; k < 3; k++)
    {
        if ((h + k) % 2 == 0)
            System.out.print((h + k) + "   ");
    }
}
```

What is printed as a result of executing the code segment?
(A) 5   3   1
(B) 6   4   2
(C) 51   31   11
(D) 6   4   2   0
(E) 51   31   11   00

2. Consider the following code segment.

```
ArrayList<String> foods = new ArrayList<String>();

foods.add("Hummus");
foods.add("Soup");
foods.add("Sushi");
foods.set(1, "Empanadas");
foods.add(0, "Salad");
foods.remove(1);
foods.add("Curry");
System.out.println(foods);
```

What is printed as a result of executing the code segment?
(A) [Salad, Empanadas, Sushi, Curry]
(B) [Hummus, Salad, Empanadas, Sushi, Curry]
(C) [Hummus, Soup, Sushi, Empanadas, Salad, Curry]
(D) [Soup, Empanadas, Sushi, Curry]
(E) [Hummus, Sushi, Salad, Curry]

GO ON TO THE NEXT PAGE

3. Consider the following output.

```
A A A A P P P P C C C C
```

Which of the following code segments will produce this output?

I.
```
String[] letters = {"A", "P", "C", "S"};
for (int i = letters.length; i > 0; i--)
{
    if (!letters[i].equals("S"))
    {
        for (int k = 0; k < 4; k++)
            System.out.print(letters[k] + "   ");
    }
}
```

II.
```
String letters = "APCS";
for (int i = 0; i < letters.length(); i++)
{
    String s = letters.substring(i, i + 1);
    for (int num = 0; num < 4; num++)
    {
        if (!s.equals("S"))
            System.out.print(s + "   ");
    }
}
```

III.
```
String[][] letters = { {"A", "P"}, {"C", "S"} };
for (String[] row : letters)
{
    for (String letter : row)
    {
        if (!letter.equals("S"))
            System.out.print(letter + "   ");
    }
}
```

(A) I only
(B) II only
(C) I and II only
(D) II and III only
(E) I, II, and III

GO ON TO THE NEXT PAGE

Questions 4–5 refer to the following two classes.

```
public class Vehicle
{
    private int fuel;

    public Vehicle(int fuelAmt)
    {
        fuel = fuelAmt;
    }

    public void start()
    {
        System.out.println("Vroom");
    }

    public void changeFuel(int change)
    {
        fuel = fuel + change;
    }

    public int getFuel()
    {
        return fuel;
    }
}


public class Boat extends Vehicle
{
    public Boat(int fuelAmount)
    {
        super(fuelAmount);
    }

    public void useFuel()
    {
        super.changeFuel(-2);
    }

    public void start()
    {
        super.start();
        useFuel();
        System.out.println("Remaining Fuel " + getFuel());
    }
}
```

GO ON TO THE NEXT PAGE

4. Assume the following declaration appears in a client program.

```
Boat yacht = new Boat(20);
```

What is printed as a result of executing the call `yacht.start()`?

(A) `Vroom`

(B) `Remaining Fuel 18`

(C) `Remaining Fuel 20`

(D) `Vroom`
`Remaining Fuel 18`

(E) `Vroom`
`Remaining Fuel 20`

5. Which of the following statements results in a compile-time error?

I. `Boat sailboat = new Boat(2);`

II. `Vehicle tanker = new Boat(20);`

III. `Boat tugboat = new Vehicle(10);`

(A) I only

(B) II only

(C) III only

(D) II and III only

(E) None of these options will result in a compile-time error.

6. Consider the following recursive method.

```
public int weird(int num)
{
    if (num <= 0)
        return num;
    return weird(num - 2) + weird(num - 1) + weird(num);
}
```

What value is returned as a result of the call `weird(3)`?

(A) `-2`

(B) `3`

(C) `4`

(D) `6`

(E) Nothing is returned. Infinite recursion causes a stack overflow error.

7. Consider the following method.

```
public boolean verifyValues(int[] values)
{
    for (int index = values.length - 1; index > 0; index--)
    {
        /* missing code */
            return false;
    }
    return true;
}
```

The method `verifyValues` is intended to return true if the array passed as a parameter is in ascending order (least to greatest), and `false` otherwise.

Which of the following lines of code could replace /* `missing code` */ so the method works as intended?

(A) `if (values[index] <= values[index - 1])`

(B) `if (values[index + 1] < values[index])`

(C) `if (values[index] >= values[index - 1])`

(D) `if (values[index - 1] > values[index])`

(E) `if (values[index] < values[index + 1])`

8. Consider the following code segment.

```
int[][] matrix = new int[3][3];
int value = 0;

for (int row = 0; row < matrix.length; row++)
{
    for (int column = 0; column < matrix[row].length; column++)
    {
        matrix[row][column] = value;
        value++;
    }
}

int sum = 0;
for (int[] row : matrix)
{
    for (int number : row)
        sum = sum + number;
}
```

What is the value of `sum` after the code segment has been executed?

(A) 0

(B) 9

(C) 21

(D) 36

(E) 72

GO ON TO THE NEXT PAGE

9. Consider the following method.

```
public int doStuff(int[] numberArray)
{
    int index = 0;
    int maxCounter = 1;
    int counter = 1;
    for (int k = 1; k < numberArray.length; k++)
    {
        if (numberArray[k] == numberArray[k - 1])
        {
            if (counter <= maxCounter)
            {
                maxCounter = counter;
                index = k;
            }
            counter++;
        }
        else
        {
            counter = 1;
        }
    }
    return numberArray[index];
}
```

Consider the following code segment.

```
int[] intArray = {3, 3, 4, 4, 6};
System.out.println(doStuff(intArray));
```

What is printed as a result of executing the code segment?

(A) 1

(B) 3

(C) 4

(D) 5

(E) 6

10. Consider the following code segment.

```
int number = Integer.MAX_VALUE;
while (number > 0)
{
    number = number / 2;
}

for (int i = number; i > 0; i++)
{
    System.out.print(i + "  ");
}
```

What is printed as a result of executing the code segment?

(A) 0

(B) 1

(C) 1073741823

(D) Nothing will be printed. The code segment will terminate without error.

(E) Nothing will be printed. The first loop is an infinite loop.

11. Consider the following class.

```
public class Automobile
{
    private String make, model;
    public Automobile(String myMake, String myModel)
    {
        make = myMake;
        model = myModel;
    }

    public String getMake()
    {  return make;  }

    public String getModel()
    {  return model;  }

    /* Additional implementation not shown */
}
```

Consider the following code segment that appears in another class.

```
Automobile myCar = new Automobile("Ford", "Fusion");
Automobile companyCar = new Automobile("Toyota", "Corolla");
companyCar = myCar;
myCar = new Automobile("Kia", "Spectre");
System.out.println(companyCar.getMake() + " " + myCar.getModel());
```

What is printed as a result of executing the code segment?

(A) Ford Spectre

(B) Ford Fusion

(C) Kia Spectre

(D) Toyota Corolla

(E) Toyota Spectre

GO ON TO THE NEXT PAGE

12. Given the String declaration

```
String course = "AP Computer Science A";
```
What value is returned by the call `course.indexOf("e")`?

(A) 9
(B) 10
(C) 18
(D) 9, 15, 18
(E) 10, 16, 19

13. Consider the code segment.

```
if (value == 1)
    count += 1;
else if (value == 2)
    count += 2;
```

Which segment could be used to replace the segment above and work as intended?

(A)
```
if (value == 1 || value == 2)
        count += 1;
```
(B)
```
if (value == 1 || value == 2)
        count += 2;
```
(C)
```
if (value == 1 || value == 2)
        count += value;
```
(D)
```
if (value == 1 && value == 2)
        count += 1;
```
(E)
```
if (value == 1 && value == 2)
        count += value;
```

14. A bank will approve a loan for any customer who fulfills one or more of the following requirements:

    - Has a credit score ≥ 640
    - Has a cosigner for the loan
    - Has a credit score ≥ 590 and has collateral

    Which of the following methods will properly evaluate the customer's eligibility for a loan?

    I.
    ```
    public boolean canGetLoan(int credit, boolean cosigner, boolean coll)
    {
        if (credit >= 640 || cosigner || (credit >= 590 && coll))
            return true;
        return false;
    }
    ```

    II.
    ```
    public boolean canGetloan(int credit, boolean cosigner, boolean coll)
    {
        if (!credit >= 640 || !cosigner || !(credit >= 590 && coll))
            return false;
        else
            return true;
    }
    ```

    III.
    ```
    public boolean canGetLoan(int credit, boolean cosigner, boolean coll)
    {
        if (coll && credit >= 590)
            return true;
        if (credit >= 640)
            return true;
        if (cosigner)
            return true;
        return false;
    }
    ```

    (A) I only
    (B) II only
    (C) III only
    (D) I and III only
    (E) II and III only

15. Consider the following method.

    ```
    public String mixItUp(String entry1, String entry2)
    {
        entry2 = entry1;
        entry1 = entry1 + entry2;
        String entry3 = entry1 + entry2;
        return entry3;
    }
    ```

    What is returned by the call mixItUp("AP", "CS")?

    (A) "APAP"
    (B) "APCSAP"
    (C) "APAPAP"
    (D) "APCSCS"
    (E) "APAPAPAP"

GO ON TO THE NEXT PAGE

16. Assume that `planets` has been a correctly instantiated and initialized array that contains the names of the planets. Which of the following code segments will reverse the order of the elements in `planets`?

(A)
```
for (int index = planets.length / 2; index >= 0; index--)
{
    String temp = planets[index];
    planets[index] = planets[index + 1];
    planets[index + 1] = temp;
}
```

(B)
```
int index = planets.length / 2;
while (index >= 0)
{
    String s = planets[index];
    planets[index] = planets[index + 1];
    index--;
}
```

(C)
```
String[] newPlanets = new String[planets.length];
for (int i = planets.length - 1; i >= 0; i--)
{
    newPlanets[i] = planets[i];
}
planets = newPlanets;
```

(D)
```
for (int index = 0; index < planets.length; index++)
{
    String temp = planets[index];
    planets[index] = planets[planets.length - 1 - index];
    planets[planets.length - 1 - index] = temp;
}
```

(E)
```
for (int index = 0; index < planets.length / 2; index++)
{
    String temp = planets[index];
    planets[index] = planets[planets.length - 1 - index];
    planets[planets.length - 1 - index] = temp;
}
```

17. Consider the program segment.

```
for (int i = start; i <= stop; i++)
    System.out.println("AP Computer Science A Rocks!!!");
```

How many times will "AP Computer Science A Rocks!!!" be printed?

(A) `stop - start - 1`
(B) `stop - start`
(C) `stop - start + 1`
(D) `stop -1`
(E) `stop`

GO ON TO THE NEXT PAGE

18. Consider the following code segment.

```
int num = (int)(Math.random() * 30 + 20);
num += 5;
num = num / 5;
System.out.print(num);
```

What are the possible values that could be printed to the console?
(A) Any real number from 4 to 10 (not including 10)
(B) Any integer from 5 to 10 (inclusive)
(C) Any integer from 20 to 49 (inclusive)
(D) Any integer from 25 to 54 (inclusive)
(E) Any real number from 30 to 50 (inclusive)

19. Consider the following code segment.

```
String word = "computer";
ArrayList<String> words = new ArrayList<String>();
for (int k = 0; k < word.length(); k++)
{
    words.add(word.substring(k));
    k++;
}

System.out.println(words);
```

What is printed as a result of executing the code segment?
(A) [computer, mputer, uter, er]
(B) [computer, comput, comp, co]
(C) [computer, computer, computer, computer]
(D) [computer, omputer, mputer, puter, uter, ter, er, r]
(E) Nothing is printed. There is an `ArrayListIndexOutOfBoundsException`.

20. Consider the following incomplete method.

```
public boolean validation(int x, int y)
{
    /* missing code */
}
```

The following table shows several examples of the desired result of a call to `validation`.

x	y	Result
1	0	true
3	6	true
1	3	false
2	6	false

Which of the following code segments should replace /* missing code */ to produce the desired return values?
(A) `return x > y;`
(B) `return (x % y) > 1`
(C) `return (x + y) % 2 == 0`
(D) `return (x + y) % x == y;`
(E) `return (x + y) % 2 > (y + y) % 2;`

21. Consider the following method that is intended to remove all Strings from words that are less than six letters long. The line numbers are used for reference only.

```
          public void letterCountCheck(ArrayList<String> words)
          {
Line 1:       int numWord = 0;
Line 2:       while (numWord <= words.size())
              {
Line 3:           if (words.get(numWord).length() < 6)
                  {
Line 4:               words.remove(numWord);
                  }
                  else
                  {
Line 5:               numWord++;
                  }
              }
          }
```

Which line of code contains an error that prevents letterCountCheck from working as intended?

(A) Line 1
(B) Line 2
(C) Line 3
(D) Line 4
(E) Line 5

22. Consider the following recursive method.

```
public void wackyOutput(String wacky)
{
    if (wacky.length() < 1)
        return;
    wacky = wacky.substring(1, wacky.length());
    wackyOutput(wacky);
    System.out.print(wacky);
}
```

What is printed as a result of executing the call wackyOutput("APCS")?

(A) PC
(B) SCPA
(C) SCSPCS
(D) PCSCSS
(E) SCSPCSAPCS

23. Consider the following method.

```
public String calculate(int num1, int num2)
{
    if (num1 >= 0 && num2 >= 0)
        return "Numbers are valid";
    return "Numbers are not valid";
}
```

Which of the following methods will give the exact same results as `calculate`?

I.
```
public String calculate1(int num1, int num2)
{
    if (!(num1 < 0 || num2 < 0))
        return "Numbers are valid";
    else
        return "Numbers are not valid";
}
```

II.
```
public String calculate2(int num1, int num2)
{
    if (num1 < 0)
        return "Numbers are not valid";
    if (num2 < 0)
        return "Numbers are not valid";
    else
        return "Numbers are valid";
}
```

III.
```
public String calculate3(int num1, int num2)
{
    if (num1 + num2 < 0)
        return "Numbers are not valid";
    return "Numbers are valid";
}
```

(A) I only
(B) II only
(C) III only
(D) I and II only
(E) I, II, and III

GO ON TO THE NEXT PAGE

24. Consider the following class declaration.

```
public class TestClass
{
    private double value;

    public TestClass(double value)
    {
        this.value = value;
    }

    public void addValue(double add)
    {
        value += add;
    }

    public void reduceValue(double reduce)
    {
        value -= reduce;
    }

    public double getValue()
    {
        return value;
    }
}
```

The following code segment is executed in the main method.

```
TestClass test1 = new TestClass(9.0);
TestClass test2 = new TestClass(17.5);
test1.reduceValue(3.0);
test2.addValue(1.5);
test2 = test1;
test2.reduceValue(6.0);
System.out.print(test2.getValue() + test1.getValue());
```

What is printed to the console as a result of executing the code segment?

(A) 0.0
(B) 3.0
(C) 12.0
(D) 19.0
(E) 27.5

25. Consider the following method.

```java
public int guess(int num1, int num2)
{
    if (num1 % num2 == 0)
        return (num2 + num1) / 2;
    return guess(num2, num1 % num2) + (num1 % num2);
}
```

What is the value of num after executing the following code statement?

```java
int num = guess(3, 17);
```

(A) 6
(B) 7
(C) 10
(D) Nothing is returned. Modulus by 0 causes an `ArithmeticException`.
(E) Nothing is returned. Infinite recursion causes a stack overflow error.

26. Consider the following method which implements an Insertion Sort algorithm.

```java
public void sortIt(int[] arr)
{
    for (int i = 1; i < arr.length; i++)
    {
        int value = arr[i];
        for (int j = i - 1; j >= 0 && arr[j] > value; j--)
        {
            arr[j + 1] = arr[j];
        }
        arr[j + 1] = value;
    }
}
```

Consider the following array which will be passed to the `sortIt` method.

```java
int[] arr = {4, 3, 7, 6, 1, 5, 2};
```

What does the array contain after the 3rd time through the outer loop (i == 3)?
(A) {4, 3, 7, 6, 1, 5, 2}
(B) {3, 4, 6, 7, 1, 5, 2}
(C) {1, 2, 3, 6, 4, 5, 7}
(D) {1, 2, 3, 4, 7, 6, 5}
(E) {1, 2, 3, 4, 5, 6, 7}

GO ON TO THE NEXT PAGE

27. Consider the following class.

```
public class Polygon
{
    /** returns true if the ordered pair is inside the polygon
     *
     *           false otherwise
     */
    // instance variables, constructor, and other methods not shown
}
```

Consider the following class.

```
public class Rectangle extends Polygon
{
    private int topLeftX, topLeftY, bottomRightX, bottomRightY;

    /**
     *  Precondition: topLeftX < bottomRightX
     *  Precondition: topLeftY < bottomRightY
     *              The y value increases as it moves down the screen.
     *  @param topLeftX The x value of the top left corner
     *  @param topLeftY The y value of the top left corner
     *  @param bottomRightX The x value of the bottom right corner
     *  @param bottomRightY The y value of the bottom right corner
     */
    public Rectangle(int topLX, int topLY, int bottomRX, int bottomRY)
    {
        topLeftX = topLX;
        topLeftY = topLY;
        bottomRightX = bottomRX;
        bottomRightY = bottomRY;
    }
}
```

Which of the following is a correct implementation of the contains method that is intended to be in the Rectangle class?

(A) ```
public boolean contains(int x, int y)
{
    return x > topLeftX && y > topLeftY &&
           x < bottomRightX && y < bottomRightY;
}
```

(B) ```
public boolean contains(int x, int y)
{
    if (topLeftX > x)
       return true;
    else if (topLeftY > y)
       return true;
    else if (bottomRightX < x)
       return true;
    else if (bottomRightY < y)
       return true;
    return false;
}
```

(C) ```
public boolean contains(int x, int y)
{   return super.contains(x, y);   }
```

(D) ```
public boolean contains(int x, int y)
{   return Polygon.contains(x, y);   }
```

(E) ```
public boolean contains(int x, int y)
{
    boolean result = false;
    if (topLeftX < x && topLeftY < y)
       result = true;
    if (bottomRightX > x && bottomRightY > y)
       result = true;
    return result;
}
```

GO ON TO THE NEXT PAGE
```

28. Consider the following method.

```
public ArrayList<String> rearrange(ArrayList<String> list)
{
    ArrayList <String> myList = list;
    for (int i = myList.size() / 2; i >= 0; i--)
    {
        String wordA = myList.remove(i);
        myList.add(wordA);
    }
    return myList;
}
```

Assume that `ArrayList<String> names` has been correctly instantiated and populated with the following entries.

```
["Nora", "Charles", "Madeline", "Nate", "Silja", "Garrett"]
```

What are the values of the `ArrayList` returned by the call `rearrange(names)`?
(A) `["Silja", "Garrett", "Nate", "Madeline", "Charles", "Nora"]`
(B) `["Madeline", "Charles", "Nora", "Nate", "Silja", "Garrett"]`
(C) `["Nate", "Silja", "Garrett", "Nora", "Charles", "Madeline"]`
(D) `["Nora", "Charles", "Madeline", "Nate", "Silja", "Garrett"]`
(E) Nothing is returned. `ArrayListIndexOutOfBoundsException`

29. Consider the following code segment.

```
int varA = -30;
int varB = 30;
while (varA != 0 || varB > 0)
{
    varA = varA + 2;
    varB = Math.abs(varA + 2);
    varA++;
    varB = varB - 5;
}
System.out.println(varA + "    " + varB);
```

What will be printed as a result of executing the code segment?
(A) -30 30
(B) -4   0
(C) 0   -4
(D) 0   4
(E) -3   -3

GO ON TO THE NEXT PAGE

30. Consider the following code segment.

```
int[][] grid = { {0,  1,  2},
                 {3,  4,  5},
                 {6,  7,  8},
                 {9, 10, 11} };

int[][] newGrid = new int[grid[0].length][grid.length];

for (int row = 0; row < grid.length; row++)
{
    for (int col = 0; col < grid[row].length; col++)
    {
        newGrid[col][row] = grid[row][col];
    }
}
```

What is the value of newGrid[2][1] as a result of executing the code segment?
(A) 3
(B) 4
(C) 5
(D) 7
(E) Nothing. There is an ArrayIndexOutOfBoundsException.

31. Consider the following code segment.

```
int[][] grid = new int[3][3];
for (int row = 0; row < grid.length; row++)
{
    for (int col = 0; col < grid[row].length; col++)
    {
        grid[row][col] = 1;
        grid[col][row] = 2;
        grid[row][row] = 3;
    }
}
```

Which of the following shows the values in grid after executing the code segment?
(A) { {1, 1, 1},
      {1, 1, 1},
      {1, 1, 1} };
(B) { {2, 2, 2},
      {2, 2, 2},
      {2, 2, 2} };
(C) { {3, 2, 2},
      {2, 3, 2},
      {2, 2, 3} };
(D) { {3, 1, 1},
      {1, 3, 1},
      {1, 1, 3} };
(E) { {3, 2, 2},
      {1, 3, 2},
      {1, 1, 3} };

32. What can the following method best be described as?

```
public int mystery(int[] array, int a)
{
  for (int i = 0; i < array.length; i++)
  {
    if (array[i] == a)
      return i;
  }
  return -1;
}
```

(A) Insertion Sort
(B) Selection Sort
(C) Binary Search
(D) Merge Sort
(E) Sequential Search

33. The following incomplete code is intended to count the number of times the letter `key` is found in `phrase`.

```
public static int countOccurrences (String phrase, String key)
{
    int count = 0;
    for (int i = 0; i < phrase.length(); i++)
        /*      missing code      */
    return count;
}
```

Which can be used to replace /* *missing code* */ so that `countOccurrences` works as intended?

(A) `if (phrase == key)`
        `count ++;`
(B) `if (phrase[i].equals(key))`
        `count ++;`
(C) `if (phrase.indexOf(i).equals(key))`
        `count ++;`
(D) `if (phrase.substring(i, i+1) == key)`
        `count ++;`
(E) `if (phrase.substring(i, i+1).equals(key))`
        `count ++;`

GO ON TO THE NEXT PAGE

34. Assume `str1` and `str2` are correctly initialized `String` variables. Which statement correctly prints the values of `str1` and `str2` in alphabetical order?

(A)
```
if (str1 < str2)
    System.out.println(str1 + " " + str2);
else
    System.out.println(str2 + " " + str1);
```
(B)
```
if (str1 > str2)
    System.out.println(str1 + " " + str2);
else
    System.out.println(str2 + " " + str1);
```
(C)
```
if (str1.compareTo(str2))
    System.out.println(str1 + " " + str2);
else
    System.out.println(str2 + " " + str1);
```
(D)
```
if (str1.compareTo(str2) < 0)
    System.out.println(str1 + " " + str2);
else
    System.out.println(str2 + " " + str1);
```
(E)
```
if (str1.compareTo(str2) > 0)
    System.out.println(str1 + " " + str2);
else
    System.out.println(str2 + " " + str1);
```

35. Assume `names` is a `String` array. Which statement correctly chooses a random element from the array?

(A) `String student = name[(int) (Math.random(names.length)];`
(B) `String student = name[(int) (Math.random(names.length - 1))];`
(C) `String student = name[(int) (Math.random() * names.length) + 1];`
(D) `String student = name[(int) (Math.random() * names.length)];`
(E) `String student = name[(int) (Math.random() * names.length) - 1];`

36. Assume that the variable declarations have been made.
```
int a = 7, b = 15, c = -6;
```

Which will evaluate to true?

```
I    (a < b) || (b < c)
II   !(a < b) && (a < c)
III  (a == b) || ! (b == c)
```

(A) I only
(B) II only
(C) III only
(D) I and III only
(E) I, II, and III

Questions 37–38 refer to the following class.

```
public class Coordinates
{
    private int x, y;

    public Coordinates(int myX, int myY)
    {
        x = myX;
        y = myY;
    }

    public void setX(int myX)
    {   x = myX;   }

    public int getX()
    {   return x;   }

    public void setY(int myY)
    {   y = myY;   }

    public int getY()
    {   return y;   }
}
```

Consider the following code segment.

```
Coordinates c1 = new Coordinates(0, 10);
Coordinates c3 = c1;
Coordinates c2 = new Coordinates(20, 30);
c3.setX(c2.getY());
c3 = c2;
c3.setY(c2.getX());
c2.setX(c1.getX());
```

37. Which of the following calls returns the value 20?

(A) `c1.getX()`
(B) `c1.getY()`
(C) `c2.getX()`
(D) `c2.getY()`
(E) `c3.getX()`

38. Which of the following calls returns the value 30?

(A) `c1.getX()`
(B) `c2.getX()`
(C) `c3.getX()`
(D) All of the above
(E) None of the above

GO ON TO THE NEXT PAGE

Questions 39–40 refer to the following classes.

Consider the following class declarations.

```
public class Building
{
    private int sqFeet;
    private int numRooms;

    public Building(int ft, int rms)
    {
        sqFeet = ft;
        numRooms = rms;
    }

    public int getSqfeet()
    {   return sqFeet;
    }

    public String getSize()
    {
        return numRooms + " rooms and " + sqFeet + " square feet";
    }

    /* Additional implementation not shown */
}

public class House extends Building
{
    private int numBedRooms;
    public House(int ft, int rms, int bedrms)
    {
        super(ft, rms);
        numBedRooms = bedrms;
    }

    public String getSize()
    {
        return super.getSqFeet() + " square feet and " + numBedRooms + " bedrooms.";
    }
}
```

39. Assume that `ArrayList<Building> list` has been correctly instantiated and populated with `Building` objects.

Which of the following code segments will result in the square feet in each building being printed?

I.
```
for (int i = 0; i < list.size(); i++)
    System.out.println(list.getSqFeet(i));
```

II.
```
for (int i = 0; i < list.size(); i++)
    System.out.println(list[i].getSqFeet());
```

III.
```
for (int i = 0; i < list.size(); i++)
    System.out.println(list.get(i).getSqFeet());
```

IV.
```
for (Building b : list)
    System.out.println(list.getSqFeet());
```

V.
```
for (Building b : list)
    System.out.println(b.getSqFeet());
```

(A) I and IV only
(B) I and V only
(C) II and IV only
(D) III and IV only
(E) III and V only

40. Consider the following code segment.

```
Building b1 = new Building(2000, 3);
Building b2 = new House(2500, 8, 4);
Building b3 = b2;
Building[] buildings = new Building[3];
buildings[0] = b1;
buildings[1] = b2;
buildings[2] = b3;
```

What will be printed by the following code segment?

```
for (int i = 0; i < buildings.length; i++)
    System.out.println(buildings[i].getSize());
```

(A) `3 rooms and 2000 square feet`
    `8 rooms and 2500 square feet`
    `8 rooms and 2500 square feet`

(B) `3 rooms and 2000 square feet`
    `2500 square feet and 4 bedrooms`
    `2500 square feet and 4 bedrooms`

(C) `2000 square feet and 3 bedrooms`
    `2500 square feet and 4 bedrooms`
    `2500 square feet and 4 bedrooms`

(D) `3 rooms and 2000 square feet`
    `2500 square feet and 4 bedrooms`
    `3 rooms and 2000 square feet`

(E) There is an error. Nothing will be printed.

STOP. End of Part I.

GO ON TO THE NEXT PAGE

AP Computer Science A
Practice Exam 2

Part II (Free Response)

Time: 90 minutes
Number of questions: 4
Percent of total score: 50

Directions: Write all of your code in Java. Show all your work.

Notes:
- You may assume import statements have been included where they are needed.
- You may assume that all preconditions are met when making calls to methods.
- You may assume that all parameters within method calls are not null.
- Be aware that you should, when possible, use methods that are defined in the classes provided as opposed to duplicating them by writing your own code. Doing so you will not receive full credit.
- You may use the Java Quick Reference sheet as needed.

1. In the seventeenth century, Location Numerals were invented as a new way to represent numbers. Location Numerals have a lot in common with the binary number system we use today, except that in Location Numerals, successive letters of the alphabet are used to represent the powers of two, starting with $A = 2^0$ all the way to $Z = 2^{25}$.

To represent a given number as a Location Numeral (LN), the number is expressed as the sum of powers of two with each power of two replaced by its corresponding letter.

$A = 2^0$ $\qquad$ $B = 2^1$ $\qquad$ $C = 2^2$ $\qquad$ $D = 2^3$ $\qquad$ $E = 2^4$ $\qquad$ and so on

Let's consider the decimal number 19.

- 19 can be expressed as a sum of powers of 2 like this: $16 + 2 + 1 = 2^4 + 2^1 + 2^0$.
- We can covert 19 to LN notation by choosing the letters that correspond with the powers of 2: EBA.

Here are a few more examples.

Base 10	Sum of Powers	LN
7	$4 + 2 + 1 = 2^2 + 2^1 + 2^0$	CBA
17	$16 + 1 = 2^4 + 2^0$	EA
12	$8 + 4 = 2^3 + 2^2$	DC

A partial `LocationNumeral` class is shown below.

```
public class LocationNumeral
{
    private String alphabet = "ABCDEFGHIJKLMNOPQRSTUVWXYZ";

    /** Returns the decimal value of a single LN letter
     *
     *  @param letter String containing a single LN letter
     *  @return the decimal value of that letter
     *  Precondition: the parameter contains a single uppercase letter
     */
    public int getLetterValue(String letter)
    {
        /* to be implemented in part (a) */
    }

    /** Returns the decimal value of a Location Numeral
     *
     *  @param numeral String representing a Location Numeral
     *  @return the decimal value of the Location Numeral.
     *  Precondition:  The characters in the parameter are
     *                 uppercase letters A-Z only.
     */
    public int getDecimalValue(String numeral)
    {   /* to be implemented in part (b) */   }
```

GO ON TO THE NEXT PAGE

```
/** Builds a Location Numeral
 *
 *   @param value int representing the LN value
 *   @return String which represents the LN
 *
 *   Precondition: 2⁰ ≤ value ≤ 2²⁶
 *   Postcondition: The letters in the returned String are in
 *                  reverse alphabetical order
 */
public String buildLocationNumeral(int value)

    {   /* to be implemented in part (c) */   }

/* Additional instance variables, constructors, and methods not shown */
}
```

(a) Write the method `getLetterValue` that returns the numerical value of a single LN letter.

The value of each LN letter is equal to 2 raised to the power of the letter's position in the alphabet string.

For example, if passed the letter "E", the method will return 16, which is 2^4.

```
/** Returns the decimal value of a single LN letter
 *
 *   @param letter String containing a single LN letter
 *   @return the decimal value of that letter
 *   Precondition: The parameter contains a single uppercase letter
 */
public int getLetterValue(String letter)
```

(b) Write the method `getDecimalValue` that takes a Location Numeral and returns its decimal value.

For example, if passed the String "ECA", the method will add the decimal values of E, C, and A and return the result. In this case: $16 + 4 + 1 = 21$.

You may assume that `getLetterValue` works as intended, regardless of what you wrote in part (a).

```
/** Returns the decimal value of a Location Numeral
 *
 *   @param numeral String representing a Location Numeral
 *   @return the decimal value of the Location Numeral.
 *   Precondition:  The characters in the parameter are
 *                  uppercase letters A-Z only.
 */
public int getDecimalValue(String numeral)
```

GO ON TO THE NEXT PAGE

(c) Write the method `buildLocationNumeral` that takes a decimal value and returns the Location Numeral representation of that decimal value.

For example, if passed the value 43, the method will return the `String` "FDBA", which represents the sum $32 + 8 + 2 + 1$.

```
/** Builds a Location Numeral
 *
 *   @param value int representing the LN value
 *   @return String which represents the LN
 *
 *   Precondition:    2^0 ≤ value ≤ 2^26
 *   Postcondition: The letters in the returned String are in
 *                  descending alphabetical order
 */
public String buildLocationNumeral(int value)
```

GO ON TO THE NEXT PAGE

2. A quadratic function is a polynomial of degree 2, which can be written in the form

$y = ax^2 + bx + c$, where a, b, and c represent real numbers and $a \neq 0$. The x-intercepts, or roots, of a quadratic function can be found by using the quadratic formula.

$$x = \frac{-b \pm \sqrt{b^2 - 4ac}}{2a}$$

The value of the discriminant $b^2 - 4ac$ determines whether the roots are real or non-real (imaginary). If the discriminant > 0, the function has 2 real roots. If the discriminant = 0 the function has 1 real root, and if the discriminant < 0, it has imaginary (0 real) roots. Examples are shown in the table.

Equation	Discriminant	Real Root(s)
$y = 1x^2 - 25$	100.0	5.0, −5.0
$y = 1.2x^2 + 3.6x + 2.7$	0.0	−1.5
$y = 2x^2 - 4.1x + 5.2$	−24.79	none

Assume that the following code segment appears in a class other than `Quadratic`. The code segment shows a sample of using the `Quadratic` class to represent the three equations shown in the table.

```
double discrim, root1, root2;
Quadratic q1 = new Quadratic(1, 0, -25);
discrim = q1.getDiscriminant();        // discrim is assigned 100.0
if (discrim > 0)
{   root1 = q1.root1();                 // root1 is assigned 5.0
    root2 = q1.root2();                 // root2 is assigned -5.0
}
else if (discrim == 0)
    root1 = q1.root1();

Quadratic q2 = new Quadratic(1.2, 3.6, 2.7);
discrim = q2.getDiscriminant();        // discrim is assigned 0.0
if (discrim > 0)
{   root1 = q2.root1();
    root2 = q2.root2();
}
else if (discrim == 0)
    root1 = q2.root1();                 // root1 is assigned -1.5

Quadratic q3 = new Quadratic(2, -4.1, 5.2);
discrim = q3.getDiscriminant();        // discrim is assigned -24.79
if (discrim > 0)
{   root1 = q3.root1();
    root2 = q3.root2();
}
else if (discrim == 0)
    root1 = q3.root1();
```

Write the `Quadratic` class. Your implementation must include a constructor that has three double parameters that represent a, b, and c, in that order. You may assume that the value of a is not zero. It must also include a method `getDiscriminant` that calculates and returns the value of the discriminant, a method `root1` and a method `root2` that will calculate the possible two roots of the equation. Your class must produce the indicated results when invoked by the code segment given above.

GO ON TO THE NEXT PAGE

3. A printing factory maintains many printing machines that hold rolls of paper.

```java
public class Machine
{
    private PaperRoll paper;

    public Machine(PaperRoll roll)
    {  paper = roll;  }

    public PaperRoll getPaperRoll()
    {  return paper;  }

    /** Returns the current partial roll and replaces it with the new roll.
     *  @param pRoll a new full PaperRoll
     *  @return the old nearly empty PaperRoll
     */
    public PaperRoll replacePaper(PaperRoll pRoll)
    {
        /* to be implemented in part (a) */
    }

    /* Additional implementation not shown */
}

public class PaperRoll
{
    private double meters;

    public PaperRoll()
    {  meters = 1000;  }

    public double getMeters()
    {  return meters;  }

    /* Additional implementation not shown */
}
```

The factory keeps track of its printing machines in array `machines`, and it keeps track of its paper supply in two lists: `newRolls` to hold fresh rolls and `usedRolls` to hold the remnants taken off the machines when they no longer hold enough paper to be usable. At the beginning of the day, `usedRolls` is emptied of all paper remnants and `newRolls` is refilled. When `newRolls` no longer has enough rolls available to refill all the machines, the factory must shut down for the day until its supplies are restocked. At that time, the amount of paper used for the day is calculated.

GO ON TO THE NEXT PAGE

A partial `PrintingFactory` class is shown below.

```
public class PrintingFactory
{
    // All machines available in the company
    private Machine[] machines;

    // The available full paper rolls (1000 meters each)
    private ArrayList<PaperRoll> newRolls = new ArrayList<PaperRoll>();

    // The used paper roll remnants (less than 4.0 meters each)
    private ArrayList<PaperRoll> usedRolls = new ArrayList<PaperRoll>();

    public PrintingFactory(int numMachines)
    {    machines = new Machine[numMachines];    }

    /** Replaces the PaperRoll for any machine that has a
     *  PaperRoll with less than 4.0 meters of paper remaining.
     *  The used roll is added to usedRolls.
     *  A new roll is removed from newRolls.
     *  Precondition: newRolls is not empty.
     */
    public void replacePaperRolls(PaperRoll roll)
    {   /* to be implemented in part (b)   */   }

    /** Returns the total amount of paper that has been used.
     *  @return the total amount of paper that has been used from the PaperRolls
     *          in the usedRolls list plus the paper that has
     *          been used from the PaperRolls on the machines.
     */
    public double getPaperUsed()
    {   /* to be implemented in part (c)   */   }

    /* Additional implementation not shown */
}
```

(a) Write the `replacePaper` method of the `Machine` class. This method returns the nearly empty `PaperRoll` and replaces it with the `PaperRoll` passed as a parameter.

```
/** Returns the current partial roll and replaces it with the new roll.
 *  @param pRoll a new full PaperRoll
 *  @return the old nearly empty PaperRoll
 */
public PaperRoll replacePaper(PaperRoll pRoll)
```

GO ON TO THE NEXT PAGE

(b) Write the `replacePaperRolls` method of the `PrintingFactory` class.

At the end of each job cycle, each `Machine` object in `machines` is examined to see if its `PaperRoll` needs replacing. A `PaperRoll` is replaced when it has less than 4 meters of paper remaining. The used roll is added to the `usedRolls` list, while a new roll is removed from the `newRolls` list.

```
/** Replaces the PaperRoll for any machine in array machines that has
 *  a PaperRoll with less than 4.0 meters of paper remaining.
 *  The used roll is added to usedRolls.
 *  A new roll is removed from newRolls.
 */
public void replacePaperRolls()
```

(c) Write the `getPaperUsed` method of the `PrintingFactory` class.

At the end of the day, the factory calculates how much paper has been used by adding up the amount of paper used from all the rolls in the `usedRolls` list and all the rolls still in the machines. A brand-new paper roll has 1000 meters of paper.

Example

The tables below show the status of the factory at the end of the day.

Paper in Machines	
Amount Left	Amount Used
900.0	100.0
250.0	750.0
150.0	850.0

Paper in usedRolls List	
Amount Left	Amount Used
3.5	996.5
2.0	998.0
1.5	998.5
3.0	997.0

Total used: 100.0 + 750.0 + 850.0 + 996.5 + 998.0 + 998.5 + 997.0 = 5690.0 meters

Complete the method `getPaperUsed`.

```
/** Returns the total amount of paper that has been used.
 *  @return the total amount of paper left on the PaperRolls
 *          in the usedRolls list plus the paper that has
 *          been used from the PaperRolls on the machines.
 */
public double getPaperUsed()
```

GO ON TO THE NEXT PAGE

4. A hex grid is a type of two-dimensional (2D) map used by many games to represent the area that tokens, ships, robots, or other types of game pieces can move around on.

The `GamePiece` class is intended to represent the various game pieces required to play different games on the `HexGrid`. The implementation of the `GamePiece` class is not shown. You may construct a `GamePiece` object with a no-argument constructor.

A hex grid is represented in the `HexGrid` class by a 2D array of `GamePiece` objects. The coordinates of a `GamePiece` represent its position on the `HexGrid` as shown in the following diagram. Many of the hex cells in the `HexGrid` will not be occupied by any `GamePiece` and are therefore `null`.

The rows in a `HexGrid` are in a staggered horizontal pattern where hexes in even columns rise higher than hexes in odd-numbered columns. The columns in a `HexGrid` always appear vertically aligned regardless of the value of the row.

The following is a representation of a `HexGrid` object that contains several `GamePiece` objects at specified locations in the `HexGrid`. The row and column of each `GamePiece` are given.

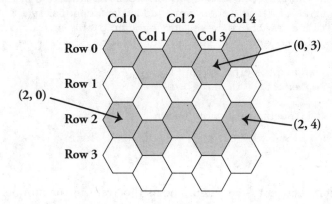

```
public class HexGrid
{
    /** A two-dimensional array of the GamePiece objects in the
     *  game. Each GamePiece is located in a specific hex cell
     *  as determined by its row and column number.
     */
    private GamePiece[][] grid;

    /** Returns the number of GamePiece objects
     *  currently occupying any hex cell in the grid.
     *
     *  @return the number of GamePiece objects currently in
     *          the grid.
     */
    public int getGamePieceCount()
    {  /* to be implemented in part (a) */  }
```

GO ON TO THE NEXT PAGE

```
/** Returns an ArrayList of the GamePiece objects
 *   in the same column as and with a lower row number than
 *   the GamePiece at the location specified by the parameters.
 *   If there is no GamePiece at the specified location,
 *   the method returns null.
 *
 *   @param row the row of the GamePiece in question
 *   @param column the column of the GamePiece in question
 *   @return an ArrayList of the GamePiece objects "above" the
 *           indicated GamePiece, or null if no such object
 *           exists
 */
public ArrayList<GamePiece> isAbove(int row, int col)
{   /*  to be implemented in part (b) */   }

/** Adds GamePiece objects randomly to the grid
 *   @ param the number of GamePiece objects to add
 *   @ return true if GamePieces were added successfully
 *           false if there were not enough blank spaces in the
 *           grid to add the requested objects
 */
public boolean addRandom(int number)
{   /*  to be implemented in part (c) */   }

/* Additional implementation not shown */
}
```

(a) Write the method getGamePieceCount. The method returns the number of GamePiece objects in the hex grid.

```
/** Returns the number of GamePiece objects
 *   currently occupying any hex cell in the grid.
 *
 *   @return the number of GamePiece objects currently in
 *           the grid.
 */
public int getGamePieceCount()
```

(b) Write the method isAbove. The method returns an ArrayList of GamePiece objects that are located "above" the GamePiece in the row and column specified in the parameters. "Above" is defined as in the same column but with a lower row number than the specified location. In the diagram below, letters represent GamePiece objects. The objects may appear in any order in the ArrayList.

- If the method is called with the row and column of C, an ArrayList containing A and B will be returned.
- If the method is called with the row and column of F, an ArrayList containing E will be returned.
- If the method is called with the row and column of E, an empty ArrayList is returned.
- If the method is called with the row and column of an empty cell, null is returned.

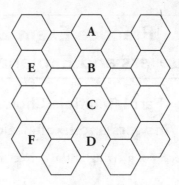

```
/** Returns an ArrayList of the GamePiece objects
 *   in the same column as and with a lower row number than
 *   the GamePiece at the location specified by the parameters.
 *   If there is no GamePiece at the specified location,
 *   the method returns null.
 *
 *   @param row the row of the GamePiece in question
 *   @param column the column of the GamePiece in question
 *   @return an ArrayList of the GamePiece objects "above" the
 *           indicated GamePiece, or null if no object exists
 *           at the specified location
 */
public ArrayList<GamePiece> isAbove (int row, int col)
```

(c) Write the addRandom method. This method takes a parameter that represents the number of GamePiece objects to be added to the grid at random locations. GamePiece objects can only be added to locations that are currently empty (null). If there are insufficient empty cells to complete the requested additions, no GamePiece objects will be added and the method will return false. If the additions are successful, the method will return true.

You may assume that getGamePieceCount works as intended, regardless of what you wrote in part (a). You must use getGamePieceCount appropriately in order to receive full credit for part (c).

```
/** Adds GamePiece objects randomly to the grid
 *   @param the number of GamePiece objects to add
 *   @return true if GamePieces were added successfully
 *           false if there were not enough empty cells in the
 *           grid to add the requested objects. In this case
 *           no objects will be added.
 */
public boolean addRandom(int number)
```

STOP. End of Part II.

Practice Exam 2
Answers and Explanations

Part I (Multiple Choice)
Answers and Explanations

Bullets mark each step in the process of arriving at the correct solution.

1. The answer is B.

   - The outer loop will start at h = 5 and then, on successive iterations, h = 3 and h = 1.
   - The inner loop will start at k = 0, then 1 and 2.
   - The `if` statement will print h + k only if their sum is even (since % 2 = 0 is true only for even numbers).
   - Since h is always odd, h + k will be even only when k is also odd. That only happens once per inner loop, when k = 1. Adding h and k, we get 5 + 1 = 6, 3 + 1 = 4, and 1 + 1 = 2, so 6 4 2 is printed.

2. The answer is A.

   - Let's picture our `ArrayList` as a table. After the first three add statements we have:

Hummus	Soup	Sushi

   - The set statement changes element 1:

Hummus	Empanadas	Sushi

   - Add at index 0 gives us:

Salad	Hummus	Empanadas	Sushi

   - Remove the element at index 1:

Salad	Empanadas	Sushi

   - And finally, add "Curry" to the end of the list:

Salad	Empanadas	Sushi	Curry

3. The answer is B.

   - Option I is incorrect. The outer loop begins at i = letters.length. Remember that the elements of an array start at index = 0 and end at index = length − 1. Starting the loop at i = letters.length will result in an `ArrayIndexOutOfBoundsException`.
   - Option II is correct. The outer loop takes each letter from the string in turn, and the inner loop prints it four times, as long as it is not an "S".
   - Option III is incorrect. It correctly traverses each element in the array, but then only prints each element once, not four times.

4. The answer is D.

   - The constructor call creates a new Boat and the super call sets the fuel variable in the `Vehicle` class to 20.
   - The call to the `Boat` class start method:
     - begins by calling the `Vehicle` class start method, which prints "Vroom",
     - then calls useFuel, which calls the useFuel method in the Boat class, which calls the `Vehicle` class `changeFuel` method, which subtracts 2 from the fuel variable, and
     - finally, the start method prints "Remaining Fuel" followed by the value in the `Vehicle` class fuel variable, which is now 18.

5. The answer is C.

- The type on the left side of the assignment statement can be the same type or a super type of the object constructed on the right side of the assignment statement. The object constructed should have an *is-a* relationship with the declared type.
- Option I is correct. A Boat *is-a* Boat.
- Option II is correct. A Boat *is-a* Vehicle.
- Option III is incorrect. Vehicle is a super class of Boat. A Boat *is* a Vehicle, but a Vehicle doesn't have to be a Boat. The super class must be on the left side of the assignment statement.

6. The answer is E.

- This is a recursive method. The first call results in:

  weird(3) = weird(3 − 2) + weird(3 − 1) + weird(3)

  = weird(1) + weird(2) + weird(3)

  A recursive method must approach the base case or it will infinitely recurse (until the Stack overflows). The call to weird(3) calls weird(3) again, which will call weird(3) again, which will call weird(3) again. . . .

7. The answer is D.

- It is important to notice that the `for` loop is traversing the array from the greatest index to the least. The array is correct if every element is greater than or equal to the one before it.
- We will return true if we traverse the entire array without finding an exception. If we find an exception, we return false, so we are looking for that exception, or values[index − 1] > values[index].
- Option A is incorrect because of the =.
- Note that since we must not use an index that is out of bounds, we can immediately eliminate any answer that accesses values[index + 1] which eliminates options B and E.

8. The answer is D.

- The first nested loop initializes all the values in the array in row-major order. The first value entered is 0, then 1, 2, etc. After these loops terminate, the matrix looks like this:

0	1	2
3	4	5
6	7	8

- The second nested loop (for-each loops this time) traverses the array and adds all the values into the sum variable. $0 + 1 + 2 + \ldots + 8 = 36$.

9. The answer is C.

- doStuff is going to loop through the array, checking to see if each item is the same as the item before it. If it is, the values of index, maxCounter, and counter all change. If it is not, only counter changes.
- Begin by setting index = 0; maxCounter = 1; counter = 1; and noting that numberArray.length() = 5.
- First iteration: k = 1, enter the loop with index = 0; maxCounter = 1; counter = 1;
  - Item 1 = item 0, execute the if clause
    - counter <= maxCounter, execute the if clause
      - maxCounter = 1; index = 1
    - counter = 2
- Second iteration: k = 2, enter the loop with index = 1; maxCounter = 1; counter = 2;
  - Item 2 != item 1, execute the else clause
    - counter = 1

- Third iteration: k = 3, enter the loop with index = 1; maxCounter = 1; counter = 1;
  - Item 3 = item 2, execute the if clause
    - counter <= maxCounter, execute the if clause
      - maxCounter = 1; index = 3
    - counter = 2
- Fourth iteration: k = 4, enter the loop with index = 3; maxCounter = 1; counter = 2;
  - Item 4 != item 3, execute the else clause
    - counter = 1
- Fifth iteration: k = 5, which fails the condition and the loop exits.
- index = 3, numberArray[3] = 4 is returned and printed.

10. The answer D.

- Integer.MAX_VALUE is a large number, but repeatedly dividing by 2 will eventually result in an answer of 0 and the loop will terminate. Remember that this is integer division. Each quotient will be truncated to an integer value. There will be no decimal part.
- In the second loop, the initial condition sets i = 0, which immediately fails the condition. The loop never executes, so nothing is printed, but the code segment terminates successfully.

11. The answer is A.

- myCar is instantiated as a reference variable pointing to an `Automobile` object with instance variables make = "Ford" and model = "Fusion".

$$myCar \longrightarrow \boxed{\begin{array}{c} \text{"Ford"} \\ \text{"Fusion"} \end{array}}$$

- companyCar is instantiated as a reference variable pointing to an `Automobile` object with instance variables make = "Toyota" and model = "Corolla".

$$myCar \longrightarrow \boxed{\begin{array}{c} \text{"Ford"} \\ \text{"Fusion"} \end{array}} \qquad companyCar \longrightarrow \boxed{\begin{array}{c} \text{"Toyota"} \\ \text{"Corolla"} \end{array}}$$

- The statement companyCar = myCar reassigns the `companyCar` reference variable to point to the same object as the `myCar` variable. They are now aliases of each other. The original `companyCar` object is now inaccessible (unless yet another variable we don't know about points to it).

$$myCar \longrightarrow \boxed{\begin{array}{c} \text{"Ford"} \\ \text{"Fusion"} \end{array}} \longleftarrow companyCar \qquad \boxed{\begin{array}{c} \text{"Toyota"} \\ \text{"Corolla"} \end{array}}$$

- The next statement instantiates a brand-new `Automobile` object with make = "Kia" and model = "Spectre". It sets the `myCar` reference variable to point to this new object. This does not change the `companyCar` variable.
- The `companyCar` variable still points to the object with instance variables make = "Ford" and model = "Fusion".

$$myCar \longrightarrow \boxed{\begin{array}{c} \text{"Kia"} \\ \text{"Spectre"} \end{array}} \qquad \boxed{\begin{array}{c} \text{"Ford"} \\ \text{"Fusion"} \end{array}} \longleftarrow companyCar$$

- So we print companyCar's make, which is "Ford" followed by myCar's model, which is "Spectre".

12. The answer is A.

- The `indexOf(str)` method returns the index of the first occurrence or `-1` if not found.
- The index position begins counting at 0. "e" is found at position 9.

13. The answer is C.

- Both of the conditions in the original segment add 1 or 2, which is value, to count.
- The conditions can be combined using an || statement.

14. The answer is D.

- Option I is correct. Note that the final condition, (credit >= 590 && coll), doesn't have to be in parentheses. Since AND has a higher priority than OR, it would be executed first, even without the parentheses. However, the parentheses make the code clearer, and that is always our goal.
- Option II is incorrect. While it seems reasonable at first glance, De Morgan's theorem tells us we can't just distribute the !. We also have to change OR to AND.
- Option III is correct. As soon as a condition evaluates to true, the method will return and no more statements will be executed. Therefore no else clauses are required. The method will return false only if none of the conditions are true.

15. The answer is C.

- To answer this problem, you need to understand that String objects are immutable (the only other immutable objects in our Java subset are Integer and Double.
- When the method begins, entry1 = "AP" and entry2 = "CS".
- Then the assignment statement reassigns entry2 so that both variables now refer to the String object containing "AP".
- When we execute the next statement, entry1 = entry1 + entry2, we would expect that to change for both variables, since they both reference the same object, but String objects don't work that way. Whenever a string is modified, a new String object is created to hold the new value. So now, entry1 references "APAP" but entry2 still references "AP".
- We put those together, and "APAPAP" is returned.

16. The answer is E.

- Remember, we only need to find one error to eliminate an option.
- Option A is incorrect. index starts in the middle of the array and goes down to zero. We swap the item at index with the item at index + 1. We are never going to address the upper half of the array.
- Option B is incorrect. The swap code is incomplete. We put planets[index] into s, but then never use s.
- Option C is incorrect. It's OK to use another array, but this code forgets to switch the order when it moves the elements into the new array. The new array is identical to the old one.
- Option D is incorrect. At first glance, there's no obvious error. The swap code looks correct. Although planets.length − 1 − index seems a bit complex, a few examples will show us that it does, indeed, give the element that should be swapped with the element at index: $0 \rightarrow 7 − 0 = 7$, $1 \rightarrow 7 − 1 = 6$, $2 \rightarrow 7 − 2 = 5$, $3 \rightarrow 7 − 3 = 4$, and so on. The trouble with this option is that "and so on" part. It swaps all the pairs and then continues on to swap them all again. After completing the four swaps listed above, we are done and we should stop.
- Option E is correct. The code is the same as option D, except it stops after swapping half the elements. The other half were the partners in those first swaps, so now everything is where it should be.

17. The answer is C.

- The loop begins at whatever value is stored in start and will continue until the value stored in stop is reached.
- Try substituting start = 1 and stop = 5. The loop will execute 5 times.
- Substituting 1 and 5 into the answer options, A, B, and D are eliminated.
- Choosing different values for start and stop such as 2 and 10 will result in option C.

18. The answer is B.

- The general form for generating a random number between *high* and *low* is

  `(int)(Math.random() * (high - low + 1)) + low`

- high − low + 1 = 30, low = 20, so high = 49
- After the first statement, num is an integer between 20 and 49 (inclusive).
- In the second statement, we add 5 to num. Now num is between 25 and 54 (inclusive).
- In the third statement we divide by 5, remembering integer division. Now num is between 5 and 10 (inclusive).

19. The answer is A.

- This loop takes pieces of the String "computer" and places them in an ArrayList of String objects.
- The loop starts at index k = 0, and adds the word.substring(0), or the entire word, to the ArrayList. The first element of the ArrayList is "computer".
- Then k is incremented by the k++ inside the loop, k = 1, and immediately incremented again by the instruction in the loop header, k = 2. It is bad programming style to change a loop index inside the loop, but we need to be able to read code, even if it is poorly written.
- The second iteration of the loop is k = 2, and we add word.substring(2) or "mputer" to the ArrayList.
- We increment k twice and add word.substring(4) or "uter".
- We increment k twice and add word.substring(6) or "er".
- We increment k twice and fail the loop condition. The loop terminates and the `ArrayList` is printed.

20. The answer is E.

- We need to plug the values of x and y into the given statements to see if they always generate the correct return value.
- Option A is incorrect. 3 > 6 is false, but should be true.
- Option B is incorrect. 1 % 0 will fail with a division by zero error.
- Option C is incorrect. (1 + 0) % 2 == 0 is false, but should be true.
- Option D is incorrect. (3 + 6) % 3 == 6 is false, but should be true.
- Option E works for all the given values.

21. The answer is B.

- The loop will continue until numWord = words.size(), which will cause an `ArrayIndexOutOfBoundsException`.
- Notice that numWord is only incremented if nothing is removed from the `ArrayList`. That is correct because, if something is removed, the indices of the elements after that element will change. If we increment numWord each time, we will skip elements.

22. The answer is C.

- This is an especially difficult example of recursion because the recursive call is not the last thing in the method. It's also not the first thing in the method. Notice that the print happens *after* the call. So each iteration of the method will print one letter less than its parameter.
- Let's trace the code. The parts in *italics* were filled in on the way back up. That is, the calls in the plain type were written top to bottom until the base case returned a value. Then the answers were filled in *bottom to top*.

  wackyOutput("APCS") ➡ *print "PCS"*   (printed fourth)
  wackyOutput("PCS") ➡ *print "CS"*   (printed third)
  wackyOutput("CS") ➡ *print "S"*   (printed second)
  wackyOutput("S") ➡ *print ""*   (printed first)
  wackyOutput("") ➡ Base Case. Return without printing.

  Remember that the returns are read bottom to top, so the output is "SCSPCS" in that order.

- Note that "S".substring(1,1) is not an error. It returns the empty string.

23. The answer is D.

- Option I is correct. It uses De Morgan's theorem to modify the boolean condition.
  ```
  !(num1 >= 0 && num2 >= 0)
  !(num1 >= 0 ) || !(num2 >= 0)
  num1 < 0 || num2 < 0
  ```
- Option II is correct. It tests the two parts of the condition separately. If either fails, it returns "Numbers are not valid".
- Option III is incorrect. If num1 is a positive number and num2 is a negative number, but the absolute value of num2 < num1 (num1 = 5 and num2 = -2, for example), option III will return "Numbers are valid" although clearly both numbers are not >= 0.

24. The answer is A.

- test1 references a `TestClass` object with value = 9.0 and test2 references a `TestClass` object with value = 17.5.

$$\text{test 1} \longrightarrow \boxed{\text{value} = 9.0} \qquad \text{test 2} \longrightarrow \boxed{\text{value} = 17.5}$$

- After the addValue and reduceValue calls, our objects look like this:

$$\text{test 1} \longrightarrow \boxed{\text{value} = 6.0} \qquad \text{test 2} \longrightarrow \boxed{\text{value} = 19.0}$$

- The assignment statement changes test2 to reference the same object as test1.

$$\text{test 1} \longrightarrow \boxed{\text{value} = 6.0} \longleftarrow \text{test 2} \qquad \boxed{\text{value} = 19.0}$$

- At this point, the object with value = 19.0 is inaccessible (unless another reference variable we don't know about is pointing to it). The next time Java does garbage collection, it will be deleted.
- The next reduceValue call changes our object to this:

$$\text{test 1} \longrightarrow \boxed{\text{value} = 0.0} \longleftarrow \text{test 2}$$

- The getValue statements in the next line get the same value, as test1 and test2 are pointing to the same object. 0.0 + 0.0 = 0.0.

25. The answer is B.

- This is a recursive method. Let's trace the calls. The parts in *italics* were filled in on the way back up. That is, the calls in the plain type were written top to bottom until the base case returned a value. Then the answers were filled in *bottom to top*.
- Be very careful to get the order of num1 and num2 correct in the modulus operation and the parameters correct in the recursive call.
  - guess(3, 17) = guess(17, 3) + 3 = *4 + 3 = 7* which gives us our final answer.
  - guess(17, 3) = guess(3, 2) + 2 = *2 + 2 = 4*
  - guess(3, 2) = guess(2, 1) + 1 = *1 + 1 = 2*
  - guess(2,1) Base case! return 3/2 = 1 (integer division)

26. The answer is B.

This method implements a standard insertion sort. In this sort, each item is taken in turn and placed in its correct position among the items to its left (with lower indices).

- The first time through the loop, i = 1, the algorithm looks at the first two values {4, 3...} and inserts the 3 in the right place {3, 4...}. The rest of the array is untouched.
- The second time through, i = 2, the algorithm looks at the first three values {3, 4, 7...}. Since the 7 is already in the right place, no changes are made.
- The third time through, i = 3, the algorithm looks at the first four values {3, 4, 7, 6...} and inserts the 6 in the right place {3, 4, 6, 7...}. Our answer is {3, 4, 6, 7, 1, 5, 2}.
- If we were to continue, the final three values, {...1, 5, 2} would be inserted in their correct locations during the remaining 3 iterations of the outside loop.

Note: Answer C is the result of the third pass of a standard selection sort algorithm.

27. The answer is A.

- In order for a rectangle to contain a point, the following conditions must be true:

  topLeftX < x < bottomRightX   and   topLeftY < y < bottomRightY

- Option A is correct. These are the exact conditions used in option A, though they are in a different order.
- Option B is incorrect because it will return true if any one of the four conditions is true.
- Options C and D are incorrect because they attempt to make invalid calls to super or `Polygon` methods that do not exist.
- Option E is incorrect. It is similar to option B, except that it will return true if two of the required conditions are true.

28. The answer is A.

- Let's show the contents of the `ArrayList` graphically and trace the code. The method is called with this `ArrayList`.

Nora	Charles	Madeline	Nate	Silja	Garrett

- The first time through the loop, i = 3. The element at index 3 is removed and added to the end of the `ArrayList`.

Nora	Charles	Madeline	Silja	Garrett	Nate

- Decrement i, i = 2, which is >= 0, so execute the loop again. The element at index 2 is removed and added to the end.

Nora	Charles	Silja	Garrett	Nate	Madeline

- Decrement i, i = 1, which is >= 0, so execute the loop again. The element at index 1 is removed and added to the end.

Nora	Silja	Garrett	Nate	Madeline	Charles

- Decrement i, i = 0, which is >= 0, so execute the loop again. The element at index 0 is removed and added to the end.

Silja	Garrett	Nate	Madeline	Charles	Nora

- Decrement i, i = -1, which fails the loop condition. The loop terminates and the `ArrayList` is returned.

29. The answer is C.

- The loop will execute while varA != 0 OR varB > 0. Another way to say that, using De Morgan's theorem, is that the loop will *stop* executing when varA == 0 AND varB <= 0.
- The only answer that fits that condition is C: varA = 0 and varB = -4.
- Instead of thinking through the logic, we could trace the execution of the loop, but it's a lot of work. Here's a table of the values of varA and varB at the end of every iteration of the loop until the loop terminates.

varA	varB
-27	21
-24	18
-21	15
-18	12
-15	9
-12	6
-9	3
-6	0
-3	-3
0	-4

30. The answer is C.

- The nested loops go through grid in row-major order, but assign into newGrid in column-major order. (Notice that newGrid is instantiated with its number of rows equal to the grid's number of columns and its number of columns equal to the grid's number of rows.) After executing the loops, newGrid looks like this:

```
{ {0, 3, 6,  9 },
  {1, 4, 7, 10 },
  {2, 5, 8, 11 } }
```

- newGrid [2][1] = 5

31. The answer is E.

- The nested loops traverse the entire array. Each time through, the three assignment statements are executed. The key to the problem is the order in which these statements are executed. We need to pay attention to which values will overwrite previously assigned values.
- On entering the loops, our array looks like this:

0	0	0
0	0	0
0	0	0

- We will execute the outer loop three times, and for each of those three times, we will execute the inner loop three times.
- The first iteration of both loops, we are changing element [0][0].
  - The first statement makes it a 1.
    - Note that this statement changes the array in row-major order.
  - The second statement makes it a 2.
    - Note that this statement changes the array in column-major order.
  - The third statement makes it a 3, so it will remain a 3.
    - Note that this statement only changes the diagonals.
- Completing the first cycle of the inner loop, the first statement assigns a 1 to [0][1] and [0][2] and the second statement assigns a 2 to [1][0] and [2][0]. The third statement repeatedly sets [0][0] to 3, and since that statement is last, it will remain a 3.

3	1	1
2	0	0
2	0	0

- The next cycle of the inner loop will assign a 1 to [1][0], [1][1], and [1][2]. A 2 will be assigned to [0][1], [1][1], and [2][1]. Then element [1][1] will be overwritten with a 3.

3	2	1
1	3	1
2	2	0

- The third (and last) cycle of the inner loop will assign a 1 to [2][0], [2][1], and [2][2]. A 2 will be assigned to [0][2], [1][2], and [2][2]. Then element [2][2] will be overwritten with a 3.

3	2	2
1	3	2
1	1	3

32. The answer is E.

   - If this were a sorting algorithm, there would be only one parameter, the array to be sorted, and a sorted array would be returned, so we can eliminate the sorting algorithms. In addition, Merge Sort is recursive, and selection and insertion sorts require nested loops, neither of which appear in this code.
   - Binary search repeatedly divides the remaining section of the array in half. There's no code that does anything like that. This is not a binary search.
   - This code goes through the array one step at a time in order. This is a sequential search algorithm.

33. The answer is E.

   - Each pass of the loop needs to check one letter to see if it is the desired key.
   - The `substring(i, i+1)` method is used to look at one letter at a time.
   - Each time the letter matches the key, then `count` is incremented by 1.

34. The answer is D.

   - The `compareTo(other)` method returns 0 if the `string` object is less than other (which means it comes first alphabetically)
   - Strings cannot be compared using ==, < , or > operators.

35. The answer is D.

   - `Math.random()` doesn't take any parameter, so options A and B can be eliminated.
   - `Math.random()` returns a value greater than or equal to 0.0 and less than 1.0.
   - Once the random `double` is returned, it must be multiplied by the size of the array and then cast into an `integer`.

36. The answer is D.

   - Only I and III evaluate to true.

37. The answer is D.

   - This question is explained along with question 38.

38. The answer is D.

- We will solve questions 37 and 38 together by diagramming the objects and reference variables.
- The first three assignment statements give us:

c1 → [x = 0 / y = 10] ← c3   c2 → [x = 20 / y = 30]

- `c3.setX(c2.getY());` results in:

c1 → [x = **30** / y = 10] ← c3   c2 → [x = 20 / y = 30]

- `c3 = c2;` results in:

c1 → [x = 30 / y = 10]   c3 —→ c2 → [x = 20 / y = 30]

- `c3.setY(c2.getX());` results in:

c1 → [x = 30 / y = 10]   c3 —→ c2 → [x = 20 / y = **20**]

- `c2.setX(c1.getX());` results in:

c1 → [x = 30 / y = 10]   c3 —→ c2 → [x = **30** / y = 20]

- Question 37: Both c2.getY() and c3.getY() return 20, but only c2.getY() is an option.
- Question 38: c1.getX(), c2.getX(), and c3.getX() all return 30.

39. The answer is E.

- Option I is incorrect. Among other errors, getSqFeet does not take a parameter.
- Option II is incorrect. Square brackets are used to access elements of arrays, but not of `ArrayLists`.
- Option III is correct.
- Option IV is incorrect. list is the name of the `ArrayList`, not the name being used for each element of the `ArrayList`.
- Option V is correct.

40. The answer is B.

- The array holds `Building` objects. As long as an object *is-a* Building, it can go into the array.
- The runtime environment will look at the type of the object and call the version of getSize written specifically for that object.
  - list[0] is a Building so the `Building` class getSize will be used to generate the String for list[0].
  - list[1] is a House so the `House` class getSize will be used to generate the String for list[1].
  - list[2] references the same object as list[1]. This will generate a duplicate of the list[1] response.

Part II (Free Response)

Answers and Explanations

Please keep in mind that there are multiple ways to write the solution to a Free-response question, but the general and refined statements of the problem should be pretty much the same for everyone. Look at the algorithms and coded solutions, and determine if yours accomplishes the same task.

General Penalties (assessed only once per problem):

-1 using local variables without first declaring them
-1 returning a value from a void method or constructor
-1 accessing an array or `ArrayList` incorrectly
-1 overwriting information passed as a parameter
-1 including unnecessary code that causes a side effect such as a compile error or console output

1. Location Numerals

   (a) **General Problem:** Write the `getLetterValue` method that returns the numerical value of the given letter.

   Refined Problem: Find the parameter letter's position in the `String` alphabet. Return 2 raised to that power.

   Algorithm:
   - Use `indexOf` to find the position of letter in the `String` alphabet.
   - Use `Math.pow` to raise 2 to the power of the position found.
   - Return the result.

   Java Code:
   ```java
   public int getLetterValue(String letter)
   {
       int position = alphabet.indexOf(letter);
       return (int) Math.pow(2, position);
   }
   ```

   (b) **General Problem:** Write the `getDecimalValue` method that takes a Location Numeral and returns its decimal equivalent.

   Refined Problem: Find the value of each letter in turn and add it to running total. Return the final answer.

   Algorithm:
   - Create a variable to hold the running total.
   - Loop through the Location Numeral `String` from the letter at index 0 to the end of the `String`.
     - Isolate each letter, using `substring`.
     - Call the method `getLetterValue`, passing the isolated letter.
     - Add the result to the running total.
     - When the loop is complete, return the total.

Java Code:

```java
public int getDecimalValue(String numeral)
{
    int total = 0;
    for (int i = 0; i < numeral.length(); i++)
    {
        String letter = numeral.substring(i, i + 1);
        total += getLetterValue(letter);
    }
    return total;
}
```

Common Errors:

- Don't end the loop at `numeral.length() - 1`. When you notice the expression `numeral.substring(i, i + 1)`, you may think that the i + 1 will cause an out of bounds exception. It would if it were the first parameter in the substring, but remember that the substring will stop *before* the value of the second parameter, so it will not index out of bounds. If you terminate the loop at `numeral.length() - 1`, you will miss the last letter in the `String`.
- Be sure that you use the method you wrote in part (a). There is generally a penalty for duplication of code if you rewrite the function in another method. The problem usually has a hint when a previously written method is to be used. In this case, the problem says, "You may assume that `getLetterValue` works as intended, regardless of what you wrote in part (a)." That's a surefire indication that you'd better use the method to solve the current problem.

(c) General Problem: Write the `buildLocationNumeral` method that returns the Location Numeral representation of the decimal value passed as a parameter.

Refined Problem: Determine which powers of 2 sum together to give the value of the parameter. Build the Location Numeral by determining the corresponding letters of the alphabet.

Algorithm:

- Initialize a variable to keep track of the position in the alphabet string starting at the end.
- Initialize a `string` variable to the empty string and add letters as appropriate.
- As long as more simplification can be done:
  - Determine the value of $2^{current}$ position in alphabet string.
    - If the power of 2 value is larger than the current value variable
    - Concatenate the corresponding alphabetic letter onto the string variable.
  - Decrease the value by the power of 2.
  - Decrease the position variable by 1.
- Return the final result.

Java Code:

```
public String buildLocationNumeral(int value)
{
    int position = 26;
    int powerOf2;
    String temp = "";
    while (value > 0)
    {
        powerOf2 = (int) Math.pow(2, position);
        if (value >= powerOf2)
        {    temp += alphabet.substring(position, position + 1);
            value -= powerOf2;
        }
        position --;
    }
    return temp;
}
```

Common Errors:
- This is a tricky piece of code. There are many places where errors can sneak in. Remember that you can earn most of the points for a question even with errors or missing sections in your code.
- The key is continuously subtracting powers of 2 from value until value becomes 0 and determining the letter of the alphabet that corresponds to that power of 2.

Scoring Guidelines: Location Numerals

Part (a)   **getLetterValue**   **2 points**
+1   Determines the correct position in the alphabet string
+1   Returns the correct value

Part (b)   **getDecimalValue**   **3 points**
+1   Accesses every individual letter in numeral; no bounds errors, no missing values
+1   Calls getLetterValue for each letter
+1   Accumulates and returns the correct total value

Part (c)   **buildLocationNumeral**   **4 points**
+1   Initializes appropriate variables
+1   Determines the appropriate power of 2 for each time through the loop
+1   Adds the appropriate letter of the alphabet to the string for each time through the loop
+1   Returns the accumulated string

Sample Driver:

There are many ways to write these methods. Maybe yours is a bit different from our sample solutions and you are not sure if it works. Here is a sample driver program. Running it will let you see if your code works and will help you debug it if it does not.

Copy the LocationNumeralDriver into your IDE along with the LocationNumeral class (including your solutions).

• Here's the `LocationNumeralDriver`:

```
public class LocationNumeralDriver
{
    public static void main(String[] args)
    {
    LocationNumeral num1 = new LocationNumeral();
    System.out.println(num1.getLetterValue("E"));
    System.out.println(num1.getDecimalValue("ECA"));
    System.out.println(num1.buildLocationNumeral(43));

    LocationNumeral num2 = new LocationNumeral();
    System.out.println(num2.getLetterValue("B"));
    System.out.println(num2.getDecimalValue("CBA"));
    System.out.println(num2.buildLocationNumeral(17));
    }
}
```

2. Quadratic

(a) **General Problem:** Write the `Quadratic` class.

Refined Problem: Create the `Quadratic` class with three instance variables and one three parameter constructor. The three methods `getDiscriminant`, `getRoot1`, and `getRoot2` will need to be defined.

Algorithm:
• Write a class header for `Quadratic`.
• Declare three instance variables to store the values of *a*, *b*, and *c*.
• Write a constructor with three parameters that represent the coefficients of the quadratic equation and assign the parameters to the corresponding instance variables.
• Write method `getDiscriminant`.
• Write methods `getRoot1` and `getRoot2`.

Java Code:
```
public class Quadratic
{
    private double a, b, c;

    public Quadratic(double a, double b, double c)
    {
        this.a = a;
        this.b = b;
        this.c = c;
    }

    public double getDiscriminant()
    {
        return b * b - 4 * a * c;
    }

    public int getRoot1()
    {
        return (-b + Math.sqrt(getDiscriminant()))/(2 * a);
    }

    public int getRoot2()
    {
        return (-b - Math.sqrt(getDiscriminant()))/(2 * a);
    }
}
```

Common Errors:
* The instance variables must be declared private.

Scoring Guidelines: Quadratic

Quadratic class	1 point
+1 Complete, correct header for `Quadratic`	

state maintenance	1 point
+1 Declares at least three private instance variables capable of maintaining the coefficients of the quadratic equation	

Quadratic Constructor	2 points
+1 Correct method header	
+1 Sets appropriate state variables based on parameters	

getDiscriminant	2 points
+1 Correct method header	
+1 Returns the correctly computed value	

getRoot1, getRoot2	3 points
+1 Correct method headers for `getRoot1` and `getRoot2`	
+1 Correctly calculates and returns `root1`	
+1 Correctly calculates and returns `root2`	

Sample Driver:

There are many ways to write these methods. Maybe yours is a bit different from the sample solutions shown here and you are not sure if it works. Here is a sample driver program. Running it will let you see if your code works, and will help you debug it if it does not.

Copy `QuadraticDriver` into your IDE along with the complete `Quadratic` class (including your solutions). You also might want to add the `toString` method to your `Quadratic` class, which will print the quadratic equation for you.

```
public String toString()
{
  return a + "x^2 + " + b + "x + " + c;
}
```

```
public class QuadraticDriver
{
  public static void main(String[] args)
  {
      Quadratic q1 = new Quadratic(1, 0, -25);
      double discrim = q1.getDiscriminant();
      System.out.println("The quadratic equation " + q1 + " with discriminant " +
                          discrim);
      if (discrim > 0)
        System.out.println("has two real roots: " + q1.root1() + " and " +
                            q1.root2());
      else if (discrim == 0)
        System.out.println("has one real root: " + q1.root1());
      else
        System.out.println("has no real roots");
      System.out.println();

      Quadratic q2 = new Quadratic(1.2, 3.6, 2.7);
      discrim = q2.getDiscriminant();
      System.out.println("The quadratic equation " + q2 + " with discriminant " +
                          discrim);
      if (discrim > 0)
        System.out.println("has two real roots: " + q2.root1() + " and " +
                            q2.root2());
      else if (discrim == 0)
        System.out.println("has one real root: " + q2.root1());
      else
        System.out.println("has no real roots");
      System.out.println();

      Quadratic q3 = new Quadratic(2, -4.1, 5.2);
      discrim = q3.getDiscriminant();
      System.out.println("The quadratic equation " + q3 + " with discriminant " +
                          discrim);
      if (discrim > 0)
        System.out.println("has two real roots: " + q3.root1() + " and " +
                            q3.root2());
      else if (discrim == 0)
        System.out.println("has one real root: " + q3.root1());
      else
        System.out.println("has no real roots");
  }
}
```

3. Printing Factory

(a) **General Problem:** Write the replacePaper method of the Machine class.

Refined Problem: Take the new PaperRoll passed as a parameter and use it to replace the current roll. Return the used roll to the caller. Notice that this is a type of swapping and will require a temp variable.

Algorithm:
- Create a temp variable of type PaperRoll.
- Assign the machine's PaperRoll paper to temp.
- Assign the new PaperRoll passed as a parameter to the machine's PaperRoll.
- Return the PaperRoll in temp.

Java Code:

```java
public PaperRoll replacePaper(PaperRoll pRoll)
{
    PaperRoll temp = paper;
    paper = pRoll;
    return temp;
}
```

Common Errors:
- It may seem like you want to do this:

```java
return paper;
paper = pRoll;
```

But once the return statement is executed, flow of control passes back to the calling method. The second statement will never be executed.

(b) **General Problem:** Write the `replacePaperRolls` method of the `PrintingFactory` class.

Refined Problem: Traverse the machines `ArrayList` checking for `Machine` object with `PaperRoll` objects that contain less than 4.0 meters of paper. Any `PaperRoll` objects containing less than 4.0 meters of paper need to be replaced. Get a new `PaperRoll` object from the newRolls `ArrayList`, and pass it to the `Machine` class `replacePaper` method. Place the returned used `PaperRoll` object on the usedRolls `ArrayList`.

Algorithm:
- Write a `for-each` loop to traverse the machines array.
  - If the current `Machine` object's `PaperRoll` object contains < 4.0 m of paper:
    - Take a `PaperRoll` object off of the newRolls `ArrayList`.
    - Call replacePaper passing the new roll as a parameter.
    - replacePaper will return the old `PaperRoll` object; put it on the usedRolls `ArrayList`.

Java Code:

```java
public void replacePaperRolls()
{
    for (Machine m : machines)
    {
        if (m.getPaperRoll().getMeters() < 4.0)
        {
            PaperRoll newRoll = newRolls.remove(0);
            PaperRoll oldRoll = m.replacePaper(newRoll);
            usedRolls.add(oldRoll);
        }
    }
}
```

Common Errors:
- The syntax for accessing the amount of paper remaining is complex, especially when using a `for` loop instead of a `for-each` loop. Remember that the `getMeters` method is not a method of the `Machine` class. We have to ask each `Machine` object for access to its `PaperRoll` object and then ask the `PaperRoll` object how much paper it has left.

Java Code Alternate Solution #1:

Use `for` loops instead of `for-each` loops.

Use just one variable for the old and new rolls.

```java
public void replacePaperRolls()
{
    for (int i = 0; i < machines.length; i++)
    {
        if (machines[i].getPaperRoll().getMeters() < 4.0)
        {
            PaperRoll roll = newRolls.remove(0);
            roll = machines[i].replacePaper(roll);
            usedRolls.add(roll);
        }
    }
}
```

Java Code Alternate Solution #2:

Combine the statements and eliminate the variables altogether. This could also be done in the `for` loop version.

```java
public void replacePaperRolls()
{
    for (Machine m : machines)
        if (m.getPaperRoll().getMeters() < 4.0)
            usedRolls.add(m.replacePaper(newRolls.remove(0)));
}
```

(c) **General Problem:** Write the `getPaperUsed` method of the `PrintingFactory` class.

Refined Problem: The amount of paper used on each roll is 1000 minus the amount of paper remaining. First traverse the usedRolls `ArrayList` and add up the paper used. Next, traverse the machines array and add up the paper used. These two amounts represent the total paper used. Return the sum.

Algorithm:
- Write a `for-each` loop to traverse the usedRolls `ArrayList`.
  - Add 1000 minus paper remaining on the current roll to a running sum.
- Write a `for-each` loop to traverse the machines array.
  - Add 1000 minus paper remaining on the current machine's roll to the same running sum.
- Return the sum.

Java Code:

```java
public double getPaperUsed()
{
    double sum = 0.0;
    for (PaperRoll p : usedRolls)
        sum = sum + (1000 - p.getMeters());

    for (Machine m : machines)
        sum = sum + (1000 - m.getPaperRoll().getMeters());

    return sum;
}
```

Java Code Alternate Solution #1:
Use for loops instead of for-each loops.
    Replace sum = sum + ... with sum += ...

```java
public double getPaperUsed()
{
    double sum = 0.0;
    for (int i = 0; i < usedRolls.size(); i++)
        sum += 1000 - usedRolls.get(i).getMeters();

    for (int i = 0; i < machines.length; i++)
        sum += 1000 - machines[i].getPaperRoll().getMeters();

    return sum;
}
```

Common Errors:
- Remember that ArrayLists and arrays use different syntax both to access elements and to find their total number of elements.

Java Code Alternate Solution #2:
There are other ways to compute the paper use. Here we add up all the leftover paper and then subtract the total from 1000 * the total number of rolls. This technique could be combined with the for loop version, as well as the for-each loop as shown here.

```java
public double getPaperUsed()
{
    double totalLeft = 0.0;
    double totalUsed = 0.0;

    for (PaperRoll p : usedRolls)
        totalLeft += p.getMeters();

    for (Machine m : machines)
        totalLeft += m.getPaperRoll().getMeters();

    totalUsed = 1000 * (usedRolls.size() + machines.length) - totalLeft;

    return totalUsed;
}
```

Scoring Guidelines: Printing Factory

Part (a)   **replacePaper**   **2 points**
+1   Assigns the PaperRoll object passed as a parameter to the Machine object's PaperRoll variable; specifically: paper = pRoll;
+1   Returns the used PaperRoll object

Part (b)   **replacePaperRolls**   **3 points**
+1   Accesses all elements of machines; no bounds errors, no missed elements
+2   Processes low-paper rolls correctly
    +1   Removes a new roll from the newRolls ArrayList; calls the replacePaper method; passing the new roll as a parameter
    +1   Adds the used roll returned from the replacePaper method to the usedRolls ArrayList

Part (c)   **getPaperUsed**   **4 points**

+1   Accesses the amount of paper remaining for all elements of the usedRolls `ArrayList`; no bounds errors, no missed elements

+1   Accesses all elements of the machines array; no bounds errors, no missed elements

+1   Accesses the amount of paper remaining on a `Machine` object's PaperRoll

+1   Correctly computes and returns total paper used

4. Hex Grid

(a) **General Problem:** Write the `getGamePieceCount` method that counts how many `GamePiece` objects are located on the grid.

Refined Problem: Traverse the 2D array of `GamePiece` objects and count the number of cells that are not null.

Algorithm:
- Create a variable to hold the count.
- Traverse the 2D array of values using nested loops.
  - Inside the loops, evaluate each cell of the grid to see if it is null. When we find an element that is not null, increment the count variable.
- Once the entire array has been traversed, the value of the count variable is returned.

Java Code:

```java
public int getGamePieceCount()
{
    int count = 0;
    for (int row = 0; row < grid.length; row++)
        for (int col = 0; col < grid[row].length; col++)
            if (grid[row][col] != null)
                count++;
    return count;
}
```

Common Errors:
- Remember that the number of rows is grid.length and the number of columns is grid[row].length or, since all columns are the same length, grid[0].length.
- The return statement has to be outside both loops.

Java Code Alternate Solution:
You can use `for-each` loops to traverse a 2D array.

```java
public int getGamePieceCount()
{
    int count = 0;
    for (GamePiece[] row : grid)
        for (GamePiece g : row)
            if (g != null)
                count++;
    return count;
}
```

(b) **General Problem:** Write the `isAbove` method that returns the `GamePiece` objects that are above an object at a given location on the grid.

Refined Problem: Create an `ArrayList` of `GamePiece` objects that are above the position passed in the parameter, where "above" is defined as having the same column number and a lower row number than another object. If there is no object at the location passed in, null is returned. If there are no objects above the parameter location, an empty `ArrayList` is returned.

Algorithm:
- Determine whether there is a `GamePiece` object at the location specified. If there is not, return null.
- Create an `ArrayList` to hold the `GamePiece` objects to be returned.
- Look in the specified column and the rows from 0 up to the specified row. If any of those cells contain `GamePiece` objects, add them to the `ArrayList`.
- Return the `ArrayList`.

Java Code:
```java
public ArrayList<GamePiece> isAbove(int row, int col)
{
    if (grid[row][col] == null)
        return null;
    ArrayList<GamePiece> above = new ArrayList<GamePiece>();
    for (int r = 0; r < row; r++)
        if (grid[r][col] != null)
            above.add(grid[r][col]);
    return above;
}
```

Common Errors:
- Do not count the object itself. That means the loop must stop at r < row, not r <= row.

(c) **General Problem:** Write the `addRandom` method that adds a specified number of `GamePiece` objects to the grid in random locations.

Refined Problem: Check to see if there are enough blank cells to add the requested objects. If there are, use a random number generator to generate a row and column number. If the cell at that location is empty, add the object; otherwise, generate a new number. Repeat until all objects have been added.

Algorithm:
- Determine whether there are enough empty cells to hold the requested number of objects.
  - If there are not, return false.
- Loop until all objects have been added.
  - Generate a random int between 0 and number of rows.
  - Generate a random int between 0 and number of columns.
  - Check to see if that cell is free. If it is, add object and decrease number to be added by 1.
- Return true.

Note that this algorithm may take a very long time to run if the grid is large and mostly full. If that is the case, a more efficient algorithm is to put all available open spaces into a list and then choose a random element from that list.

Java Code:

```java
public boolean addRandom(int number)
{
    if (getGamePieceCount() + number > grid.length * grid[0].length)
        return false;
    while (number > 0)
    {
        int row = (int)(Math.random() * grid.length);
        int col = (int)(Math.random() * grid[0].length);
        if(grid[row][col] == null)
        {
            grid[row][col] = new GamePiece();
            number--;
        }
    }
    return true;
}
```

Scoring Guidelines: Hex Grid

Part (a)   **getGamePieceCount**   **2 points**

+1   Compares every element to null; no bounds errors, no missed elements

+1   Returns the correct count

Part (b)   **isAbove**   **3 points**

+1   Returns null if the specified location is null

+1   Compares to null all elements in the given column with a row number from 0 up to but not including the given row number; no bounds errors, no missed elements

+1   Creates and returns `ArrayList` of all elements "above" the given location

Part (c)   **addRandom**   **4 points**

+1   Returns false if there is not sufficient room to add requested elements; must use getGamePieceCount; returns true after requested number of elements have been added

+1   Generates a random location; no bounds errors, no missed elements

+1   Adds the element only if the generated location is null; continues to generate locations in the context of a loop until an element is successfully added (a non-null location is found)

+1   Continues to add elements in the context of a loop until requested number of elements has been added

Scoring Worksheet

This worksheet will help you to approximate your performance on Practice Exam 2 in terms of an AP score of 1–5.

Part I (Multiple Choice)
Number right (out of 40 questions)   = _____

Part II (Short Answer)
See the scoring guidelines included with the explanations for each of the questions and award yourself points based on those guidelines.

Question 1: Points Obtained (out of 9 possible)   _____

Question 2: Points Obtained (out of 9 possible)   _____

Question 3: Points Obtained (out of 9 possible)   _____

Question 4: Points Obtained (out of 9 possible)   _____

Add the points and multiply by 1.1111   _____ × 1.1111   = _____

Add your totals from both parts of the test   Total Raw Score _____
(round to nearest whole number)

Approximate conversion from raw score to AP score

Raw Score Range	AP Score	Interpretation
62–80	5	Extremely Well Qualified
44–61	4	Well Qualified
31–43	3	Qualified
25–30	2	Possibly Qualified
0–24	1	No Recommendation

Appendix

Java Quick Reference

Accessible methods from the Java library that may be included in the exam

Class Constructors and Methods	Explanation
String Class	
`String(String str)`	Constructs a new `String` object that represents the same sequence of characters as `str`
`int length()`	Returns the number of characters in a `String` object
`String substring(int from, int to)`	Returns the substring beginning at index `from` and ending at index `to` `-1`
`String substring(int from)`	Returns `substring(from, length())`
`int indexOf(String str)`	Returns the index of the first occurrence of `str`; returns `-1` if not found
`boolean equals(String other)`	Returns `true` if `this` is equal to `other`; returns `false` otherwise
`int compareTo(String other)`	Returns a value <0 if `this` is less than `other`; returns zero if `this` is equal to `other`; returns a value >0 if `this` is greater than `other`
Integer Class	
`Integer(int value)`	Constructs a new `Integer` object that represents the specified `int` value
`Integer.MIN_VALUE`	The minimum value represented by an `int` or `Integer`
`Integer.MAX_VALUE`	The maximum value represented by an `int` or `Integer`
`int intValue()`	Returns the value of this `Integer` as an `int`
Double Class	
`Double(double value)`	Constructs a new `Double` object that represents the specified `double` value
`double doubleValue()`	Returns the value of this `Double` as a `double`
Math Class	
`static int abs(int x)`	Returns the absolute value of an `int` value
`static double abs(double x)`	Returns the absolute value of a `double` value
`static double pow(double base, double exponent)`	Returns the value of the first parameter raised to the power of the second parameter
`static double sqrt(double x)`	Returns the positive square root of a `double` value
`static double random()`	Returns a `double` value greater than or equal to 0.0 and less than 1.0

ArrayList Class	
`int size()`	Returns the number of elements in the list
`boolean add(E obj)`	Appends `obj` to end of list; returns `true`
`void add(int index, E obj)`	Inserts `obj` at position index(0 <= index <= size), moving elements at position `index` and higher to the right (adds 1 to their indices) and adds 1 to size
`E get(int index)`	Returns the element at position `index` in the list
`E set(int index, E obj)`	Replaces the element at position `index` with `obj`; returns the element formerly at position `index`
`E remove(int index)`	Removes element from position `index`, moving elements at position `index +1` and higher to the left (subtracts 1 from their indices) and subtracts 1 from size; returns the elements formerly at position `index`
Object Class	
`boolean equals(Object other)`	
`String toString()`	

Free-Response Scoring Guidelines

When grading your exam, the AP Computer Science A reader will compare your code for each question to the rubric for each question. After this process is complete, penalty points may be deducted from your score based on the list below. A penalty point can only be deducted once per question (even if you make the same mistake multiple times in the same question). You can't get a negative total. These are the guidelines as of the 2019 exam. Be aware that they are sometimes modified from year to year.

General Penalties (assessed only once per problem)

-**1**   using local variables without first declaring them

-**1**   returning a value from a void method or constructor

-**1**   accessing an array or ArrayList incorrectly

-**1**   overwriting information passed as a parameter

-**1**   including unnecessary code that causes a side effect like a compile error or console output

No Penalty (*These may change from year to year!*)

- Extra code that doesn't cause any side effects
- Minor spelling mistakes such as "wile" for "while"
- Code that includes private or public on a local variable
- Using local variables but forgetting to declare at least one of them
- Forgetting to put public when writing a class or constructor header
- Accidentally using the mathematical symbols for operators ($\times$, $\bullet$, $+$, $\leq$, $\geq$, $<>$, $\neq$)
- Confusing the use of [ ] and < > and ( )
- Accidentally using "=" rather than "==" and vice versa
- Confusing length with size for either String, ArrayList, or array
- Accidentally putting the size in array declaration such as int[25] myArray = new int[25];
- Missing a semicolon if you write the majority of them and you provide proper spacing
- Missing curly braces when your indenting is proper and you used them elsewhere
- Accidentally forgetting to put parentheses on no-argument method or constructor calls
- Forgetting to put parentheses on `if` statements or `while` loops provided indenting is proper

Note: Suppose your code declares "Bunny bunny = new Bunny()" and then uses "Bunny.hop()" instead of "bunny.hop()". The mistake is not treated as a grammatical error. Instead, you will not earn points, because the grader is not allowed to assume that you know the difference between "Bunny" and "bunny" in the context of this problem.

List of Keywords in Java

The following is a sample of some of the keywords in Java and cannot be used as identifiers (variable names, class names, etc.).

abstract	assert	boolean	break	byte	case	catch	char
class	const	continue	default	do	double	else	enum
extends	final	finally	float	for	goto	if	implements
import	instanceof	int	interface	long	native	new	package
private	protected	public	return	short	static	strictfp	super
switch	synchronized	this	throw	throws	transient	try	void
volatile	while	true*	false*	null*	*Not keywords but can't be used!		

Glossary

access-level modifiers *see visibility modifiers*

accessor method methods that return the value of an instance variable

accumulating to add (or subtract) a value from a variable

actual parameter *see argument*

algorithm a process to be followed to solve a problem

alias an alternate name (identifier) used to reference an object

application programming interface (API) a set of classes and files for building software in Java

argument (actual parameter) the actual value that is passed to a constructor or method

arithmetic overflow the result of adding one (or more) to the maximum value of a number which will lead to unexpected values.

array a complex data structure that can store a list of primitive or objects that can be referenced by an index

ArrayList a complex data structure that can store a list of objects that can be accessed and modified using methods in the ArrayList class.

assignment operator a single equals, =, used for assigning values to a variable

attribute describes the characteristic or feature of the class by using instance variables.

autobox the automatic process of converting between primitive types and the corresponding object wrapper class

autounbox the automatic conversion from the wrapper class to the primitive type

base case used in a recursive method to determine whether or not the method should call itself again

binary search a searching algorithm for a list that is in sorted order that repeatedly eliminates half of the list by comparing the desired value with the middle of the list. It continues to eliminate half of the list until the desired value is found or the entire list has been eliminated.

black box the idea that an output is produced based on inputs without any knowledge of the internal workings of the function

block of code a group of instructions inside a pair of curly braces

bottom-up a way of approaching class hierarchy design that starts with the details

boundary error also known as an off by one (obo) error, a boundary error is a logical error or runtime error that occurs as a result of executing a for or while loop one too many or one two few times

bytecode computer object code that is Java Virtual Machine–readable code

camel case a naming convention where all primitive variable names start with a lowercase letter; then for each new word in the variable name, the first letter of the new word is assigned an uppercase letter

case-sensitive upper- and lowercase letters are not considered equal

cast temporarily changing the data type of a variable for the sake of performing some action such as division or assigning

child (subclass) a class that inherits the instance variables and methods of the parent class

class the blueprint, or description of characteristics, for constructing all objects that derive from it

class hierarchy describes the relationship between classes

class variables *see static variables*

client any object (client) that is using another object

client program *see runner class*

column-major the process of traversing a 2D array by starting at the top left cell and move toward the bottom along the first column until you reach the end of the column and continue in the same manner for the rest of the columns

compile time the time period when the program code is being translated to machine code. The compiler translates and verifies if program code can be executed.

compiler a program that converts your Java program into bytecode. It checks for syntax errors and generates a new program that is readable by a Java virtual machine.

compile-time error an error caused by using incorrect syntax that is identified at compile-time

complex data structure a variable that can store a list of other variables

compound assignment operator a way to modify the value of a variable that only uses the variable name one time rather than twice. A compound assignment operator exists for addition, subtraction, multiplication, division, and modulo.

compound conditional statement a Boolean expression that tests more than one condition

concatenation joining strings together

condition a Boolean expression that evaluates to either true or false

console the text-based interface that allows the user to interact with the program

constant a variable whose value doesn't change during the execution of a program. Any attempt to change the value will generate a compiler error.

constructor a block of code that is executed when an object is being instantiated

dangling else an else that attaches itself to the if statement directly above the else when curly braces are not used

data structure a variable used to organize, manage, and store information

data type a classification of data or a variable

De Morgan's Law a law that handles the negation of a compound conditional statement by showing how it is equivalent to another Boolean expression. !(a && b) is equivalent to !a || !b and !(a || b) is equivalent to !a && !b according to De Morgan's Law.

decrement subtract from the value stored in the variable

default value the value of a variable if not explicitly initialized

documentation comments see Javadoc comments

downcasting casting a reference variable of a parent class to one of its child classes

dynamic binding the process of deciding which method the parent reference will perform during run-time

efficiency used to describe algorithms that does its job in the fastest way it can or describe programs that reduce CPU time and memory usage

element the values stored in a data structure

empty string a string where the value exists (it is not null), but there are no characters in the String literal. It has the length of 0 characters.

encapsulate protecting information by restricting its access

enhanced for loop (for-each loop) a special looping structure that can be used by either arrays or

ArrayLists. It traverses every element of the list starting from the beginning.

escape sequence special codes that are embedded in String literals that indicate special meaning

field a property of a class (like an instance variable)

for-each loop *see enhanced for loop*

formal parameter the variable (defined by the header's parameter) used by a constructor or method

functional decomposition a process of breaking down a complex program into smaller more manageable parts

garbage collection an action by Java that automatically deletes any objects that no longer have any references to the object in scope

identifier the name used for a variable

immutable an attribute of an object that means the state cannot be modified after it is created

implicit parameter (this) a reference to the current object, or rather, the object whose method or constructor is being called

increment add to the value stored in the variable

index (indices) an integer that refers to the location of a String or list

infinite loop a loop that never ends

infinite recursion indefinite method calls to itself in recursion

inheritance deriving a class from another class to create a hierarchy of classes that share a set of instance variables and methods

initializer list an alternate way to initialize an array's contents by explicitly assigning the values of the elements as a list

inline comment documentation ignored by the compiler that begins with two forward slashes and continues to the end of the line

inner loop control variable a variable used to control the inside loop

insertion sort a sorting algorithm that inserts each element of the list, one at a time, into the sorted position of the sorted portion of the list, and repeats this process until the entire list is sorted

instance variables virtual attributes (variables) that describe the state of an object. They are created when the object is instantiated.

instantiate the word used to describe the action of constructing (or creating) a new object

integer division dividing an integer by an integer, which results in an integer answer, where the decimal is truncated

Integrated Development Environment (IDE) a piece of software that allows you to write code more easily by providing tools like word processing

invoke to call on or execute a method by passing a value to the parameter

is-a relationship a relationship that describes a class hierarchy where a child class is-a parent class

iteration repeating a statement more than once

Java a general-purpose, object-oriented computer programming language that is designed to be machine-independent, meaning that a Java program can be run on any platform

Java Runtime Environment (JRE) a program that runs on top of a computer's operating system software and provides resources that specific Java programs need to run

Java virtual machine (JVM) a virtual machine that translates the bytecode into machine code, which enables a computer to run Java programs. It is part of the Java Runtime Environment (JRE) that is provided by Oracle.

Javadoc comments (documentation comments) comments begin with /** and end with */ that summarize a class, including its constructor, instance variables, methods, etc. in a readable format

keyword a reserved word in Java that has specific meaning and cannot be used as an identifier

length describes the number of elements in a String or array

lexicographically a case-sensitive ordering of words similar to a dictionary but using the UNICODE codes of each character

linear search *see sequential search*

logic error when your program compiles and runs without crashing, but does not do what you expected it to do

logical operator a symbol used to form compound conditional statements

loop control variable (LCV) a variable (typically an int) whose value determines whether a loop continues to executes or terminates

machine code a computer program that is written in the elemental language of computers, which is composed of binary numbers

machine-dependent a program must be run on the same type of machine that the program was written on

machine-independent a program can be written on any platform and run on any platform

merge sort a sorting algorithm that repeatedly divides the list into two groups and subsequently merges the smaller groups together and sorts them as it joins them

method a block of code that performs a service or returns an answer

method declaration a line of code that includes the access modifier, the return type, the name of the method, and the parameter list

method signature includes the name of the method and the parameter list. It does not include the access modifier or the return type.

multiple line comments comments that begin with /* and end with */ and may span over multiple lines

mutuator (modifier) method method that changes the value of an instance variable

naming convention the rules in which you choose a variable name

nested loop a loop that is inside of another loop

no-argument constructor a constructor with no parameters. An implicit, empty, no-argument constructor exists in every class unless explicitly defined.

null a reference that does not contain the address of any object

null check comparing a reference variable using the == or != to determine if the reference variable has been created and has an address location in memory

object a virtual entity that is created using a class as a blueprint

object-oriented programming (OOP) an approach to programming that uses the concept of classes and objects

outer loop control variable a variable used to control the outer loop

overloaded constructor two constructors with the same name but different parameter lists

overloaded methods two methods with the same name but different parameter lists

override when a child class provides a different implementation of a method that is already defined by the parent or ancestor (any other class in the hierarchy) class

parameter list used when a method or constructor uses more than one parameter. A parameter list is a series of parameter definitions separated by commas.

parametrized constructor a constructor that takes one or more parameters

parent (superclass) a class that is inherited from

polymorphism describes how different child classes of the same parent class can act differently depending on the object type instantiated and if the methods have been overridden in the class hierarchy

postcondition a condition that must always be true after the execution of a section of program code. Postconditions can also describe the outcome of the execution in terms of what is being returned or the state of an object.

precondition documentation on what you are allowed to assume about a parameter

preprocessing the preliminary processing of information to prepare the information for input into another function

primitive variable a simple data structure that can store a single numerical value. These numerical values may be read as something other than a number as is the case with char and boolean

procedural abstraction the idea that when a program is broken down into pieces and each piece has a responsibility

program specifications descriptions of what the program should look like and how it should operate

pseudocode an informal code like language that does not use the syntax of any programming language

recursion process of repeating instructions by making a recursive call (a method call to itself) using a parameter that is incrementally moving towards the base case

reference a value that represents the location (memory address) of data but not the data itself

reference variable a variable used to hold the location (memory address) of an object

relational operator a symbol that represents the comparison of two values

reusable using existing code in some part in a client class

row-major the process of traversing a 2D array by starting at the top-left cell and moving toward the right along the first row until you reach the end of the row and continue in the same manner for the rest of the rows

runner class (client program) a class that contains a main method, which is the point of entry for a program

run-time the time period when the program code is executing

run-time error an error that causes the program to crash while running because an exception has occurred

scope the area of code where a variable is visible and accessible

selection sort a sorting algorithm that repeatedly finds and selects the smallest item in a list and puts it in its proper place

sequential (linear) search the process of looking at each of the elements in a list, one at a time, until you find what you are looking for

short-circuit evaluation when one or more conditions in a compound conditional statement are not tested because the result of the final evaluation is known and the remaining evaluations are irrelevant

simple data structure a variable that can store a single value, such as a primitive variable

software engineering the study of designing, developing, and maintaining software

stack a complex data structure that stores the result of a method call in Java

stack overflow error an error that occurs where is no valid base case in a recursive method due to infinite recursion

state the values of all attributes of an object at a particular point in time

static binding the process of deciding which method the child reference variable will perform during compile-time

static variables (class variables) a variable that is shared by all the objects that come from the class

string literal a sequence of characters enclosed in double quotation marks

subclass *see child*

superclass *see parent*

syntax technical way of writing code and describes the correct way to type the code so the program will run

syntax errors errors due to code not following the syntax rules of the programming language

this *see implicit parameter*

top-down a way of approaching class hierarchy design that starts with the big picture

traverse to systematically visit each of the elements of a list

truncated the decimal portion of a number is excluded

truth table a table that shows all the possible truth values of a Boolean expression

two-dimensional (2D) array a data structure that is an array of arrays and simulates a rectangular grid with coordinates for each location based on the row and the column

UNICODE an international encoding standard where each letter, digit, or symbol is assigned a unique numeric value

unit test short methods that test whether or not a specific method is performing its task correctly

variable a simple data structure that allows the programmer to store a value in the computer. The programmer can retrieve or modify the variable at any time in the program.

visibility modifiers (access level modifiers) a reserved word in Java (public or private) that specifies internal or external access

wrapper class a class that wraps or contains primitive data types. It is a way for Java to convert a primitive data type to an object of the same type.

List of Required Runtime Exceptions

Runtime Exception	Possible Reason for Error
`ArithmeticException`	You divided by zero. You performed a mod by zero.
`NullPointerException`	You tried to make a null object reference perform a method. You tried to access or modify a field of a null object reference.
`IndexOutOfBoundsException`	Attempting to access indices outside the range of a `String` object, such as a negative value or a value larger than length-1. This error occurs when doing ArrayList handling like add, get, remove and so on. The index for the `ArrayList` method is greater than or equal to the size of the ArrayList. The index for the `ArrayList` method is negative.
`ArrayIndexOutOfBoundsException`	You are attempting to use an index that is larger than (or equal to) the length of the array. You are attempting to use a negative array index.
`StringIndexOutOfBoundsException`	You are attempting to use an index that is larger than (or equal to) the length of the String. You are attempting to use a negative index.
`ConcurrentModificationException`	Changing the size of an ArrayList while traversing it using an enhanced `for` loop.

Language Features and Other Testable Topics

Tested on the AP CS A Exam	Not tested on the AP CS A Exam, but potentially relevant/useful
Comments /* */, //, and /** */	Javadoc tool
Primitive Types	
```int Integer.MIN_VALUE/MAX_VALUE Overflow double boolean (values: true, false)```	```char, byte, short, long, float```

Operators
Arithmetic: +, -, *, /, %
Increment/Decrement: ++, --
Assignment: =, +=, -=, *=, /=, %=
String concatenation: +, +=
Numeric casts: (int), (double)
Relational: ==, !=, <, <=, >, >=
Logical: !, &&, ||
 	
Short circuited evaluation
De Morgan's Laws
	```StringBuilder```
	```(char), (float)```
	
	```&, |, ^```
	Shift: ```<<, >>, >>>```
	Bitwise: ```~, &, |, ^```
	Conditional: ```?:```

Escape Sequences \", \\, \n inside strings	```\', \t, \unnnn```
Input/Output ```System.out.print, System.out.println```	```Scanner, System.in, System.out, System.err, Stream``` input/output, GUI input/output Parsing input: ```Integer.parseInt, Double.parseDouble``` Formatting output: ```System.out.printf, String.format```

Control Statements	
if	
if-else	
if-else-if	switch
Nested if	
while	break, continue, do-while
for, enhanced for (for-each)	
Nested iteration	
return	

Variables	
Parameter variables	final parameter variables
Local variables	final local variables
Instance variables visibility (private)	final instance variables
Static (class) variables visibility (public, private)	
final	

Methods	
Visibility (public, private)	visibility (protected)
Static vs. non-static	public static void main(String[] args), command line arguments
Method signatures	variable number of parameters, final parameters
Overloading, overriding	
Formal vs. actual parameters passed using call-by-value	
Dot (.) operator	
Void method	
Non-void method	
Precondition	
Postcondition	
toString	

Constructors	
new	default initialization of instance variables, initialization blocks
super(), super(args)	this(args)
Visibility (public)	visibility (private, protected)
Initialize state of the object	
No-argument	
Overloading	

Classes	
Visibility (`public`)	visibility (`private`, `protected`)
Accessor methods	final class
Modifier (mutator) methods	nested classes
Design/create/modify class	inner classes, enumerations
Encapsulation	
Inheritance	
`extends`	
`super.`*method(args)*	
Understand inheritance hierarchies, (subclass/superclass relationship)	
Design/create/modify subclasses	
Declare/create objects of subclasses	
Polymorphism	
Object Comparison	
object identity (`==`, `!=`) vs. object equality (`equals`)	
implementation of `equals`	
`String compareTo`	`Comparable` interface
Miscellaneous OOP	
"is-a" and "has-a" relationships	`instanceof`, (*ClassName*) cast
`null`	
`this`	`this.`*var*, `this.`*method(args)*
Packages	
`import` *packageName.className*	`import` *packageName.**, static import, package packageName, class path
Standard Java Library	
`Object`	clone
`Integer`, `Double`	
`String`	
`Math`	
`ArrayList<E>`	`Collection<E>`, `Arrays`, `Collections`
Autoboxing	
Unboxing	

Arrays	

1-dimensional arrays
  Capacity: `arr.length`
  Default values: `0, 0.0, false, null`
	new *type*[] {...}

2-dimensional rectangular arrays	ragged arrays (non-rectangular), arrays with 3 or more dimensions
Initializer list: { ... } Row-major and column-major order traversals of 2-D array elements	
Exceptions	

`ArithmeticException`
`NullPointerException`
`IndexOutOfBoundsException`
`ArrayIndexOutOfBoundsException`
`StringIndexOutOfBoundsException`
`ConcurrentModificationException`
	`try/catch/finally`
	`throw, throws`
	`assert`

Common Algorithms	
Identify if integer is(not) divisible by another; identify individual digits in an integer	
Determine min/max value; Compute sum/average/mode	
Array (1-D, 2-D) traversal	
(minimum/maximum value, sum, average, mode, element found, access consecutive pairs, determine if duplicates, count elements meeting criteria, shift or rotate elements left/right, reverse order of elements)	
`ArrayList` traversal	
(insert elements, delete elements, and all listed for arrays above)	
Sequential/linear search	
Binary search	
Selection sort, Insertion sort, and Merge sort	
Informal run-time comparisons	
Recursion	
Base case, recursive call	writing recursive methods

Common Syntax Errors for Beginning Java Programmers

Incorrect Code	Explanation	Correct Code
`int count = 0`	Forgot the semicolon	`int count = 0;`
`system.out.println("smile);`	Forgot the second double quote	`System.out.println("smile");`
`double gpa = true;`	Assigned a `boolean` to a `double`	`double gpa = 3.75;`
`double a = 6.45;` `int b = a;`	Loss of precision since an integer will not accept the decimal portion	`double a = 6.45;` `double b = a;`
`system.out.println("OMG");`	System starts with uppercase letter	`System.out.println("OMG");`
`System.out.println('Yo');`	Need double quotes rather than single quotes	`System.out.println("Yo");`

`if (x > 5);`
`{`
`    // some random code`
`}`
	Semicolon before the curly brace	`if (x > 5)`
		`{`
		`    // some random code`
		`}`

`while(x > 5);`
`{`
`    // some random code`
`}`
	Semicolon before the curly brace	`while(x > 5)`
		`{`
		`    // some random code`
		`}`

College Board AP Computer Science A Exam
https://apstudents.collegeboard.org/courses/ap-computer-science-a

Java API
http://docs.oracle.com/javase/8/docs/api/

If you have any questions, suggestions, or would like to report an error, we'd love to hear from you. Email us at 5stepstoa5apcsa@gmail.com.